# FIRSTS, SECONDS AND THIRDS:

## AFRICAN AMERICAN LEADERS IN LOS ANGELES DURING THE 1960S AND '70S FROM THE ROLLAND J. CURTIS COLLECTION

Edited by KRISTINE PROTACIO

Preface by CHRISTINA RICE

photo
friends

LOS ANGELES PUBLIC LIBRARY

Hands all in at the Testimonial Dinner for Assemblyman Leon Ralph.
*Left to right*: Senator Mervyn Dymally, Attorney Charles Lloyd,
Congresswoman Yvonne Brathwaite Burke, Attorney General Tom Lynch,
Assemblyman Leon Ralph, Senator Bill Greene. October 6, 1966

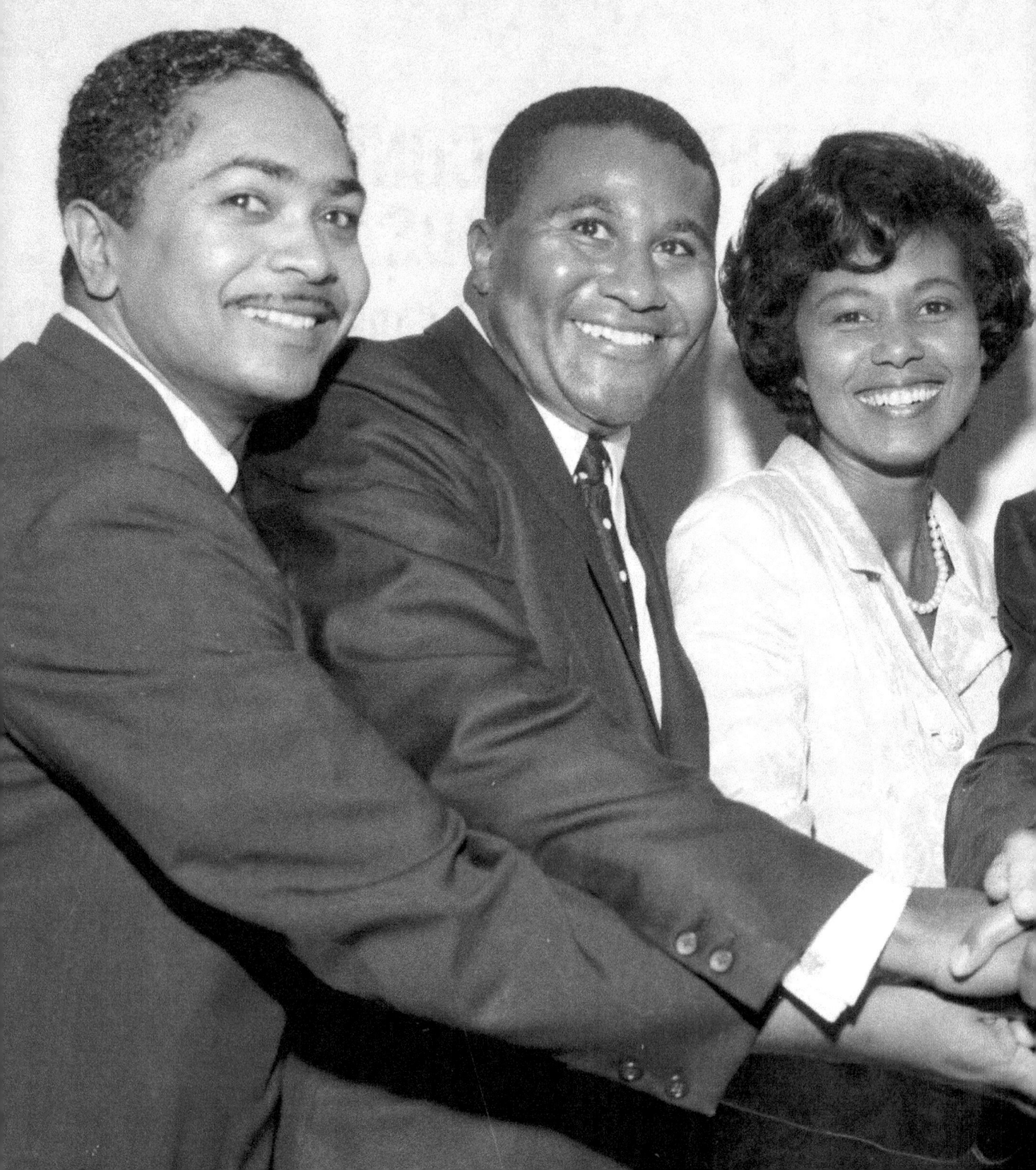

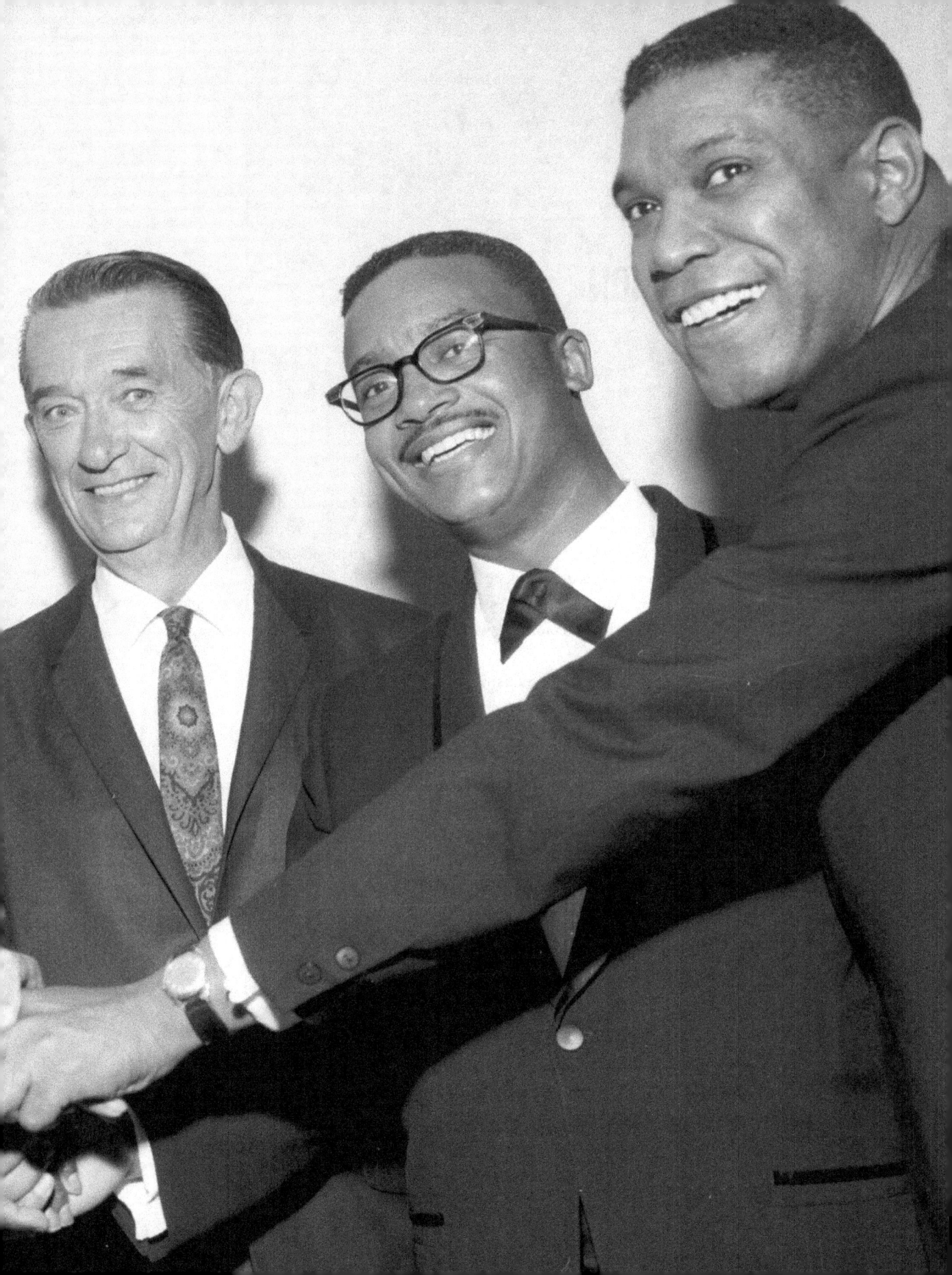

# INTRODUCTION

African Americans living in Los Angeles in the first half of the twentieth century faced a different, though by no means less challenging, experience than their counterparts across the country. Instead of having to face voter disenfranchisement and legal segregation in schools and businesses, black citizens in Los Angeles were still subject to lawful discrimination in the form of racial covenants, which restricted where they could own land, as well as segregation in community gathering spots like beaches and public pools.

A mass migration to the wealth of industrial jobs before and after World War II saw the African American population swell in Los Angeles county. However, the growing numbers of African American residents failed to correlate with increased political power in Los Angeles. To guarantee that they never gained enough votes, districts were gerrymandered and white politicians courted black voters, promising to be agents of change, but they seldom delivered. African Americans remained a fiercely segregated race in the state through the 1950s.

Civil rights took hold in Los Angeles in the 1960s as African Americans broke color barriers and began to occupy positions in government. Progress during this time extended beyond politics, to the realms of entertainment, commerce, public service, sports, and activism. African Americans flexed their newfound power, changing their own destiny and the destiny of Los Angeles in the process.

During this turbulent and thrilling time, photographer Rolland J. Curtis was one of the many African Americans eager and ready to change the world. After graduating from USC and serving a brief stint with the LAPD, Curtis became a field deputy for Tom Bradley, a newly-elected Los Angeles city councilman, and later, Councilman Billy G. Mills. Curtis spent much of his time taking pictures of Los Angeles' tightly-knit black leaders—newly-elected men and women who knew that in order to improve the lives of those they represented, they had to work together and form a united front. Community groups were formed for nearly every cause, attacking problems from multiple fronts so as to effect social change through political and community action.

Rolland Curtis' images provide a unique view of the African American experience in South Los Angeles during the 1960s and 1970s and document the city's black leaders of the period. Some famous, some forgotten, these individuals were true trailblazers: the first, second, or third African Americans in the history of Los Angeles to accomplish their feats. The men and women in these photographs helped change the face of Los Angeles and eventually the entire nation. Their efforts and unwavering crusade for civil rights were instrumental in the development of Los Angeles as one of the most diverse cities in the world, and a shining example of the rich culture that emerges when we value and fight for equality.

Over a decade after their donation by Gloria Curtis, Rolland Curtis' wife, and funded by a grant from the John Randolph Haynes and Dora Haynes Foundation, the Los Angeles Photo Collection is proud to present the Rolland J. Curtis Photo Collection.

KRISTINE PROTACIO
Archivist
January 2016

# PREFACE

I was at a party recently where I struck up a conversation with a woman who was especially interested in my position overseeing the Los Angeles Public Library's vast photographic collection. Her first question was, "What is the biggest challenge working with the collection?" I didn't recall ever being asked this and I paused before answering, not wanting to bore her with an avalanche of archival-speak. "I guess it's the sheer size," I responded, "and never having enough time or staff to get to everything."

This indeed is probably the biggest challenge, especially in an era when we have the ability to make the images in the collection so readily available online. However, getting those photos up on the website takes much more time than running a photo though a scanner—and even though we manage to get anywhere from five to seven thousand photos on the LAPL website every year—that still represents a small fraction of the collection. Try as we might, it sometimes seems like some collections may never see the light of day. This was certainly the case with the Rolland J. Curtis Collection.

The Los Angeles Public Library acquired the collection from Curtis' widow, Gloria, in the late 1990s. When I took the reins in 2009, only 100 of the 17,000+ images in the Curtis archive had been digitized. The only person who had worked with the collection was a volunteer who had facilitated the donation and had been dutifully coming to Central Library for a decade, identifying people in the photos. While thumbing though the 4×5 envelopes labeled with names like Bobby Kennedy, Martin Luther King Jr., Muhammad Ali, and Angela Davis, I knew the collection was special, but the sheer size, largely comprised of negatives, was not a project I was able to personally dedicate my time to. When we failed to secure a grant from the National Endowment of the Humanities, I was fearful that Rolland Curtis would remain on the back burner indefinitely.

The archival stars aligned when Kristine Protacio came to me in the summer of 2015 looking for an internship while pursuing her MLIS (Master of Library and Information Science) degree. I gave her the Curtis collection to work with, and she was off an running, though her limited time only allowed her to skim the surface. A few months later, her graduation coincided with a grant award from the John Randolph Haynes and Dora Haynes Foundation, and she was able to return, dedicating six months of full-time work to the collection. When she leaves at the end of January 2016, the Rolland J. Curtis Collection will be completely organized and ready for digitization. What does that mean exactly? Well, it means we're still a ways off from the 17,000+ images being available on the Los Angeles Public Library's website, but we're getting there!

In the meantime, Kristine, who now has a deep connection to this collection, has compiled some of her favorite photos which are presented in these pages. Thanks to passionate archivists like her and institutions like the Haynes Foundation, who believe in what we do, my job has become a little bit less challenging and work of Rolland Curtis will be accessible and ready to appreciate that much sooner.

CHRISTINA RICE
Senior Librarian
Los Angeles Public Library Photo Collection
January 2016

Portrait of Rolland J. Curtis. Rolland J. Curtis ("Speedy" to his friends) moved to Los Angeles from Louisiana in 1942, and in 1960 joined the LAPD, where he met Tom Bradley. In 1964, shortly after Bradley was elected to the city council, Curtis joined his staff as field deputy, and then Billy G. Mills' staff in 1967. Curtis was murdered in his home in 1979 after spending the day delivering Mother's Day bouquets to the community. An obituary in the *Los Angeles Sentinel* recalled, "Whenever there was a community affair, "Speedy" would be seen right down in front, sometimes taking pictures with his huge view camera, or sometimes just there to lend his support to community projects. But he was always there and he always wore a smile."

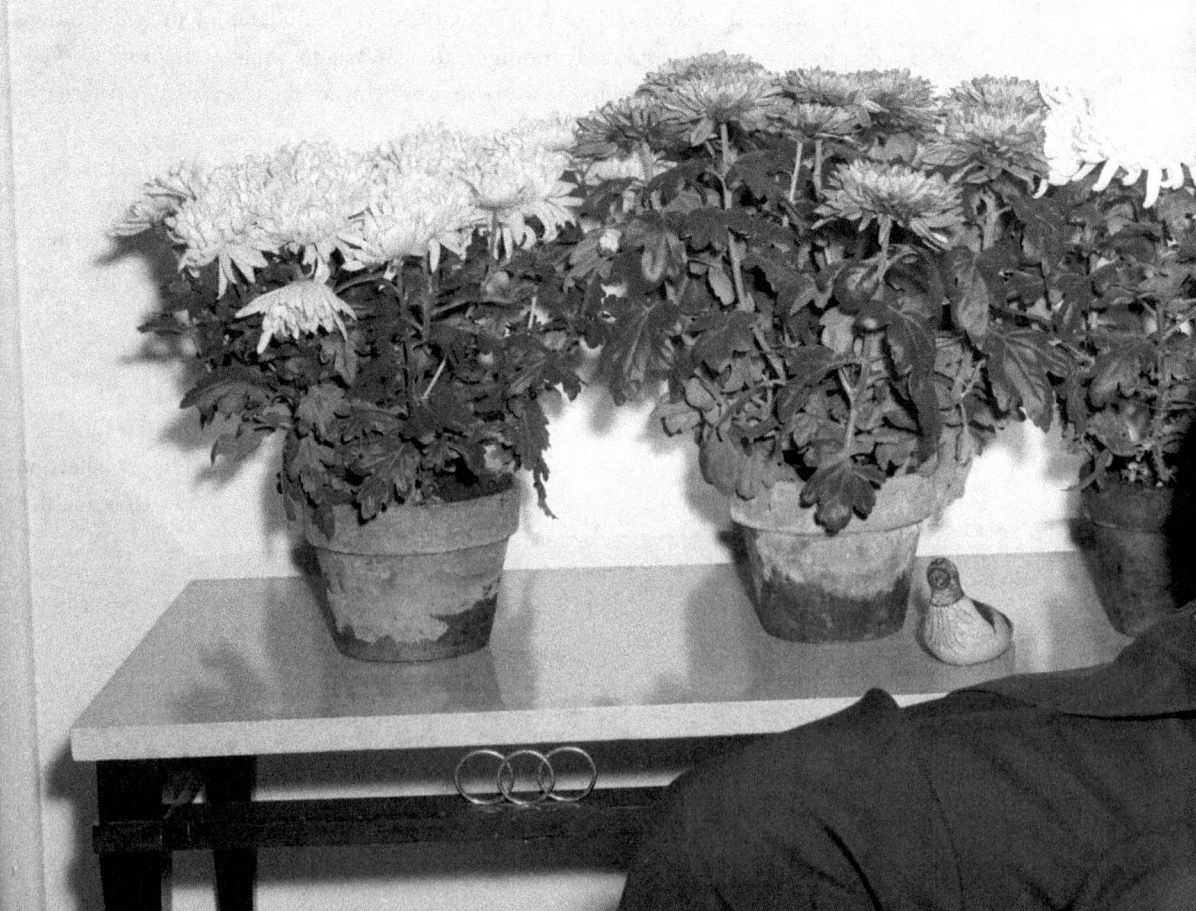

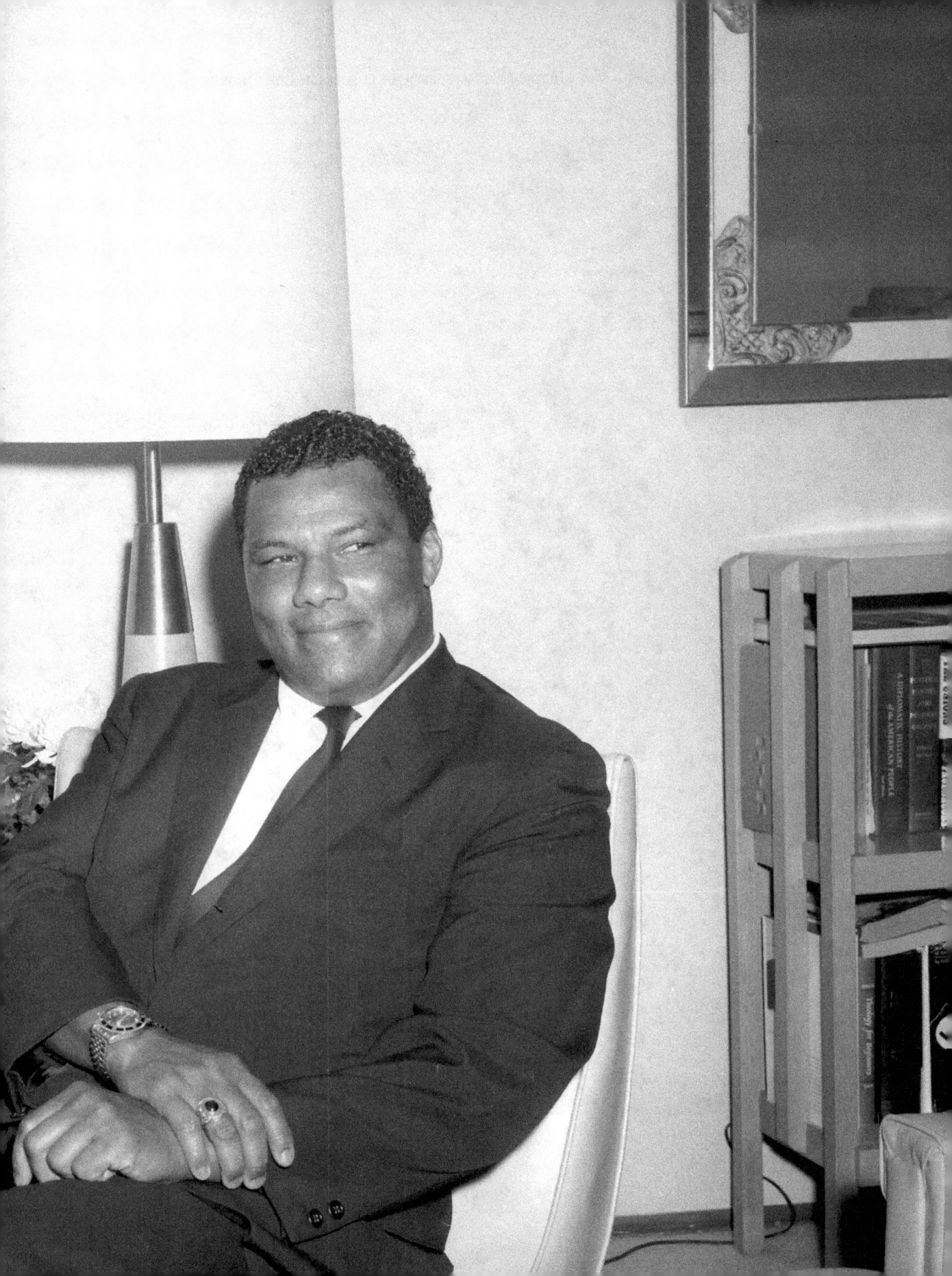

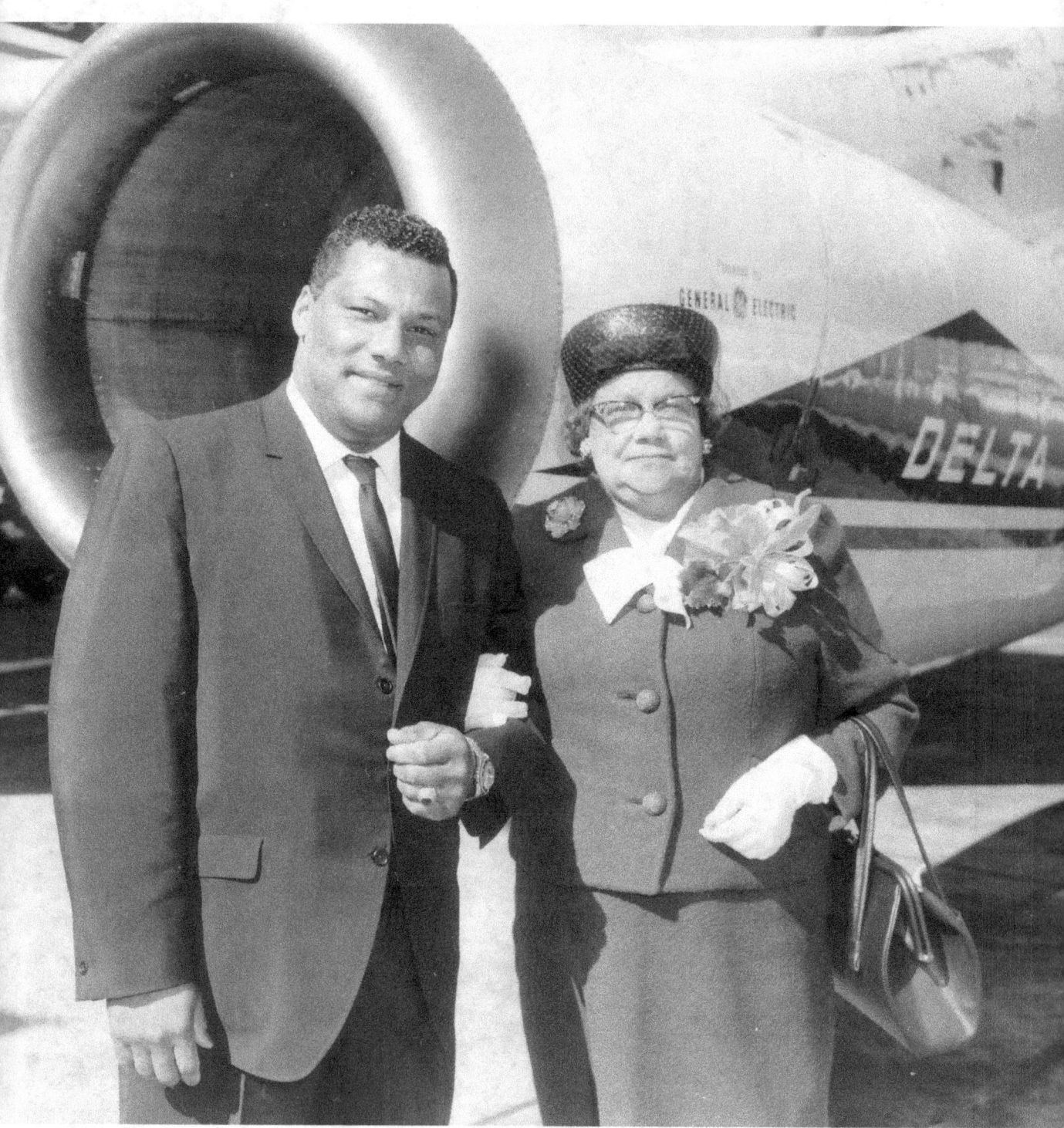

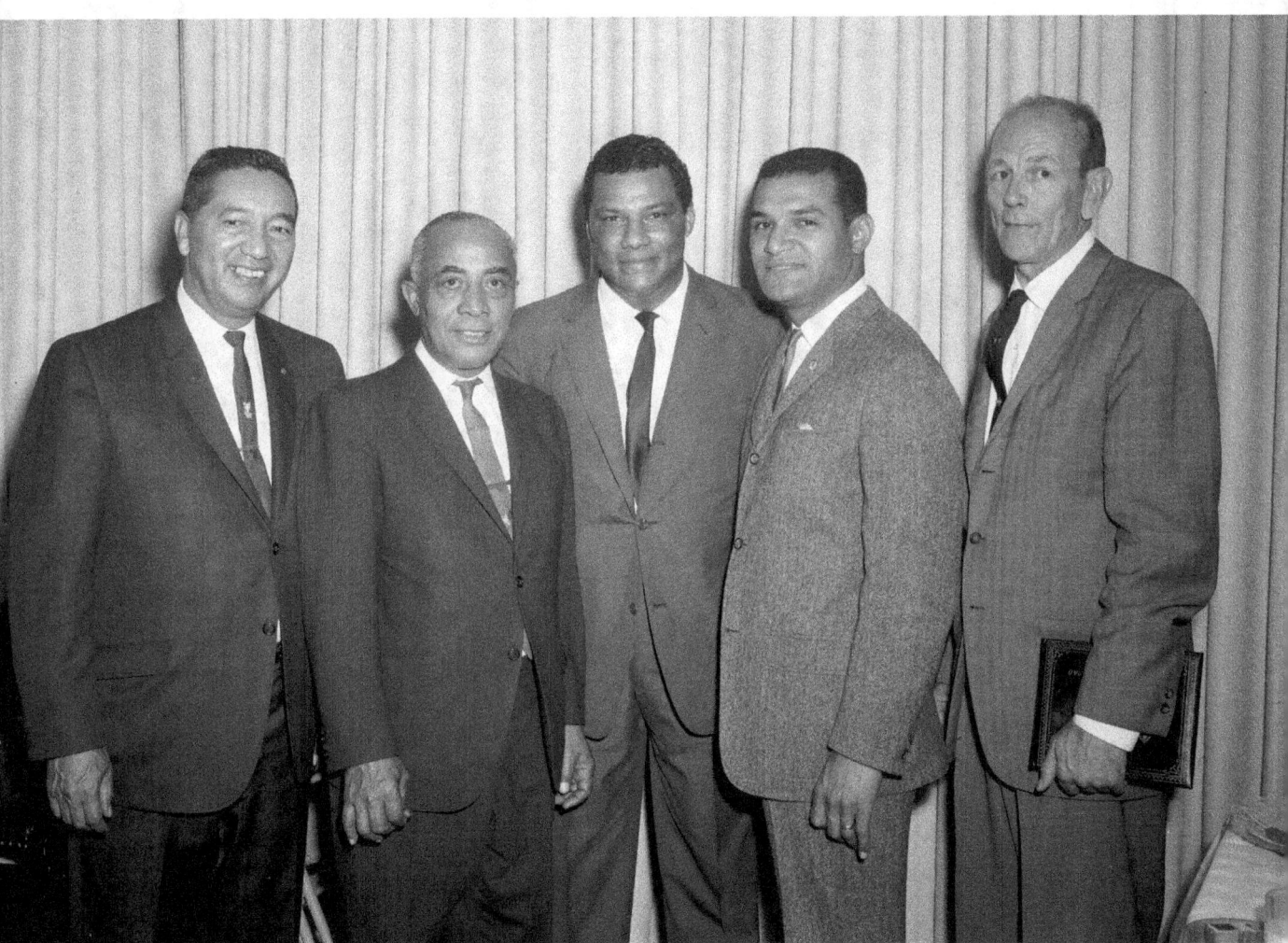

Rolland Curtis (*center*) with Gilbert Lindsay (*left*) and Billy G. Mills (*right*) at a victory
celebration for Gilbert Lindsay. c1964
*Opposite*: Rolland J. Curtis with his mother Mathilda at LAX. c1960s

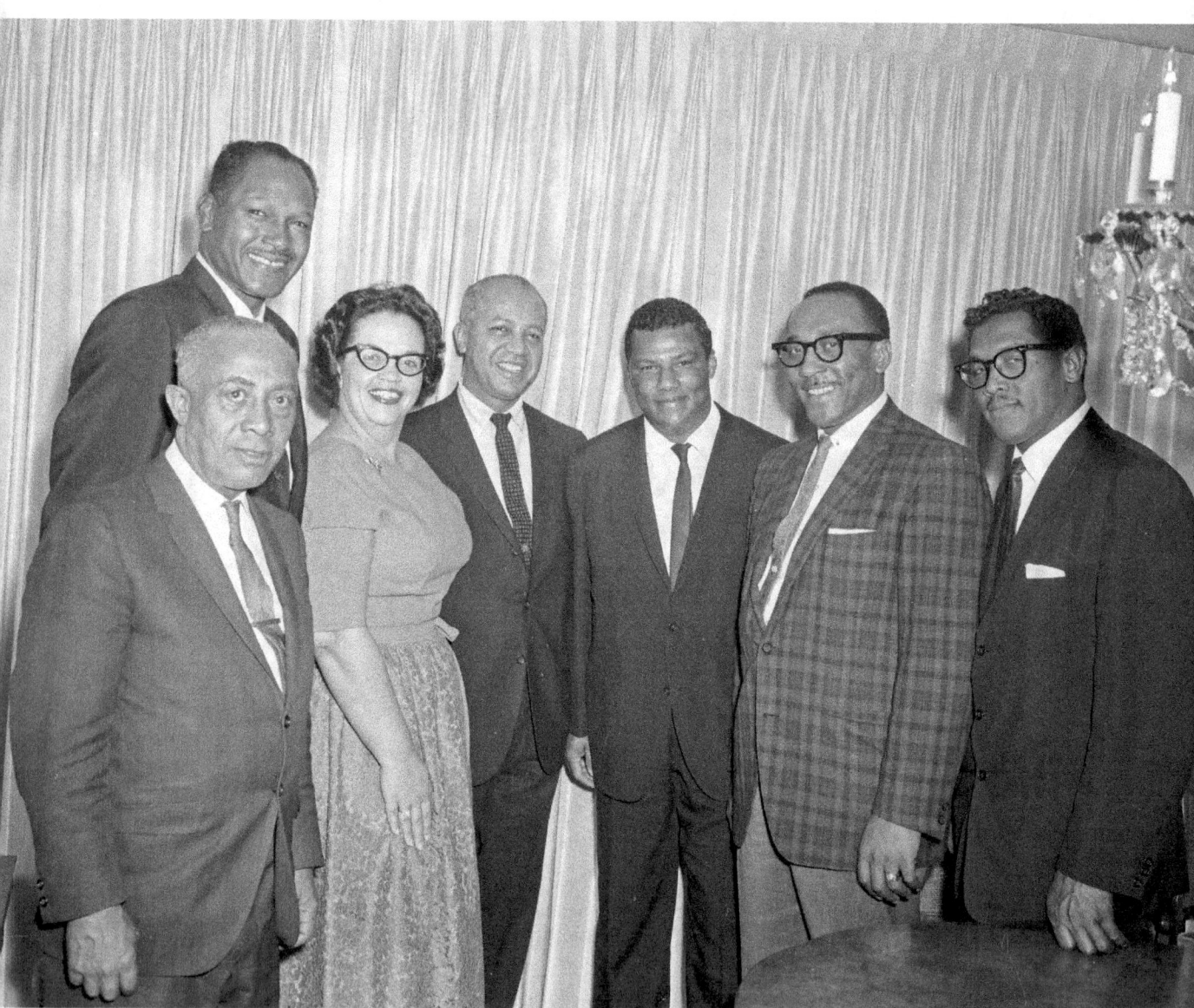

Rolland Curtis (*center right*) with Gilbert Lindsay (*far left*), Tom Bradley (*left*), Gloria Curtis (*center left*), Rev. H.H. Brookins (*right*) and Dr. Clarence Littlejohn (*far right*) at home. c1963

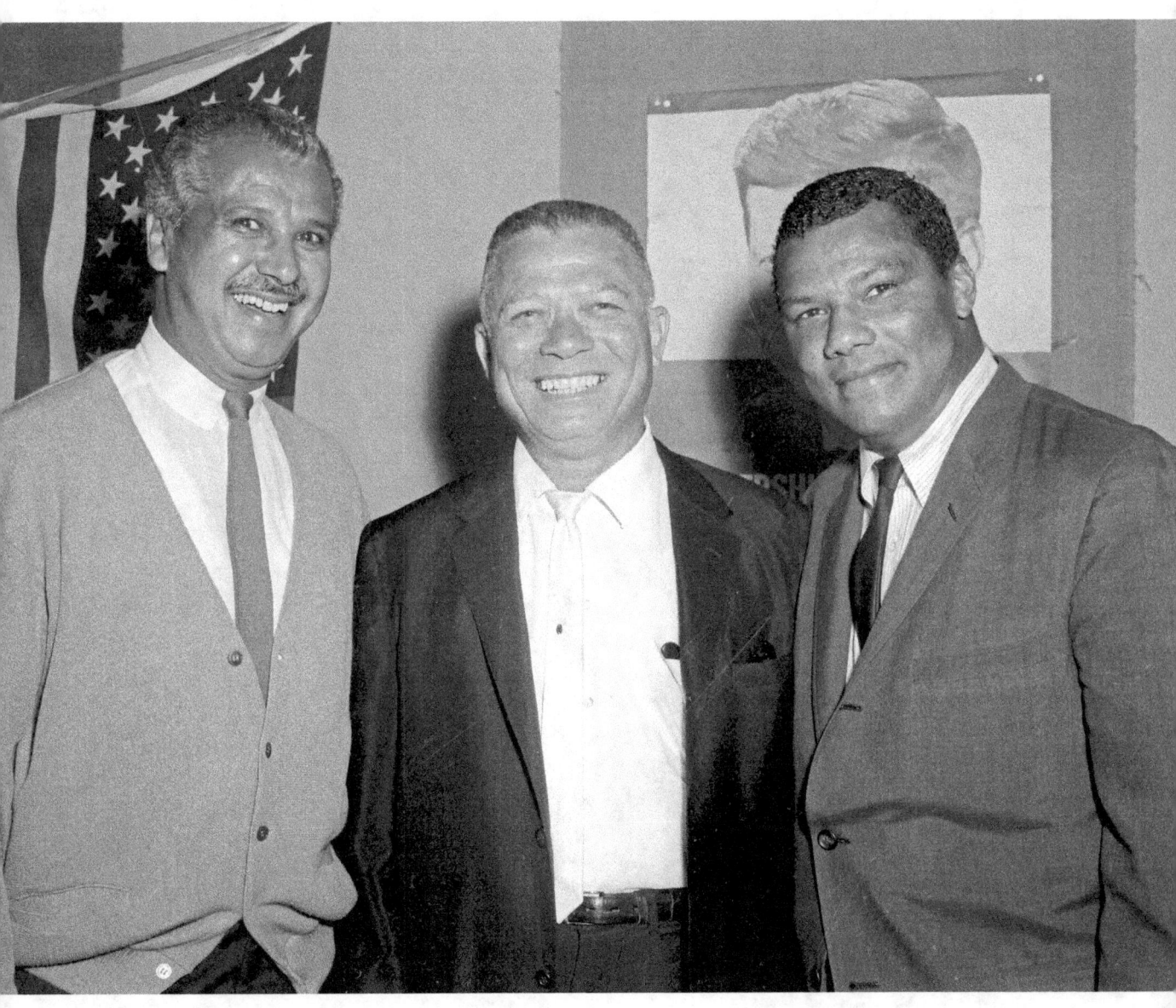

Rolland Curtis (*right*) with Leon Aubry SR. (*left*) and Rip Roberts SR (*center*). c1963

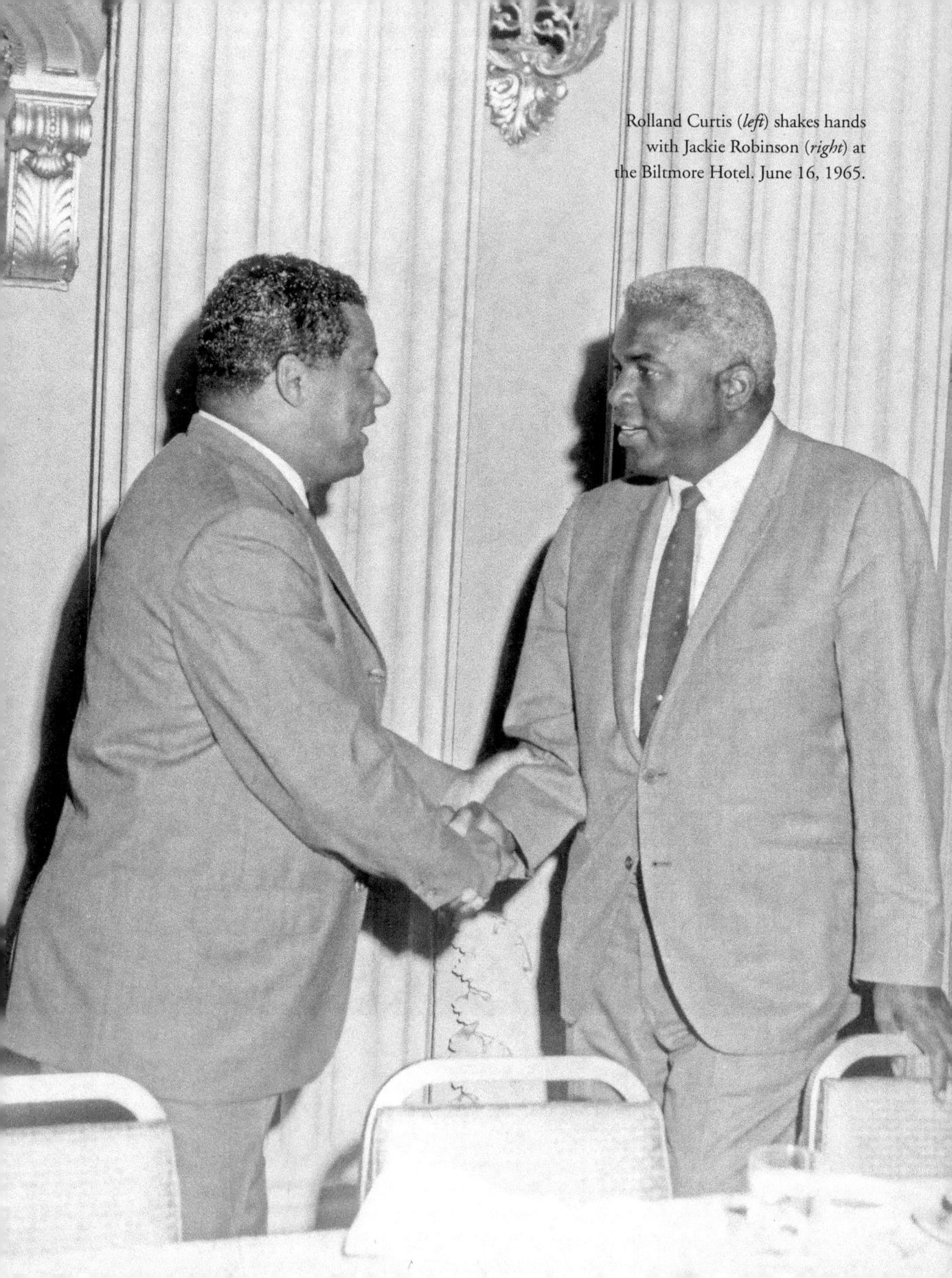

Rolland Curtis (*left*) shakes hands with Jackie Robinson (*right*) at the Biltmore Hotel. June 16, 1965.

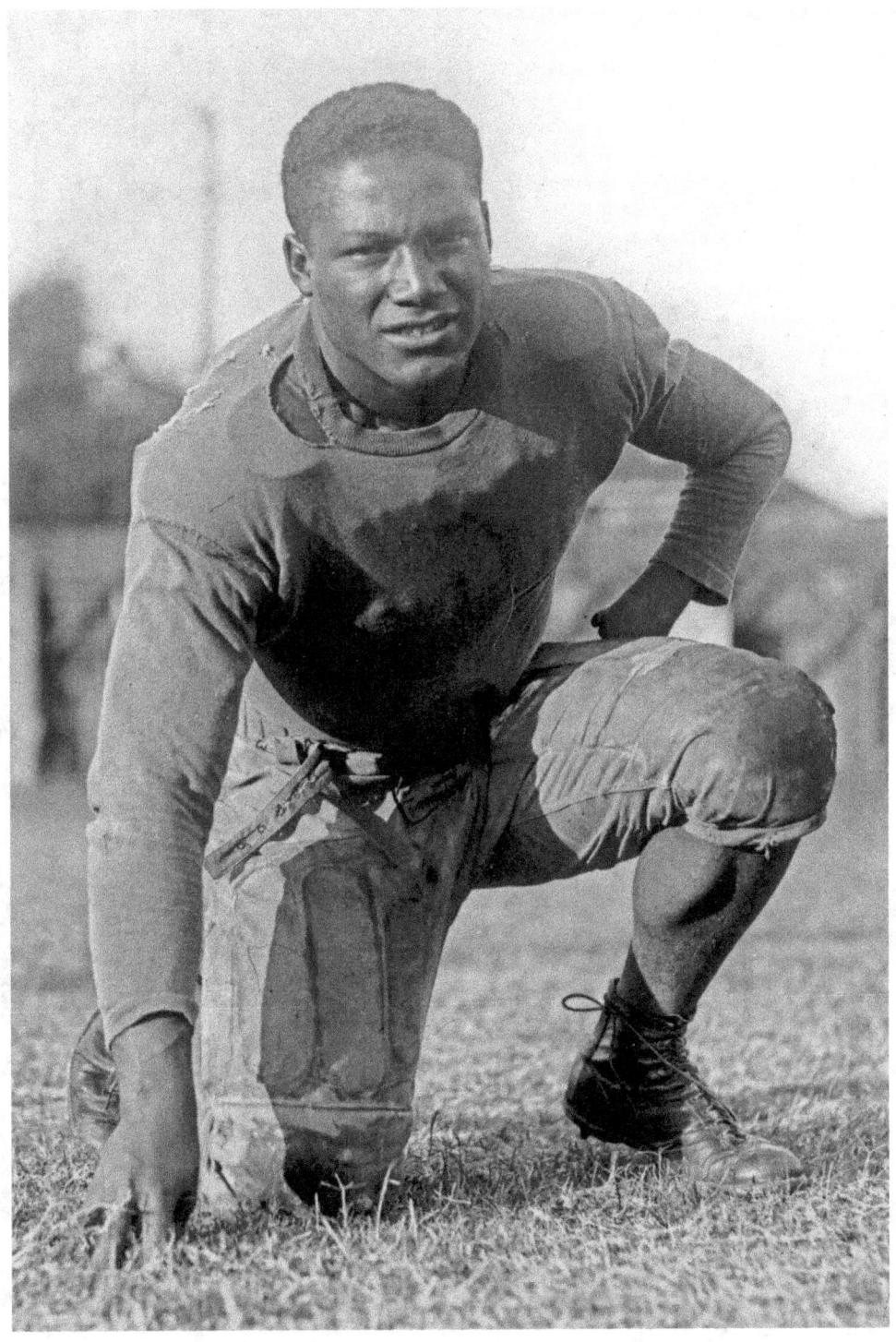

Rolland Curtis in a football uniform at USC. c1952

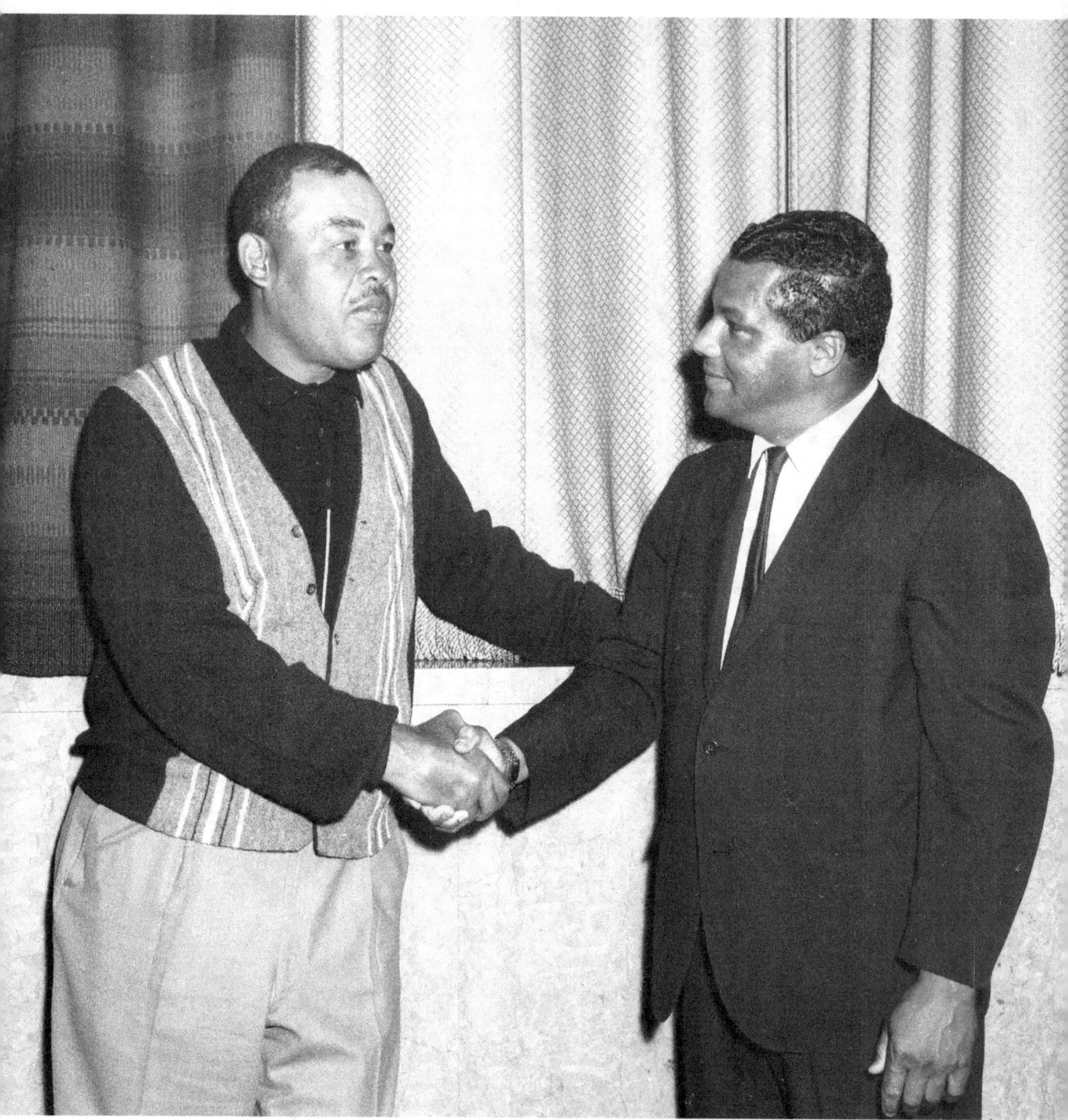

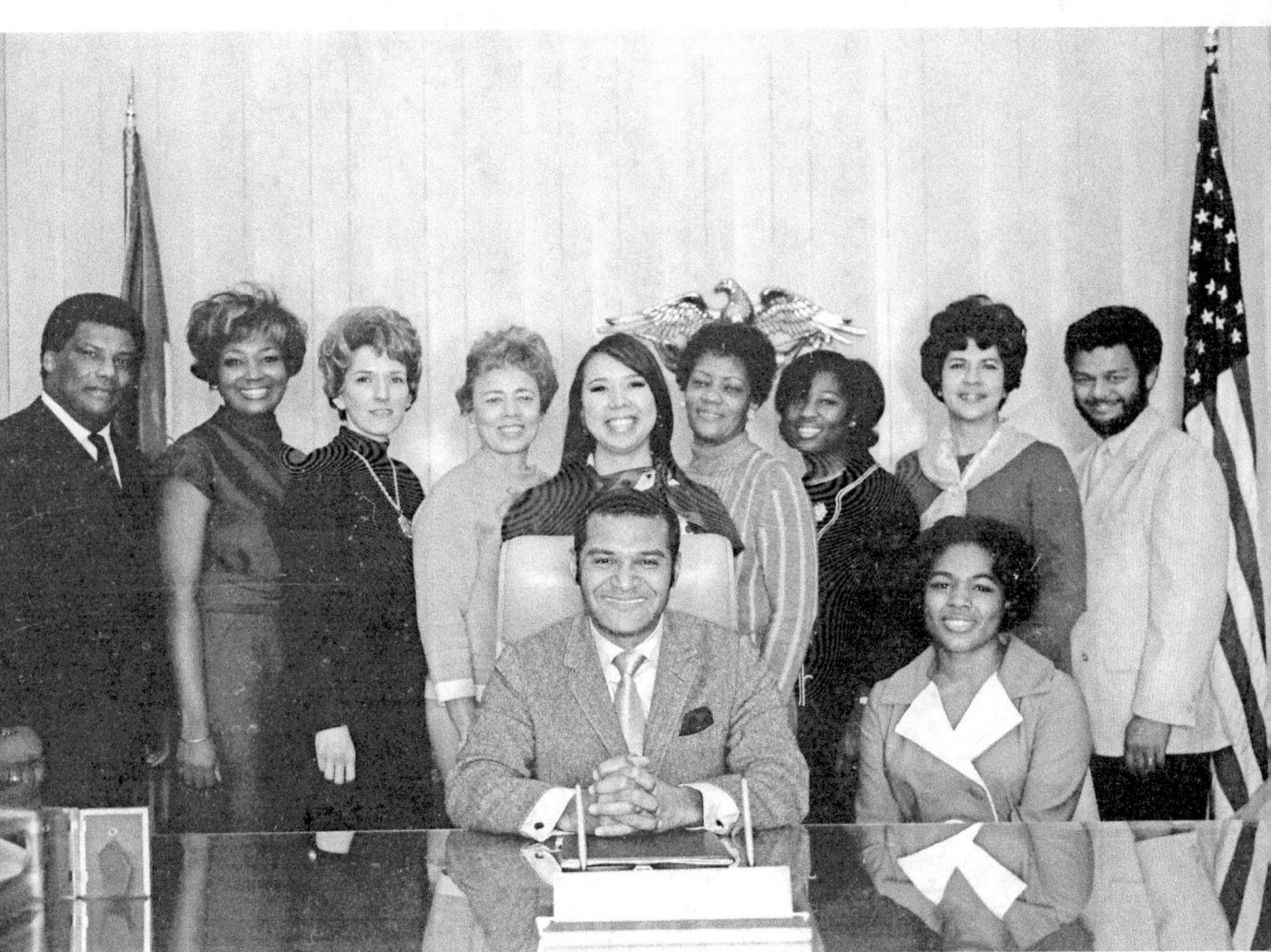

Councilman Billy G. Mills with his staff, including Robert Farrell (*far right*), Flossie Burnley (*seated right*), Rolland Curtis (*far left*), Ruby Williams (*right of Curtis*) and Ferdia Harris (*left of center*).
*Opposite*: Rolland Curtis (*right*) shakes hands with boxer Joe Louis (*left*) at City Hall. c1963

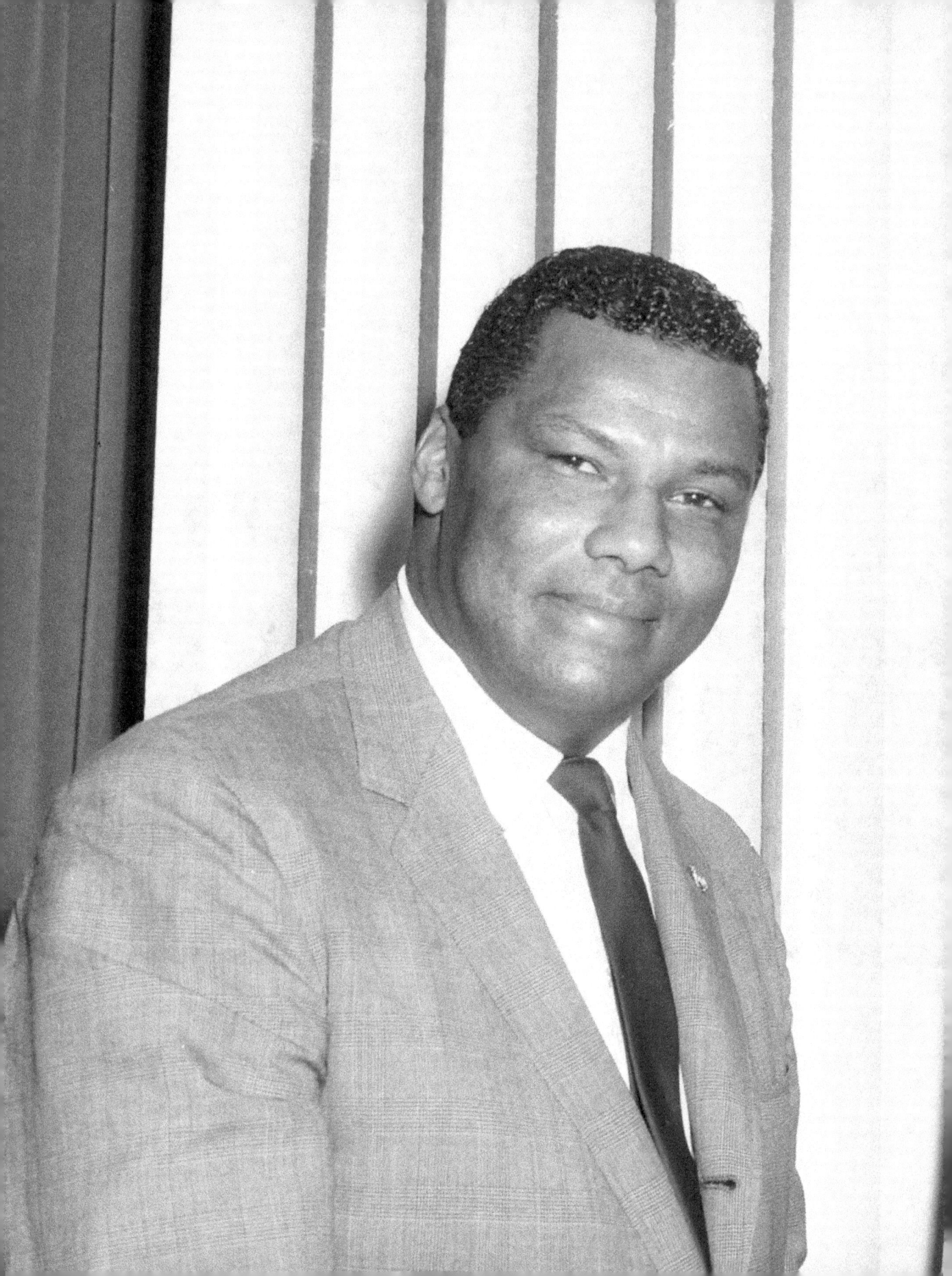

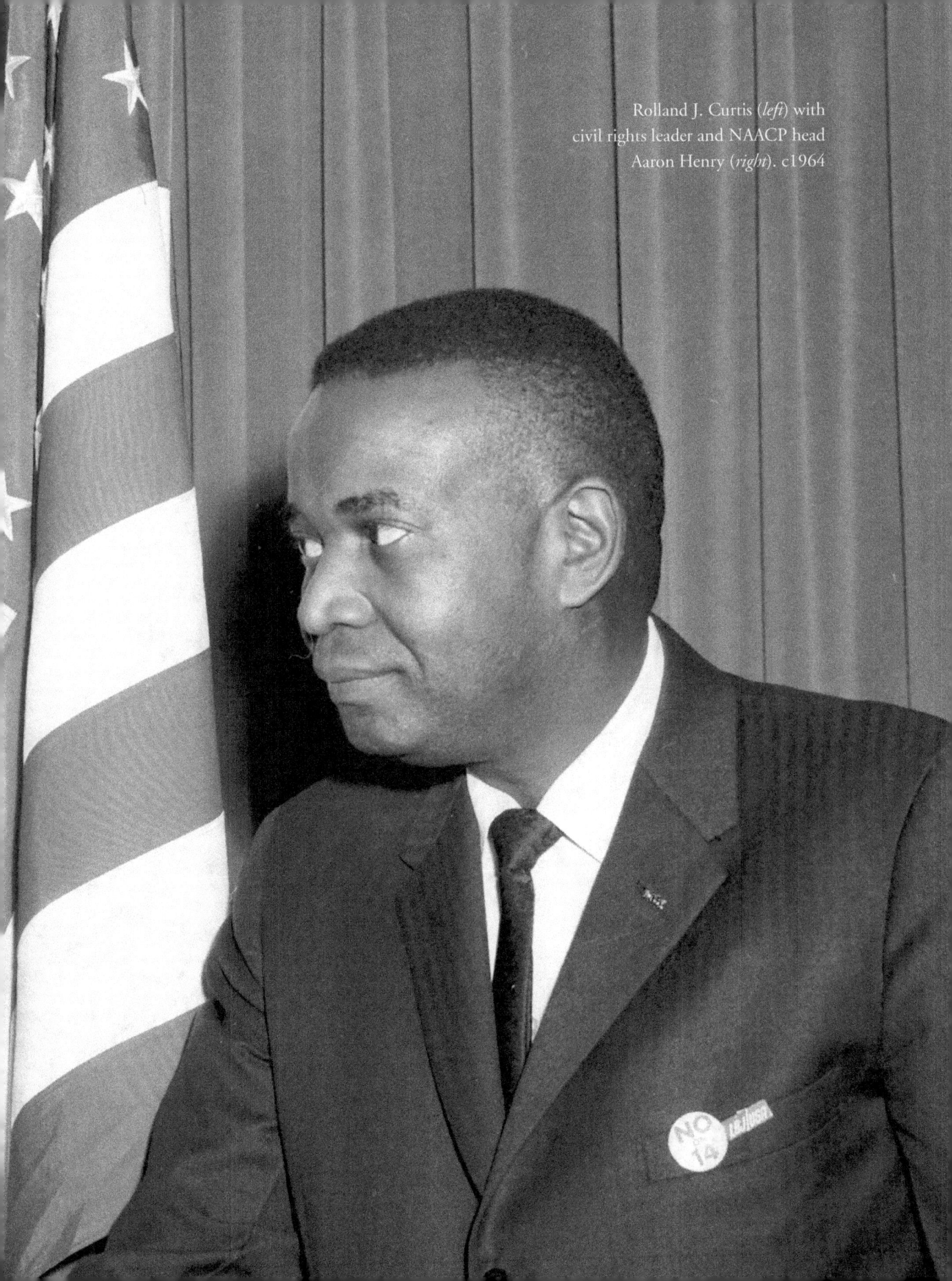

Rolland J. Curtis (*left*) with
civil rights leader and NAACP head
Aaron Henry (*right*). c1964

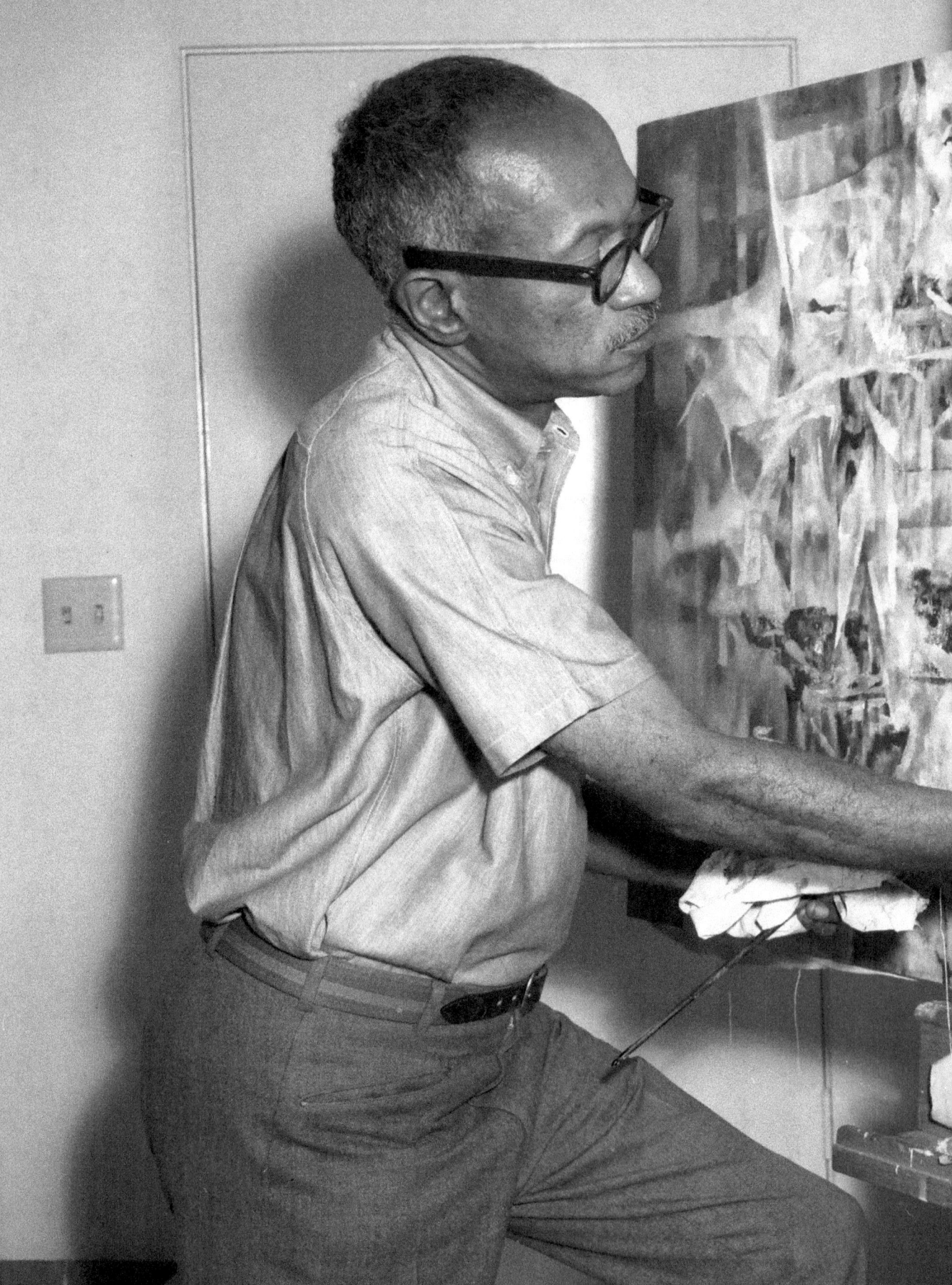

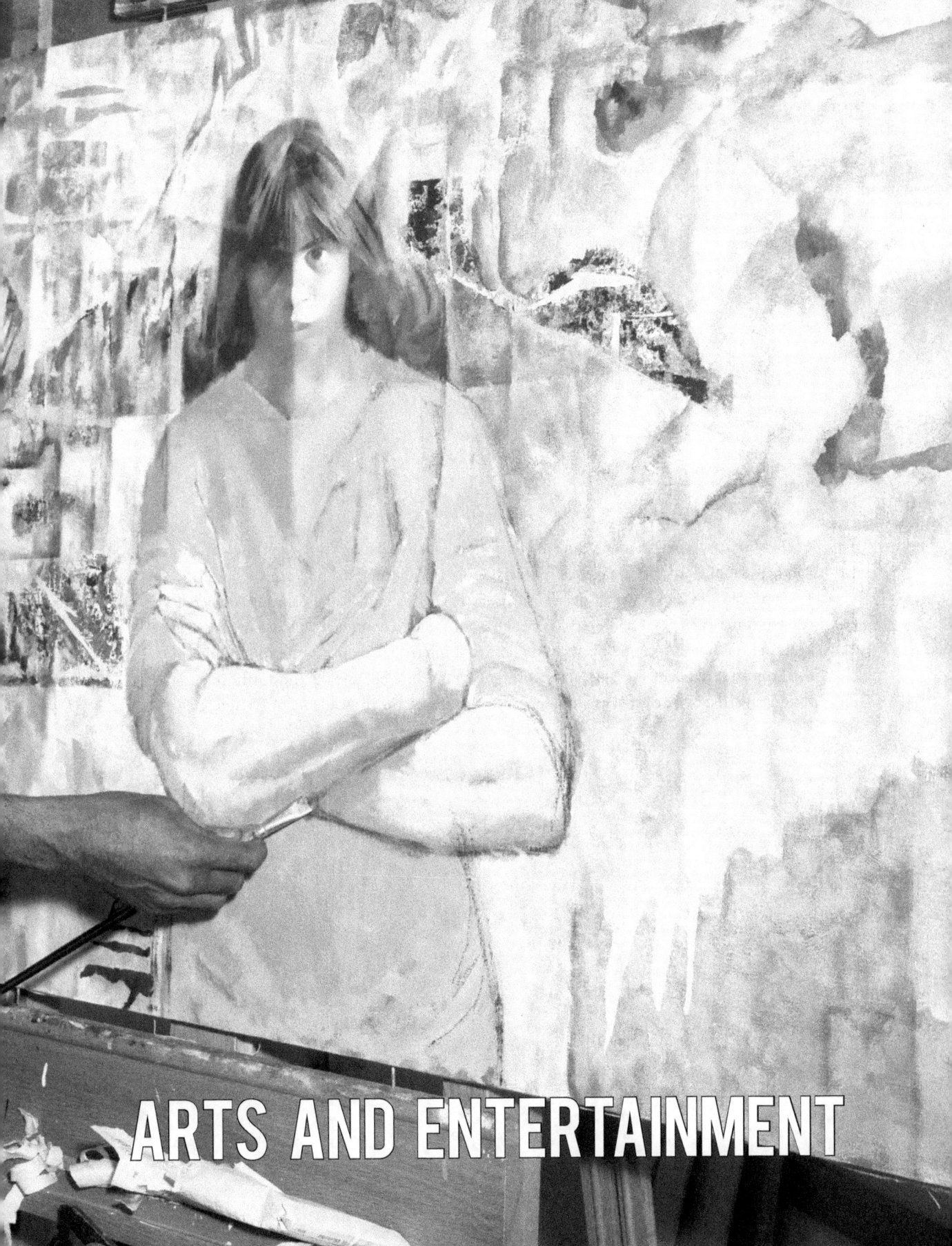

ARTS AND ENTERTAINMENT

*Overleaf and opposite*: Charles White paints at home. When young Charles White raised his hand at school to ask if there were any black heroes in American history, his wife recalled, "He was told to shut up and sit down." Years later, White's murals and paintings depicted African American heroes and everyday people, and came to epitomize the idea of "black is beautiful." When White and his wife were the first interracial couple in the community, their son later recalled "for sale signs went right up." White became the third African American artist to be elected as a full member into the National Academy of Design. c1968

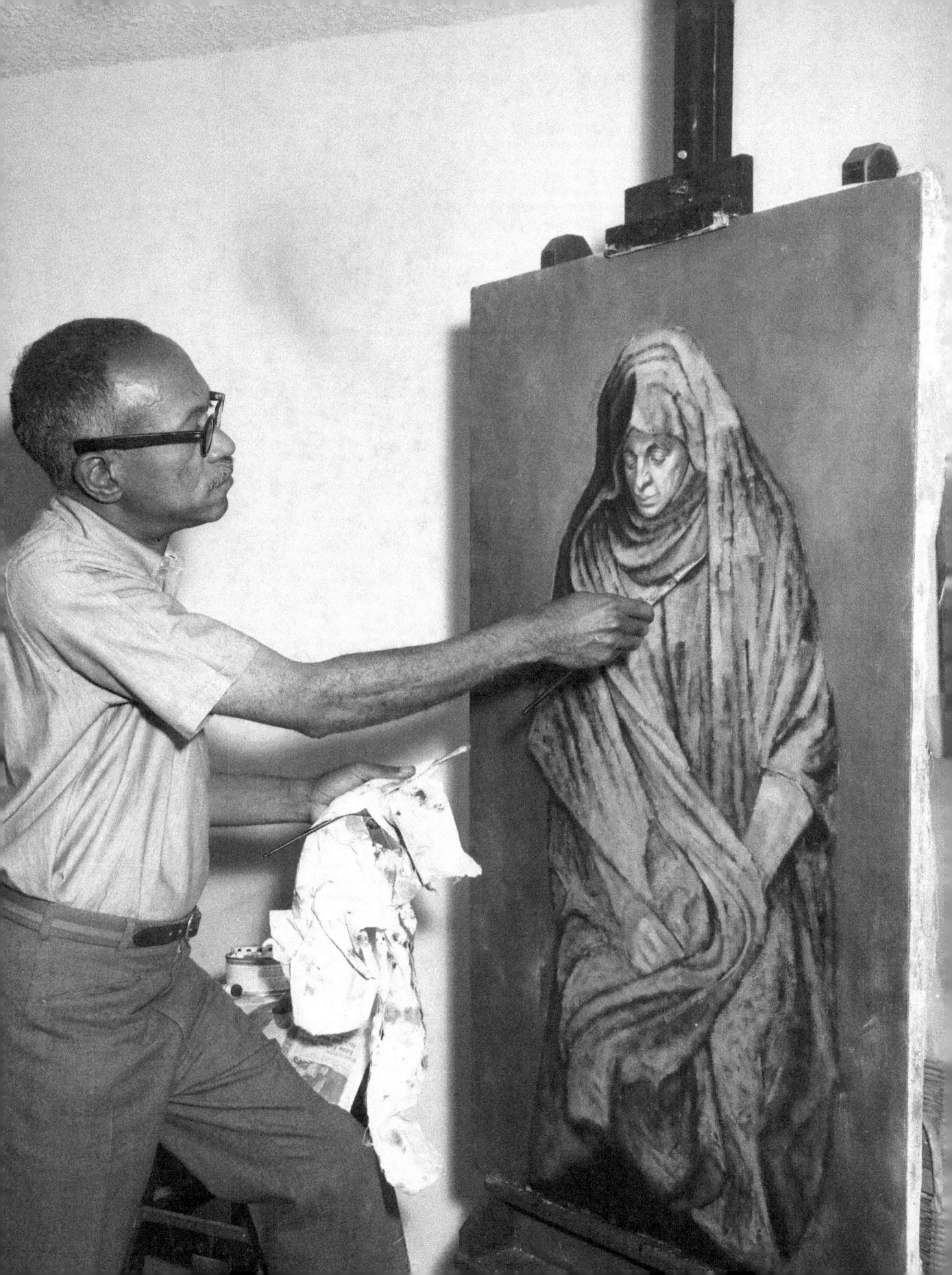

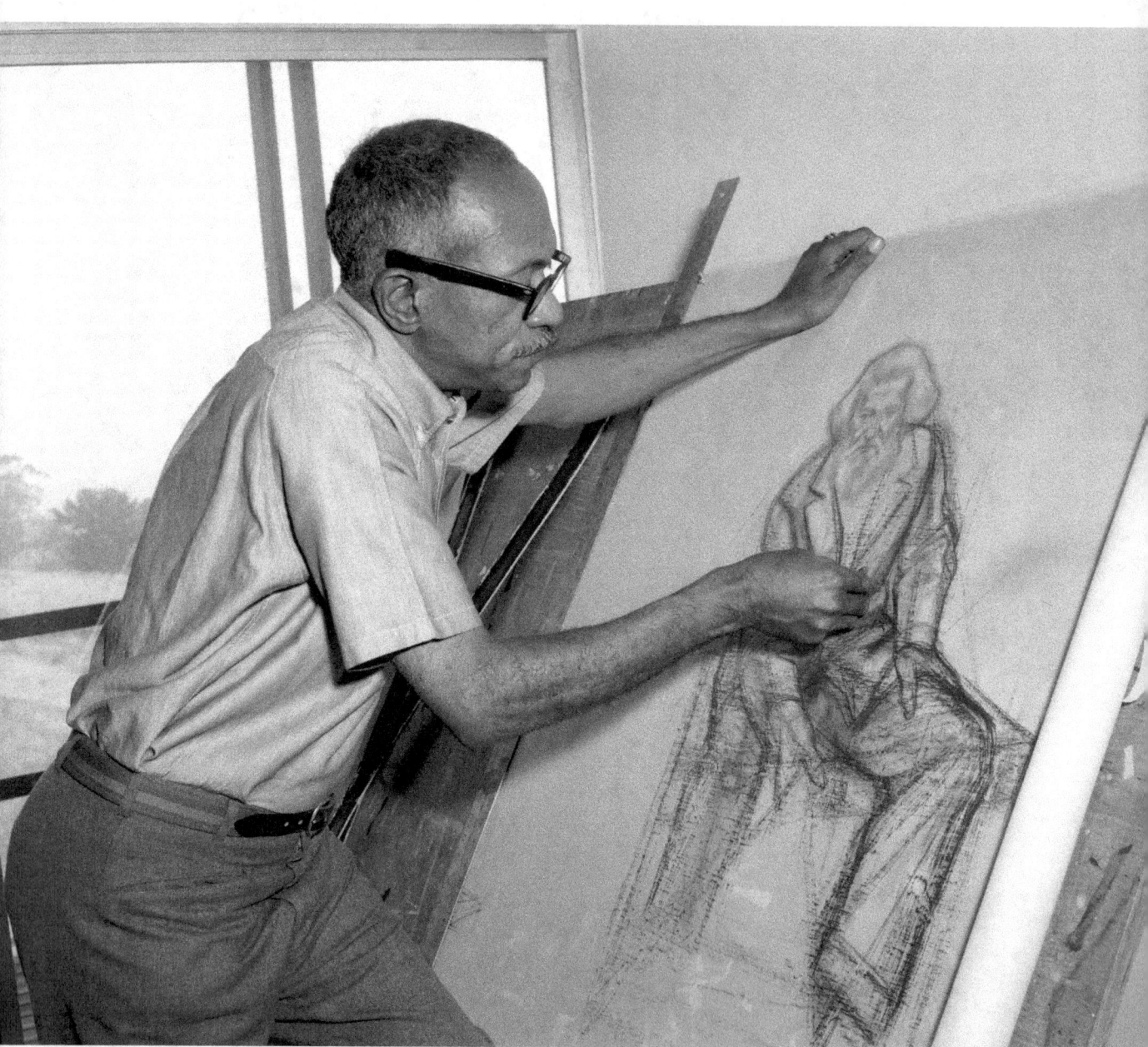

Charles White paints at home.

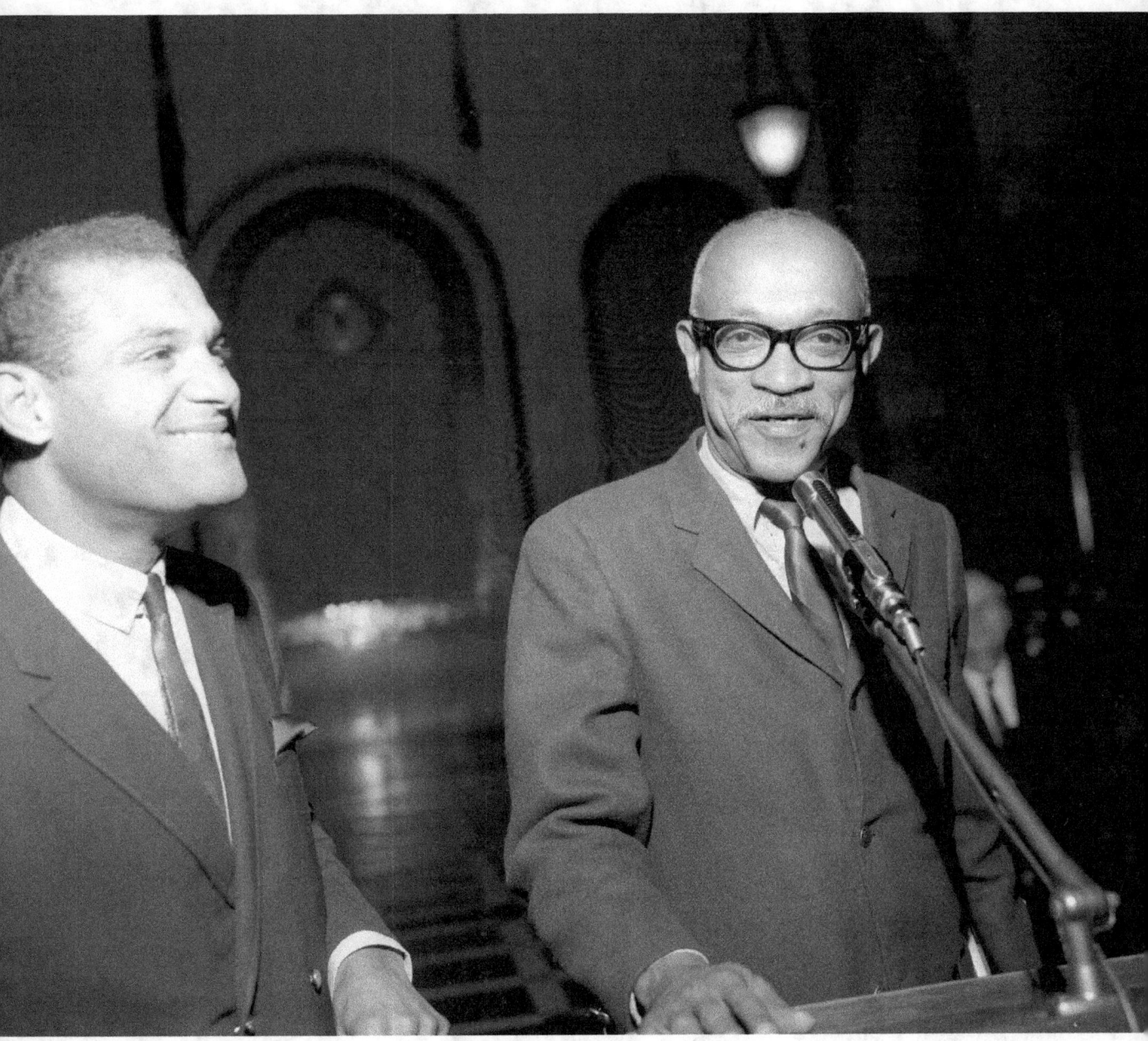

Billy G. Mills presents Charles Wilbert White with a resolution at City Hall.
January 10, 1968

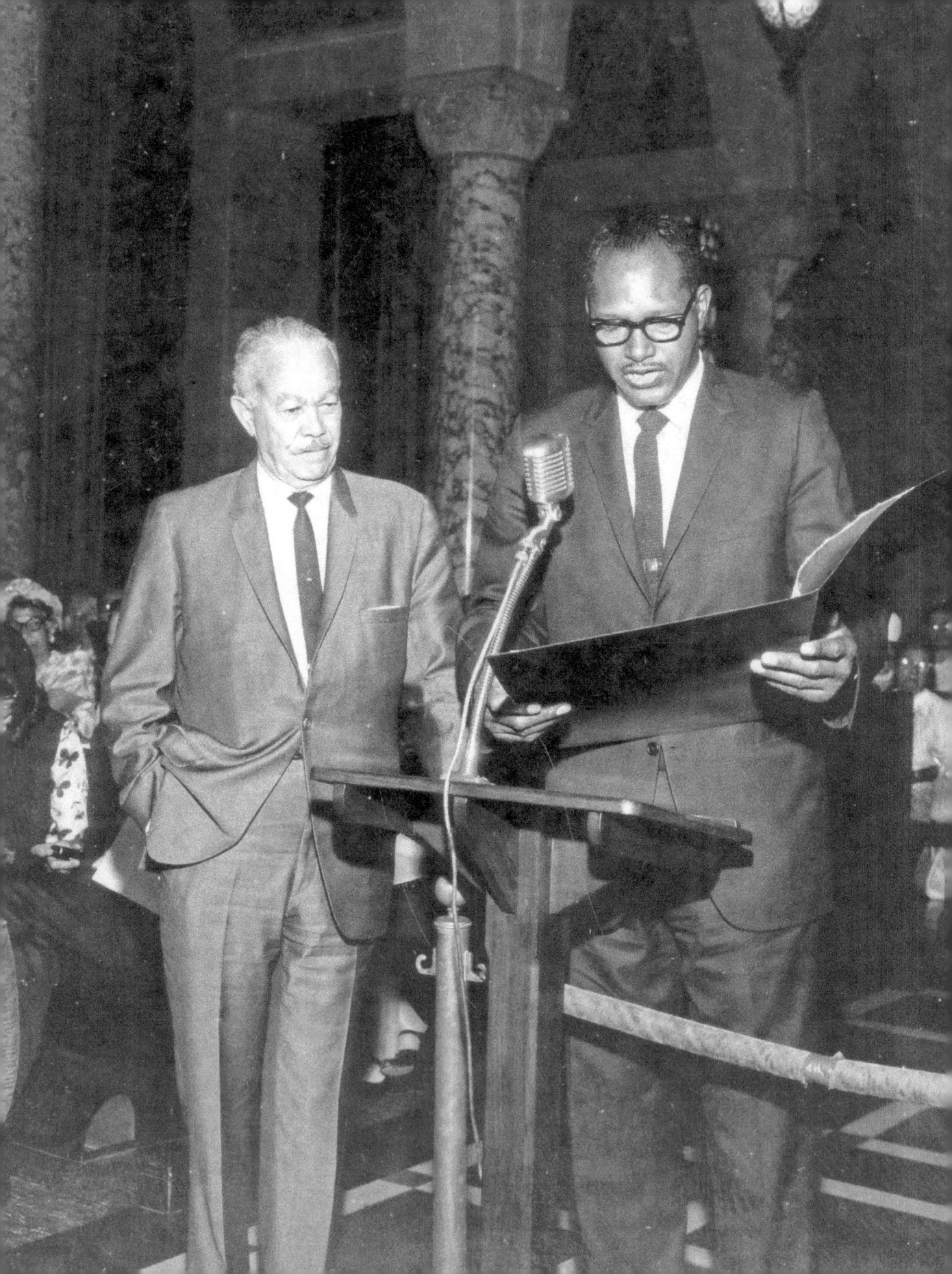

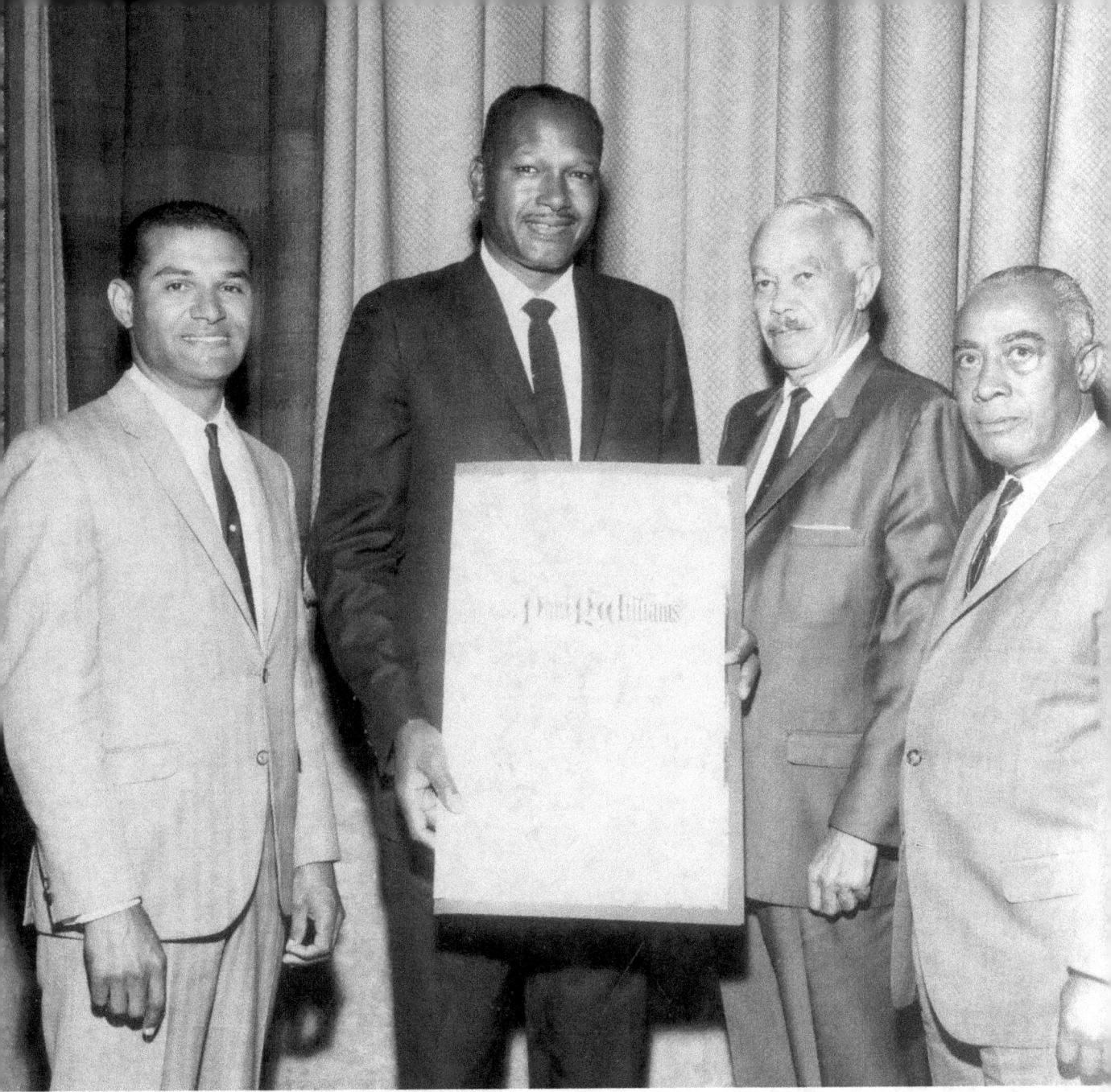

*Above and opposite*: Paul Williams receives a resolution from city council. At an early age, Williams knew he wanted to be an architect, despite his high school teacher advising him that, "Your own people can't afford you, and white clients won't hire you." Williams learned to draw upside-down so that white clients wouldn't have to sit next to him while he drew. When touring construction sites, his hands were clasped behind him, to allow white people to extend their hand first if they wished to shake his. Williams became the first African American member of the American Institute of Architects in 1923. September 14, 1965

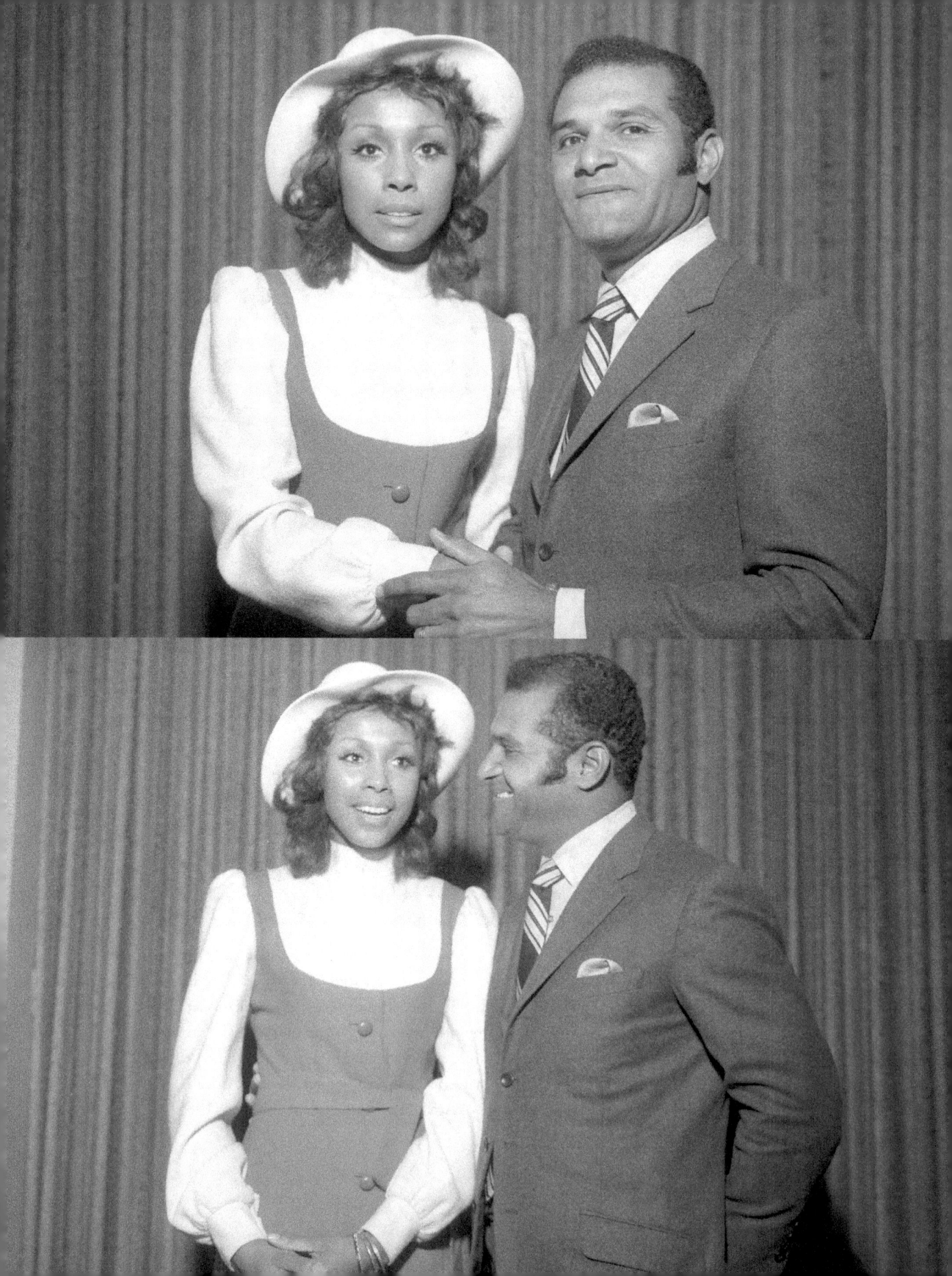

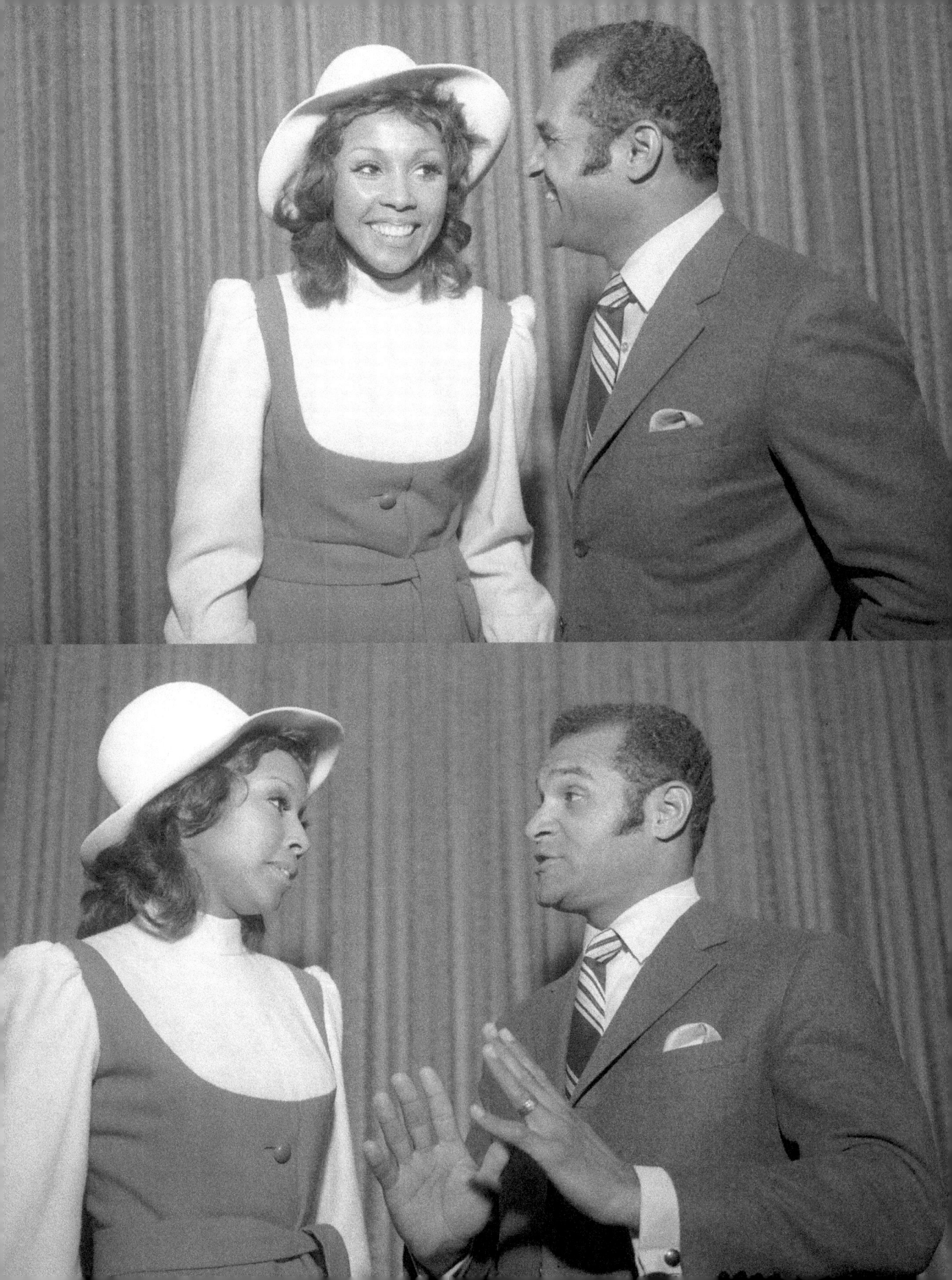

*Overleaf:* Billy G. Mills meets Diahann Carroll. Perhaps best known for her role as Dominique Deveraux in the nighttime soap opera *Dynasty*, Carroll's career began in some of the earliest major films featuring black casts. In 1962, she became the first African American to win a Tony award for best actress, and six years later broke an entertainment racial stereotype by starring in the television show, *Julia*, where she played a professional instead of a domestic worker. c1970

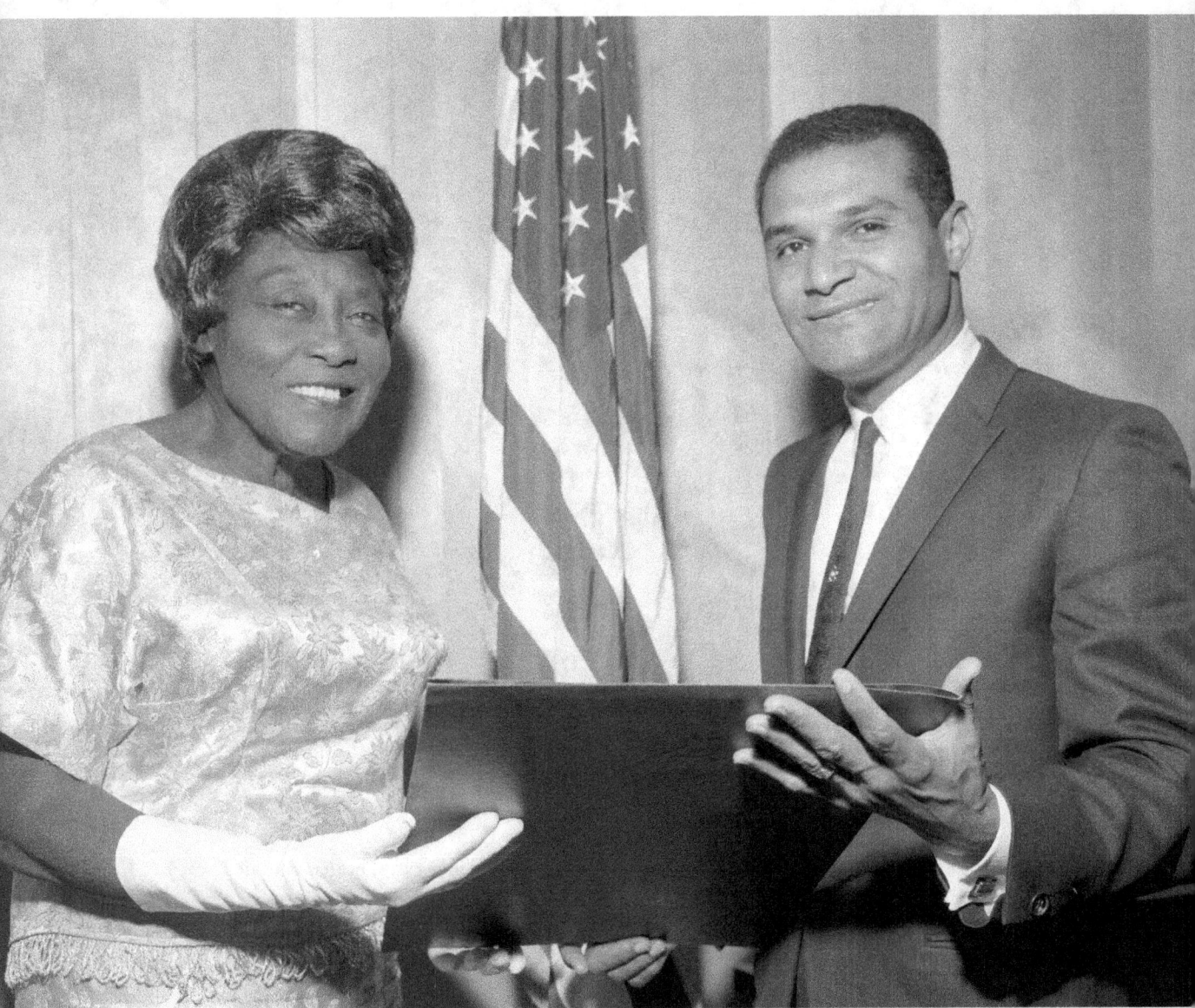

Madame A.C. Bilbrew receives a resolution from Billy G. Mills. Bilbrew was the director of the first black choir featured in a film, 1928's *Hearts of Dixie,* which also happened to be the first black "talkie." She was also a pioneer in radio, becoming the first African American soloist on the radio in 1923, and later, the first African American to have and host a show in 1942. Bilbrew was a champion of women's rights and childhood literacy. October 27, 1956

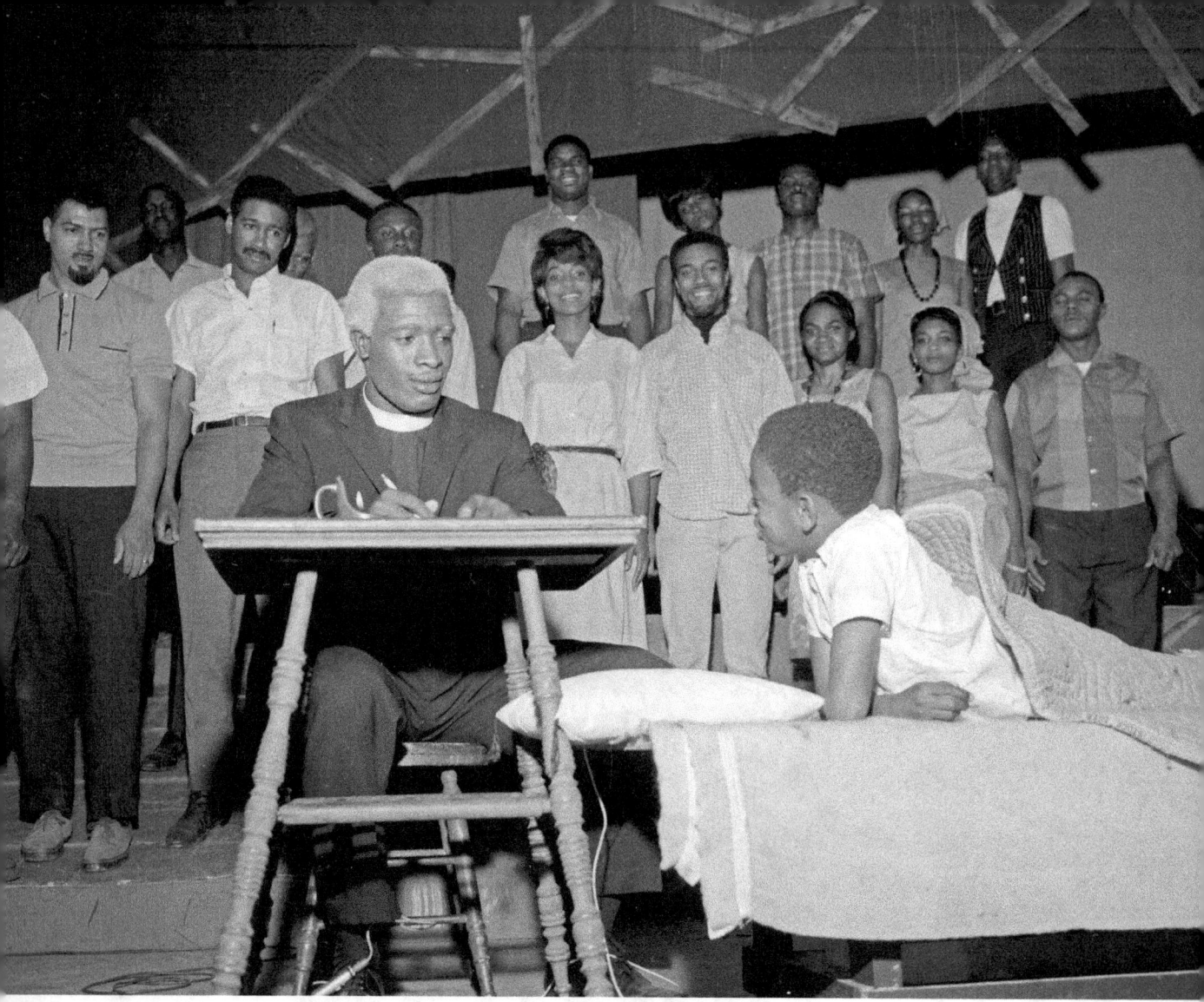

Actor Joseph Washington (*seated*) in *Lost in Stars* at the Ebony Showcase Theater. Founded by Nick and Edna Stewart in 1950, the Ebony Showcase Theater was the first African American owned theater in Los Angeles. Nick Stewart, who was most famous for his portrayal of "Lightnin'" on the TV show *Amos and Andy,* and voicing Brer Rabbit in Disney's *Song of the South,* sought to build a place where African Americans could act in roles outside of traditional stereotypes. The theater has been credited for starting the careers of many young black actors, including Nichelle Nichols, John Amos and Isabel Sanford. It was demolished in 1998. c1967

*Opposite*: Production of *Lost in Stars* at Ebony Showcase Theater with Laurine Nevels (*left*) and Joseph Washington (*right*). c1967

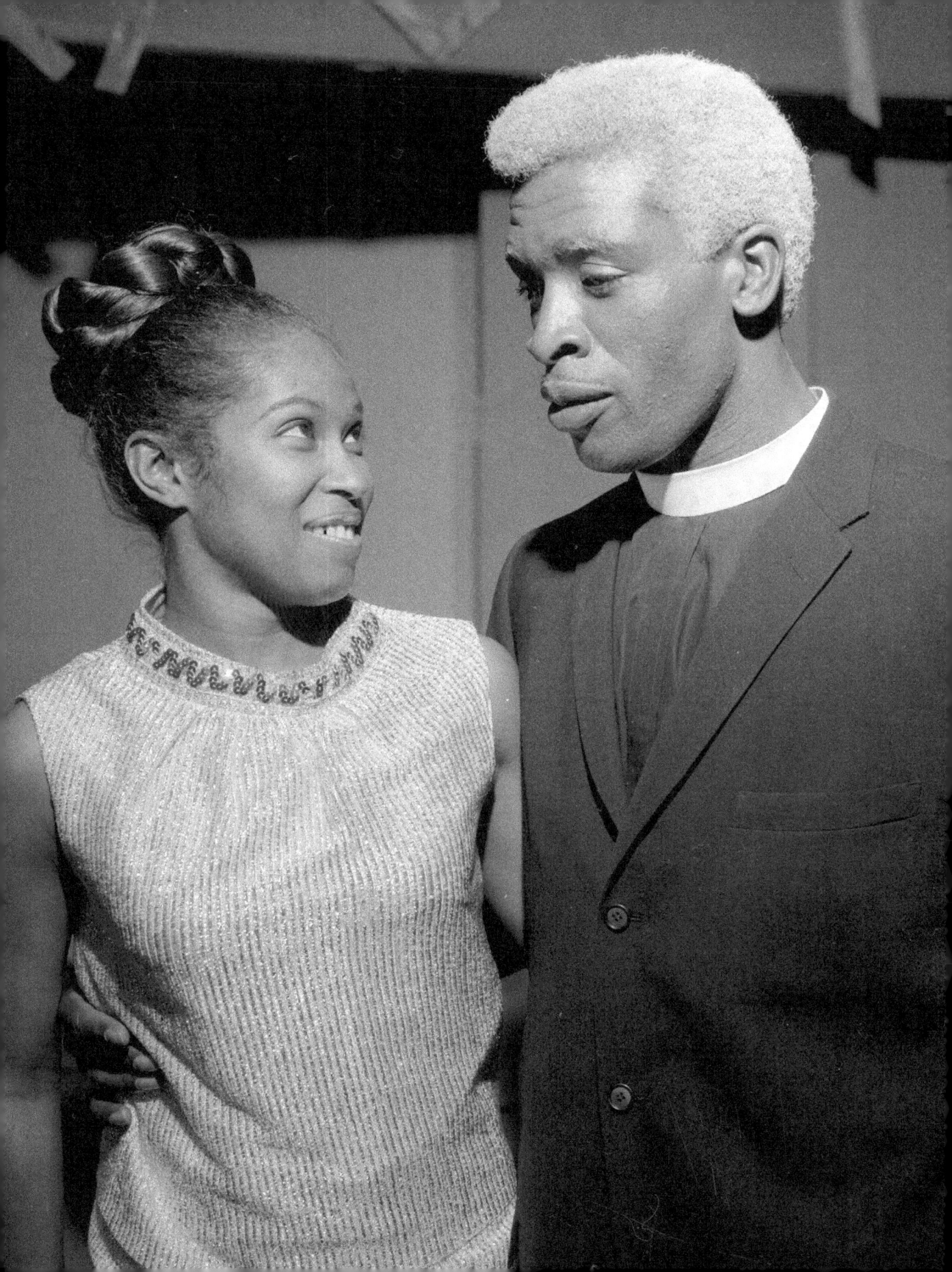

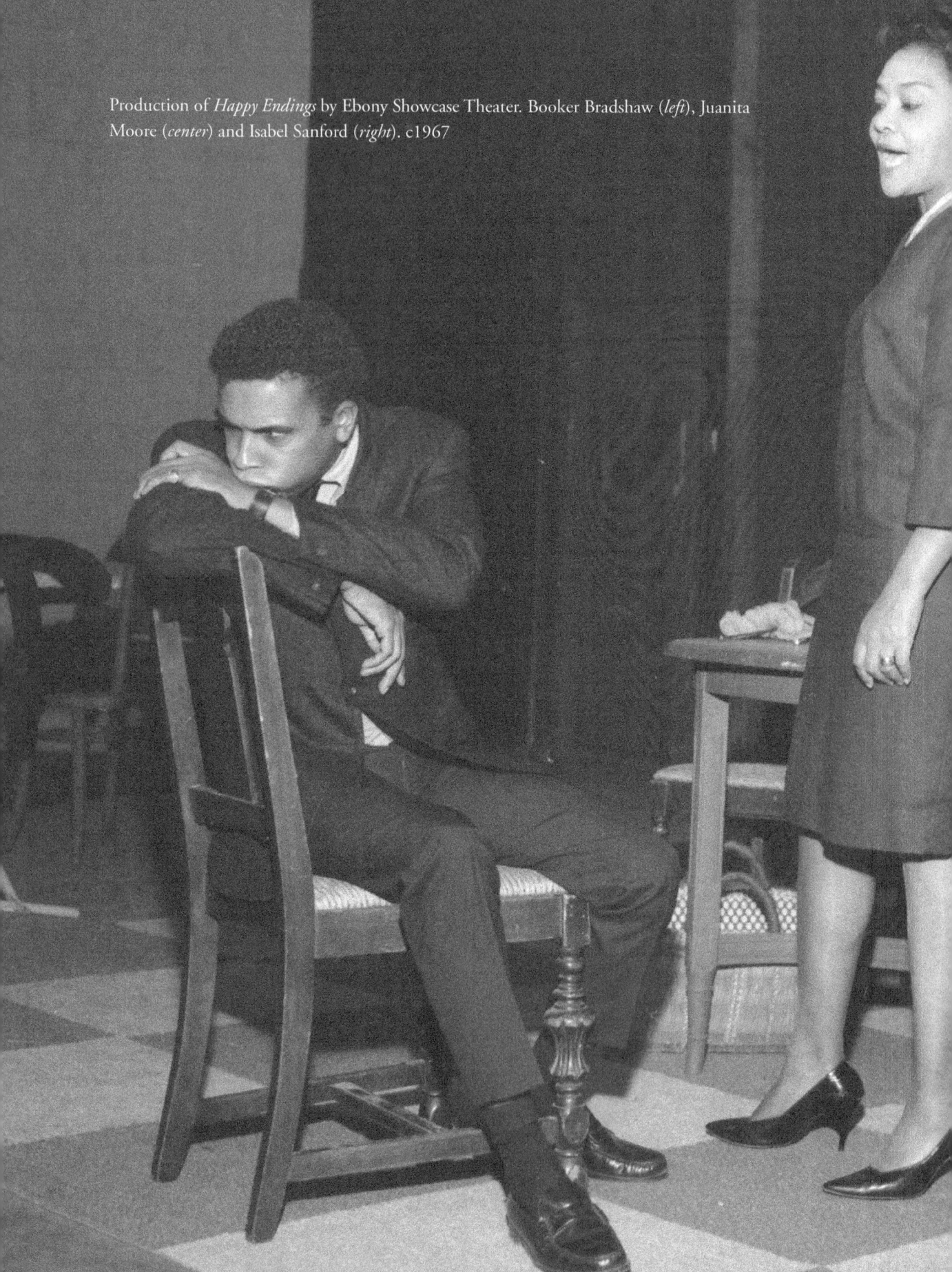

Production of *Happy Endings* by Ebony Showcase Theater. Booker Bradshaw (*left*), Juanita Moore (*center*) and Isabel Sanford (*right*). c1967

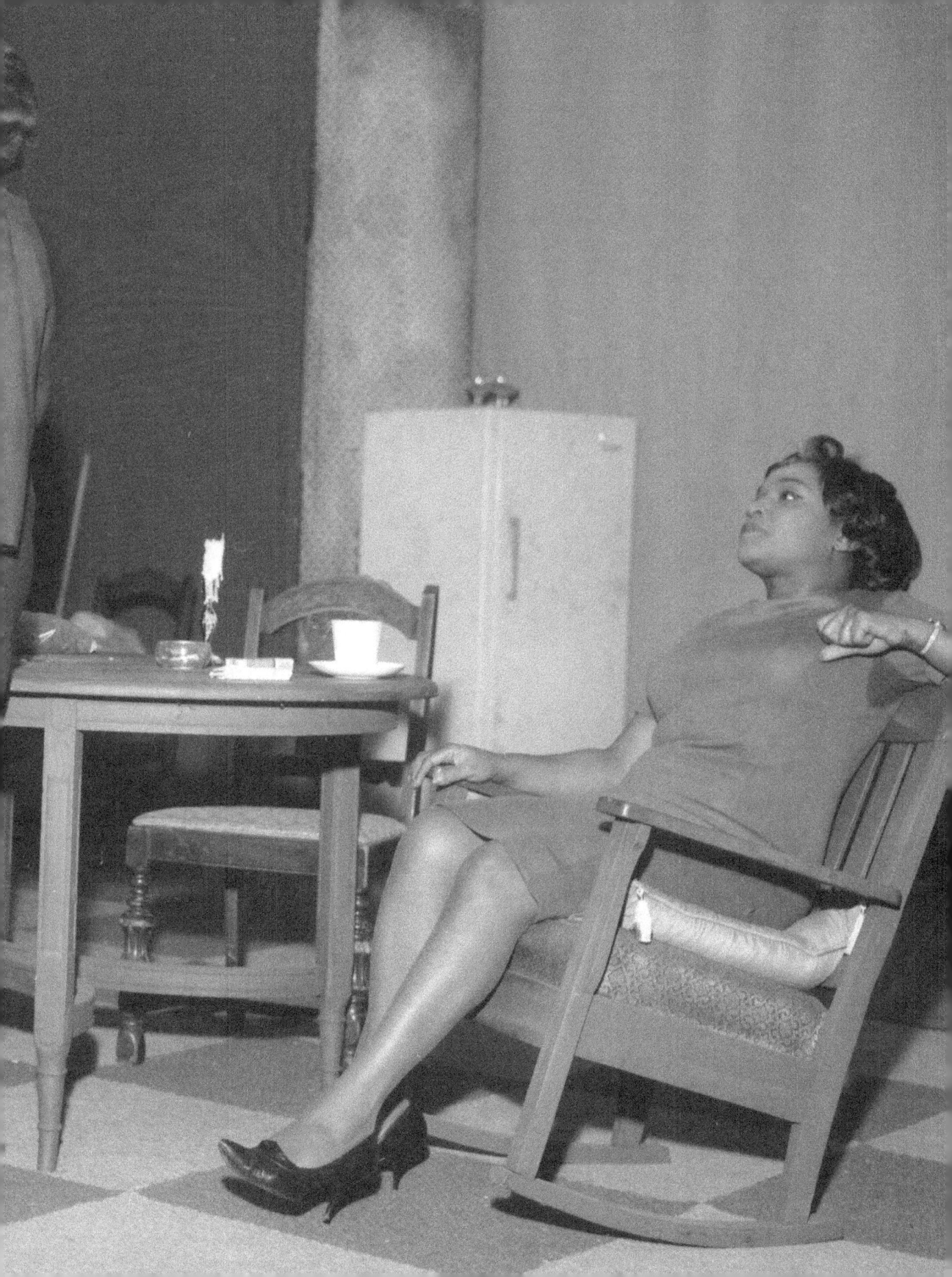

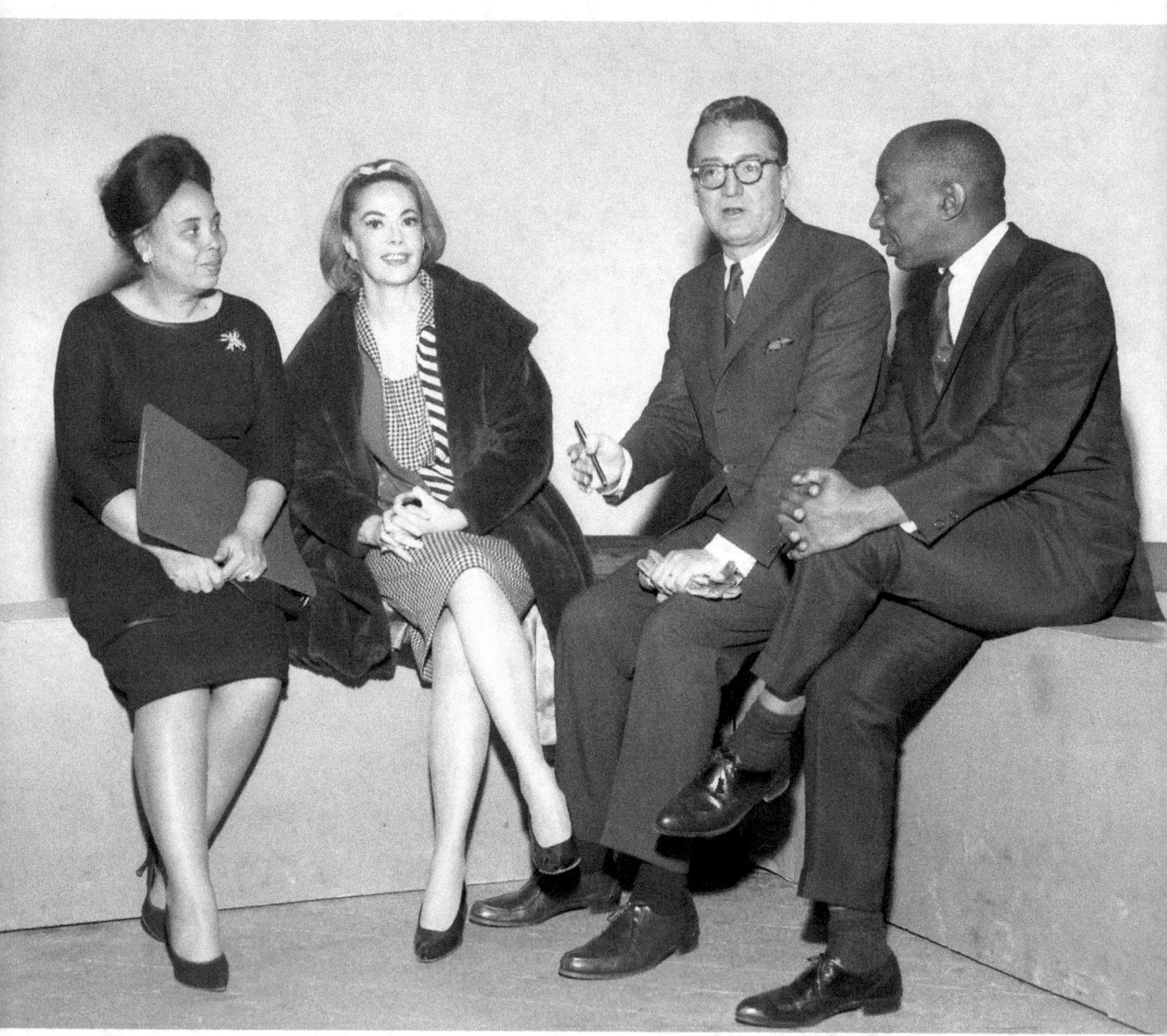

*Left to right*: Edna Stewart, Jayne Meadows, Steve Allen and Nick Stewart chat after the Stewarts receive a resolution from the city council. January 18, 1966

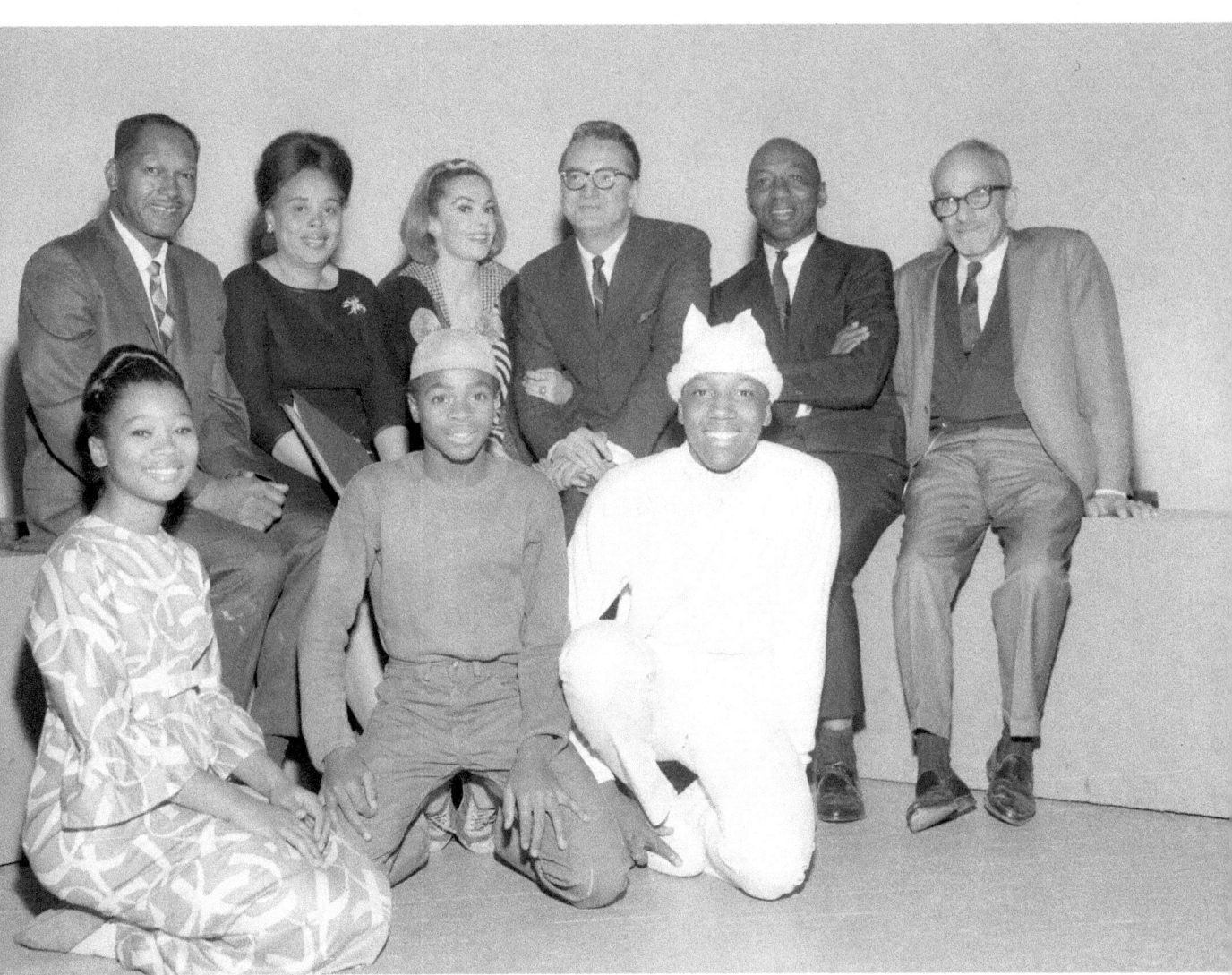

*Left to right*: Tom Bradley, Edna Stewart, Jayne Meadows, Steve Allen and Nick Stewart with Ebony Showcase Theater actors after the Stewarts receive a resolution from the city council. January 18, 1966

*Opposite*: Actors in full costume and make-up for a production of *Day of Absence* at the Ebony Showcase Theater. Morris Erby (*far left*), Isabel Sanford (*left*), Juanita Moore (*right*) and Billy G. Mills (*far right*). c1967

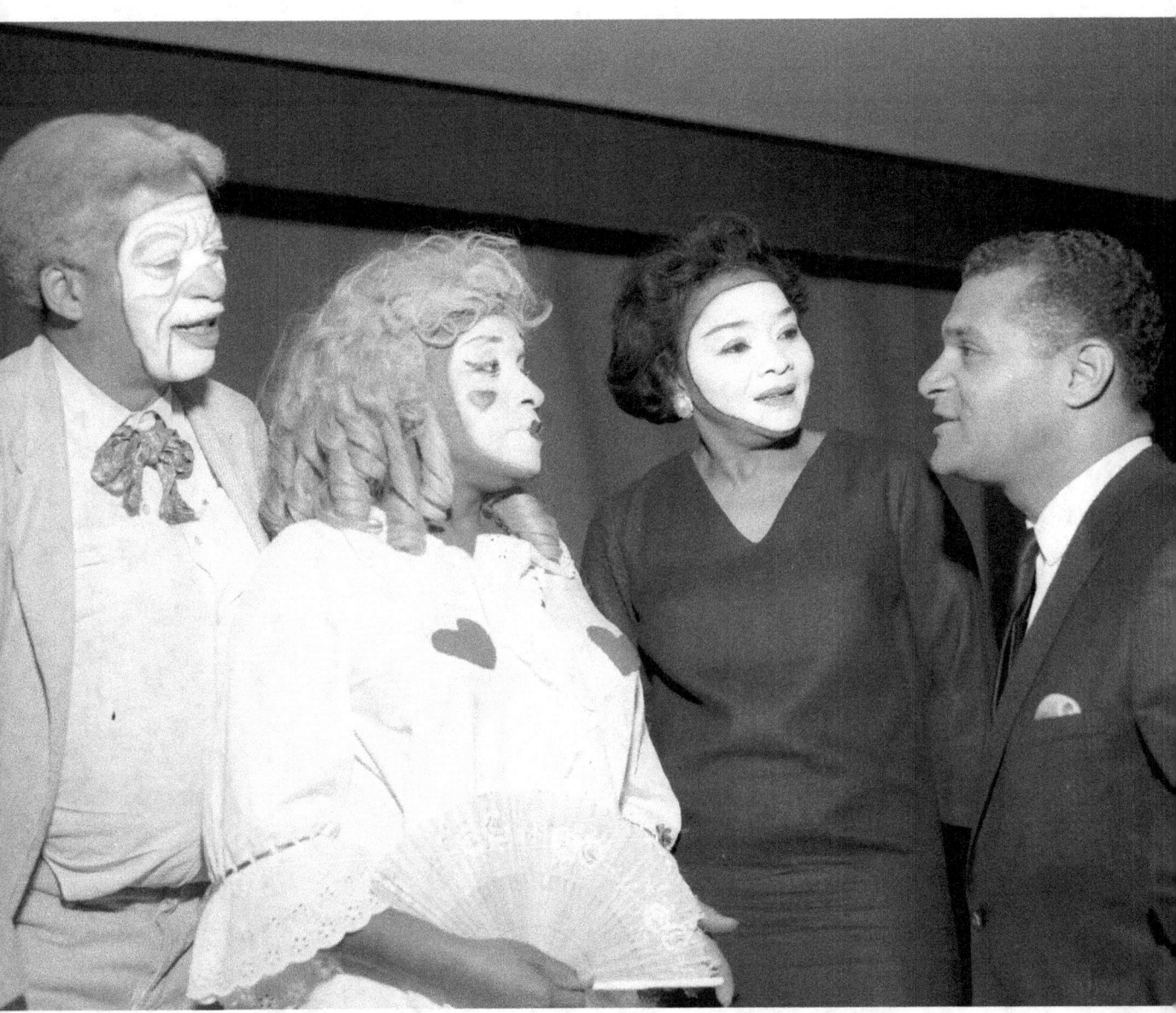

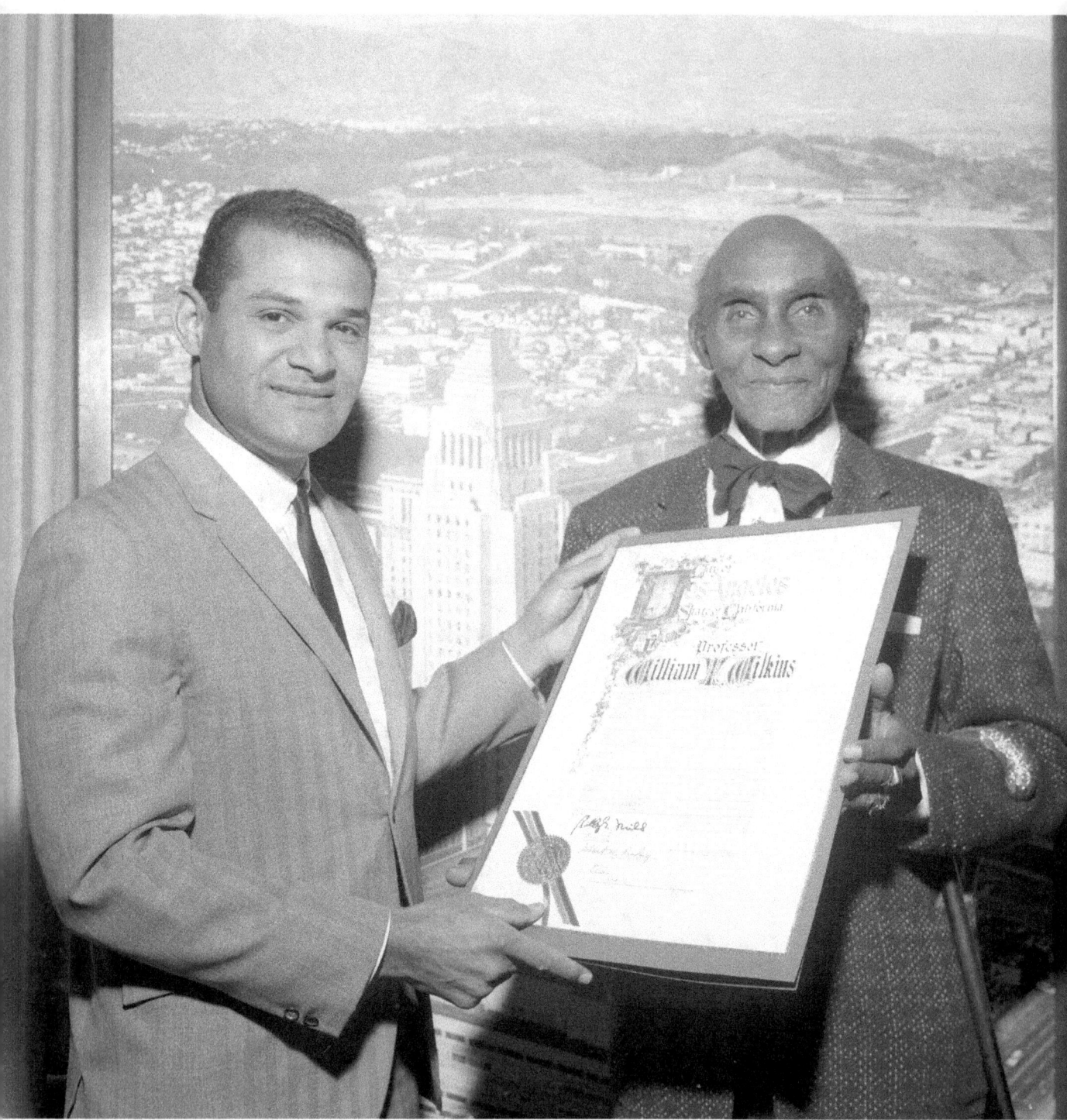

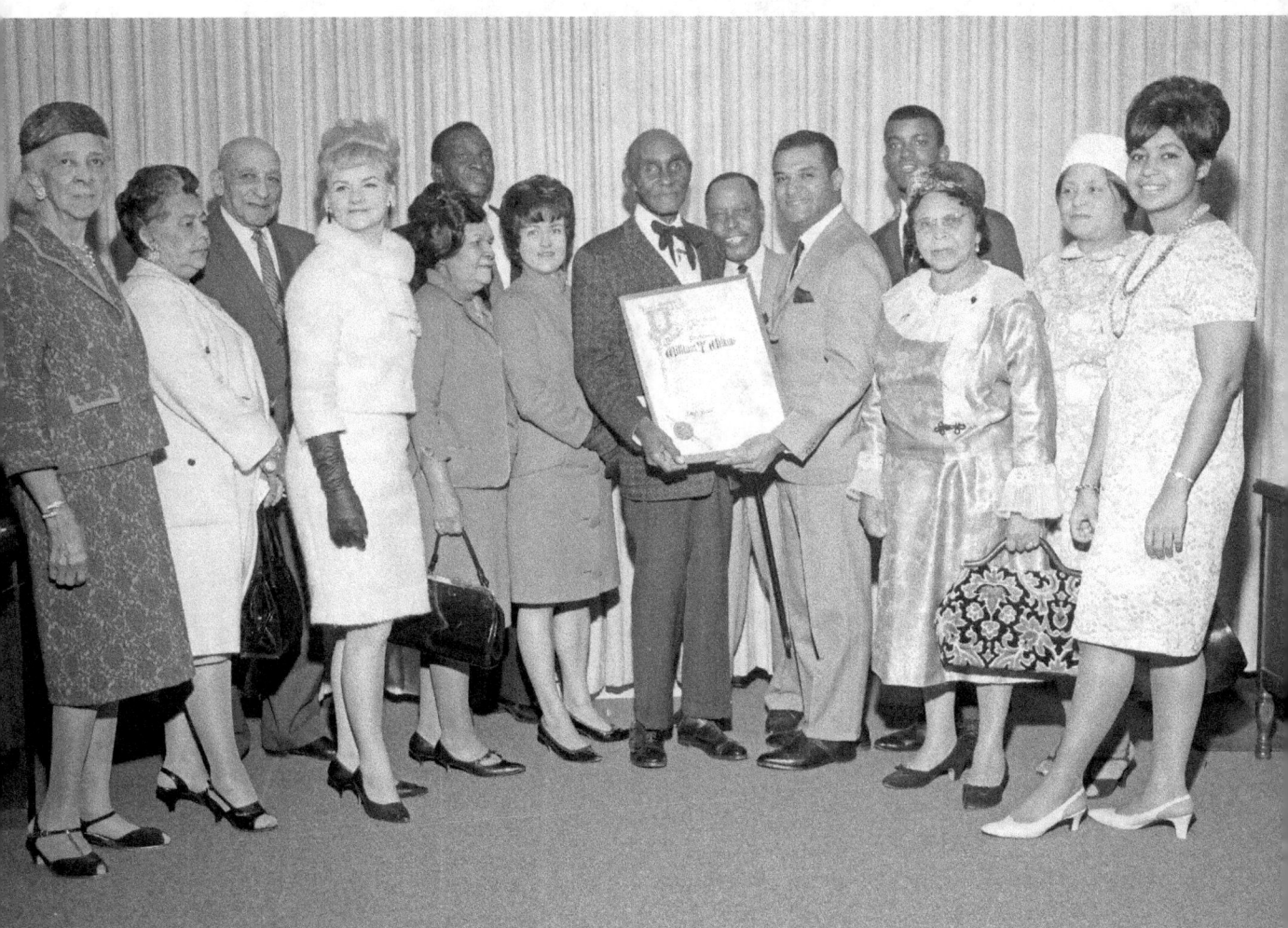

*Above and opposite*: Professor William T. Wilkins receives a resolution from Billy G. Mills. Wilkins opened the first interracial piano school in the city of Los Angeles in 1912, known as the Wilkins Piano Academy. Though Wilkins was taught to play musical instruments at a young age, his father intended for Wilkins to become a tinsmith and mechanic. While he became the first African American to be employed at the Edison Light and Power Company, Wilkins continued to pursue his dream, mowing lawns for six years to pay for advanced piano classes. He eventually received a certificate of completion along with his professor's blessing to teach piano. March 15, 1967

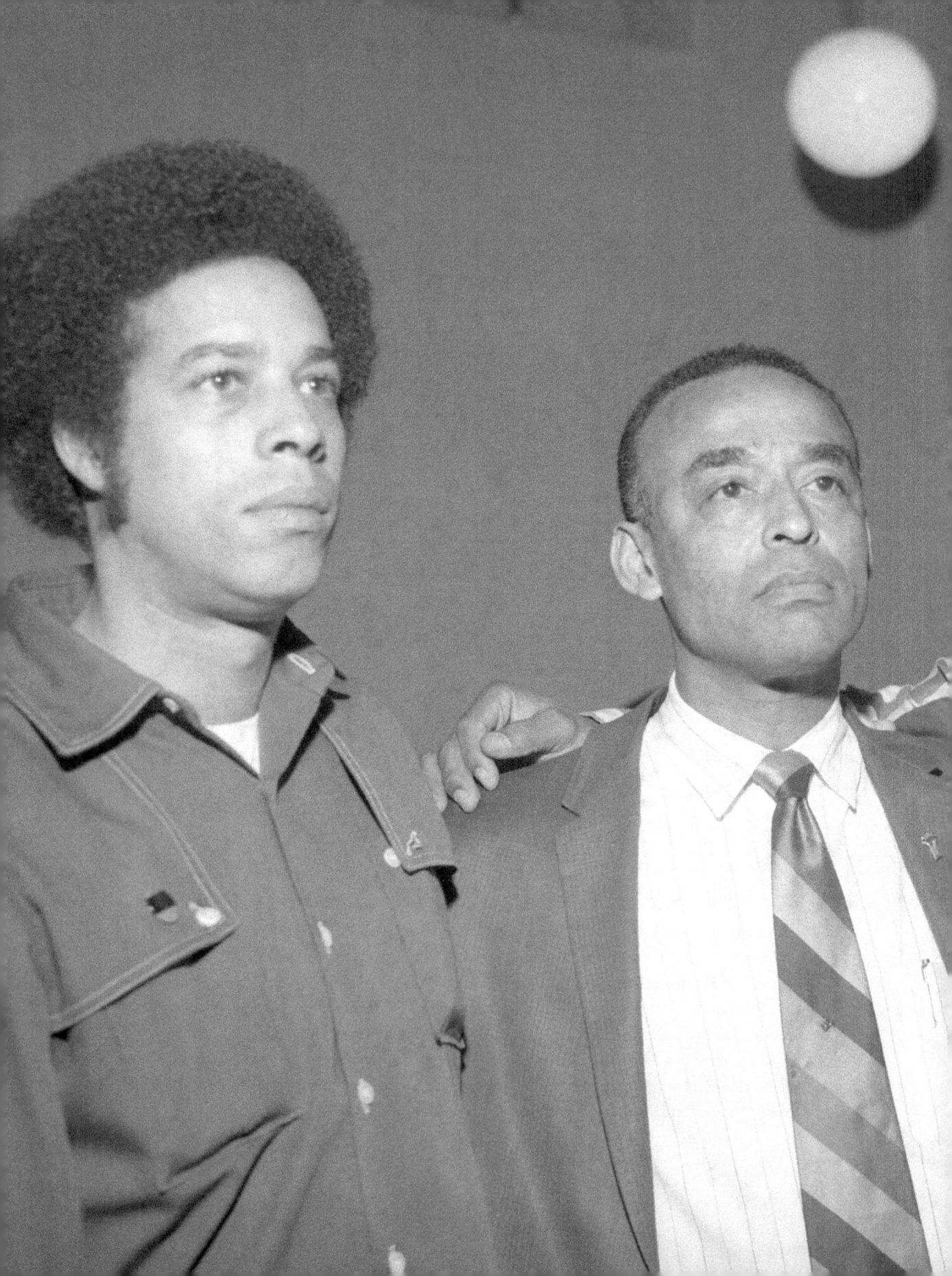

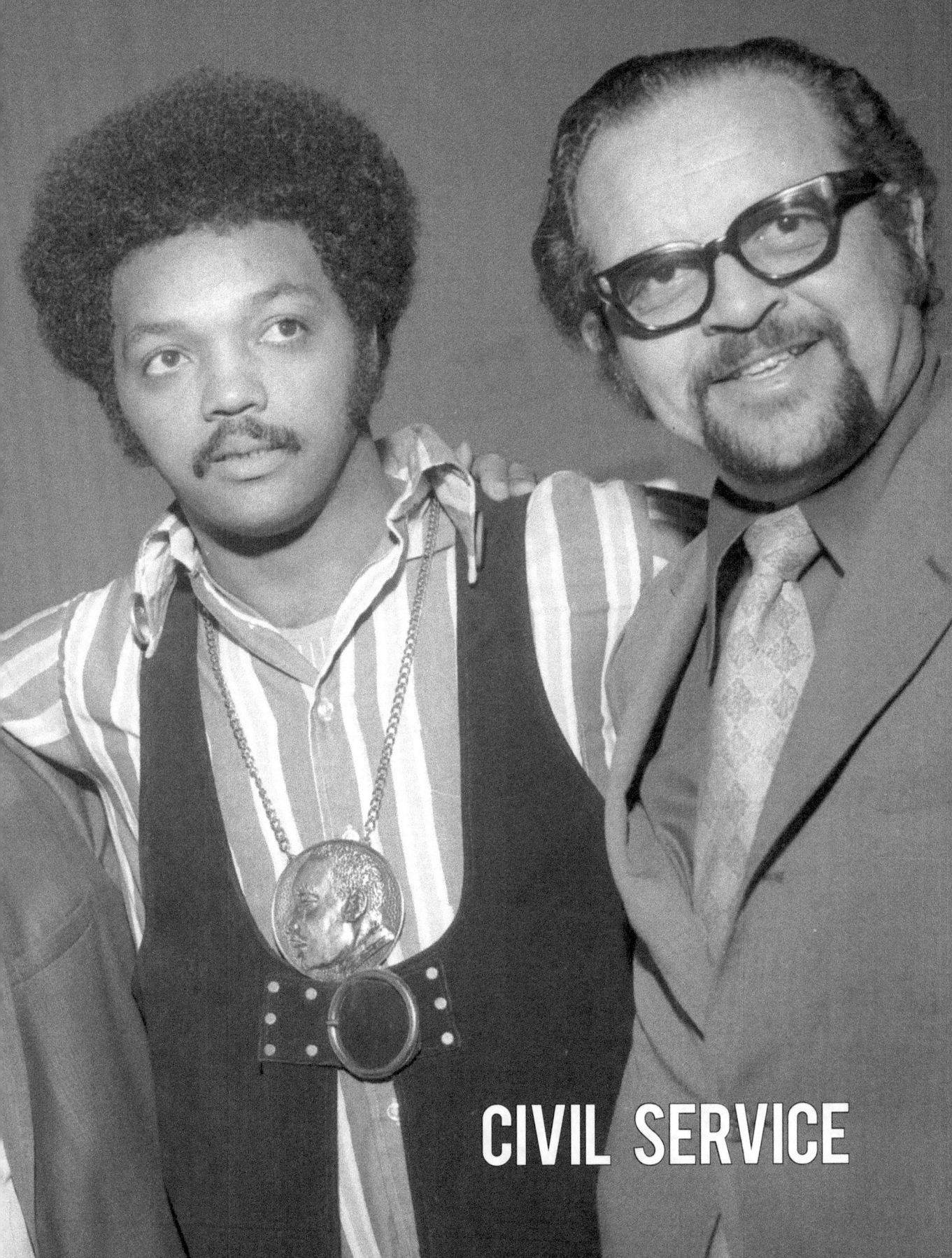

CIVIL SERVICE

*Overleaf*: Arnett Hartsfield (*left*) with Reverend Jesse Jackson (*right*) and Dr. Kenneth Washington (*far right*) at Operation Breadbasket meeting. May 1971

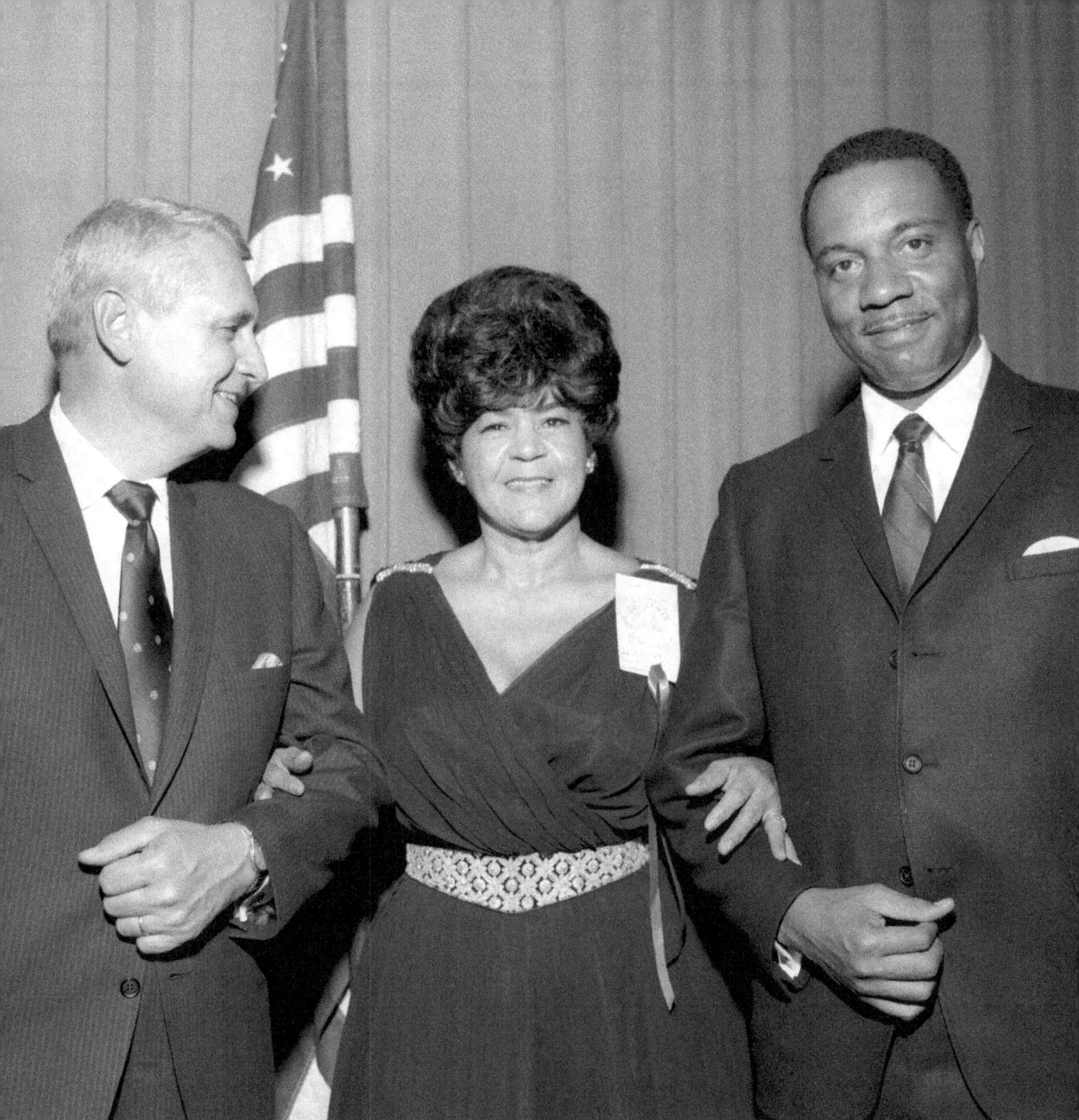

Marguerite Justice (*center*) with Homer Broome (*right*) at an awards ceremony. Marguerite Justice was appointed to the Los Angeles Police Commission in 1971, becoming the second woman, and the first African American woman, to be named to the commission. Justice, or "Mama J" as she was affectionately called, was well-regarded as a great supporter of the LAPD, and for her extensive community work. October 1969

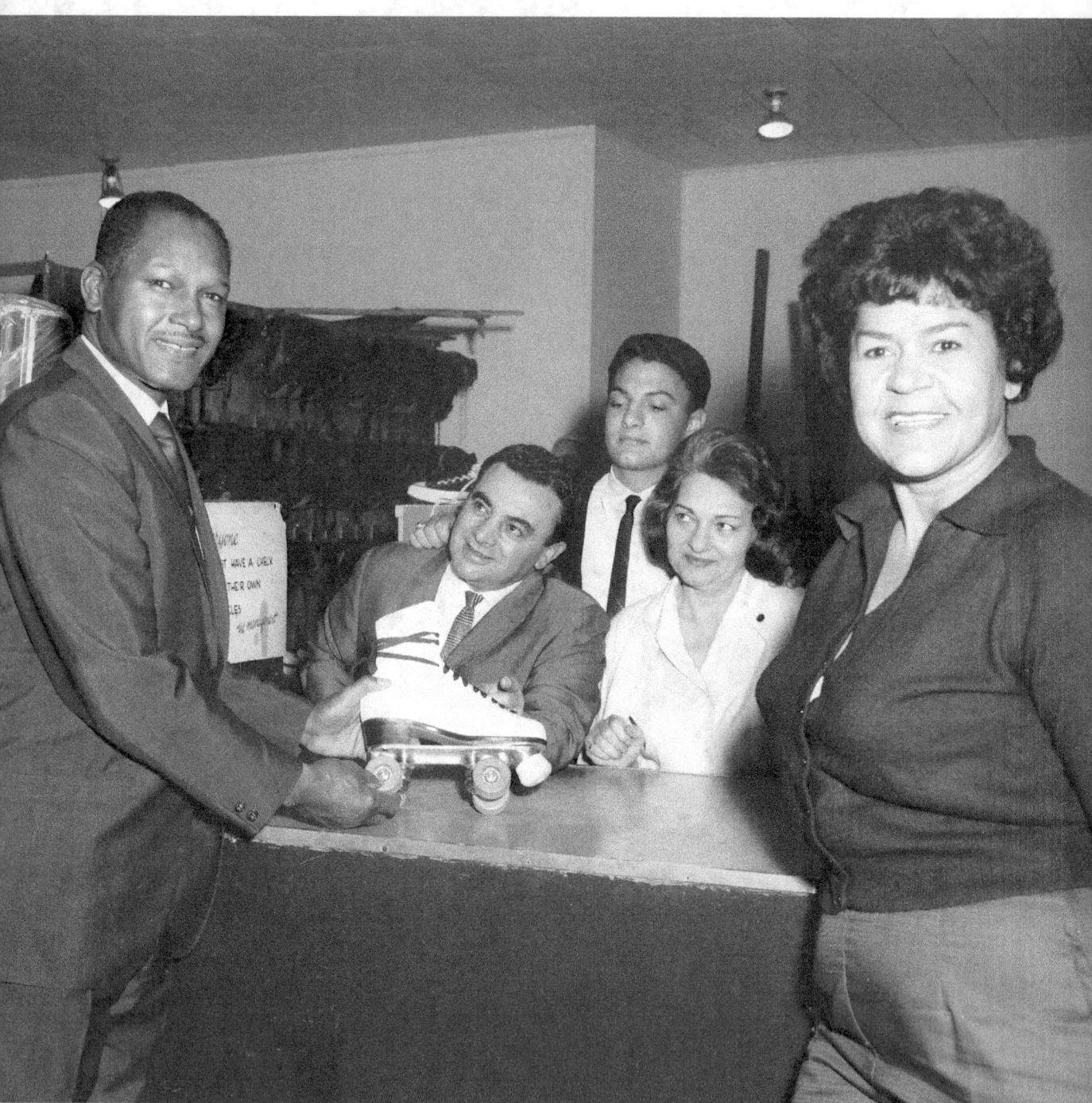

Marguerite Justice (*right*) with Tom Bradley (*left*) at skating rink. c1964

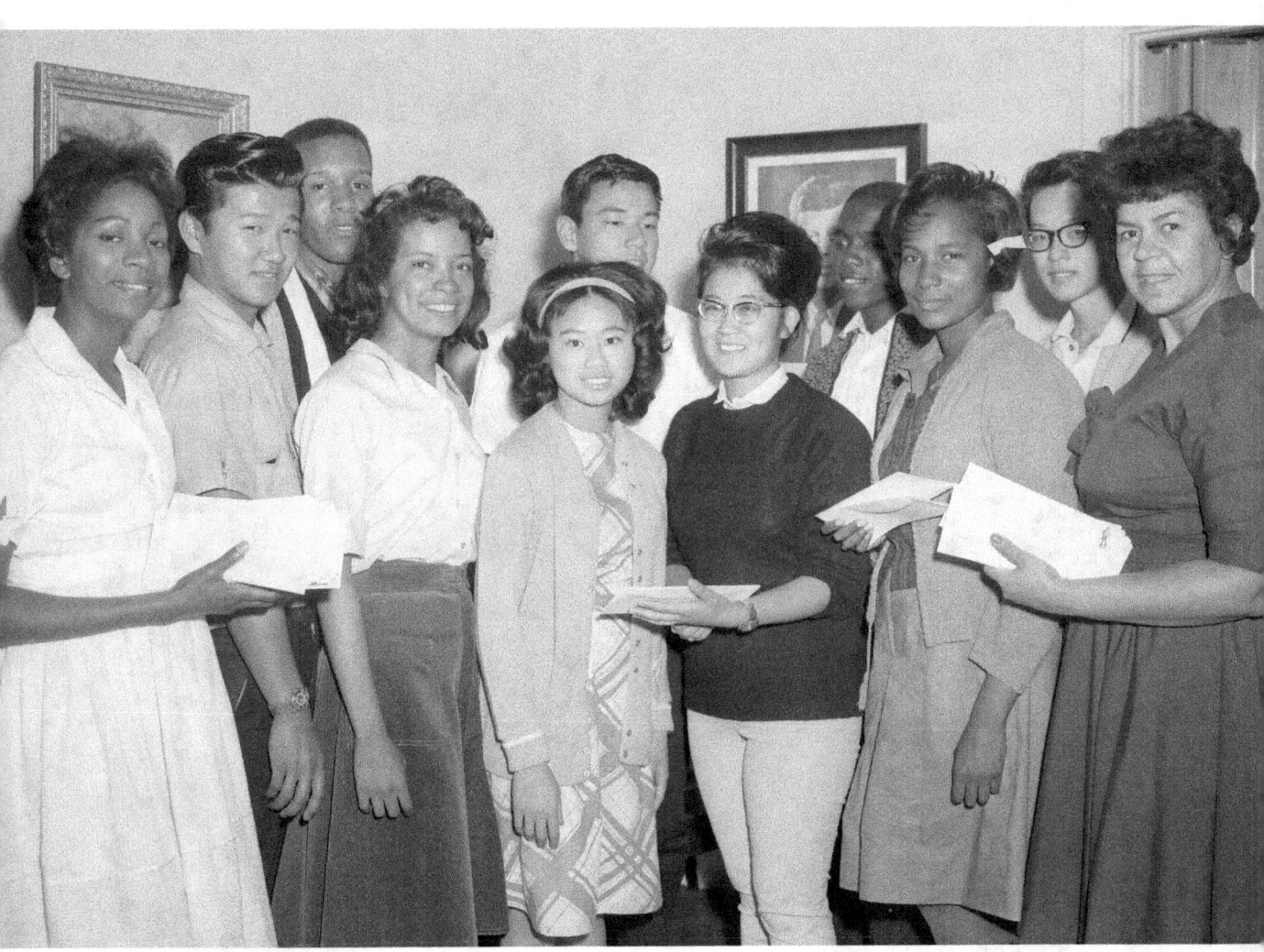

Marguerite Justice (*far right*) with teens in her office. Justice was known for her community work, especially with teens. c1964

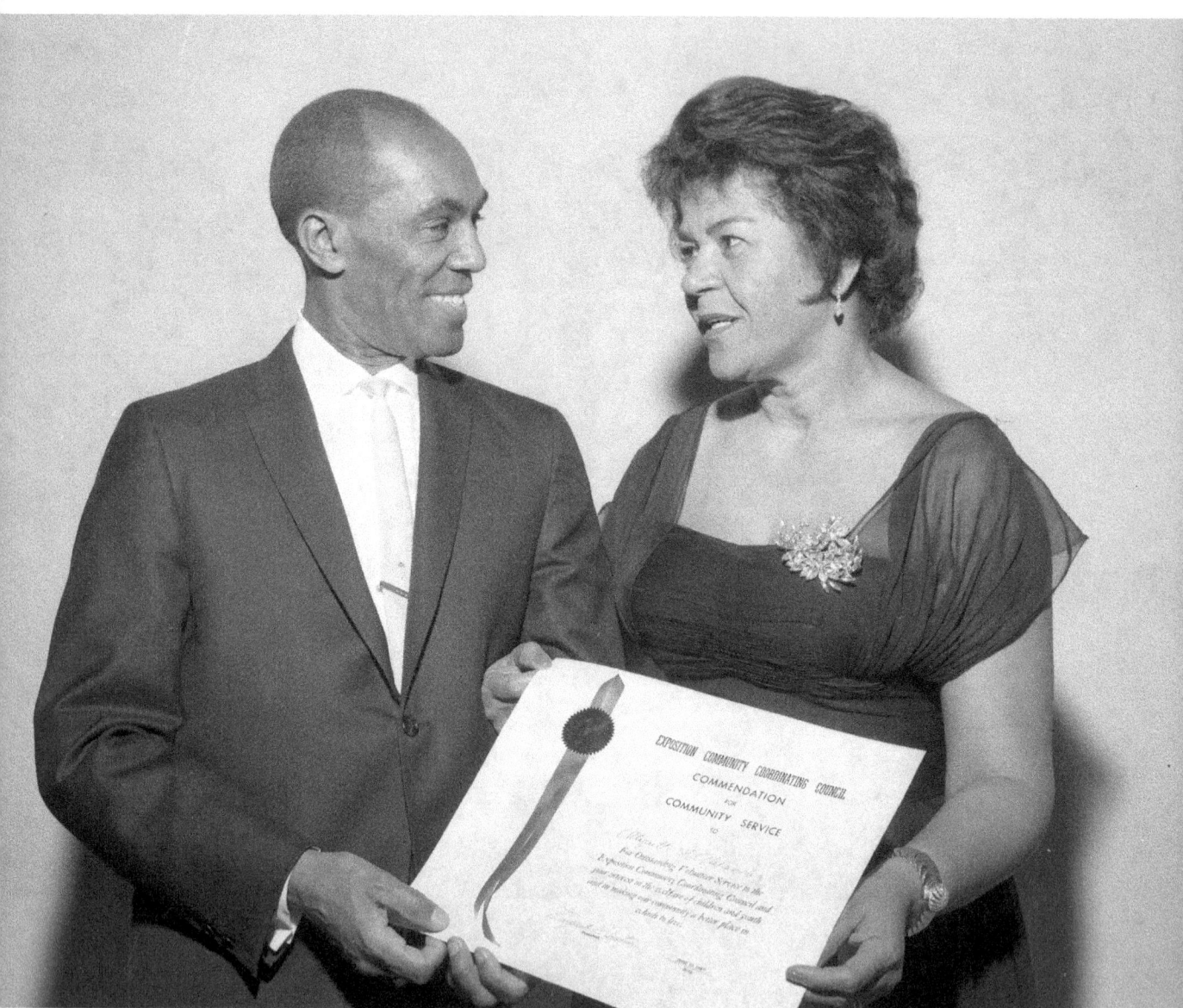

Marguerite Justice (*right*) presents Allegretto Alexander (*left*) with commendation at Exposition Community Coordinating Council meeting. June 10, 1967

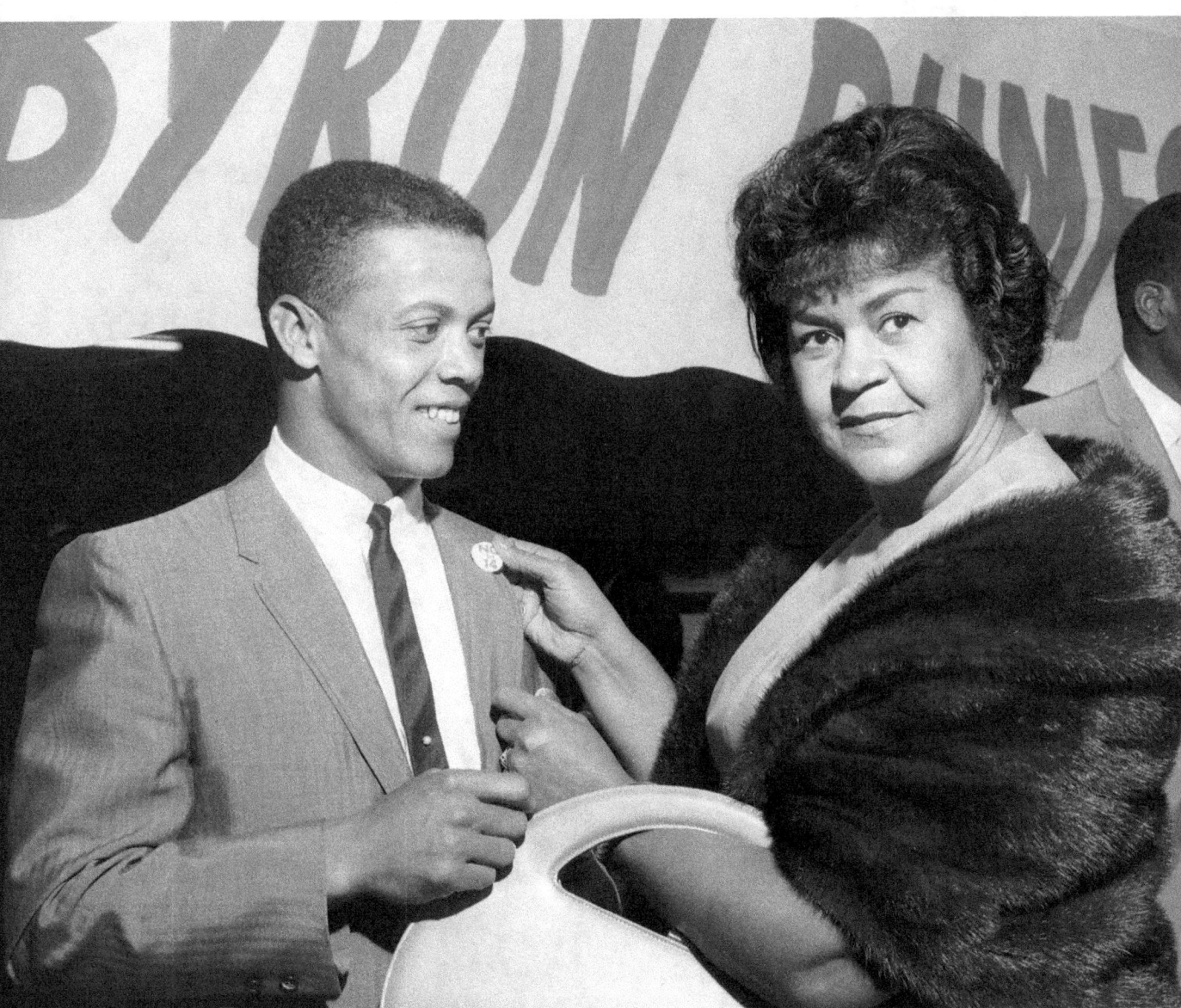

Marguerite Justice (*right*) pins button on baseball player Maury Wills (*left*) during a garden party for Byron Rumford. September 17, 1964

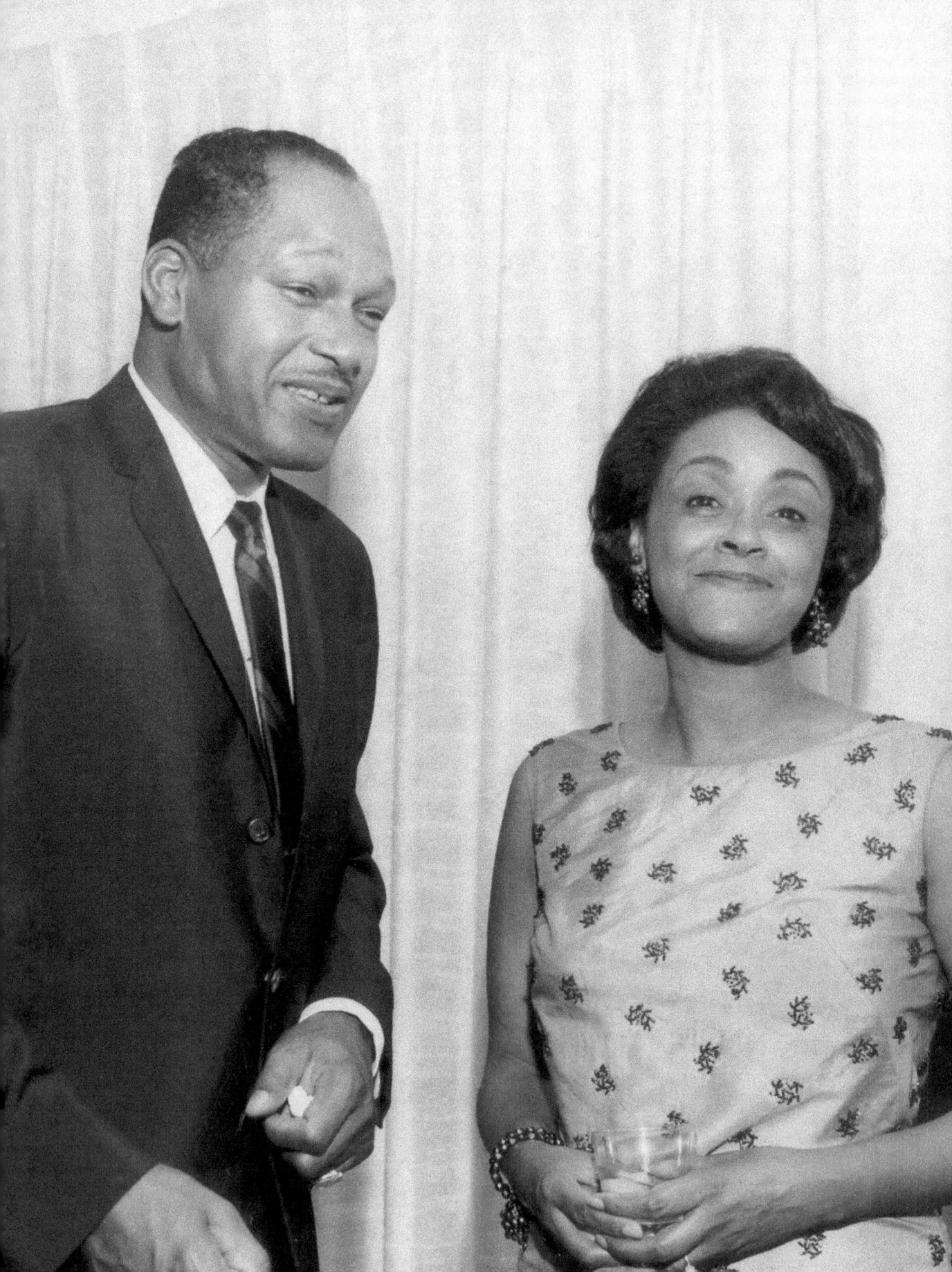

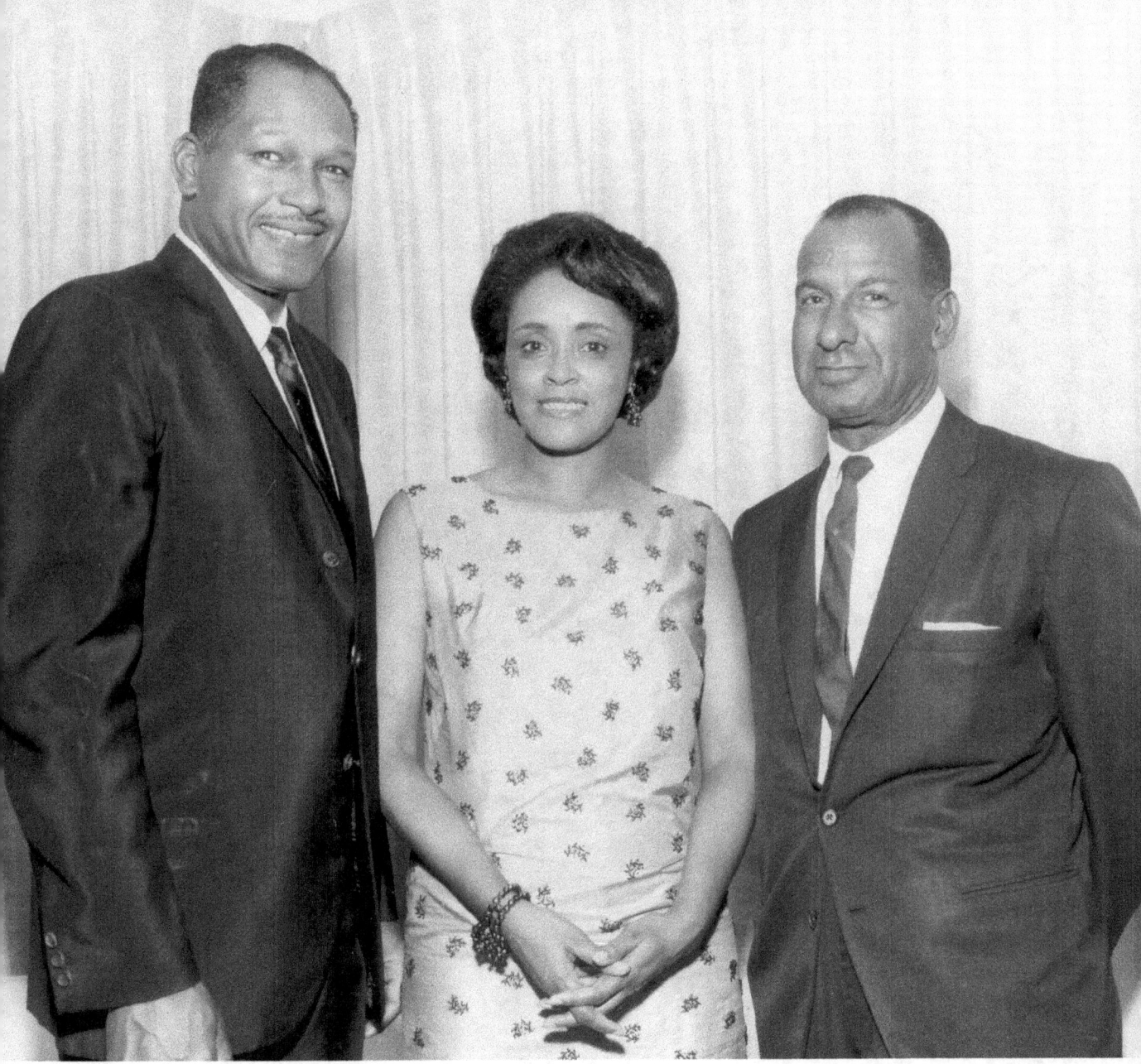

Vivian Strange (*center*) with Tom Bradley (*left*) and Vernon Strange (*right*) at home. Vivian Strange was the first African American woman to be promoted to the rank of sergeant at the LAPD. She served for twenty-three years in the public relations department before she retired. Strange had a complicated relationship with other LAPD officers, refusing to ride in the same car with many white officers when driving to South Los Angeles. She opted to drive herself, understanding that black women who rode in cars with white men were likely to be seen as prostitutes, which would undermine her authority and respect in the eyes of the community. c1960s

*Opposite*: Tom Bradley (*left*) speaks to Vivian Strange (*right*) at home.

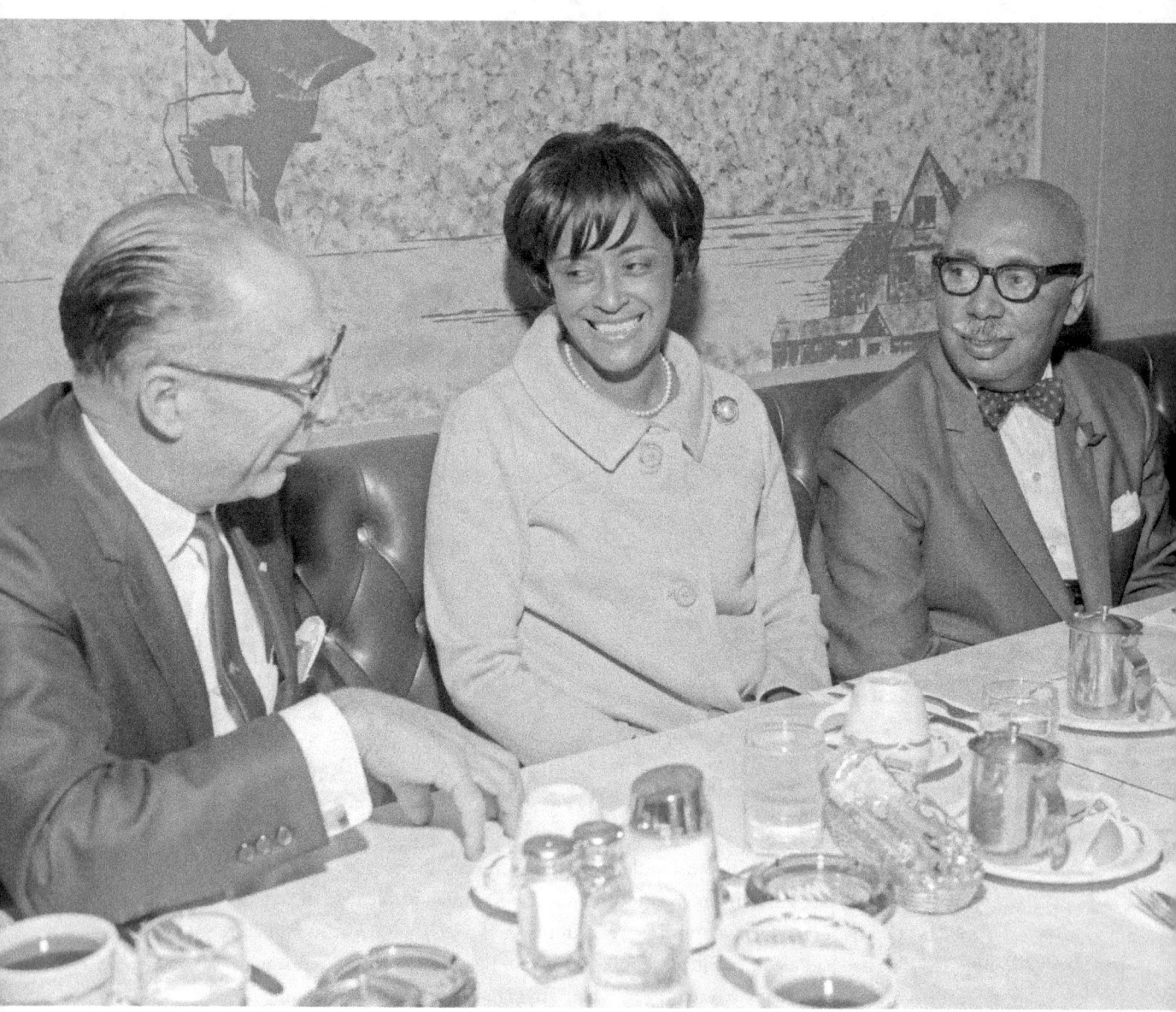

Vivian Strange (*center*) and Leon Washington (*right*) celebrating her community service award from the *Los Angeles Sentinel.* December 8, 1966

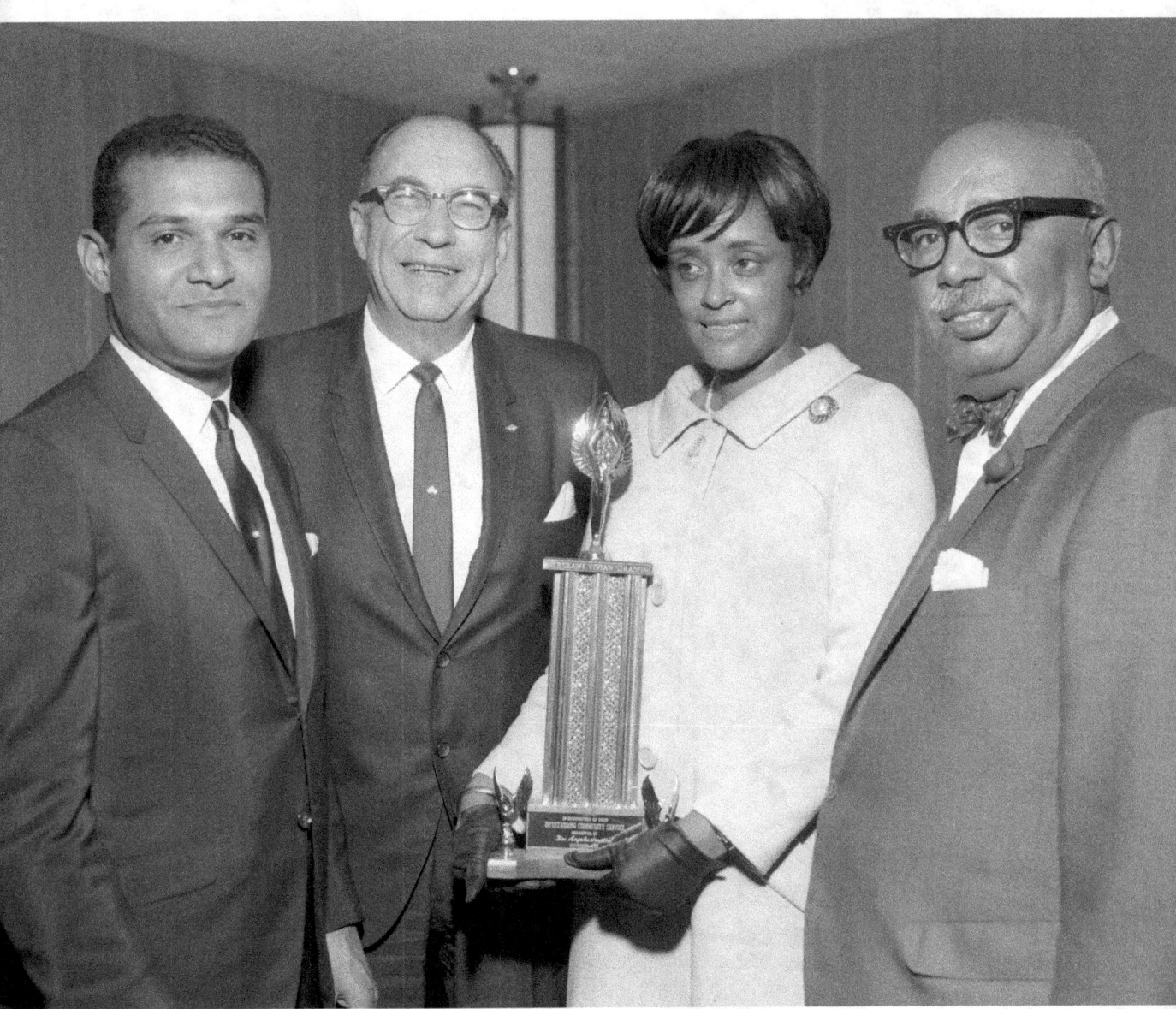

Vivian Strange (*right*) with Billy G. Mills (*far left*) and Leon Washington (*far right*) receives
community service award from the *Los Angeles Sentinel*. December 8, 1966

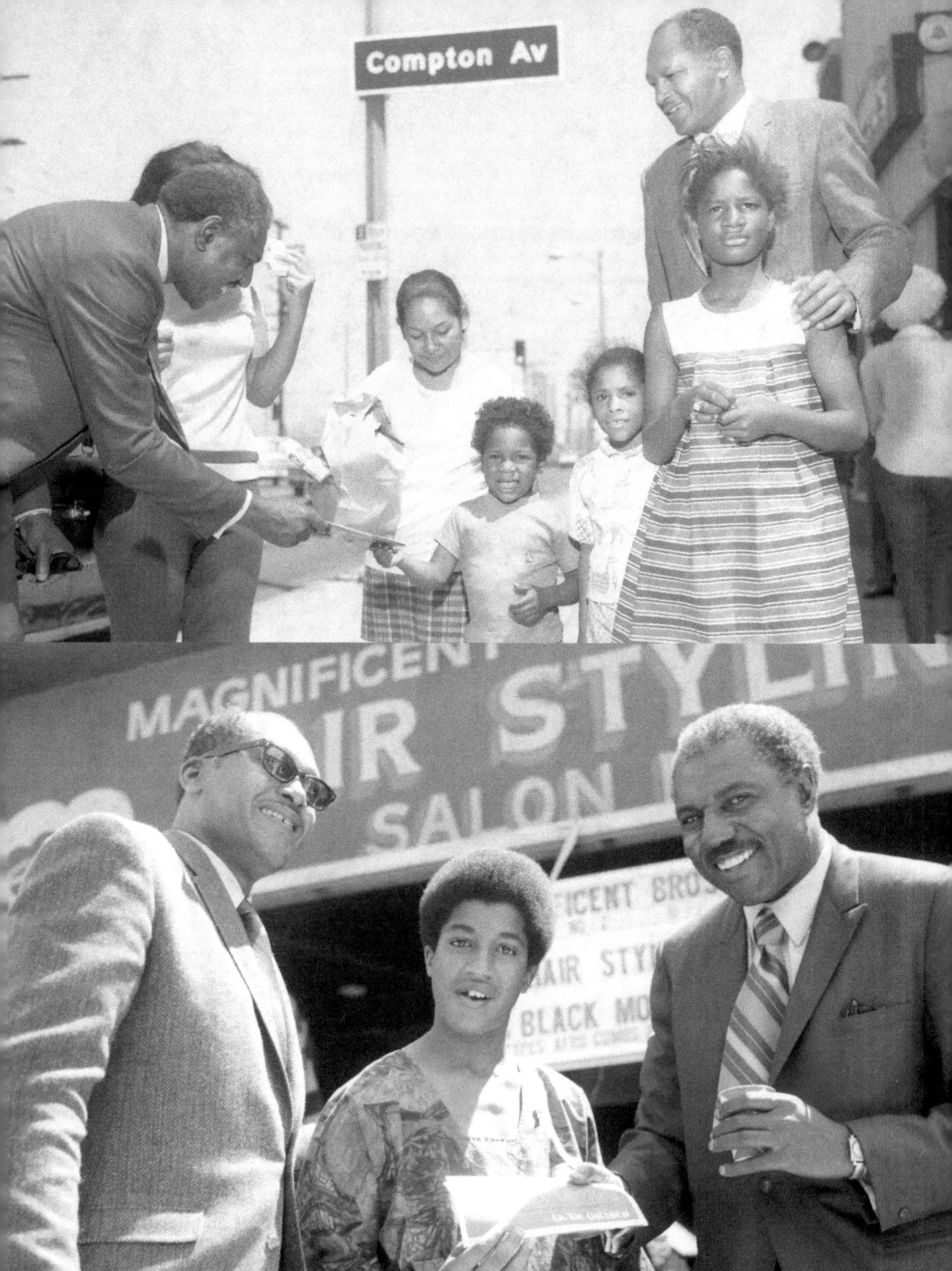

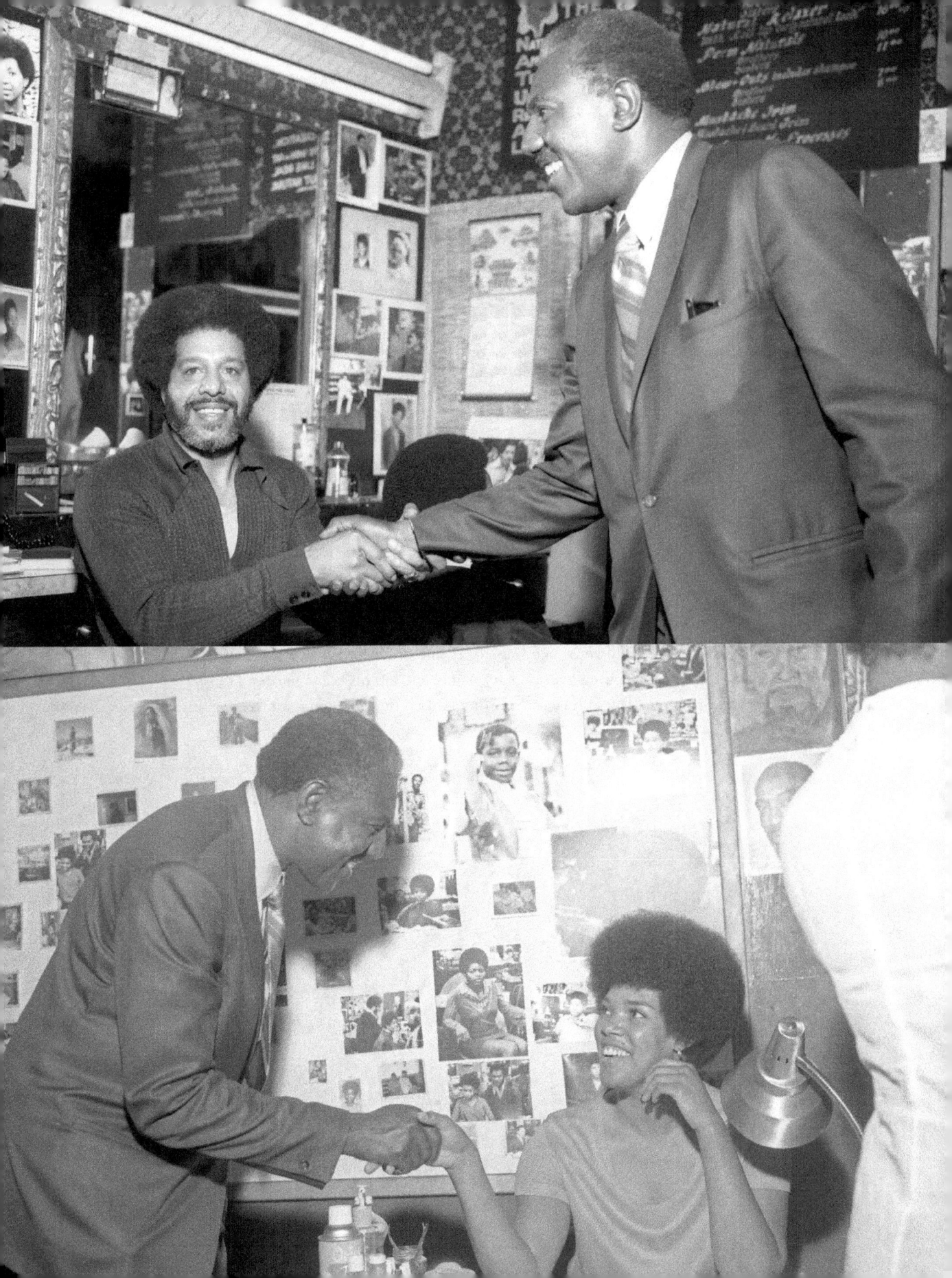

*Overleaf and opposite*: Wilson Riles campaigns for Superintendent with Tom Bradley at Magnificent Bros Hair Salon 2. Wilson Riles was the first African American to be elected to statewide office in California, as well as the first to be elected to as State Superintendent of Schools in the nation. Riles held the seat of California State Superintendent of Public Instruction for three terms, serving from 1970–1982. Riles was a champion of education for poor and disadvantaged children, which was largely influenced by his own experience. As a child, he'd worked his way through elementary school and left his home in rural Louisiana to attend high school in New Orleans, supporting himself by selling milk for $2.50 a week. c1790s

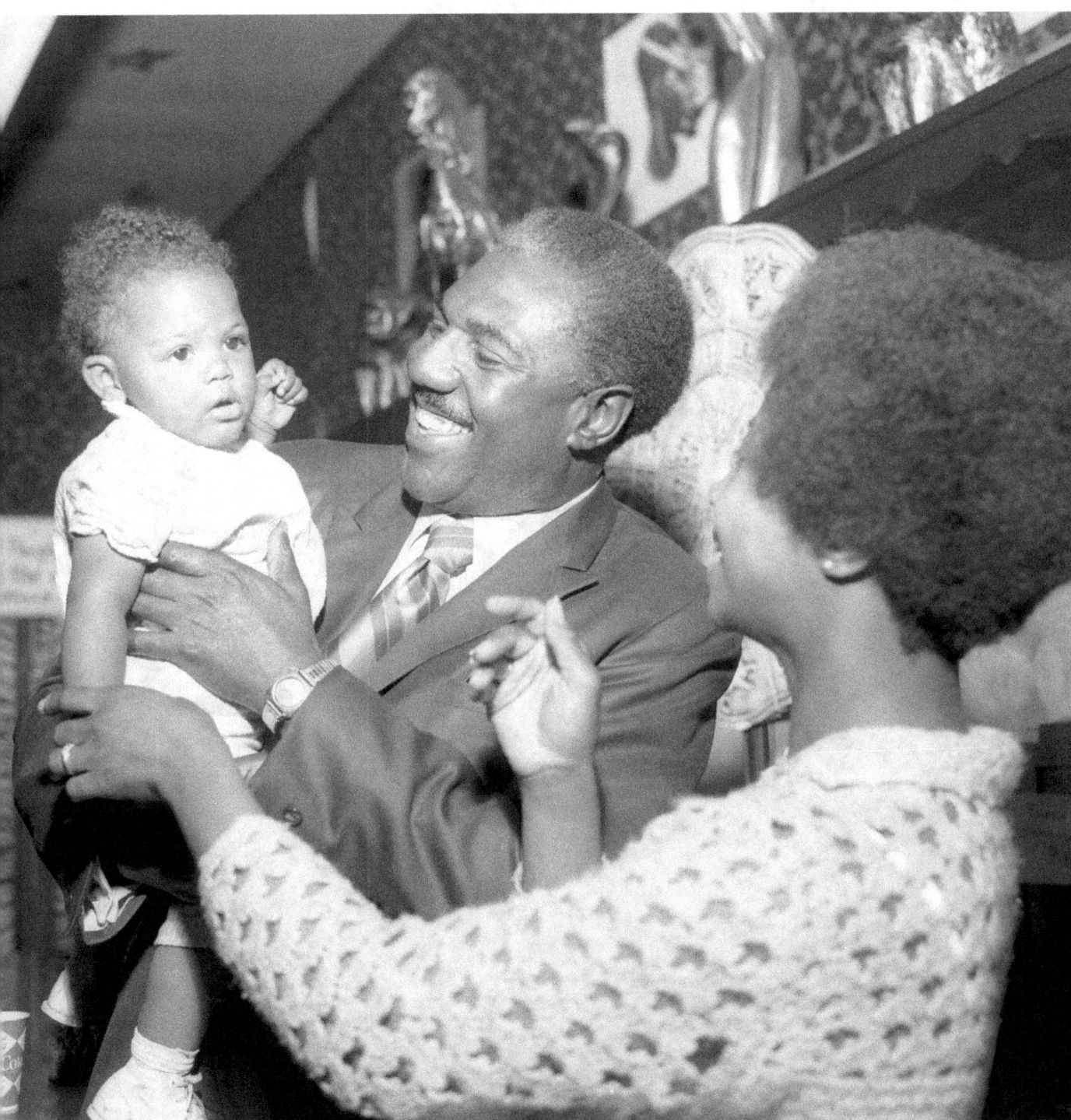

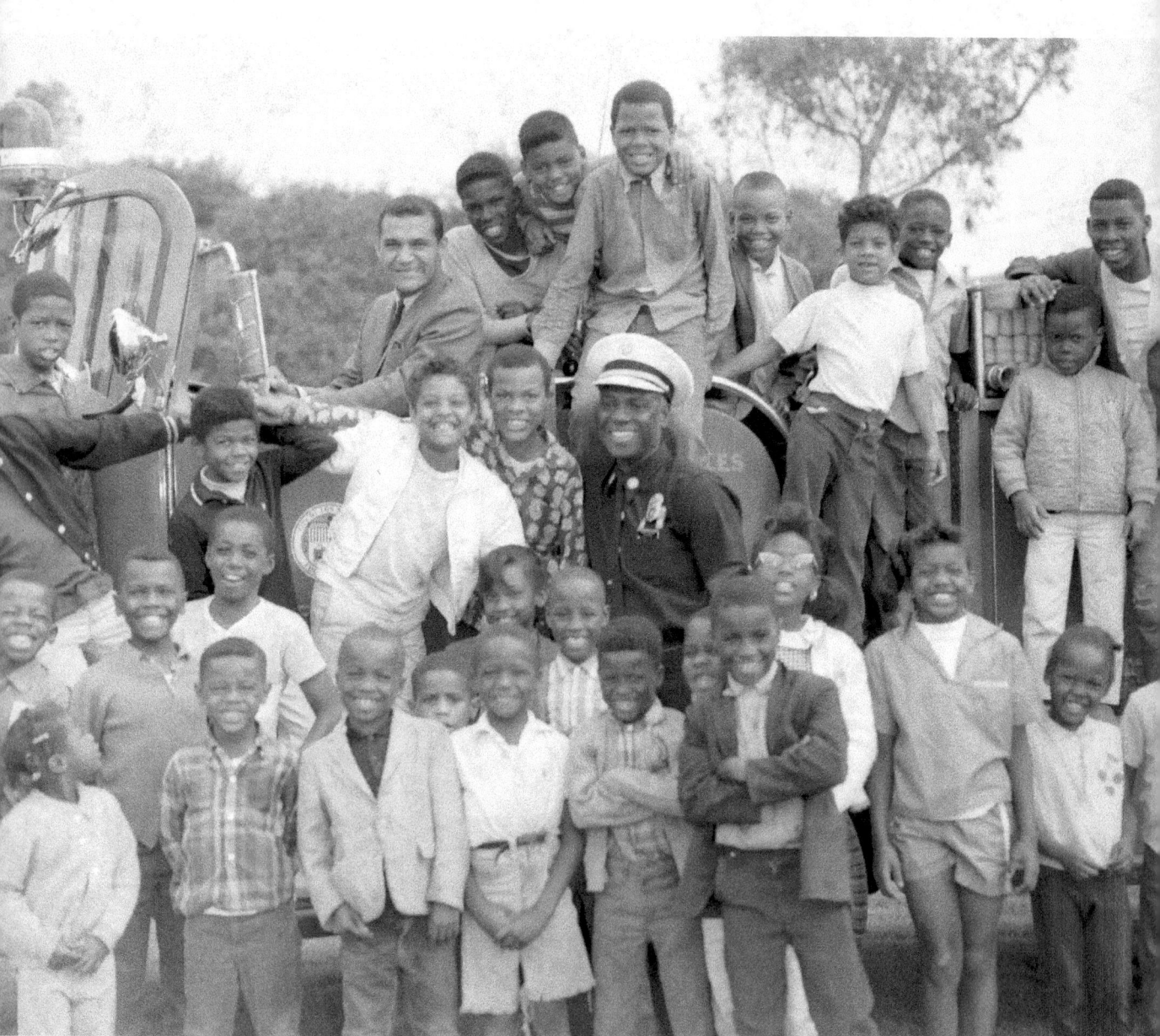

James Shern (*center*) with Billy G. Mills (*top row, left of center*) and children at park. c1968

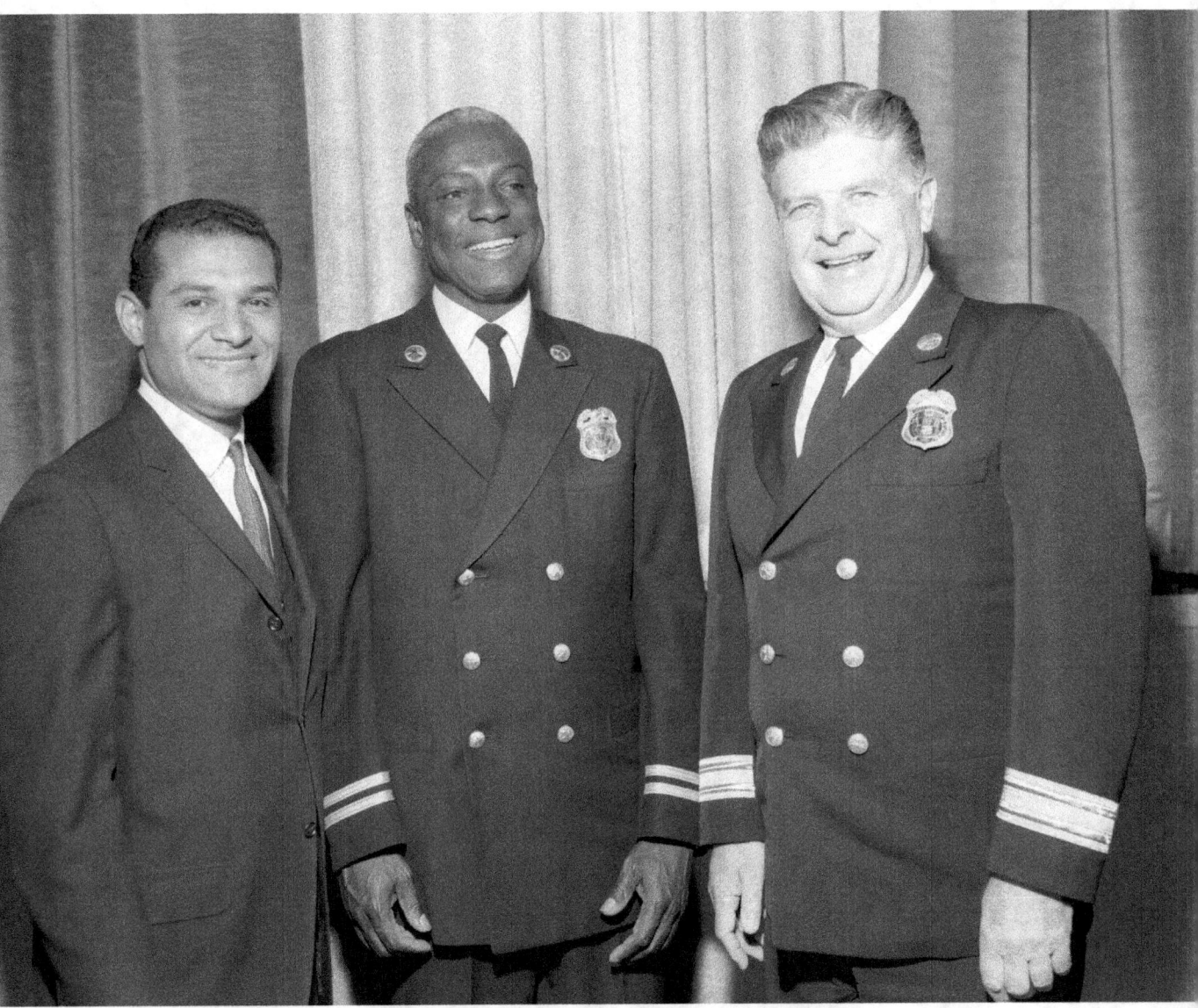

James Shern (*center*) with Billy G. Mills (*left*) and Raymond Hill (*right*) at City Hall. When Shern joined the LAFD in 1948, the highest rank any African American firefighter had achieved up to that point was captain, a distinction held by William Hall, who upon passing the battalion chief exam in 1931, was told that there would never be an African American promoted to that position. Thirty-seven years later, in 1968, James Shern became the LAFD's first black battalion chief. By 1972, Shern retired from the LAFD and became the fire chief for the city of Pasadena, the first African American to hold that position in a major California city. October 1969

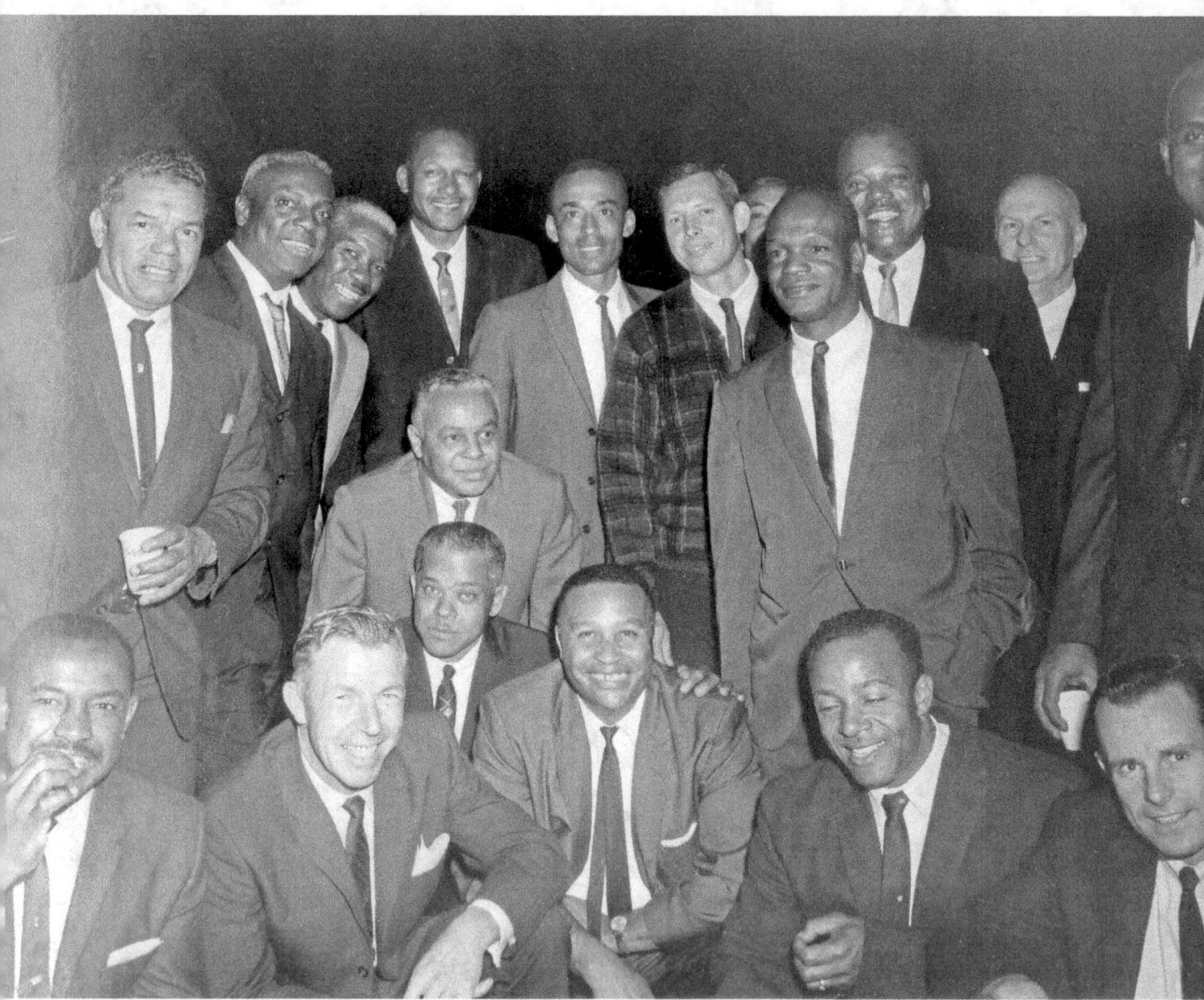

James Shern (*back row, second from left*) with Tom Bradley (*back row, fourth from left*) and Arnett Hartsfield (*center left*) with firemen at party. c1960s
*Opposite*: James Shern (*right*) with Tom Bradley (*left*) in his office. c1960s

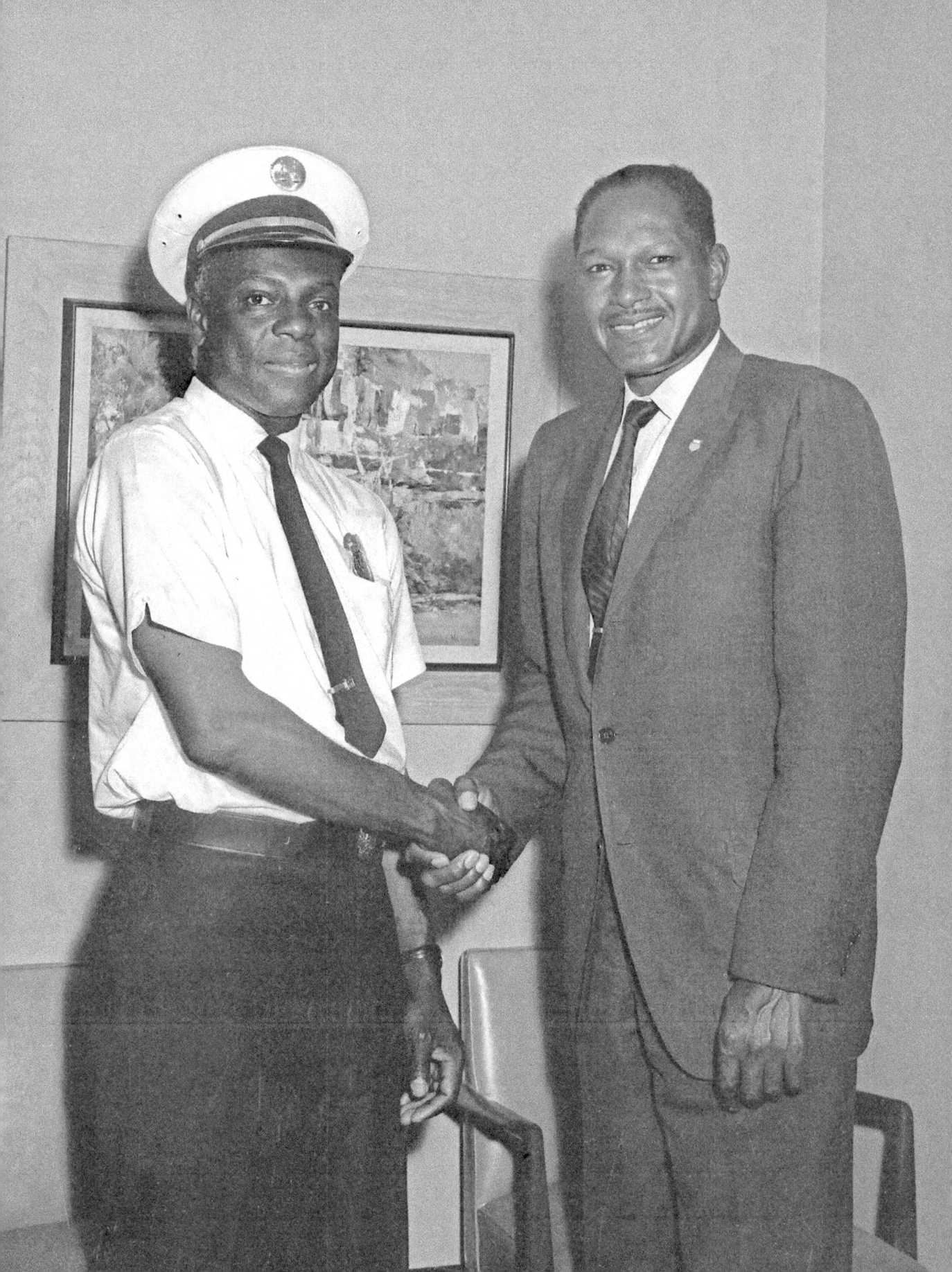

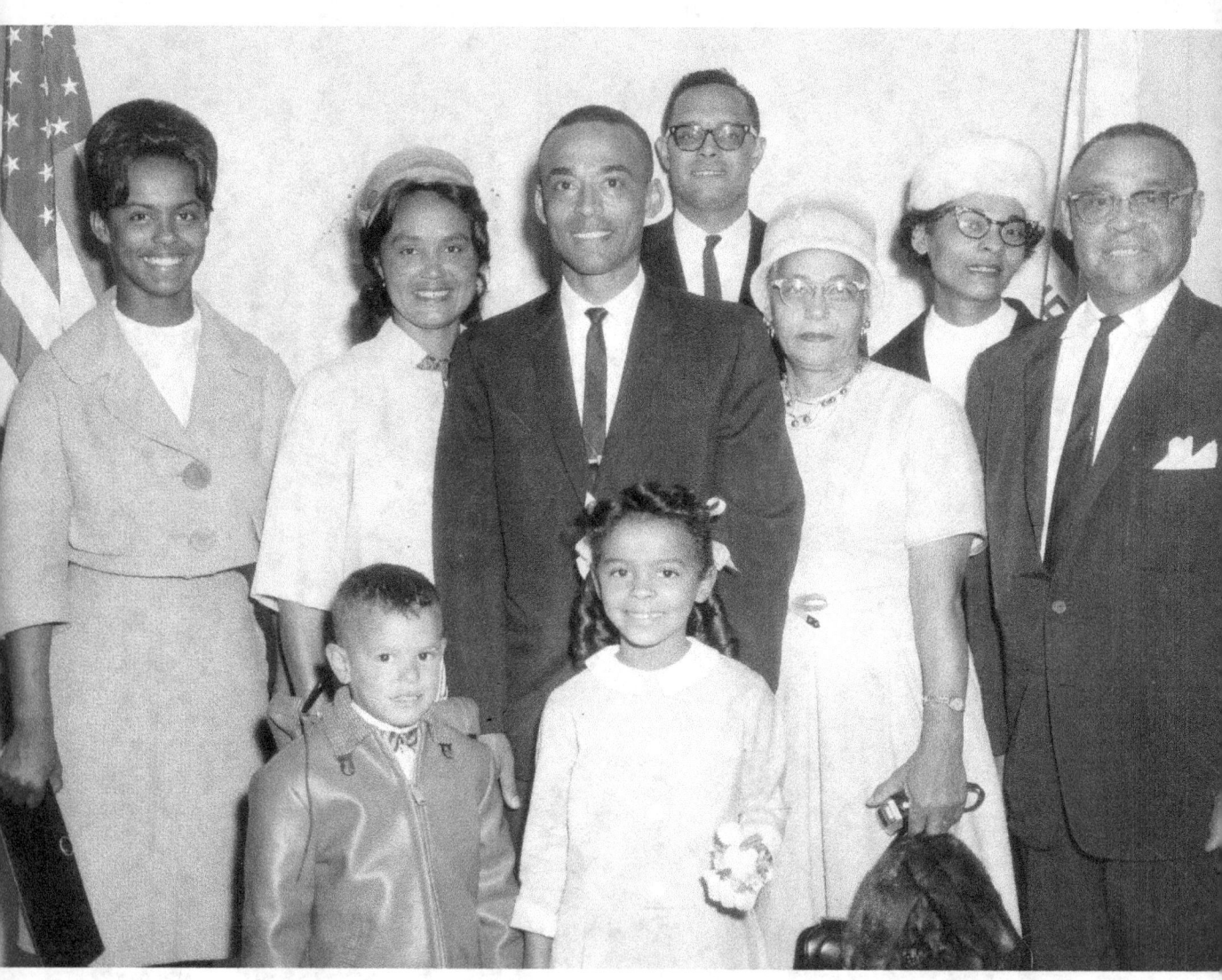

Arnett Hartsfield (*center*) with family. c1955

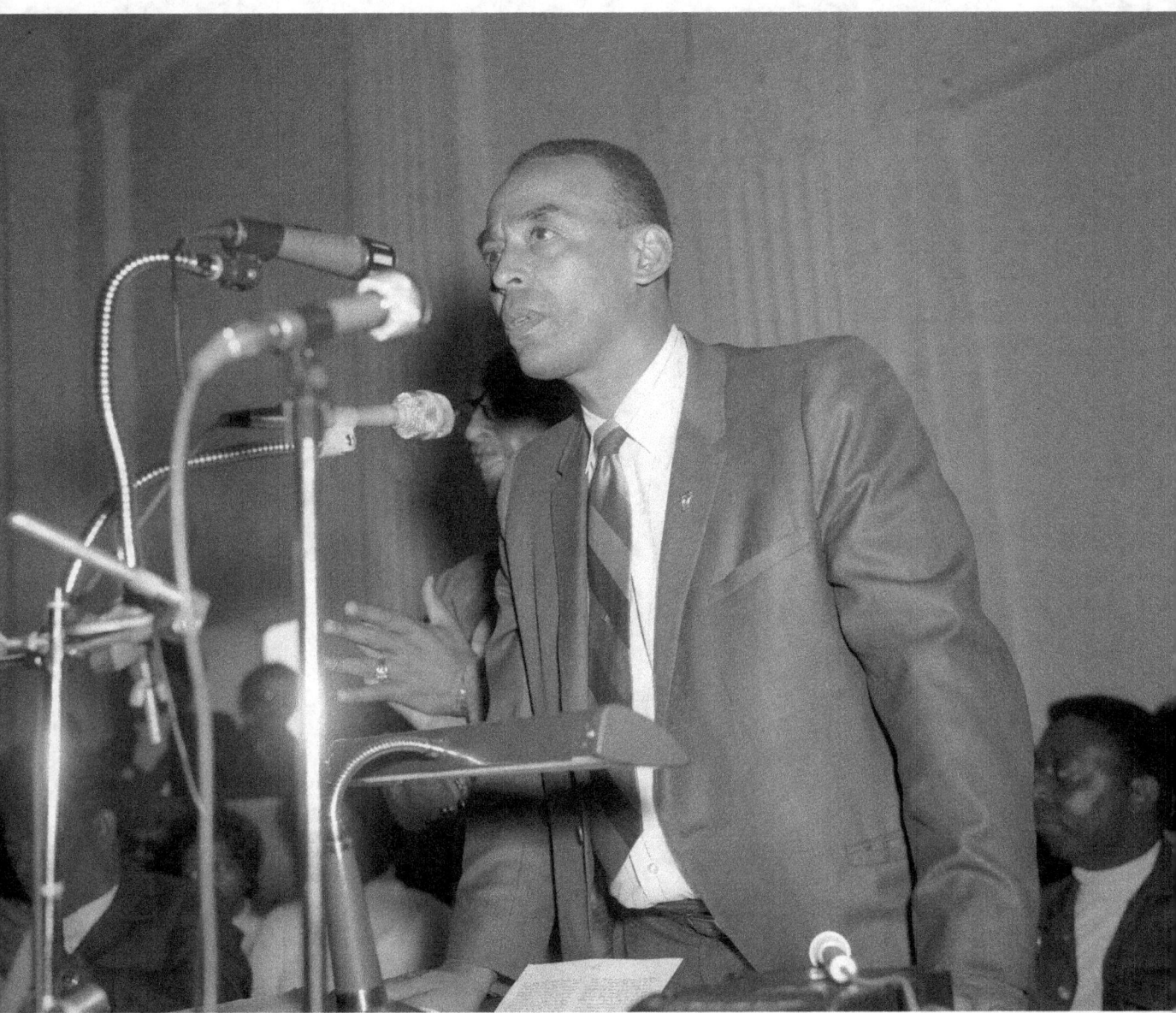

Arnett Hartsfield speaks at an Operation Breadbasket meeting. In 1955, LAFD firefighters received the notice to desegregate all of the fire houses. Arnett Hartsfield, who had been a firefighter for fifteen years and had just passed the bar exam, was the first to join a white station in order to begin desegregation. Hartsfield recalled, "The captain met me at the door and gave me a direct order never to enter the kitchen when the white firemen were eating, to use my own pots and pans and to shower only when no whites were using the washroom. I was already an attorney, and every day I came to work and scrubbed toilets." May 1971

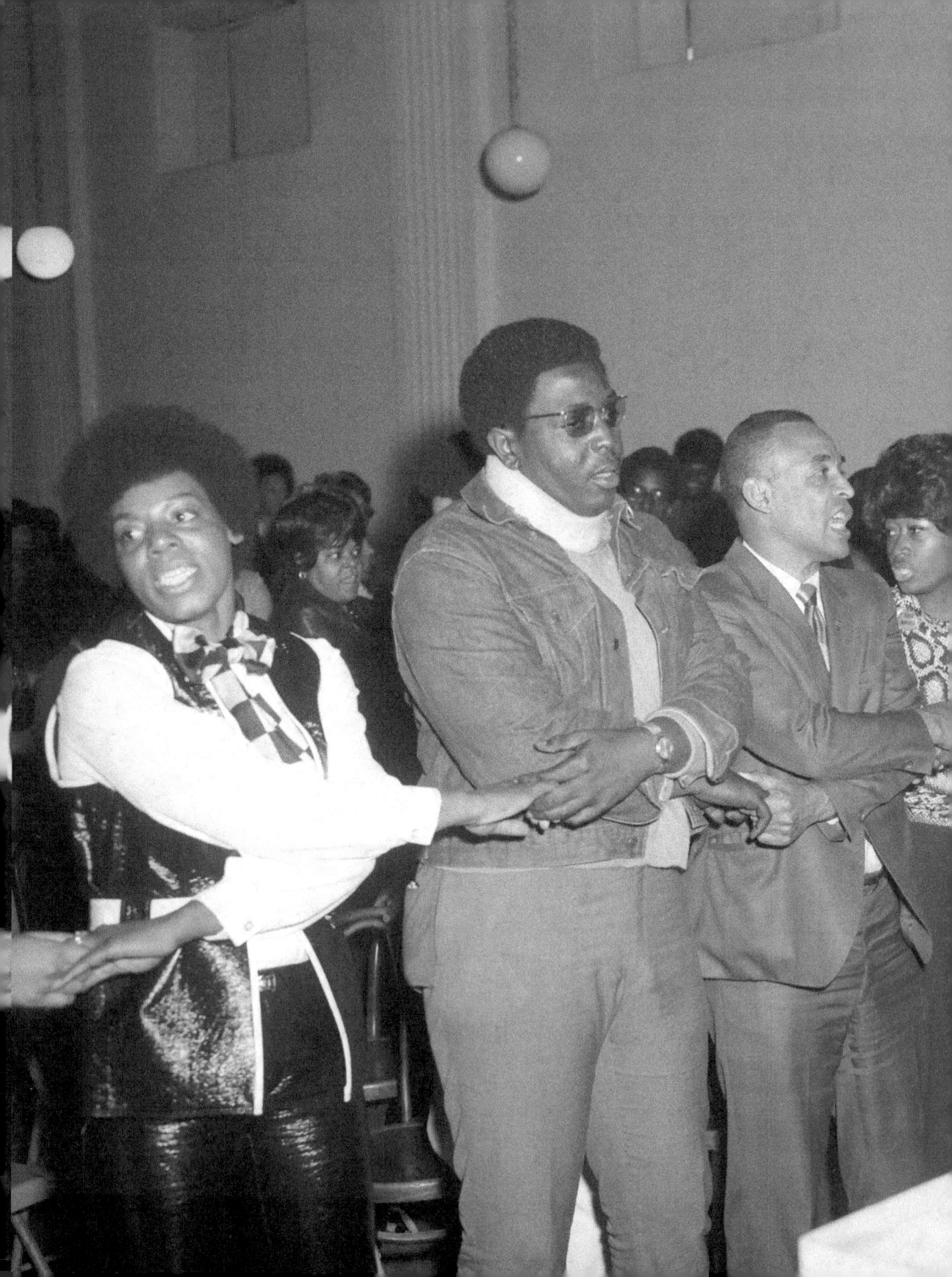

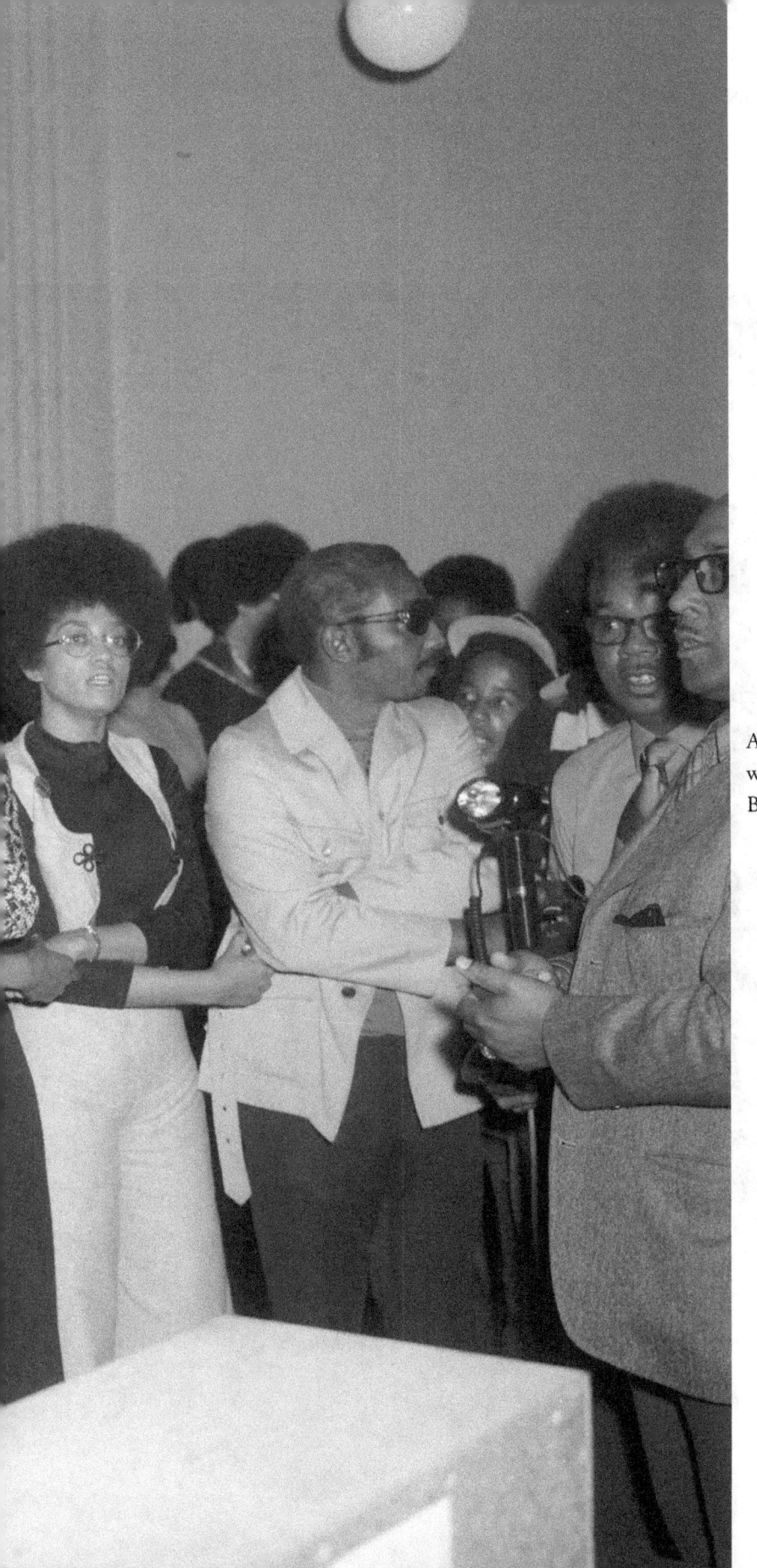

Arnett Hartsfield links hands
with crowd at Operation
Breadbasket meeting. May 1971

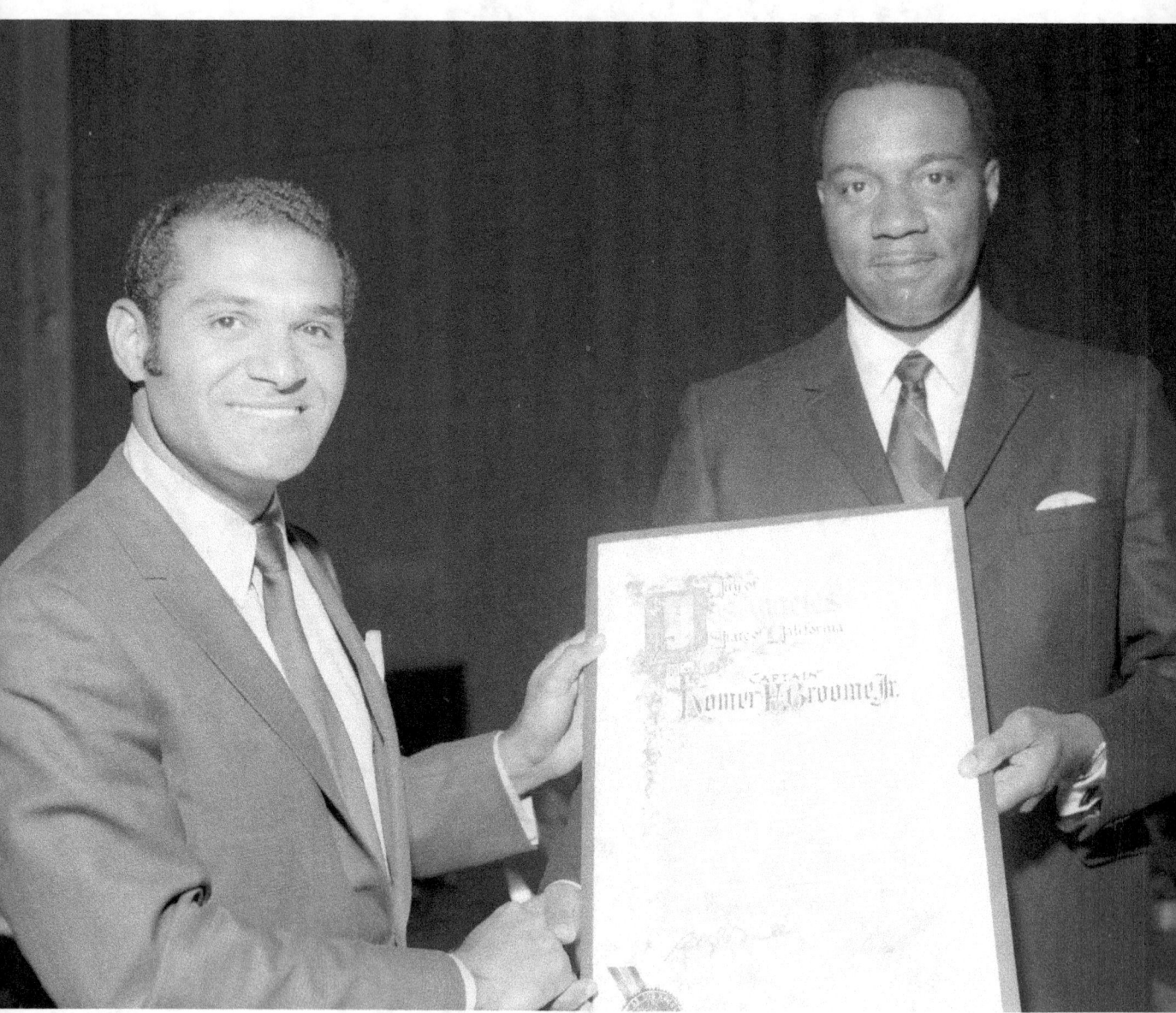

Homer Broome (*right*) receives a resolution from Councilman Billy G. Mills (*left*).
October 16, 1969

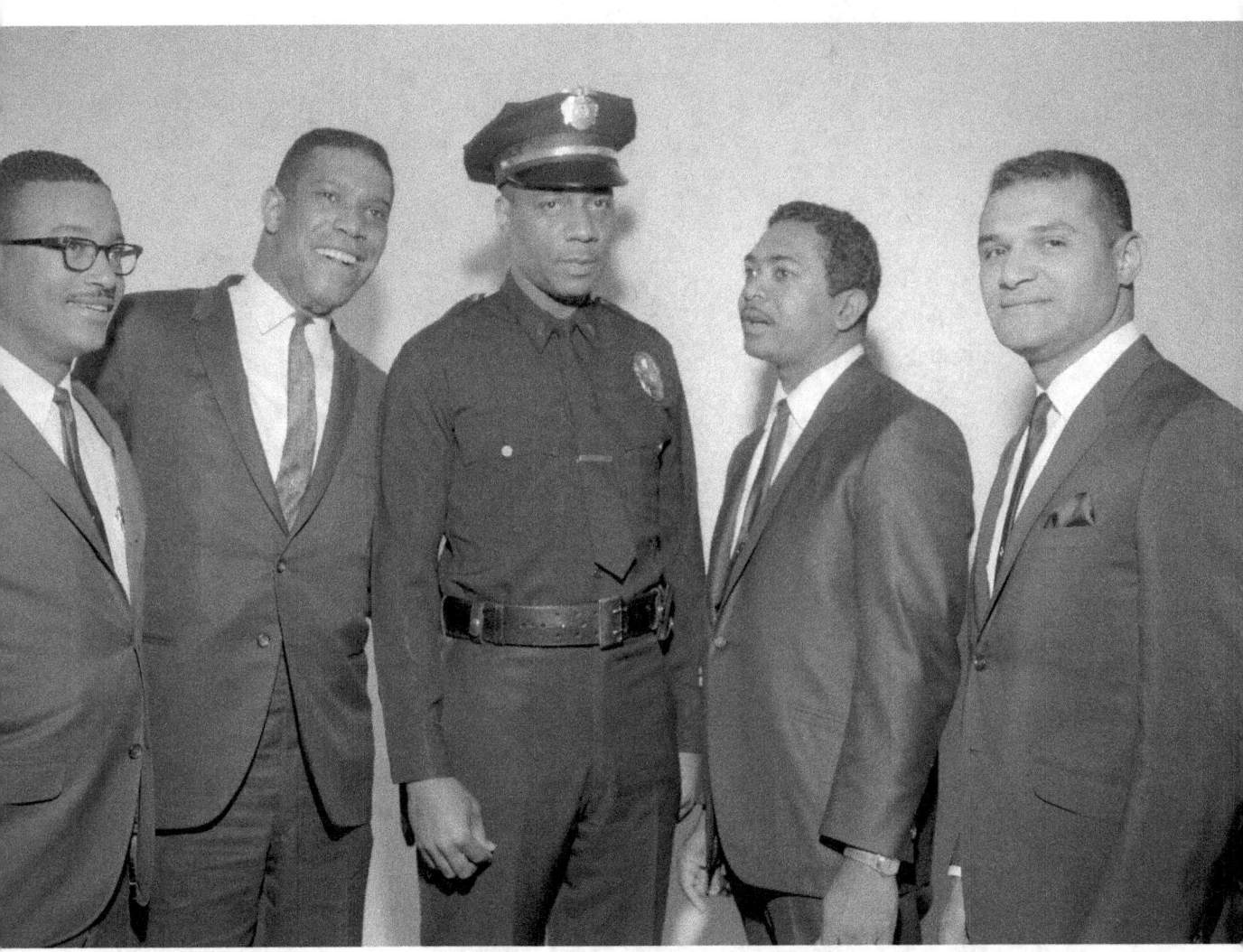

Homer Broome (*center*) at Grass Roots Conference with Assemblyman Leon Ralph (*far left*), Assemblyman Bill Greene (*left*), Senator Mervyn Dymally (*right*) and Councilman Billy G. Mills (*far right*). April 1, 1967

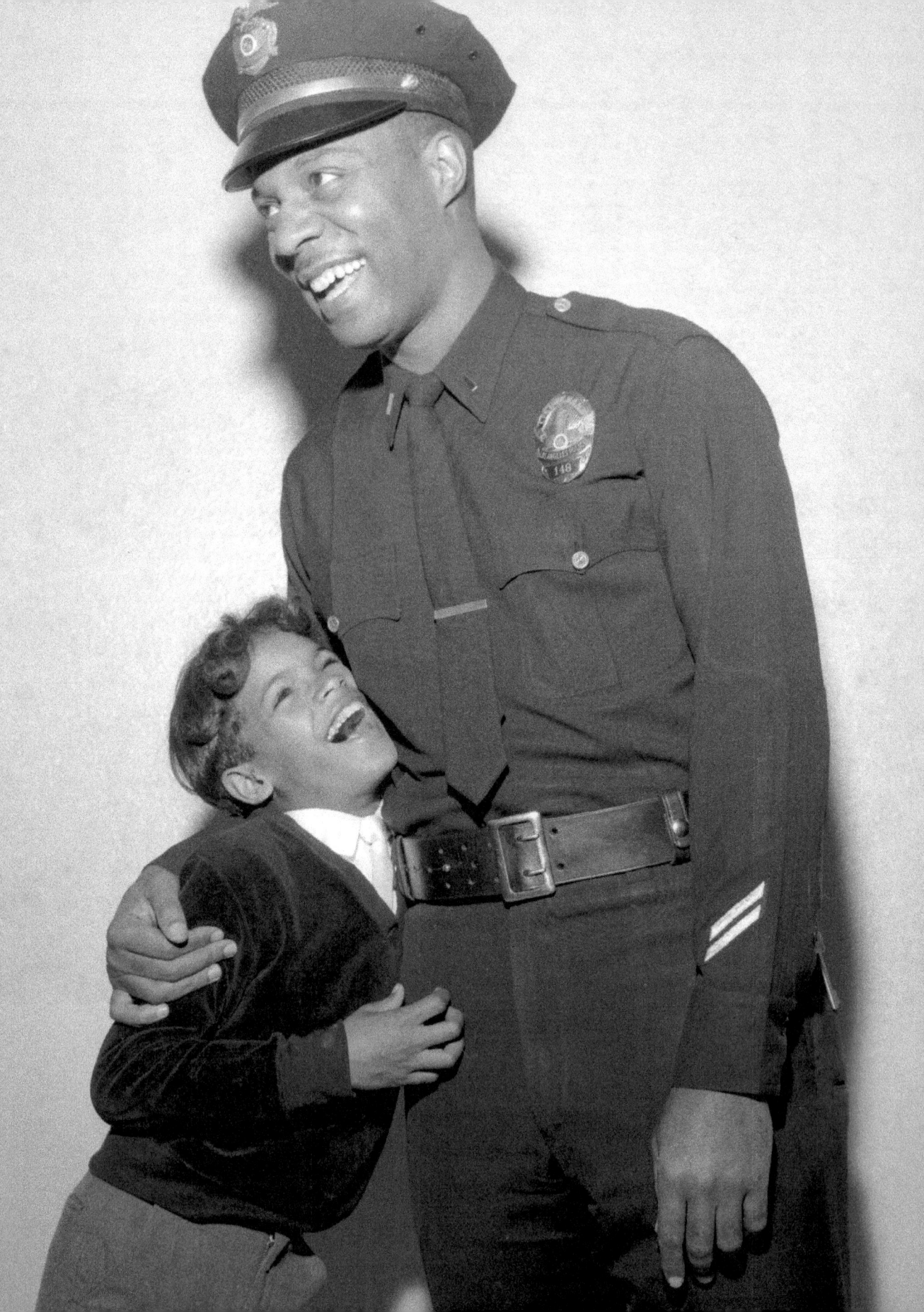

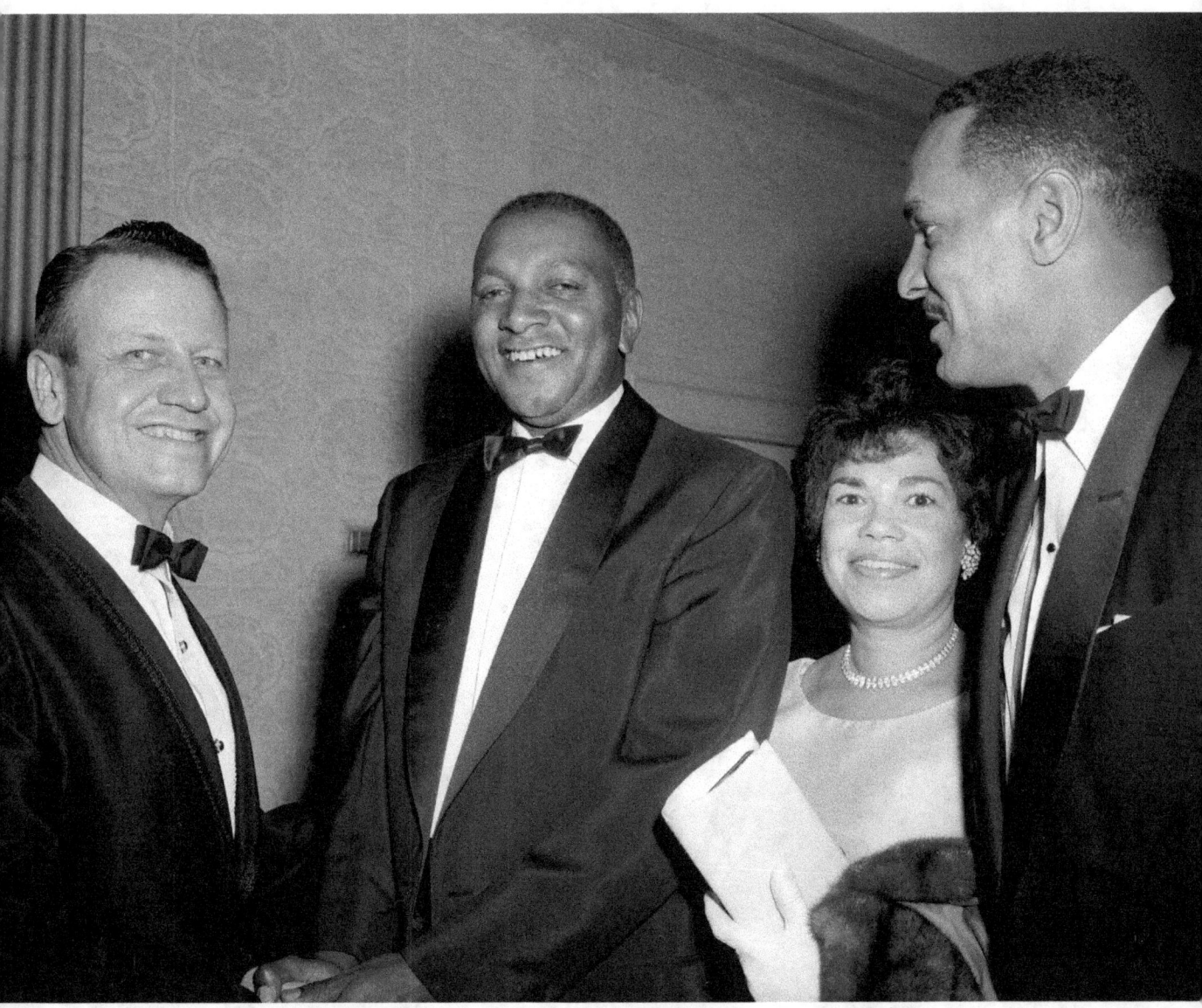

Leslie Shaw shakes hands with Speaker Jesse Unruh at the Ambassador Hotel. His wife (*right*), civic activist Ann Shaw, was the first African American to head the YMCA of Greater Los Angeles. April 12, 1964

*Opposite*: Homer Broome with child at a conference. Broome joined the LAPD in 1954, and by 1969 became the first black captain of the LAPD. He was promoted in 1975 to the rank of commander, also the first African American to do so. Broome is credited with opening the doors for many minority law enforcement officers throughout Los Angeles and across the country, including Chief Bernard Parks. April 1, 1967

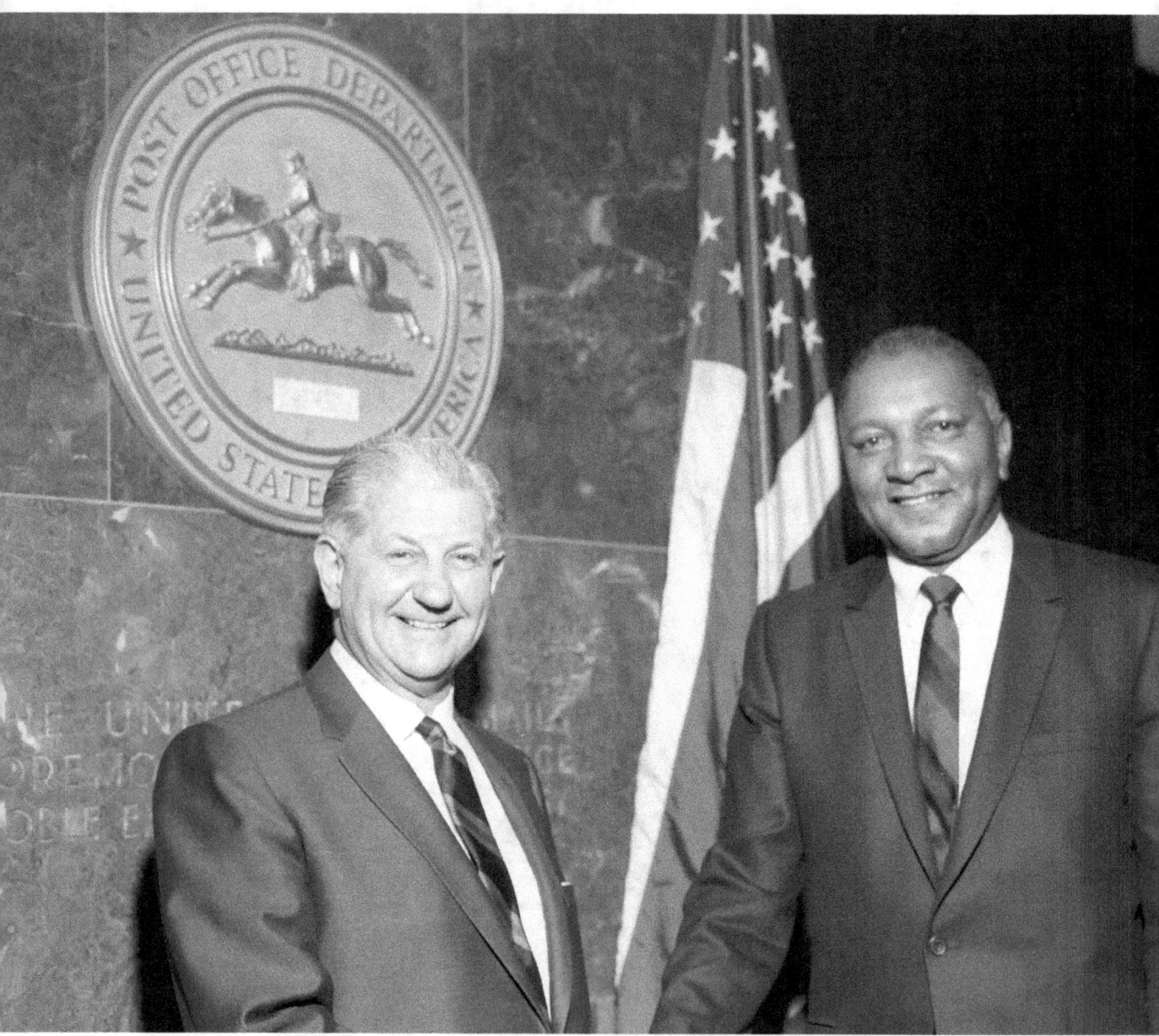

Leslie Shaw (*right*) with Compton Postmaster Joseph Causey (*left*) at a postal service meeting. Shaw was named the postmaster of Los Angeles in 1963, under the direction of President John F. Kennedy. He was the first African American postmaster of Los Angeles, and the first black male to be appointed postmaster of a major U.S. city. He was preceded only by Nancy Avery, who was appointed postmaster of Pacoima in 1961 and was the first African American postmaster of a major office in California. c1963

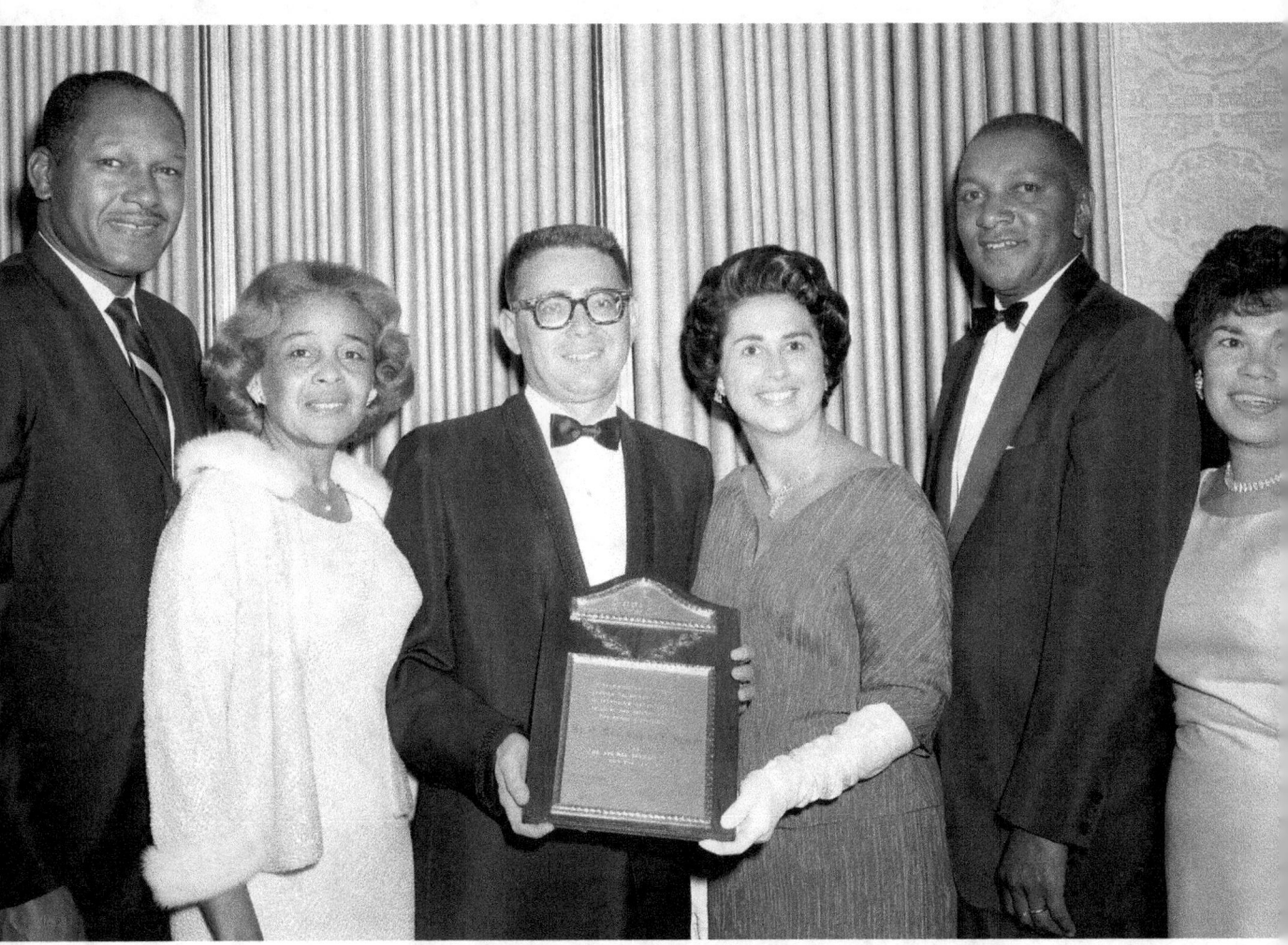

Leslie and Ann Shaw (*far right*), and Tom and Ethel Bradley (*far left*) attend awards ceremony for Eugene and Rosalind Wyman (*center*) at the Cocoanut Grove. April 12, 1964

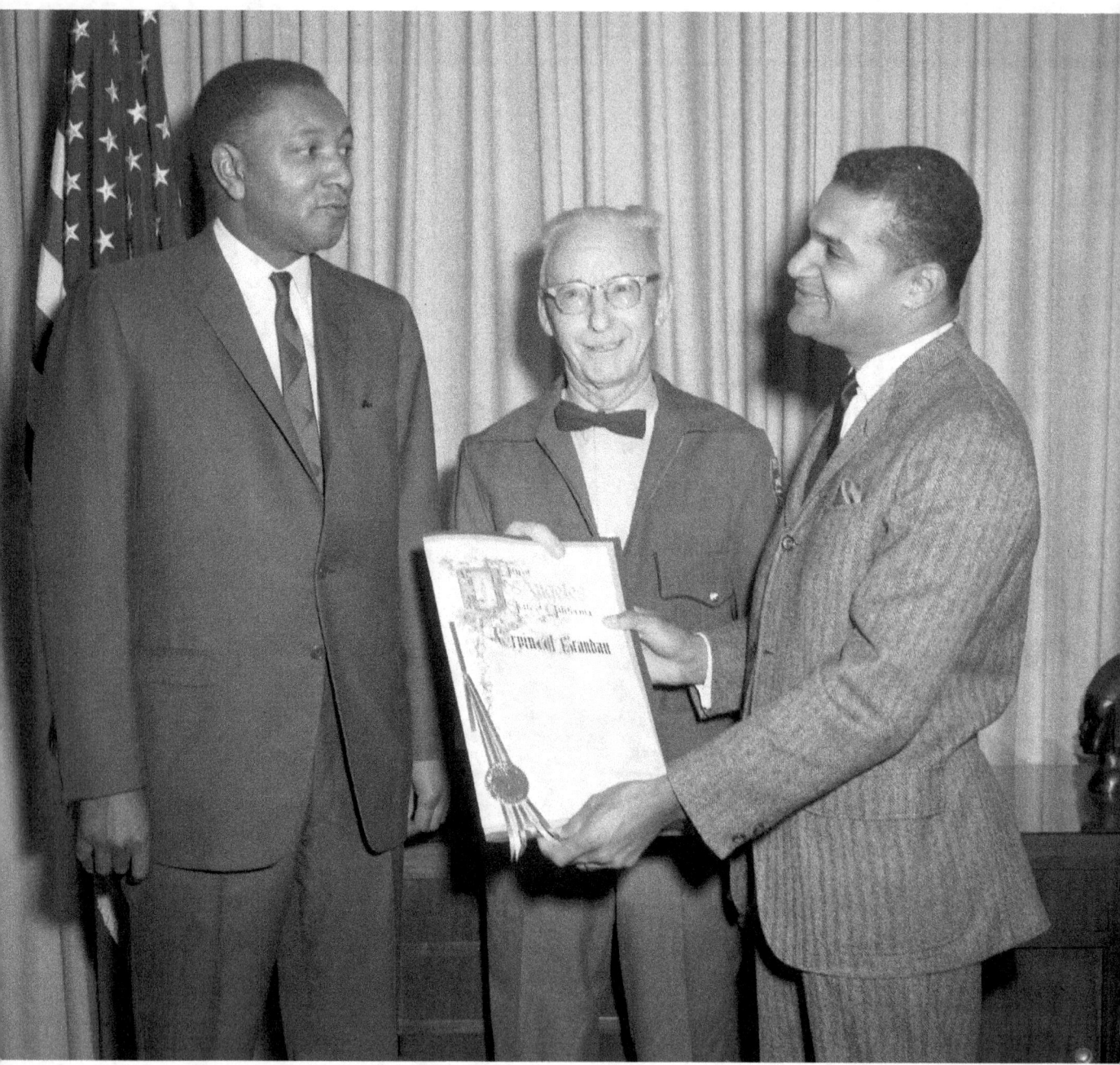

Leslie Shaw (*left*) receives a resolution from Councilman Billy G. Mills (*right*). Irvin W. Brandau (*center*) also received a resolution that day.

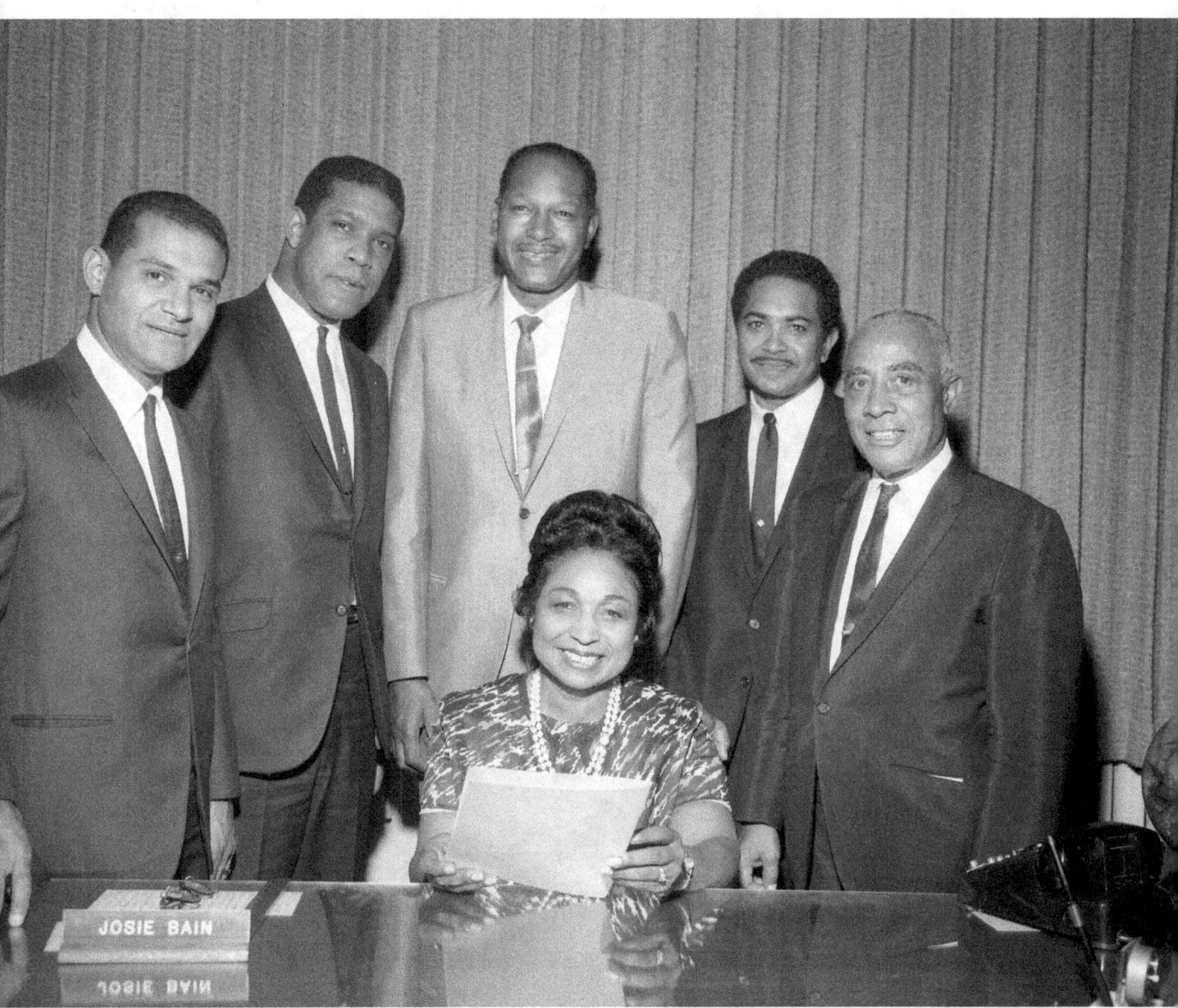

Josie Bain at desk, surrounded by Councilman Billy G. Mills (*far left*), Assemblyman Bill Greene (*left*), Councilman Tom Bradley (*center*), Senator Mervyn Dymally (*right*) and Councilman Gilbert Lindsay (*far right*). c1967

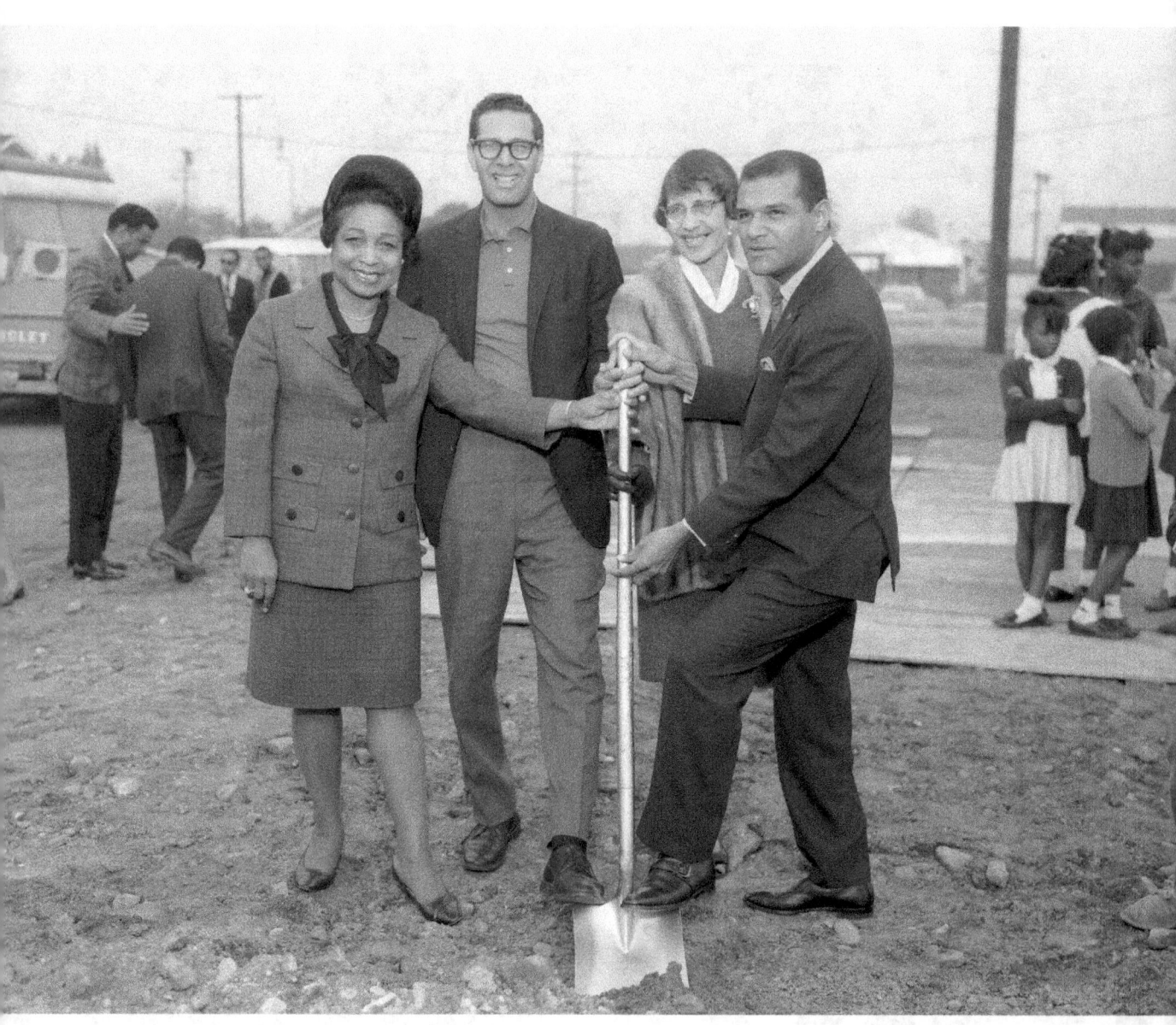

Josie Bain (*left*) joined by Loren Miller III (*left center*), Mrs. Juanita Miller (*right center*) and Councilman Billy G. Mills (*right*) at the groundbreaking ceremony for Loren Miller Elementary School. January 18, 1969

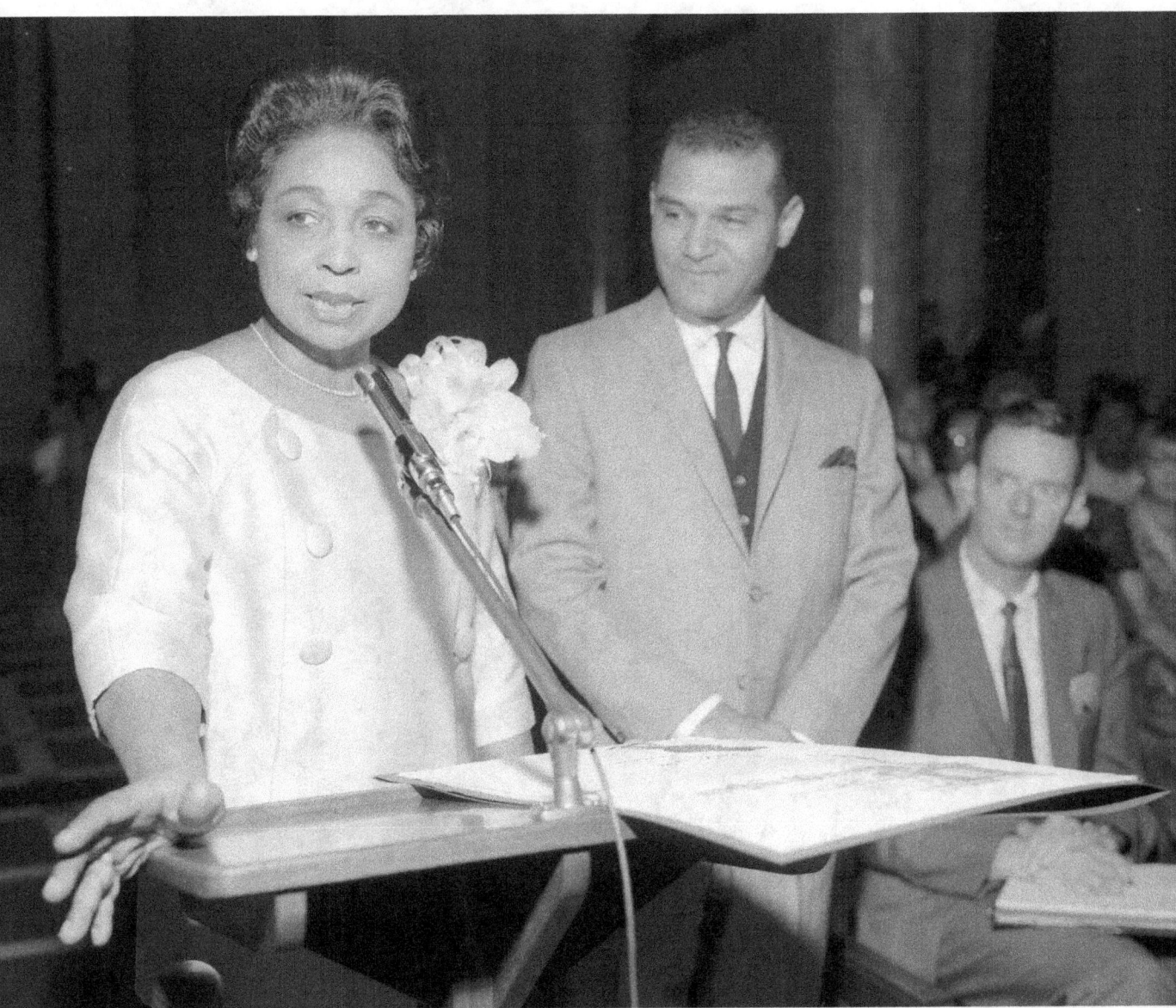

Josie Bain receives a resolution at City Hall from Billy G. Mills. Bain became a teacher in Los Angeles during a time when there were few African Americans doing so. Working her way through the ranks, she became the first black districtwide associate superintendent of the Los Angeles Unified School District in the early 1970s. She also became the highest paid woman in the district. January 11, 1968

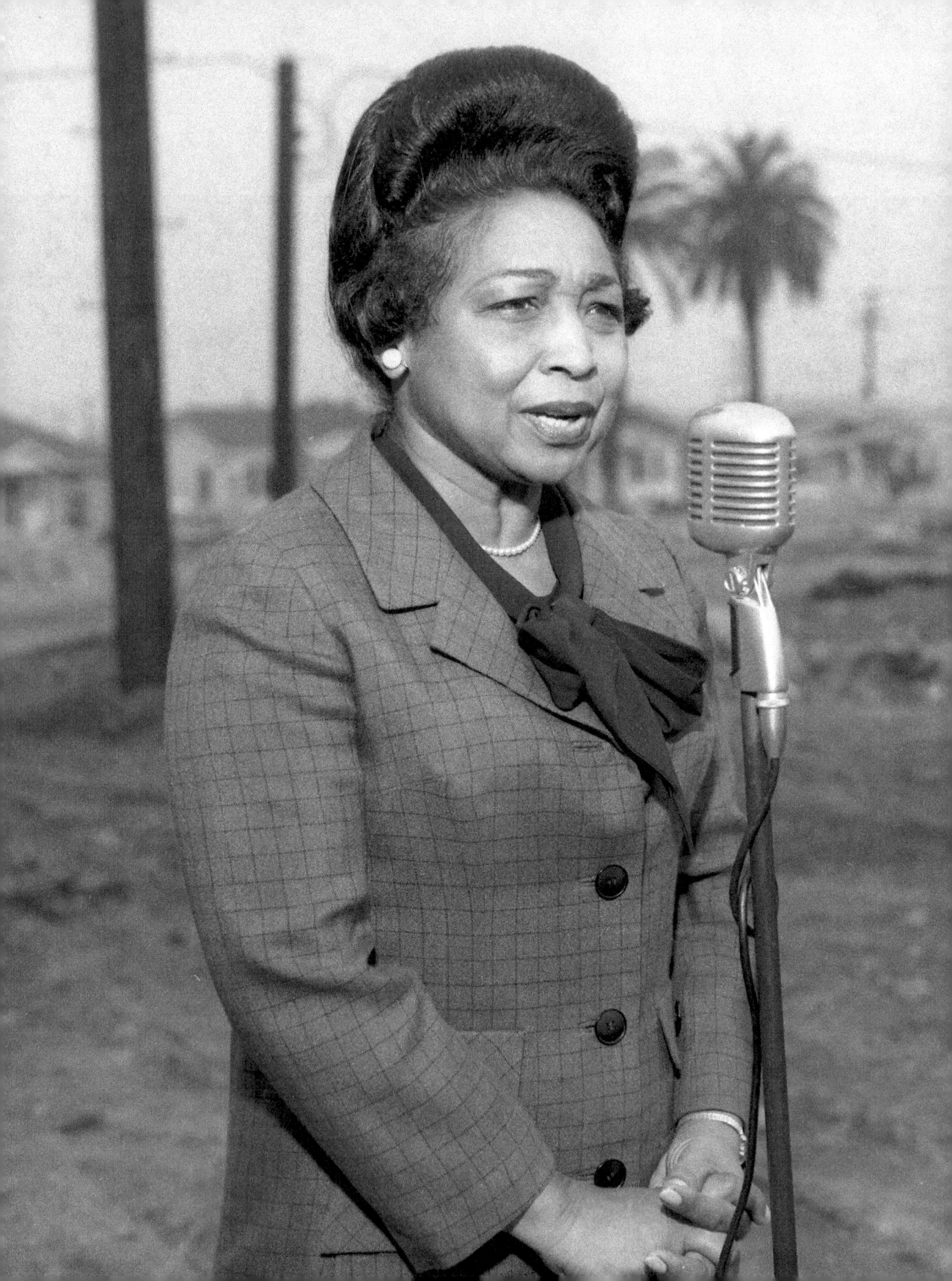

Josie Bain speaks at the groundbreaking
ceremony for Loren Miller Elementary
School. January 18, 1969

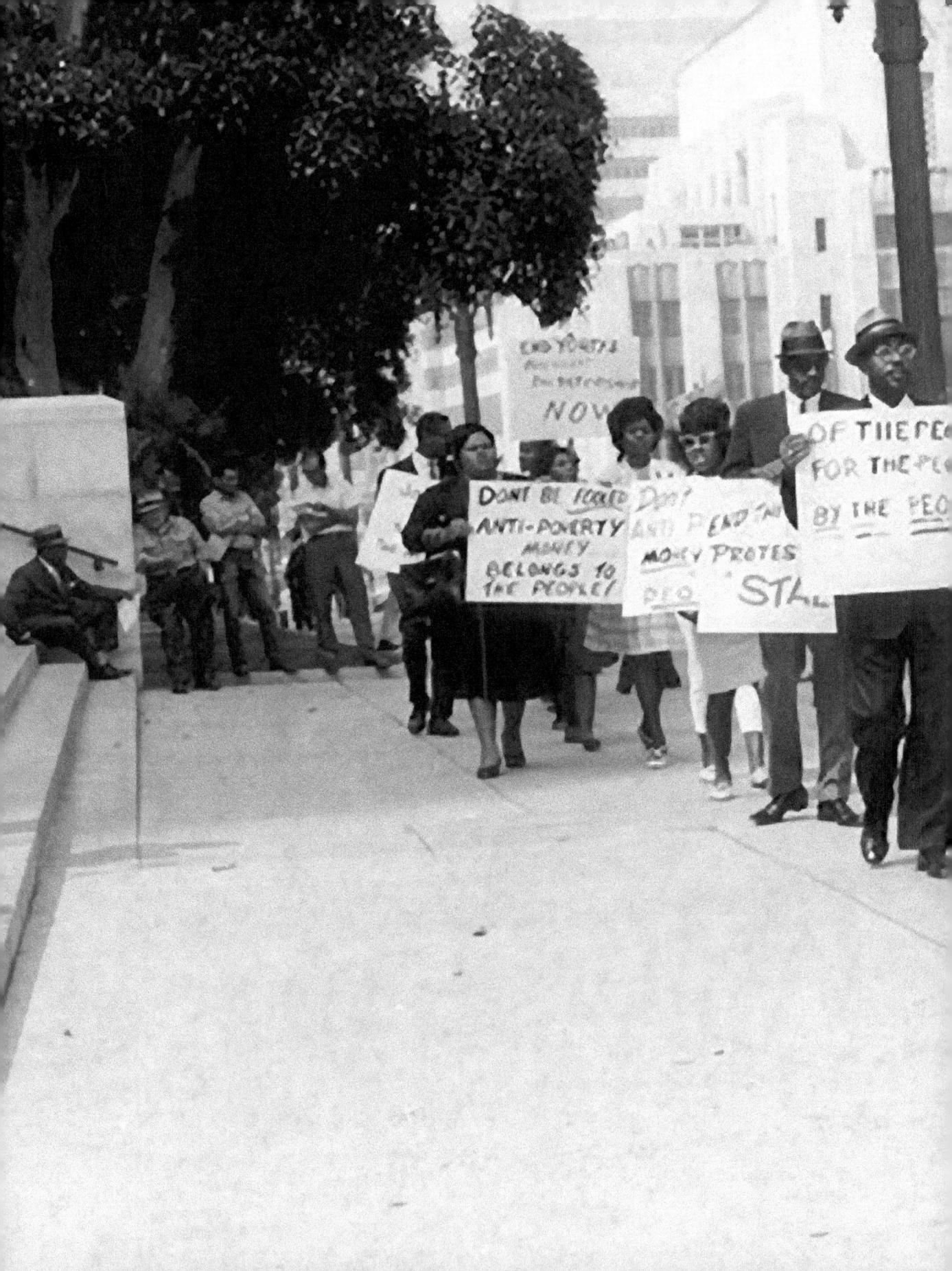

LET THE POOR SPEAK for themselves

COMMUNITY LEADERS AND ACTIVISTS

*Overleaf*: Leon Washington protests the election of the board to oversee anti-poverty funds in front of City Hall. Washington became the first African American to serve on the board of directors of the California Newspaper Publishers Association. His own newspaper, the *Los Angeles Sentinel* began publication in 1933, and is currently the oldest and largest running African American newspaper in Los Angeles. Washington became best known for his "Don't Spend Where You Can't Work" campaign, which boycotted businesses that operated in black communities, but refused to hire black workers. July 12–13, 1965

*Opposite*: Ralph Bunche shakes hands with Finnie Jackson (*right*), field deputy for Councilman Leonard Timberlake. c1960s

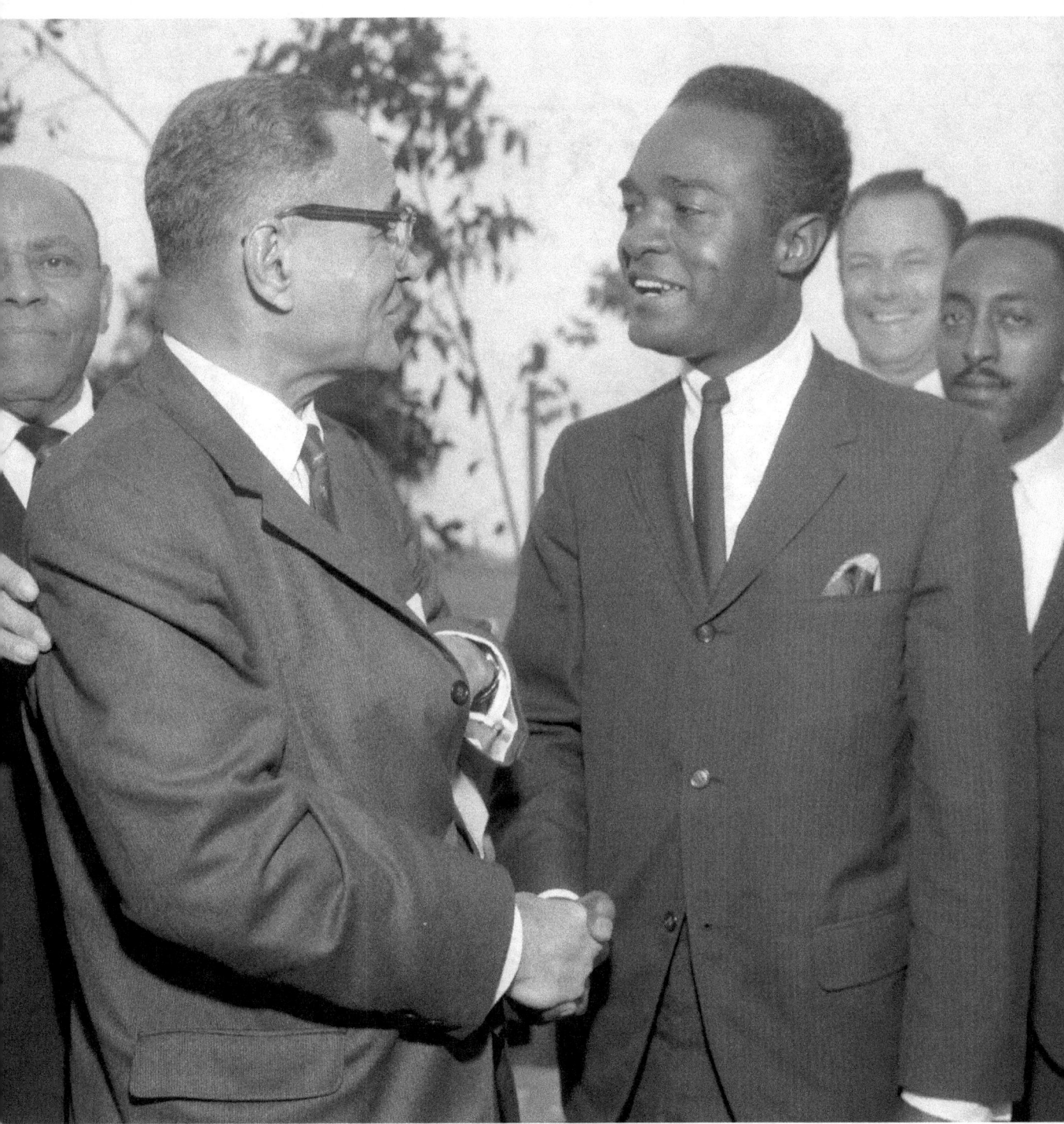

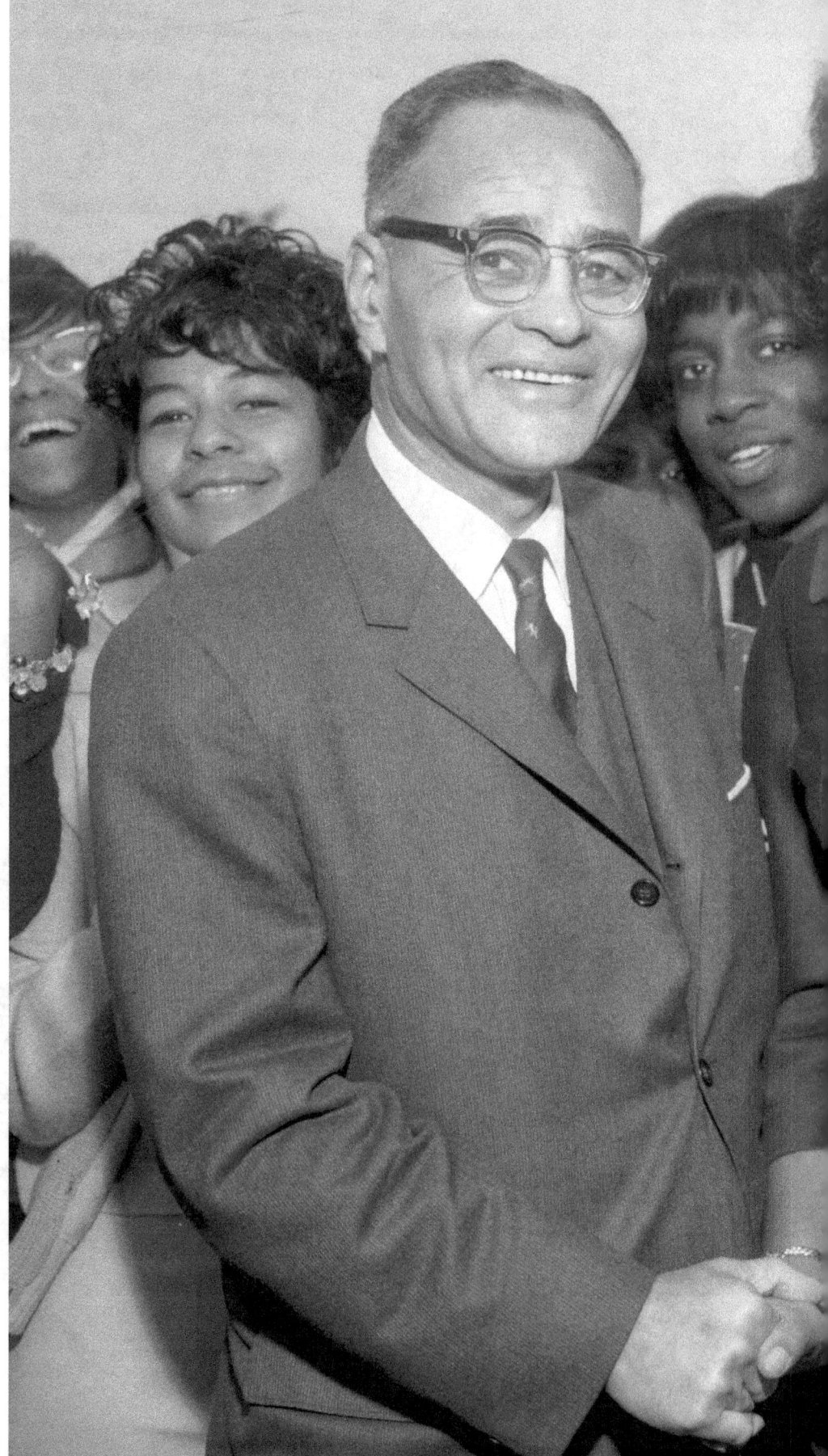

Ralph Bunche
with crowd.
Gilbert Lindsay
(*far right*). c1960s

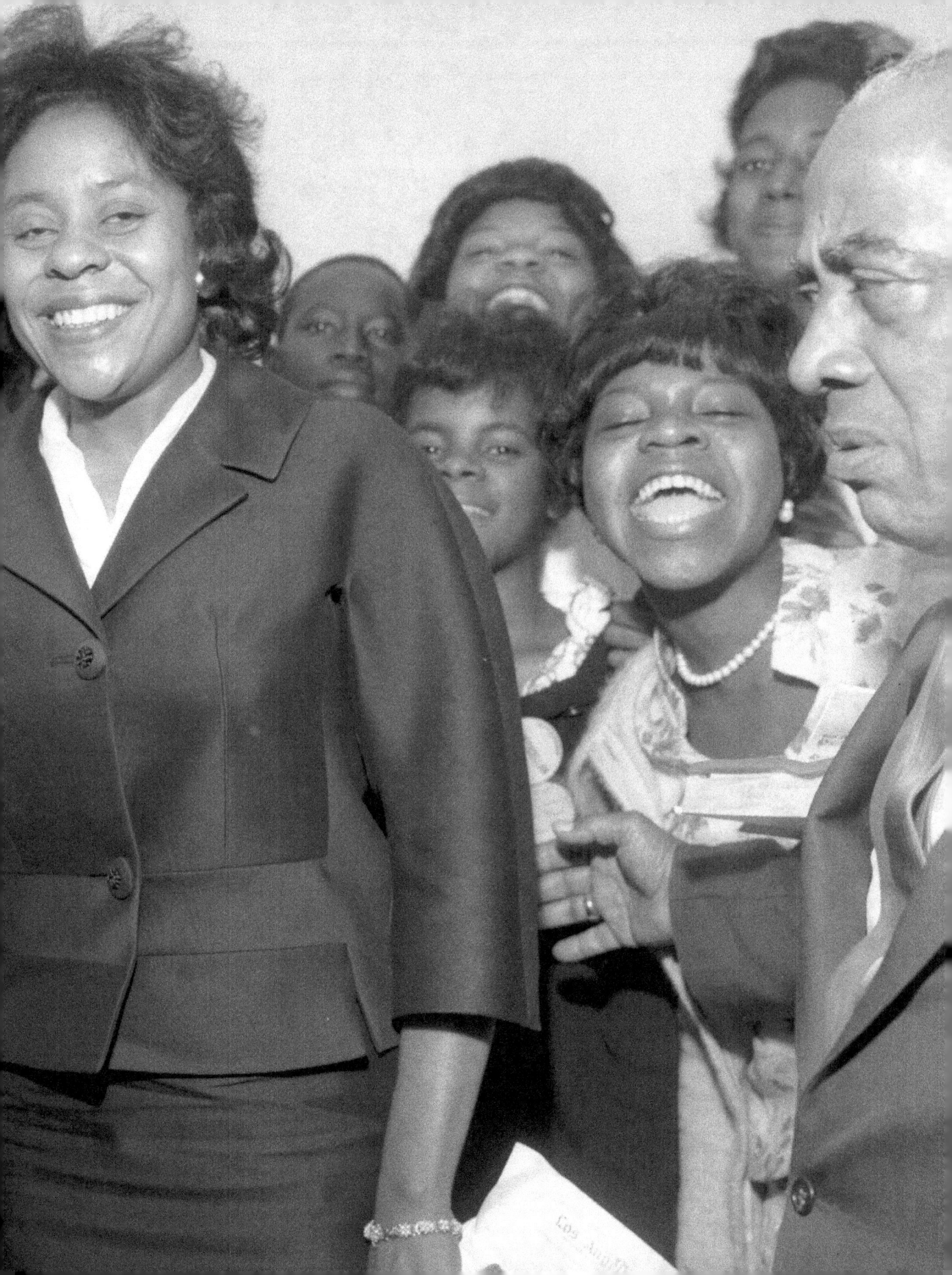

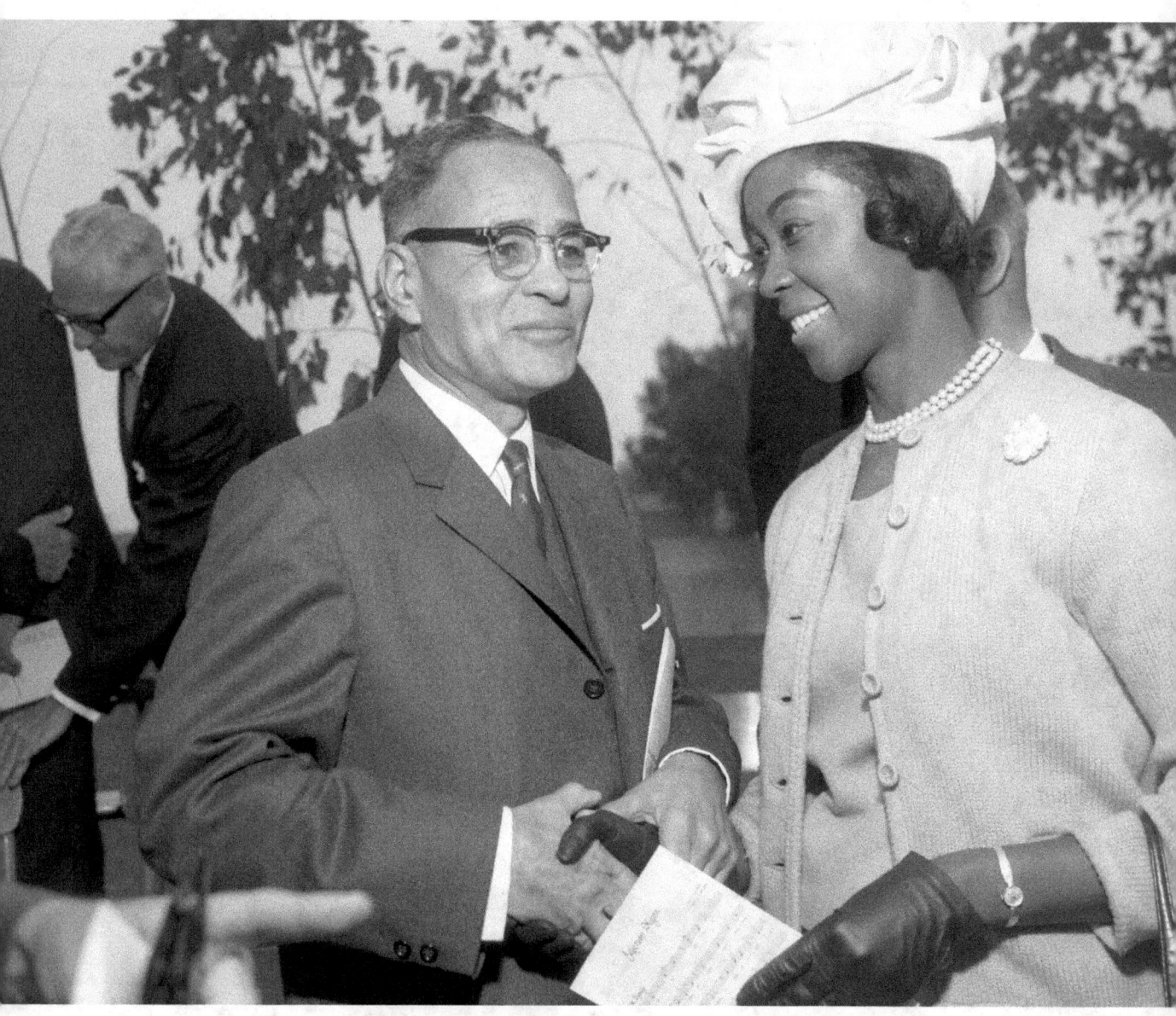

Ralph Bunche (*left*) shakes hands with Louise Ridgle. Bunche was the first African American to receive the Nobel Prize in 1950 for his mediation during the Israeli–Arab War. During World War II, Bunche worked for the OSS, a predecessor to the CIA. He was awarded the Medal of Freedom by President John F. Kennedy, and marched with Martin Luther King Jr. during the March on Washington in 1963 and from Selma to Montgomery in 1965. c1960s

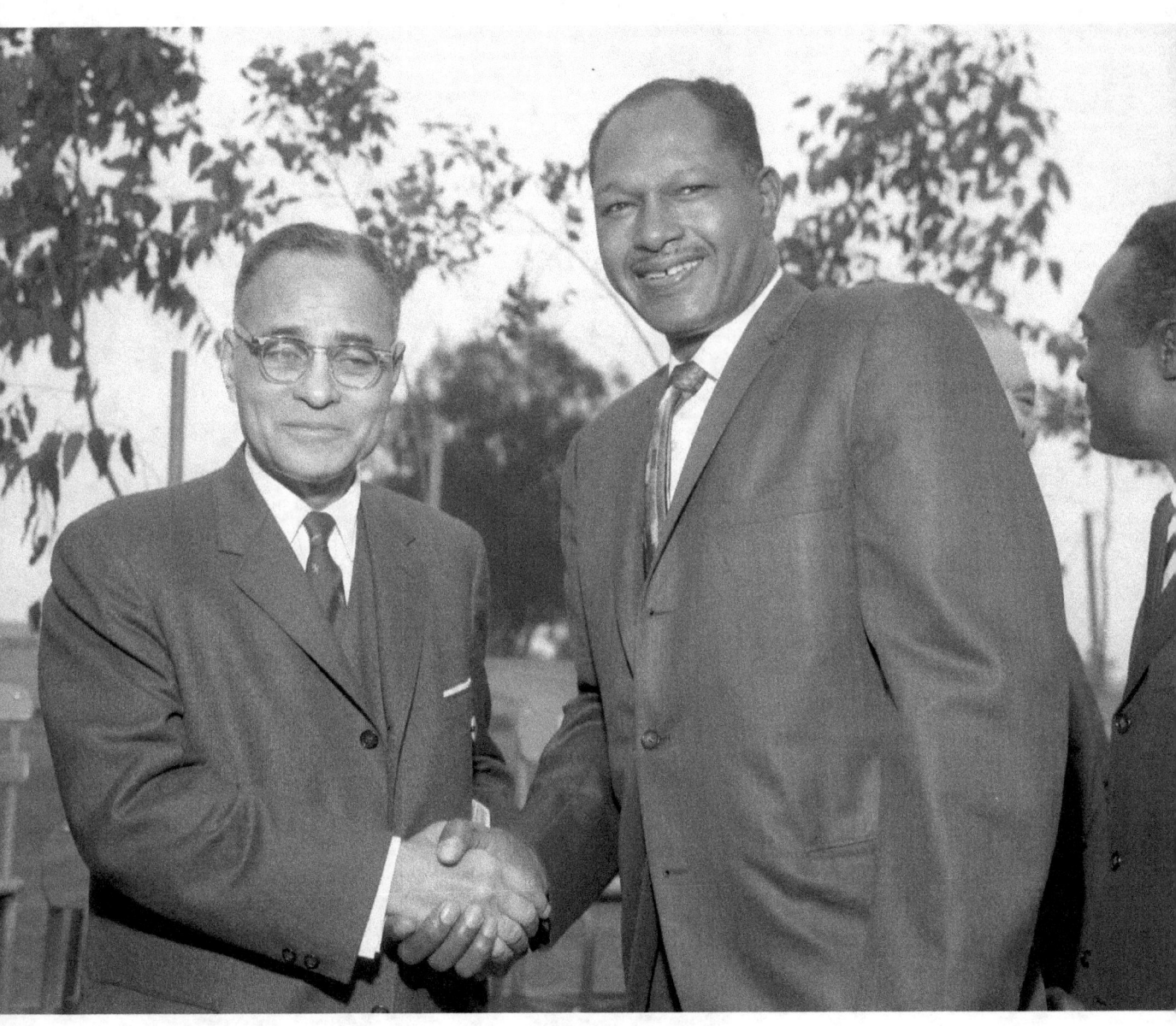

Ralph Bunche (*left*) shakes hands with Councilman Tom Bradley (*right*). c1960s

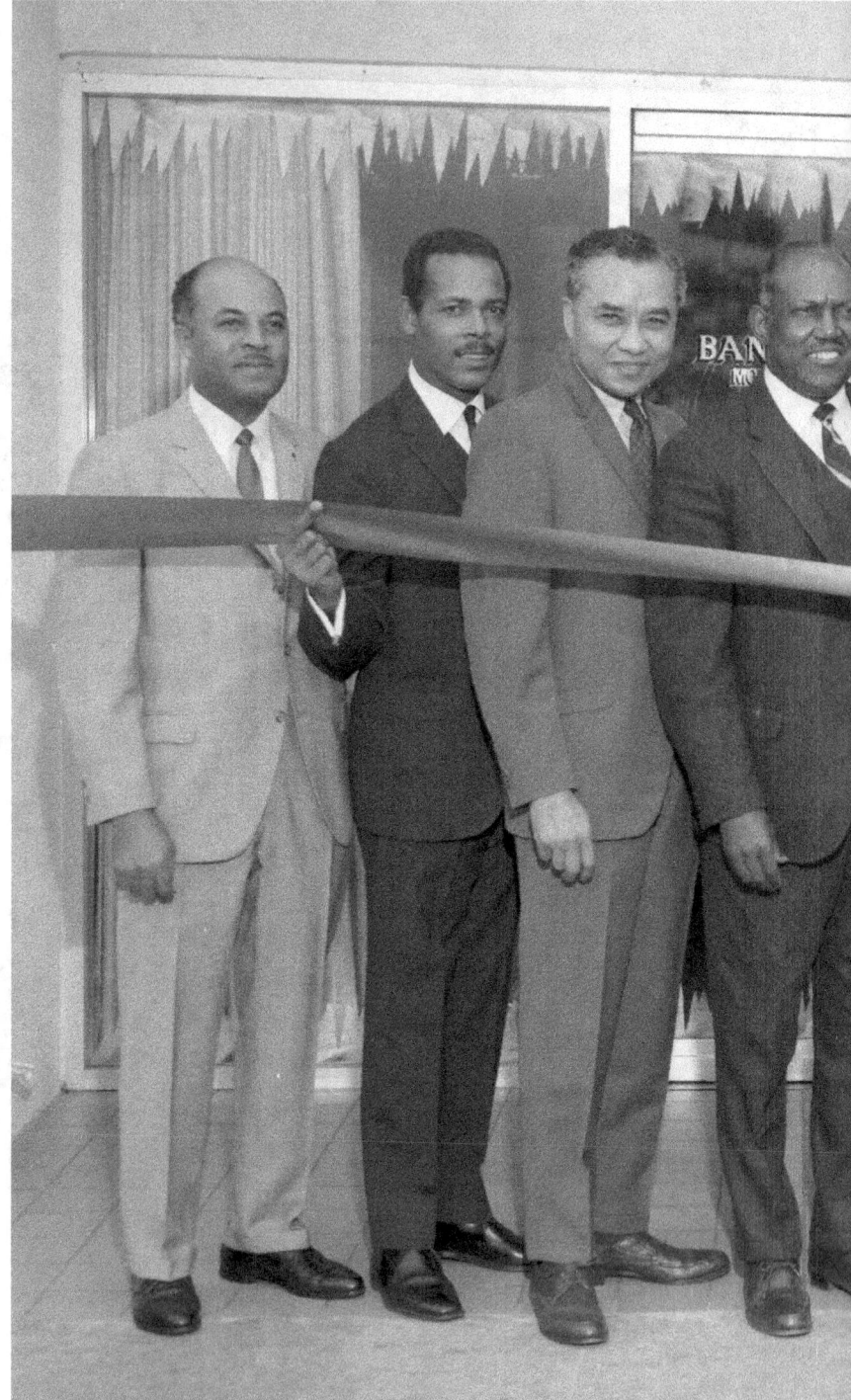

Community leaders and bank officers attend a Bank of Finance ribbon cutting ceremony. The Bank of Finance was the first African American organized bank in California. Opened in 1964, it catered to small businesses in the community. During its time, it nursed local businesses to fruition and provided financial assistance for necessary community resources like medical centers, day care centers and homes for the elderly. Members of the organizing committee included Dr. Edward H. Ballard, Dr. Perry W. Beal, Wilton A. Clarke, Onie B. Granville, Mrs. Bernice M. Malbrue, Tom Bradley and Lorenzo V. Spencer. c1968

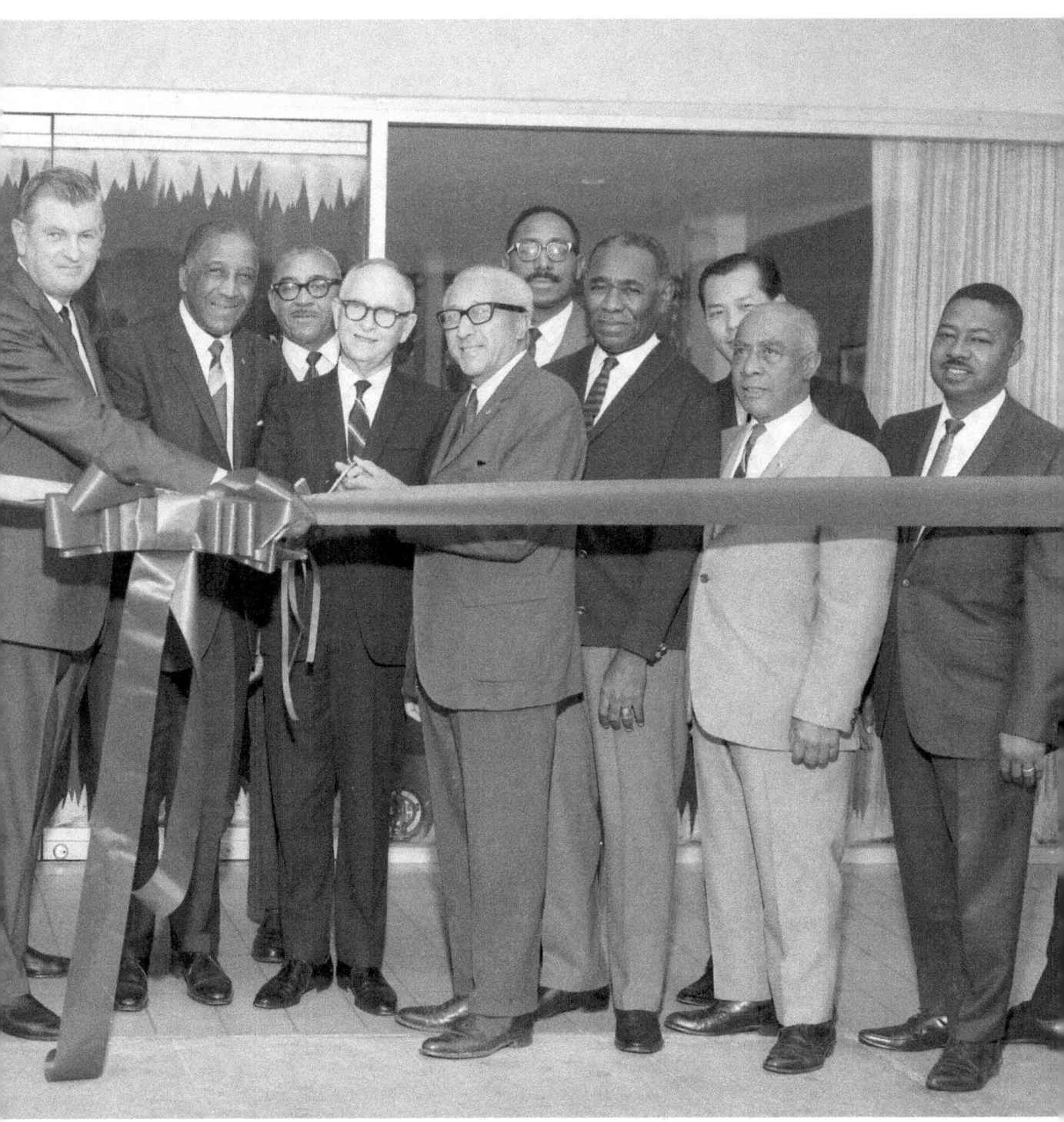

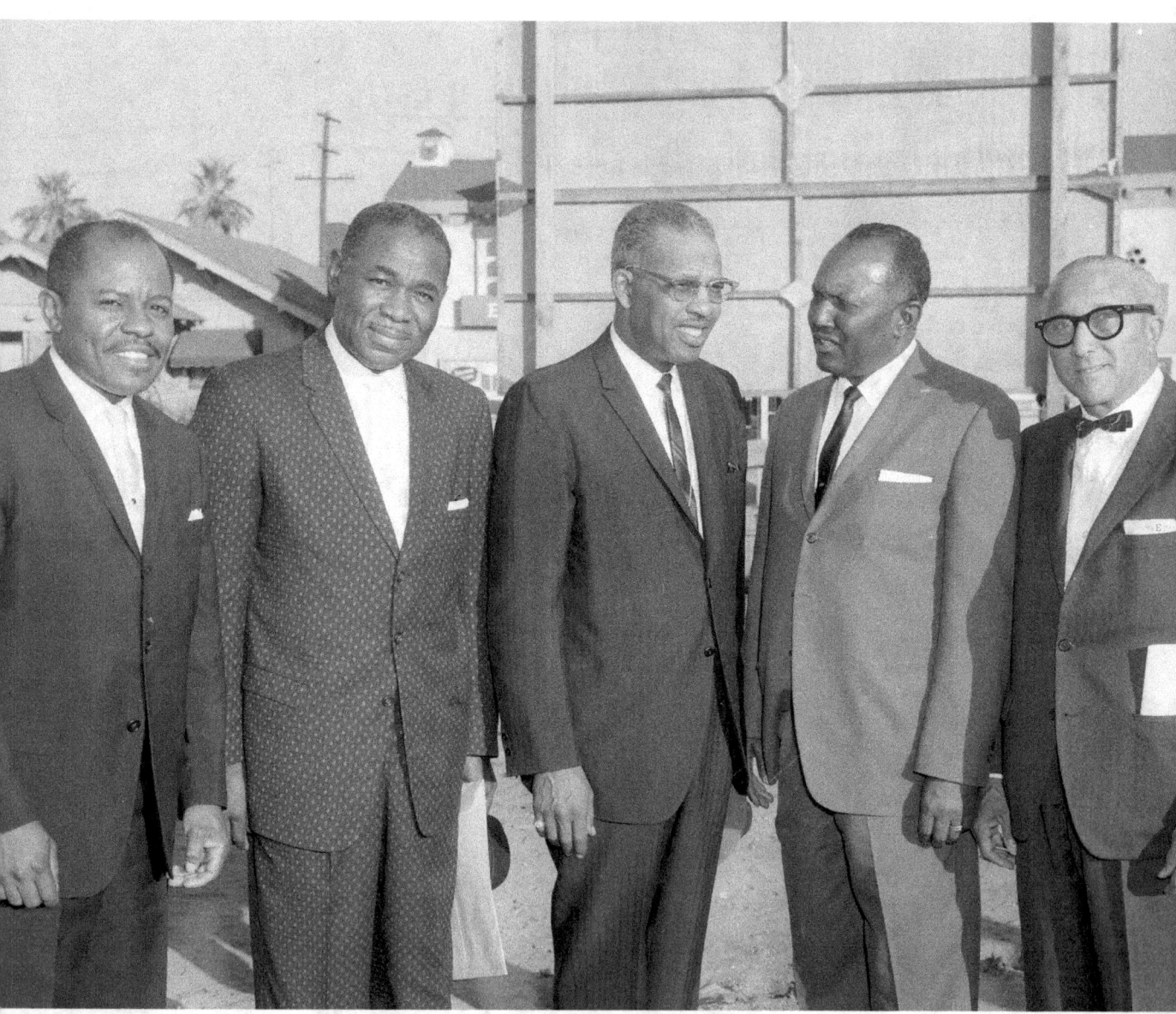

Bank of Finance officers at the groundbreaking ceremony. c1964

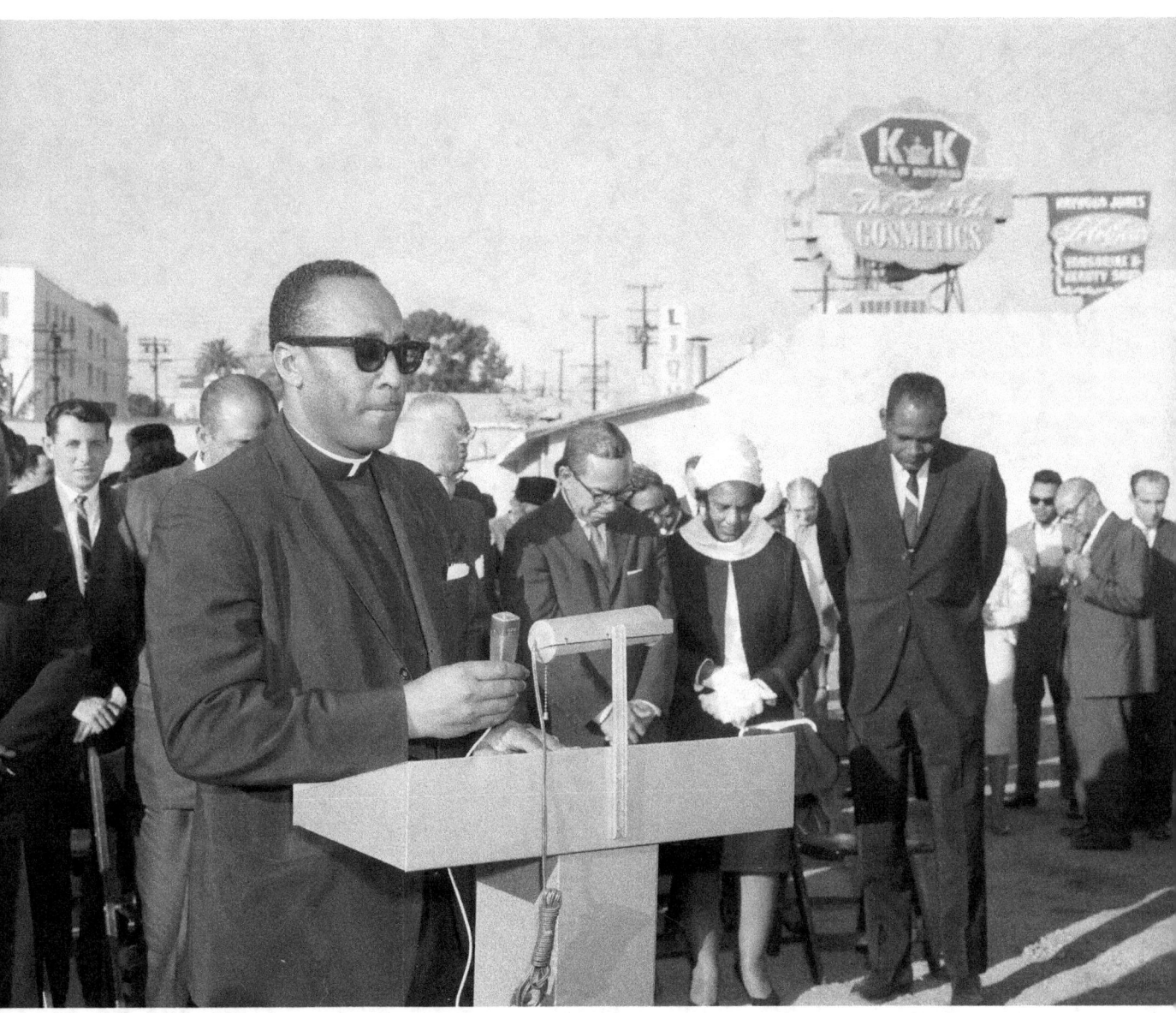

Reverend H.H. Brookins speaks at groundbreaking ceremony for Bank of Finance. Tom Bradley is in striped tie on right. c1964

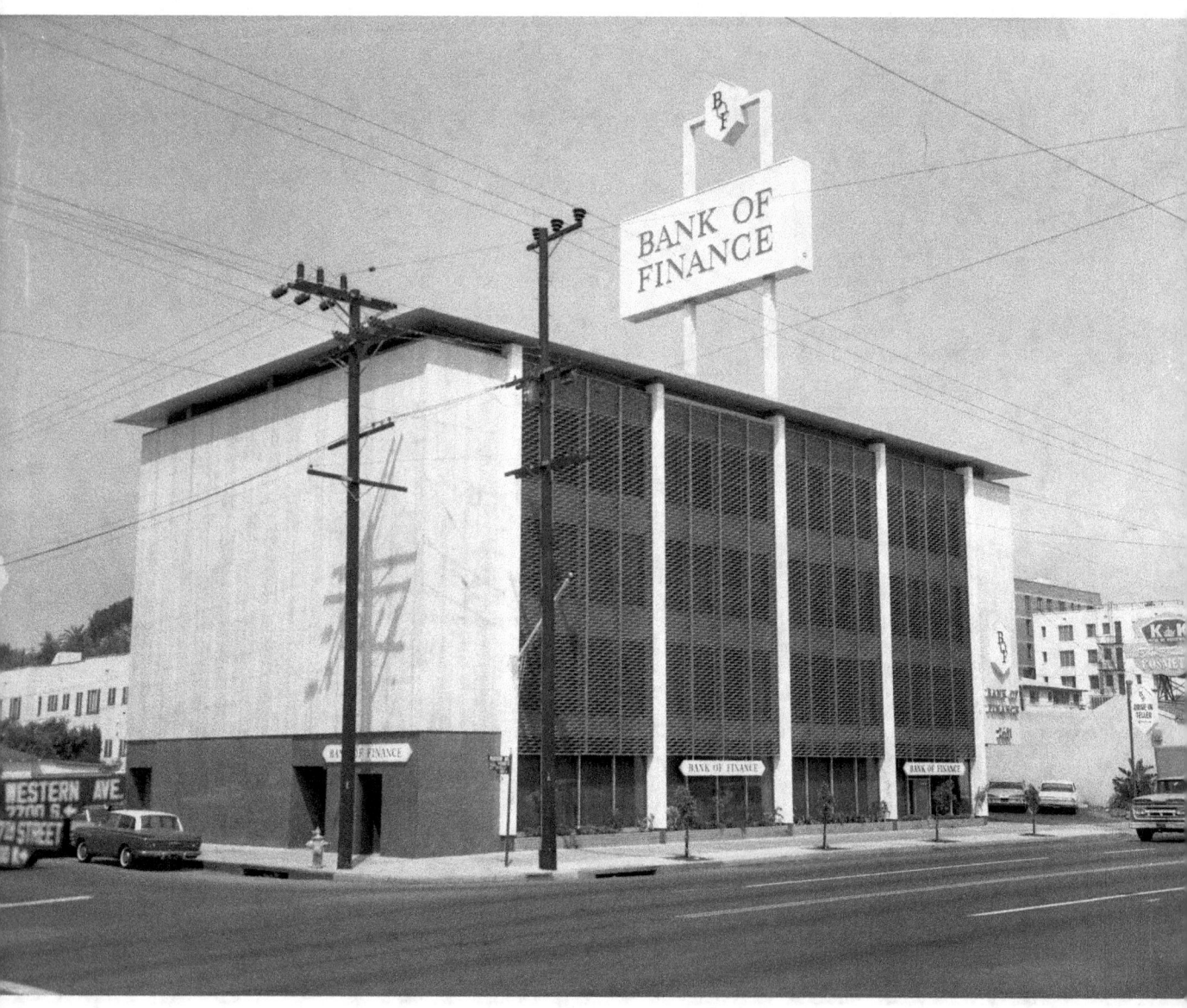

Bank of Finance building on Western Ave. and 27th. c1960s

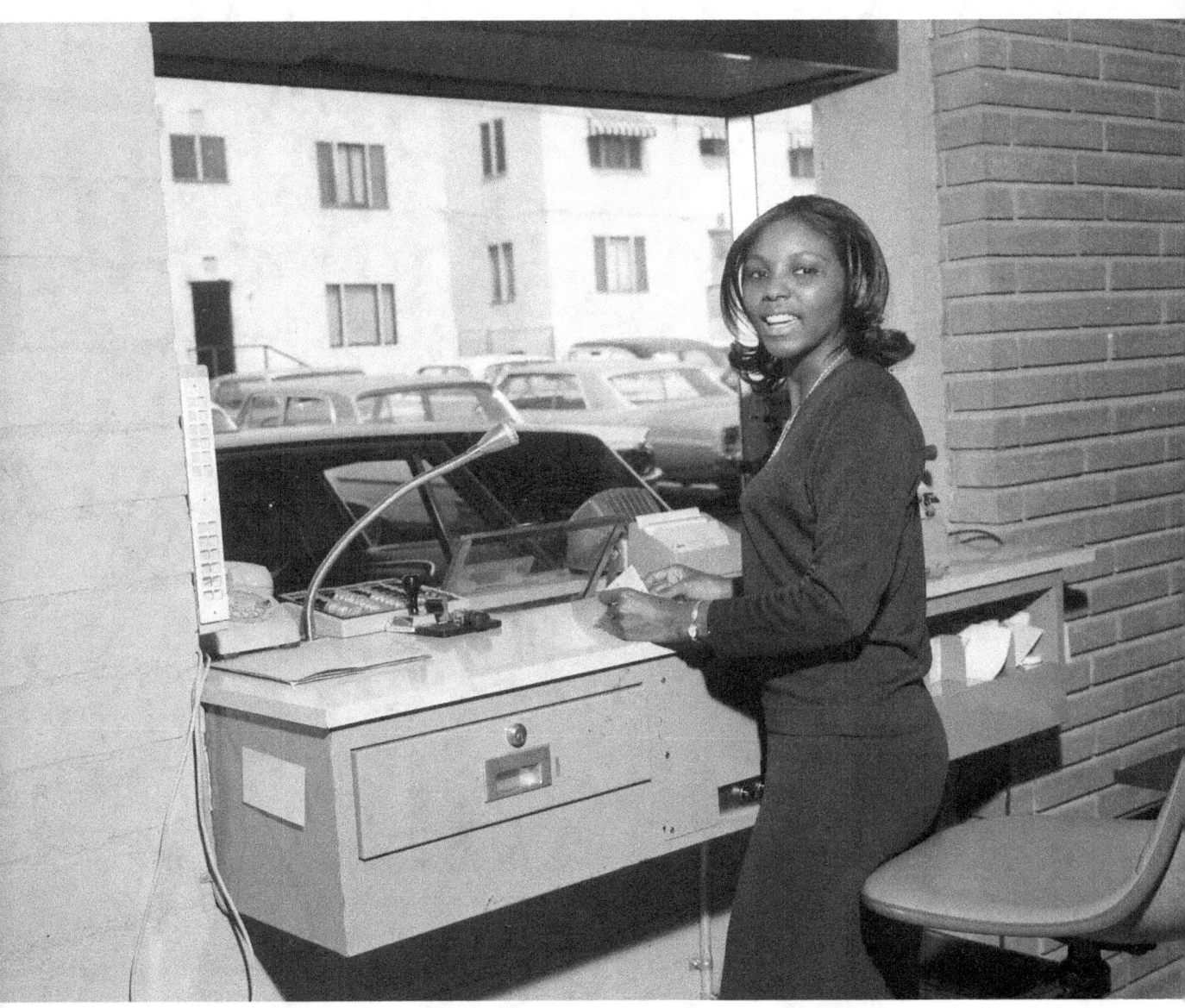

Bank teller at Bank of Finance branch. c1964

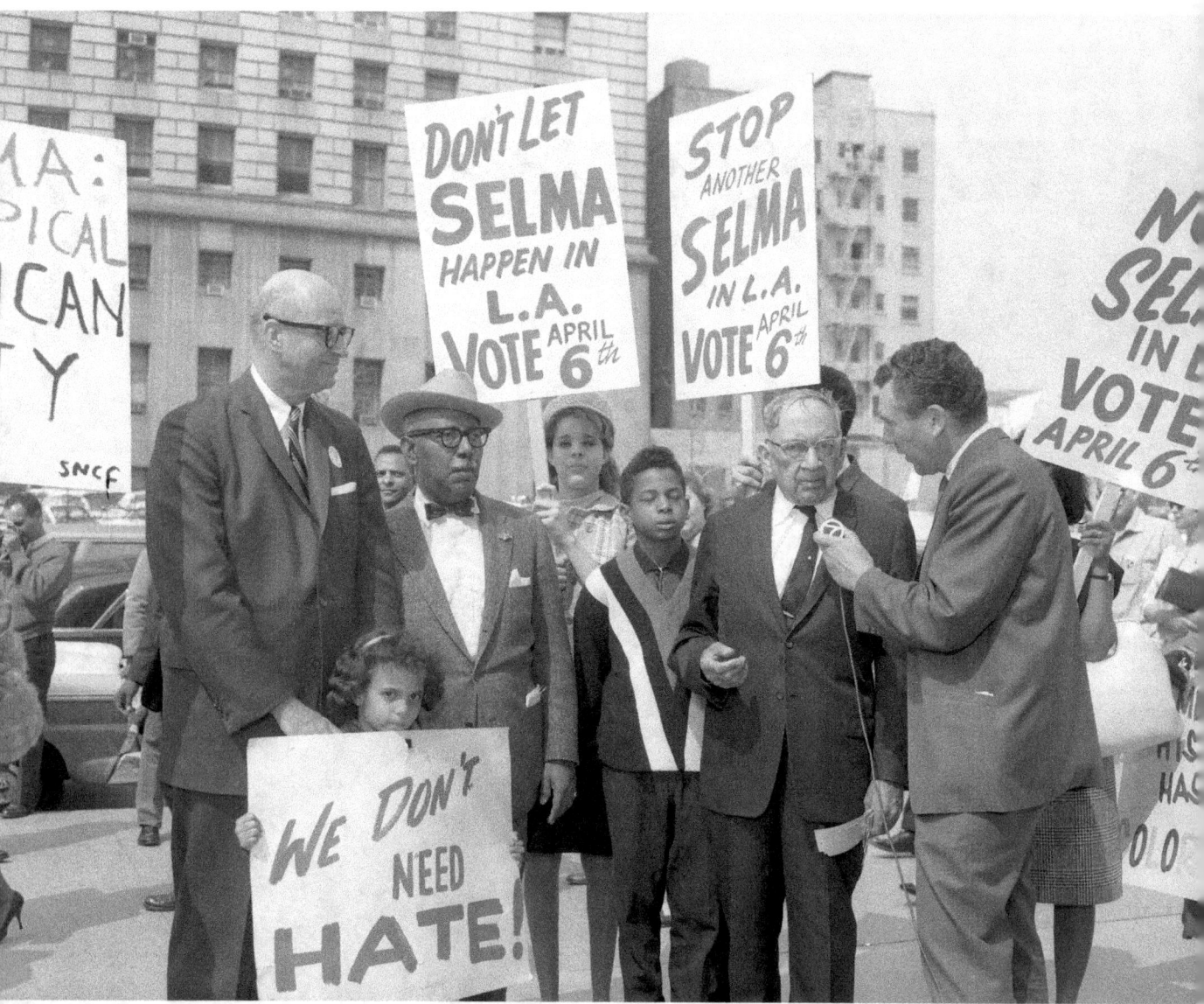

Claude Hudson (*speaking into the mic*) at a Prop. 14 protest with Congressman James
Roosevelt (*far left*) and Leon Washington (*left*). Hudson, a dentist who became the first
African American to receive a law degree from Loyola University in 1931, was one of the
founding members of the NAACP, known at the time as Niagara Movement. He was one of
the most revered civil rights leaders in Los Angeles, and is credited with desegregating Los
Angeles beaches, an accomplishment he celebrated by, "taking the blackest little boy I could
find to the beach with me. We ran along the beach from the Inkwell all the way up the
coast, and no one bothered us." c1964

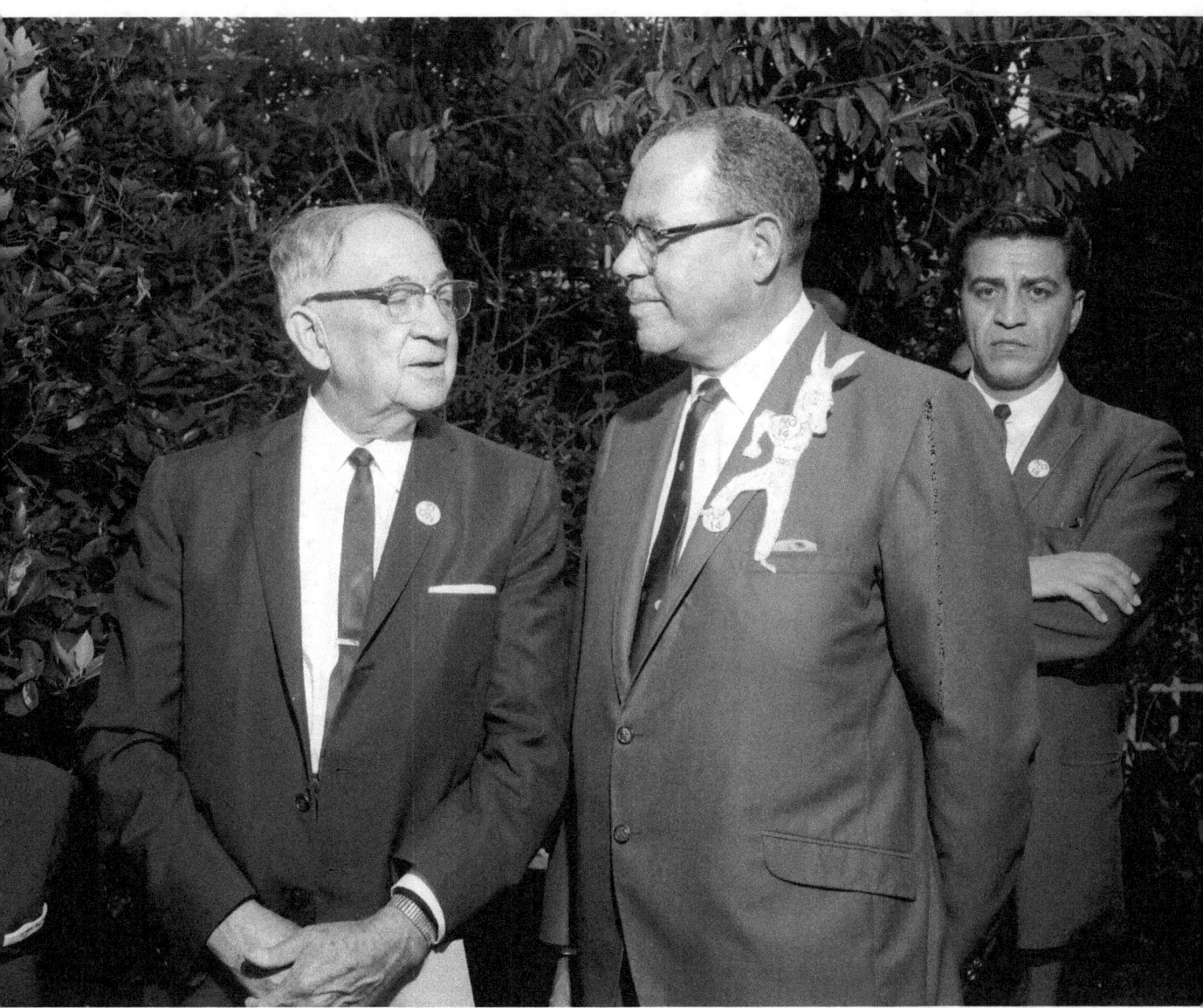

Claude Hudson (*left*) chats with Assemblyman Byron Rumford (*right*) at a garden party in Rumford's honor. Rumford was the first African American elected to state public office in Northern California. September 17, 1964

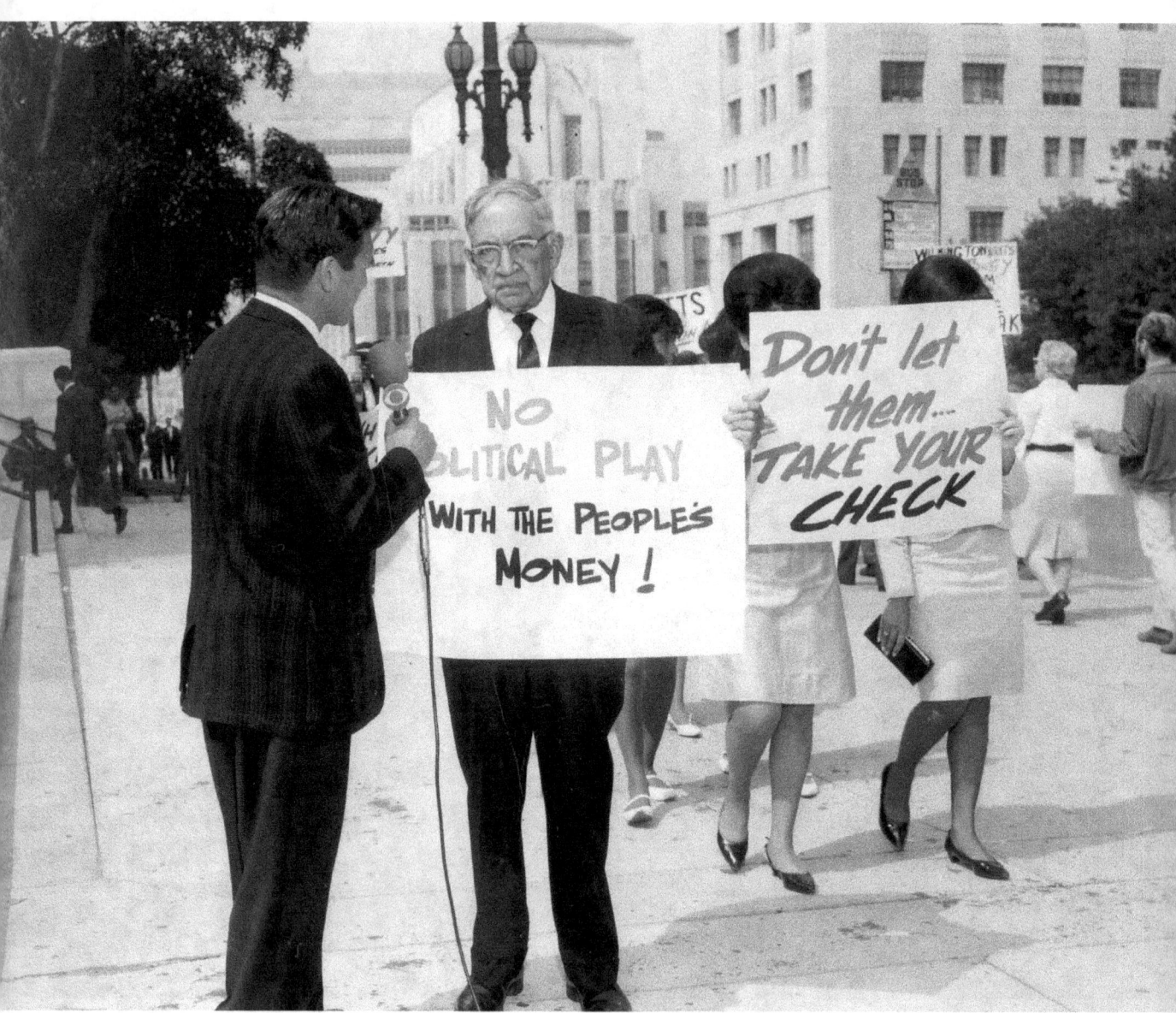

Dr. Claude Hudson speaks to reporter during protests over the election of the board to oversee anti-poverty funds in front of City Hall. July 12–13, 1965

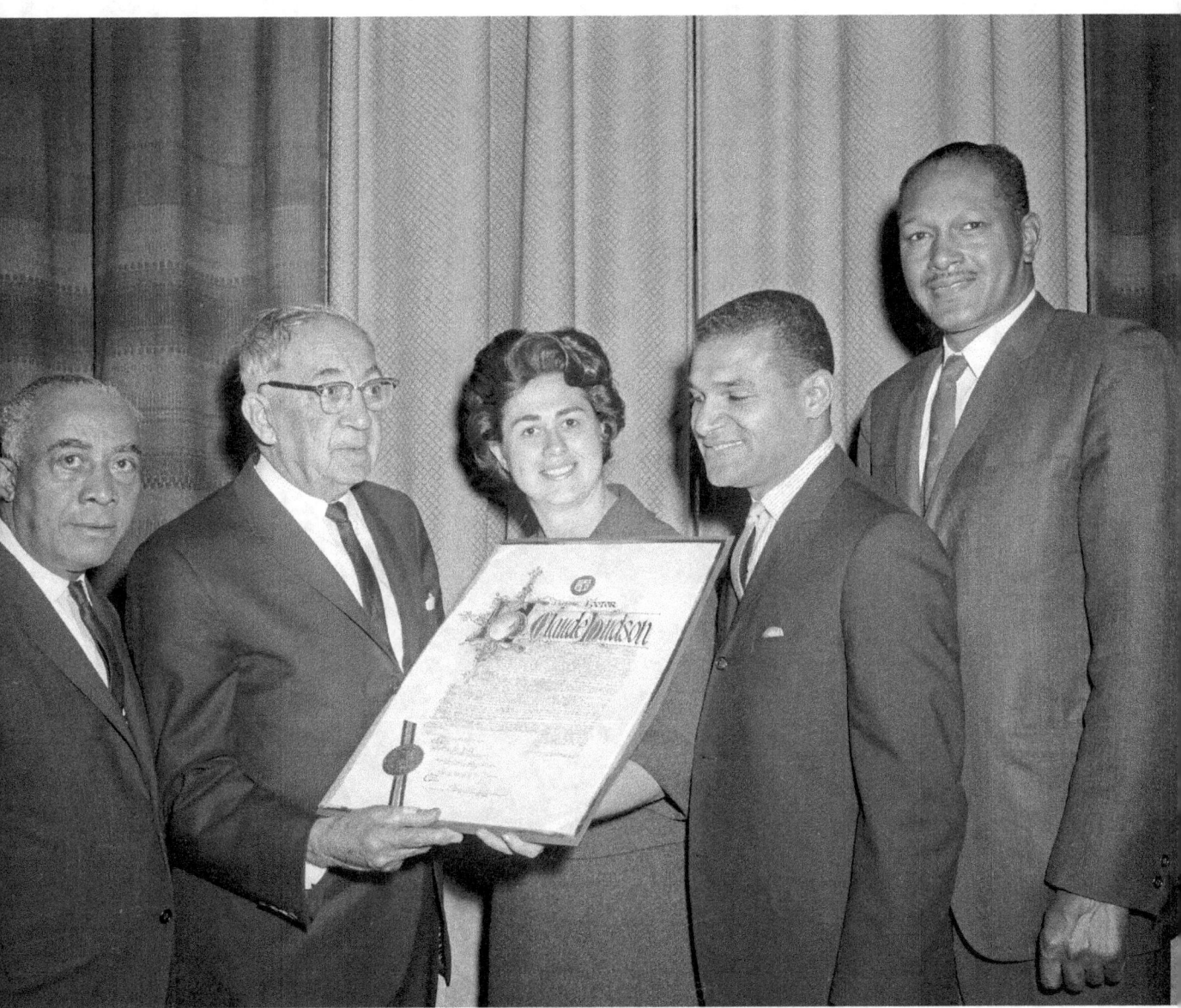

Dr. Claude Hudson receives a resolution. Councilman Gilbert Lindsay (*far left*), Claude Hudson (*left*), Councilwoman Rosalind Wyman (*center*), Councilman Billy G. Mills (*right*) and Councilman Tom Bradley (*far right*). March 19, 1964

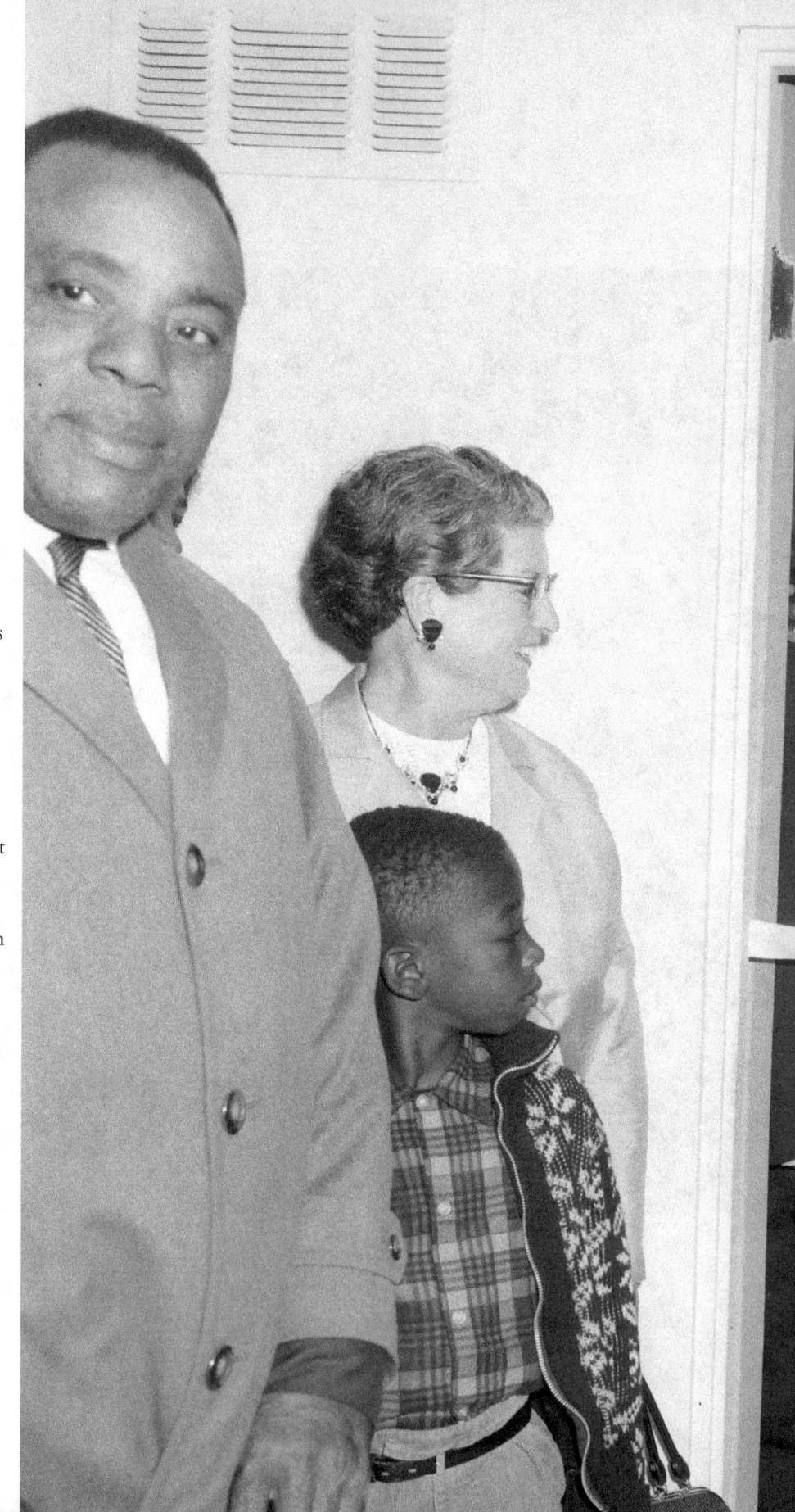

Rev. Thomas Kilgore (*right*) accompanies Martin Luther King Jr. during a ribbon-cutting ceremony. Kilgore was the first African American to become president of the American Baptist churches, during a time when African Americans only made up 20% of the members. He was a friend to Martin Luther King Jr., and helped organize the 1963 March on Washington. He was a senior pastor at Second Baptist Church, the oldest African American Baptist church in Los Angeles. Kilgore combined spirituality and community work, believing that serving God and serving your community were intertwined. c1964

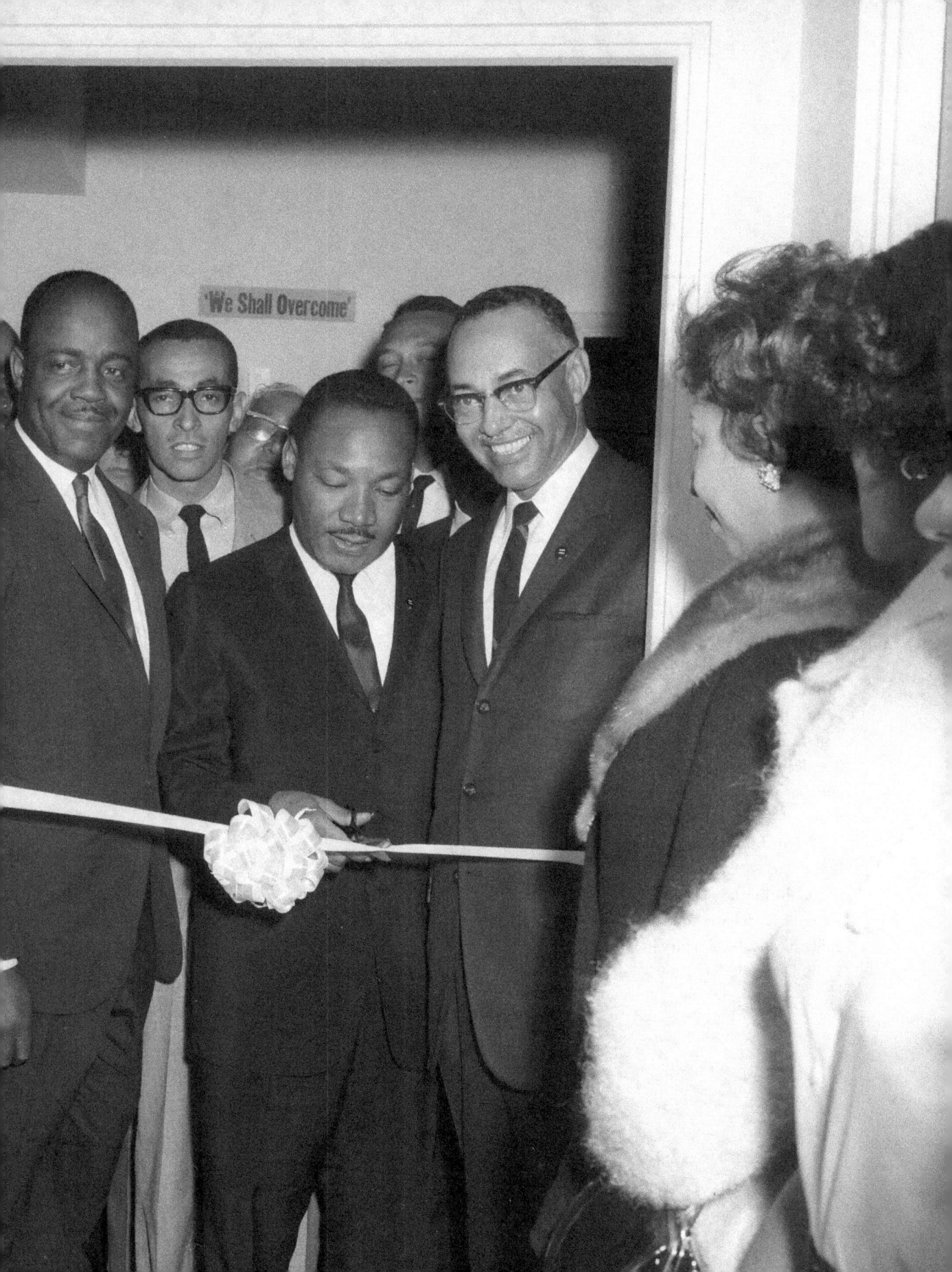

Angela Davis speaks a Black Panther rally. In 1969, Angela Davis became an assistant professor of Philosophy at UCLA. Due to her affiliation with the Communist Party in the United States and close ties to the Black Panther movement, the UCLA Board of Regents, at the urging of Governor Ronald Reagan, fired her from her position. A year later, Angela Davis was named to the FBI's Ten Most Wanted fugitive list, the third woman, and the second African American woman to be added. She was charged aggravated kidnapping and first degree murder when guns she purchased were used during the escape attempt by the Soledad Brothers, resulting in the death of the trial judge, the brothers and their accomplice. She was found not guilty by an all-white jury in 1972. December 11, 1969

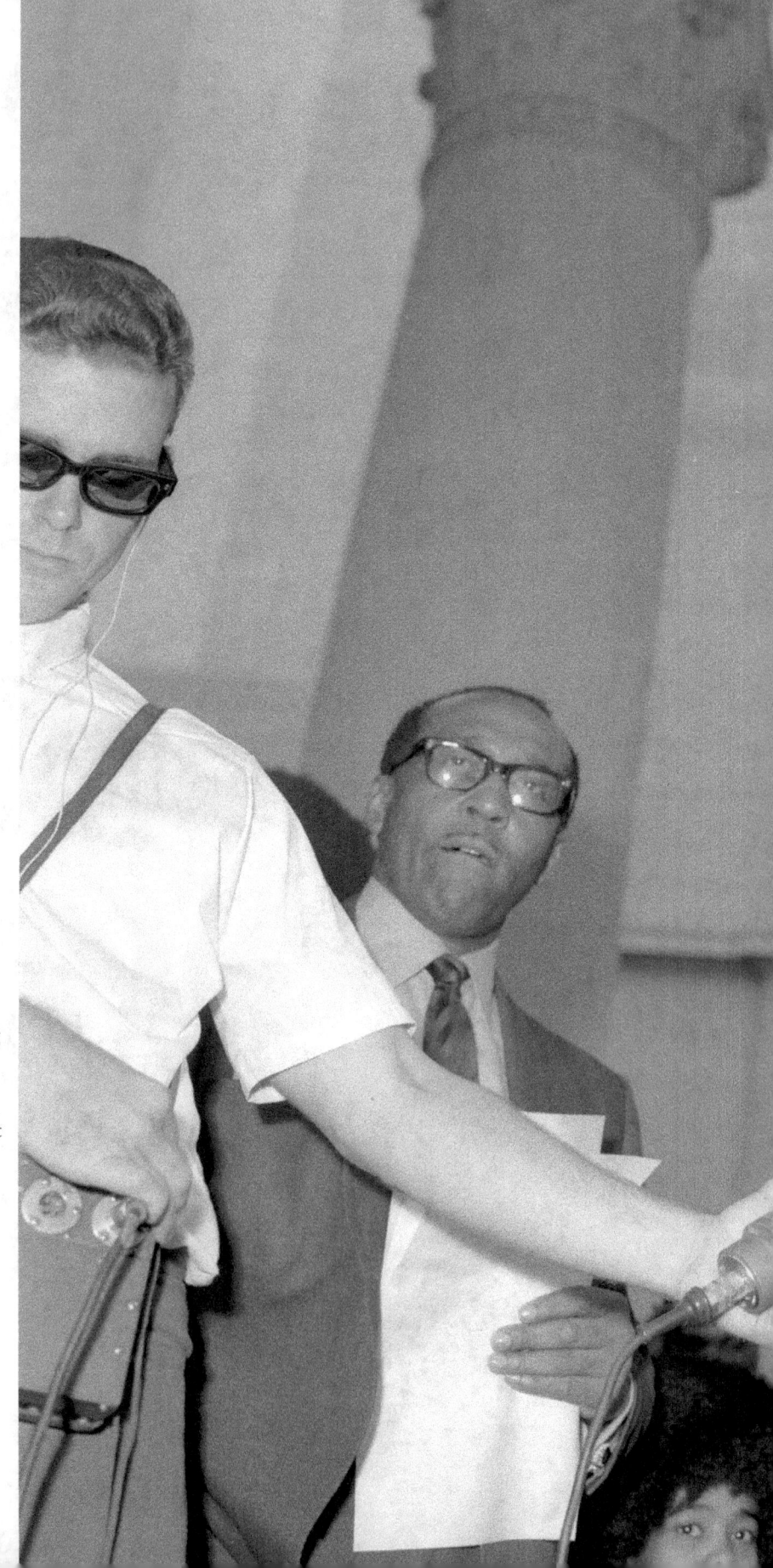

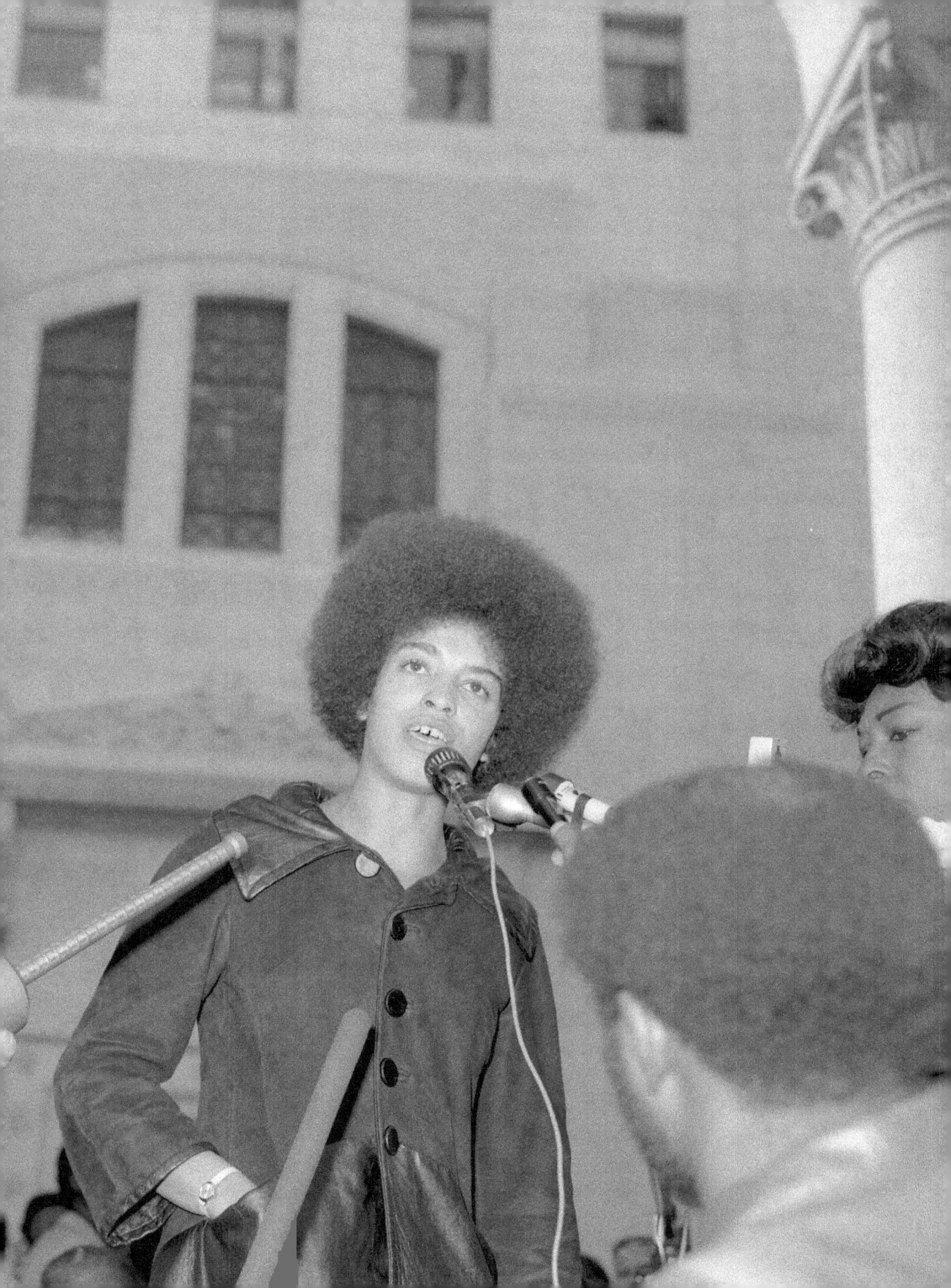

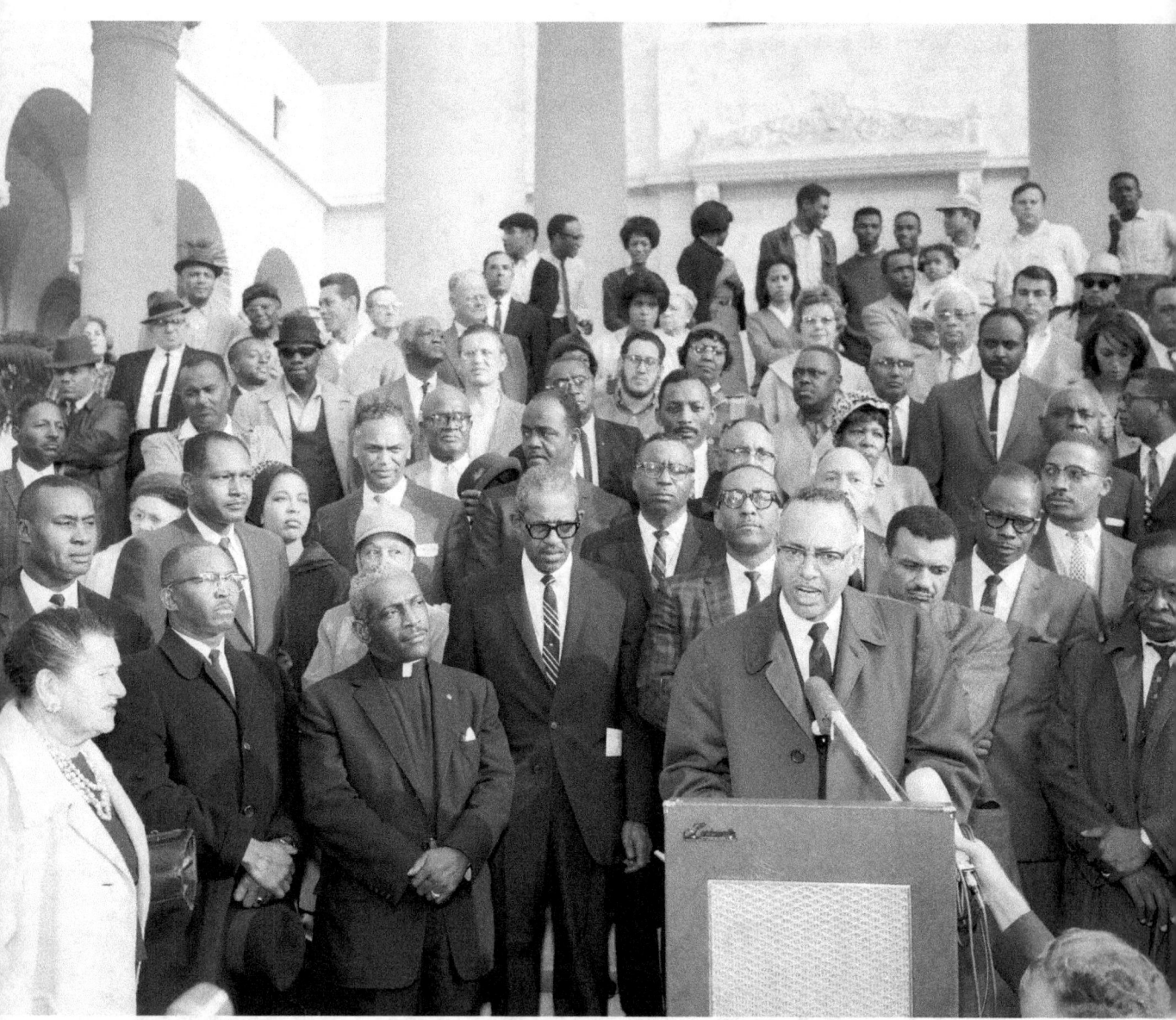

Rev. Thomas Kilgore speaks to crowd in front of City Hall. c1964

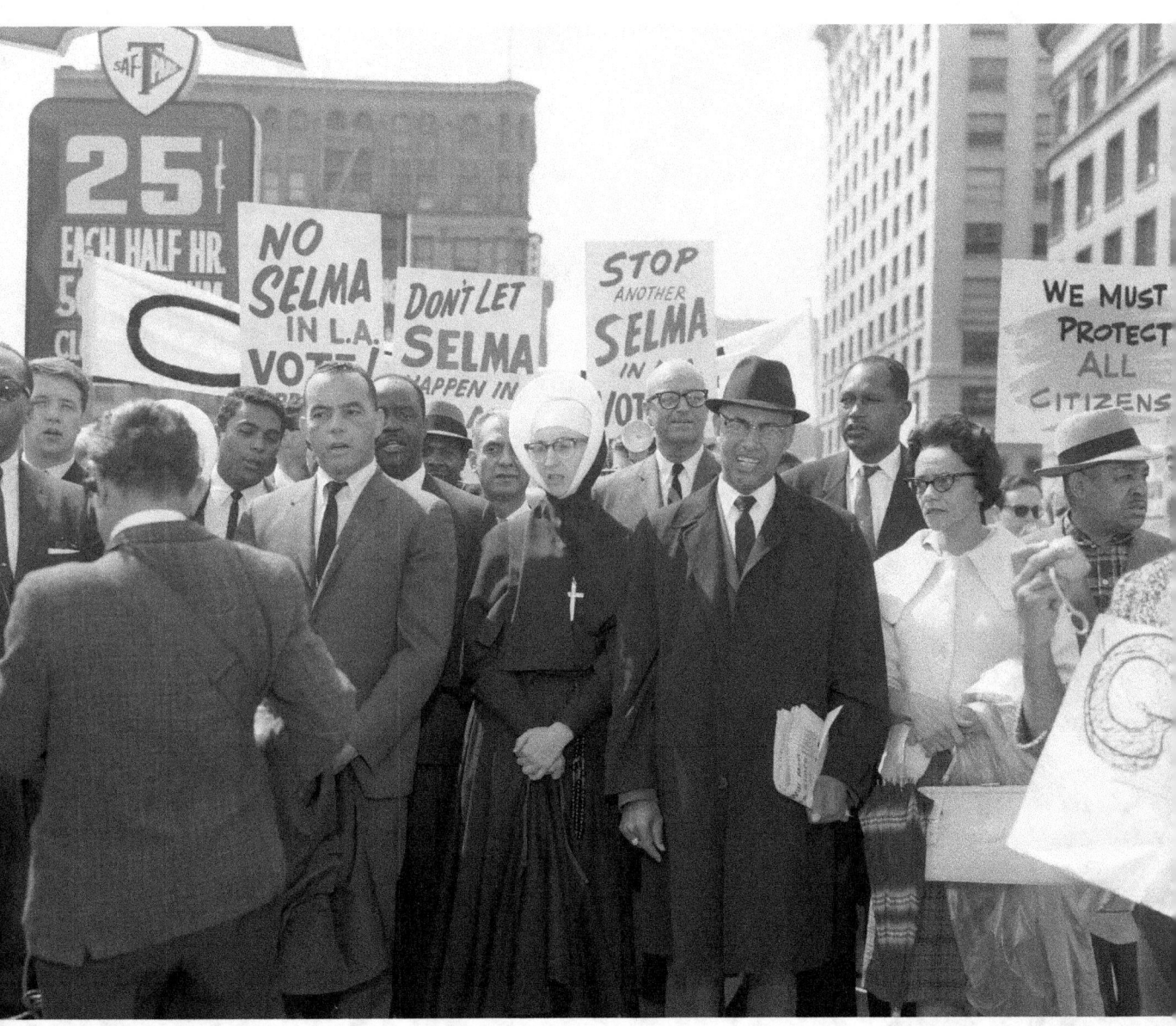

Rev. Thomas Kilgore (*right of center*) walks in protest against Prop. 14 at the Hall of Justice. c1964

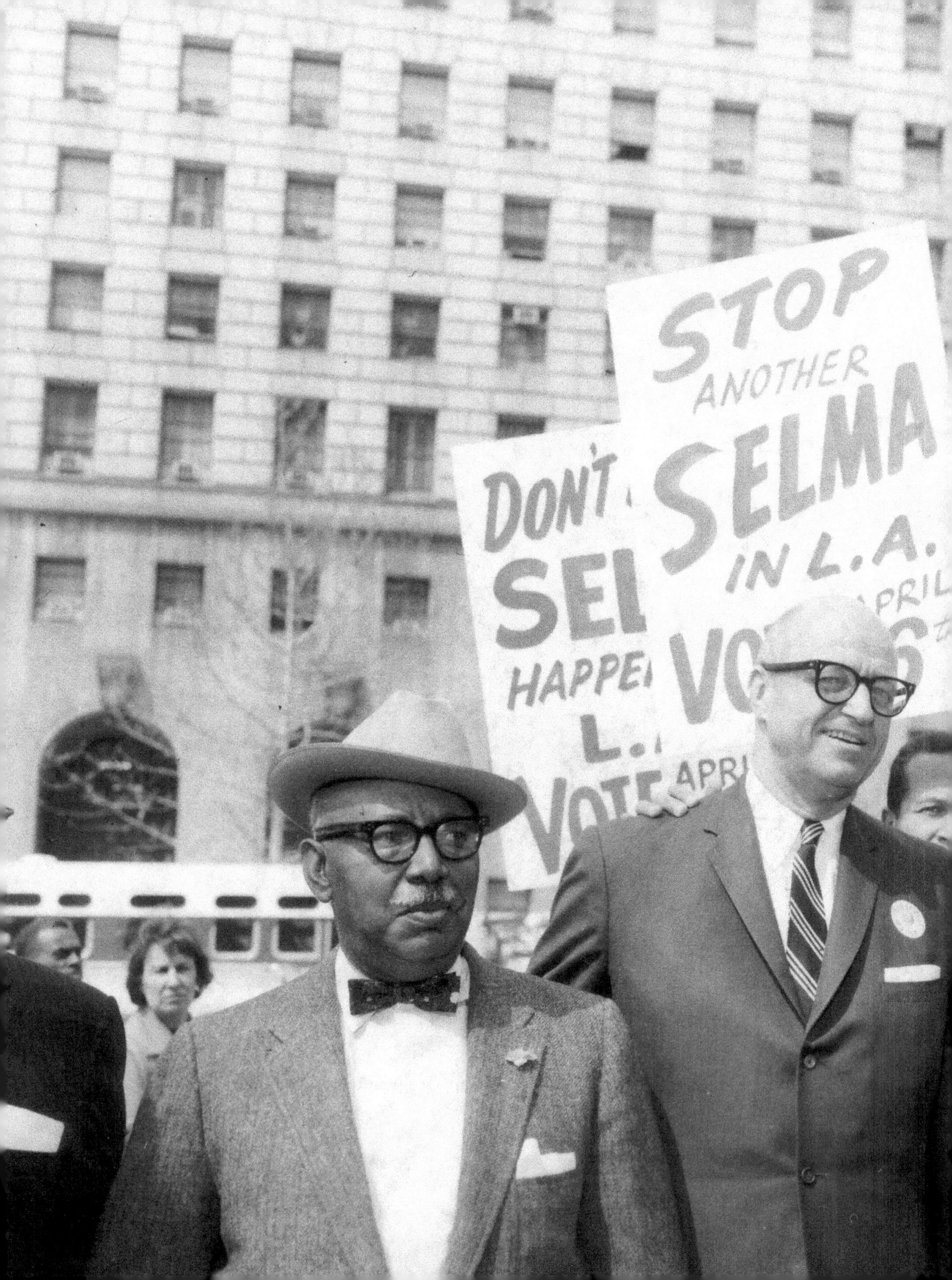
DON'T
STOP
ANOTHER
SELMA
IN L.A.

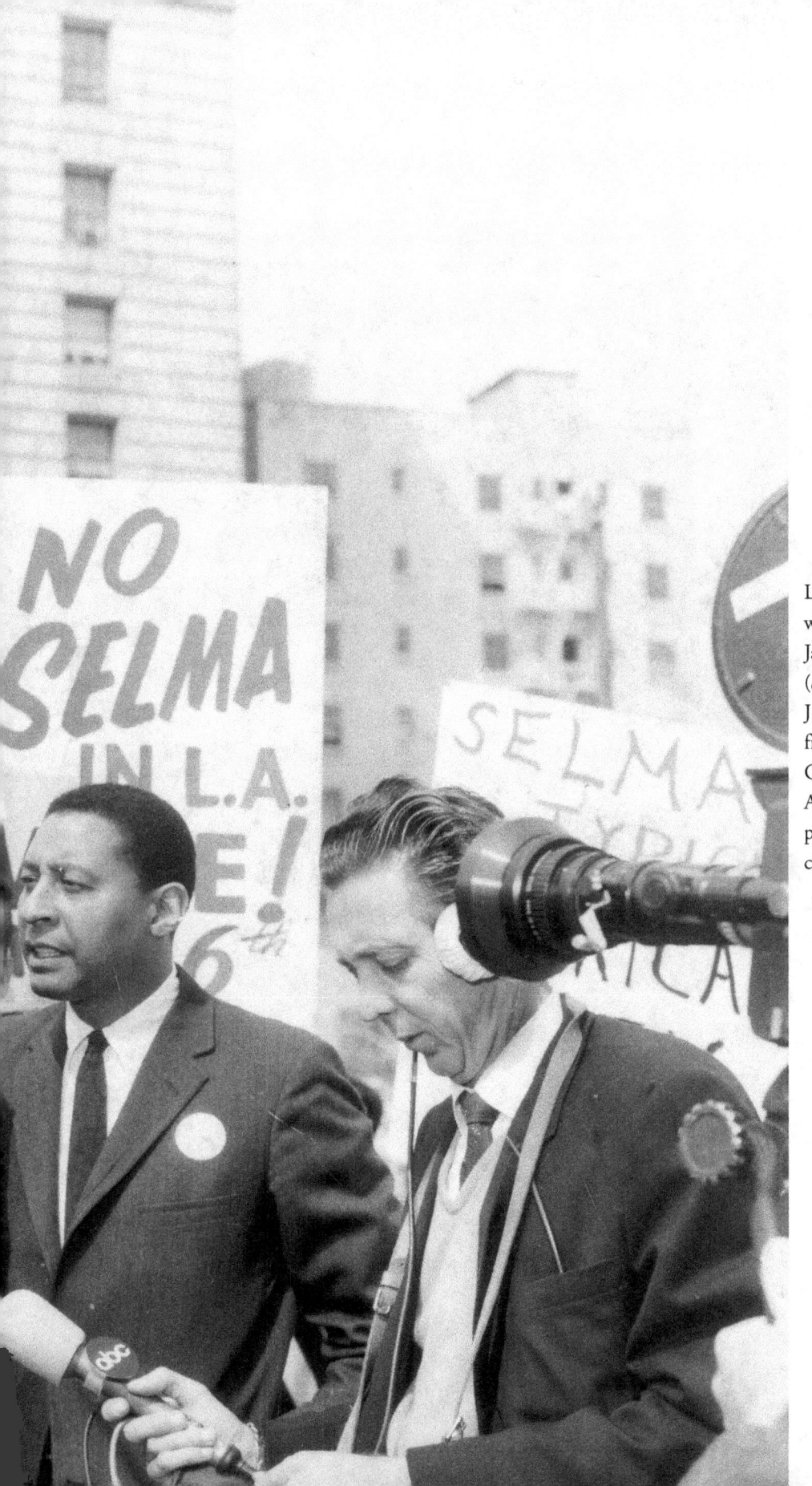

Leon Washington with Congressman James Roosevelt (*center*) and William J. Williams (*right*), field deputy for Congressman Augustus Hawkins, protesting Prop. 14. c1964

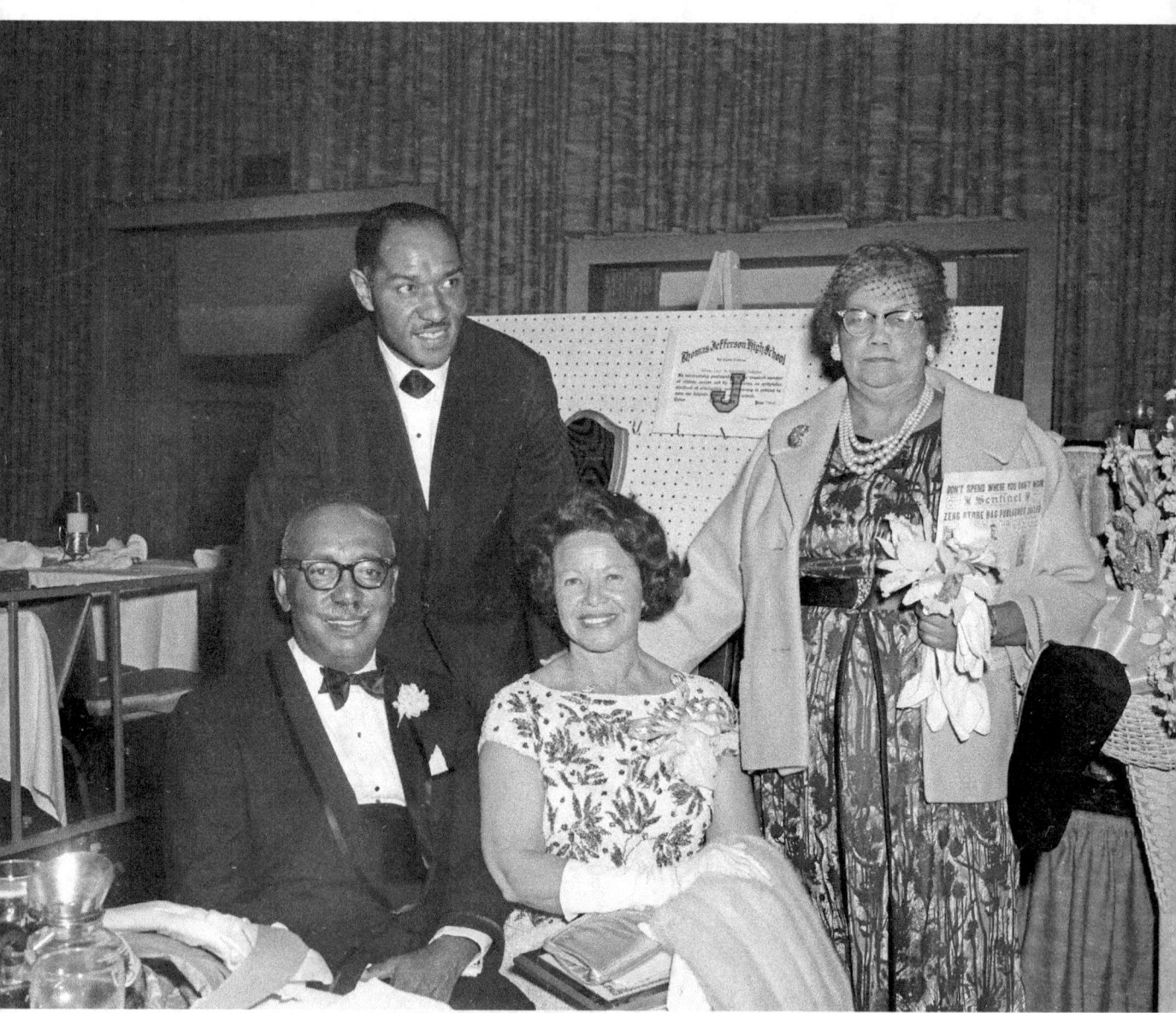

Leon Washington (*seated left*) at salute in his honor by *Los Angeles Sentinel.* His wife Ruth Washington (*seated right*), Leroy Beavers (*standing left*) and Mathilda Curtis (*standing right*), join him. April 23, 1964

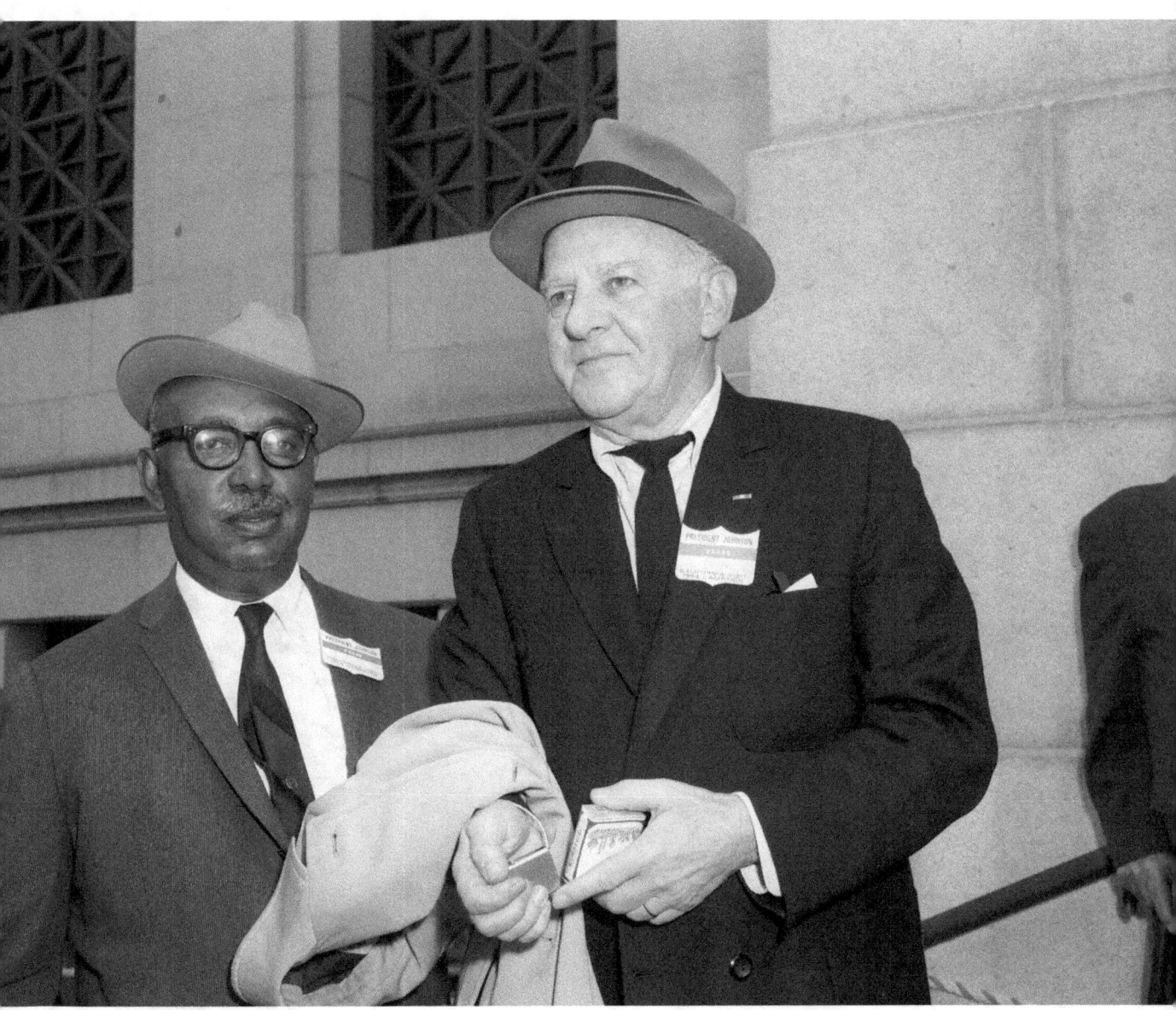

Leon Washington (*left*) at City Hall for visit by President Lyndon B. Johnson. c1964

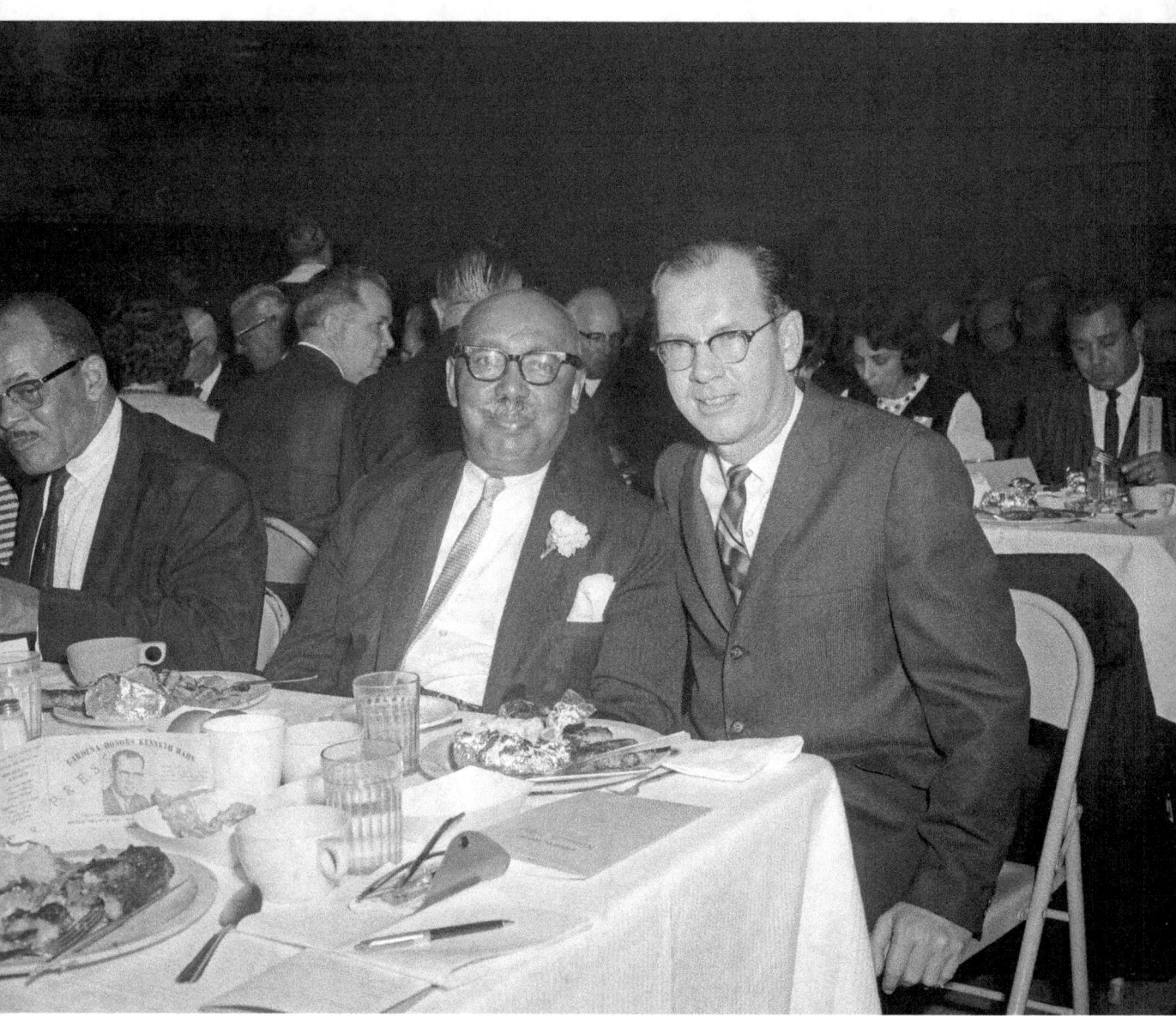

Leon Washington (*left*) with friend Supervisor Kenneth Hahn (*right*) at Hahn's testimonial in Gardena. February 2, 1964

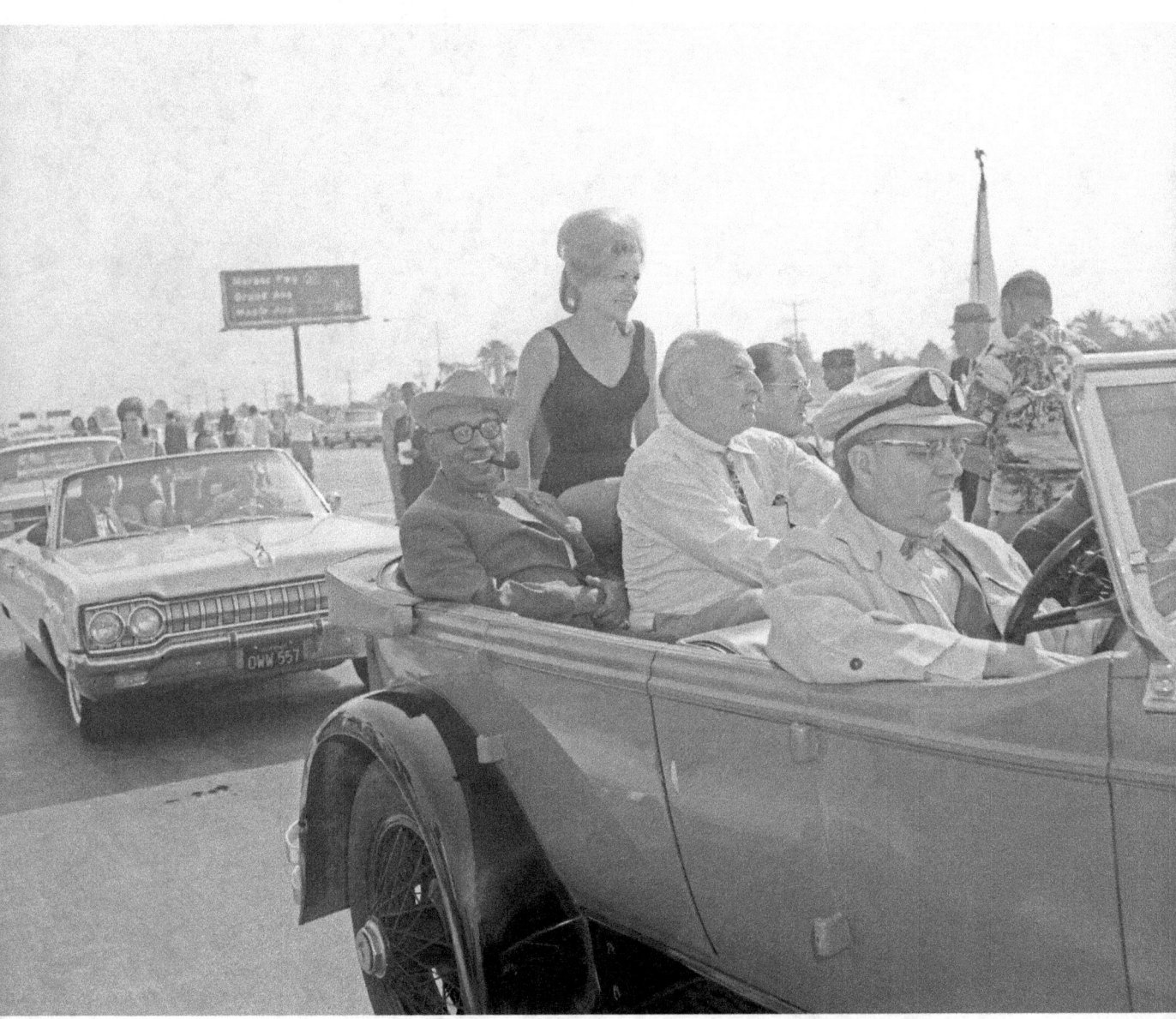

Leon Washington (*seated left*) with Kenneth Hahn at parade. c1964

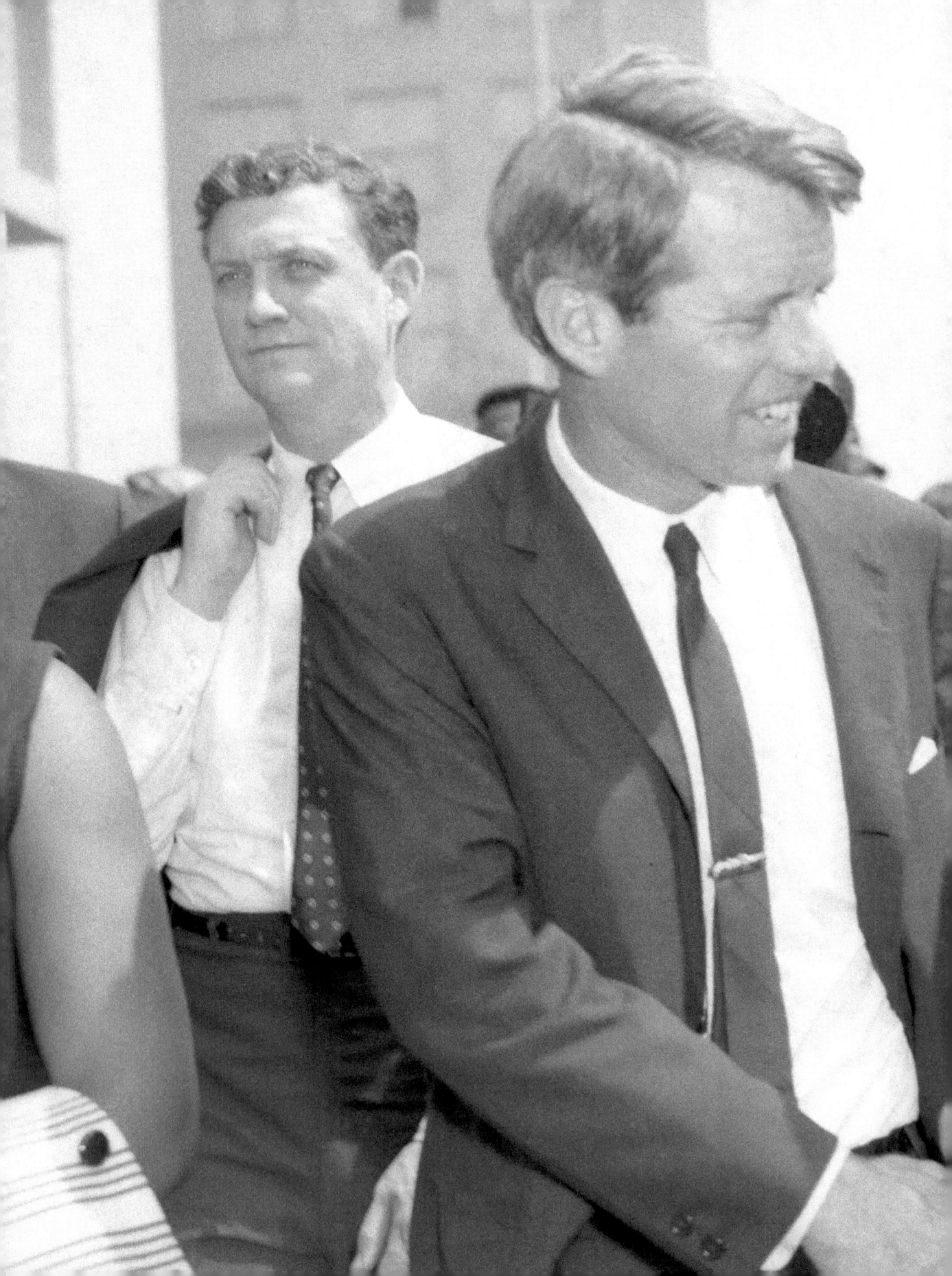

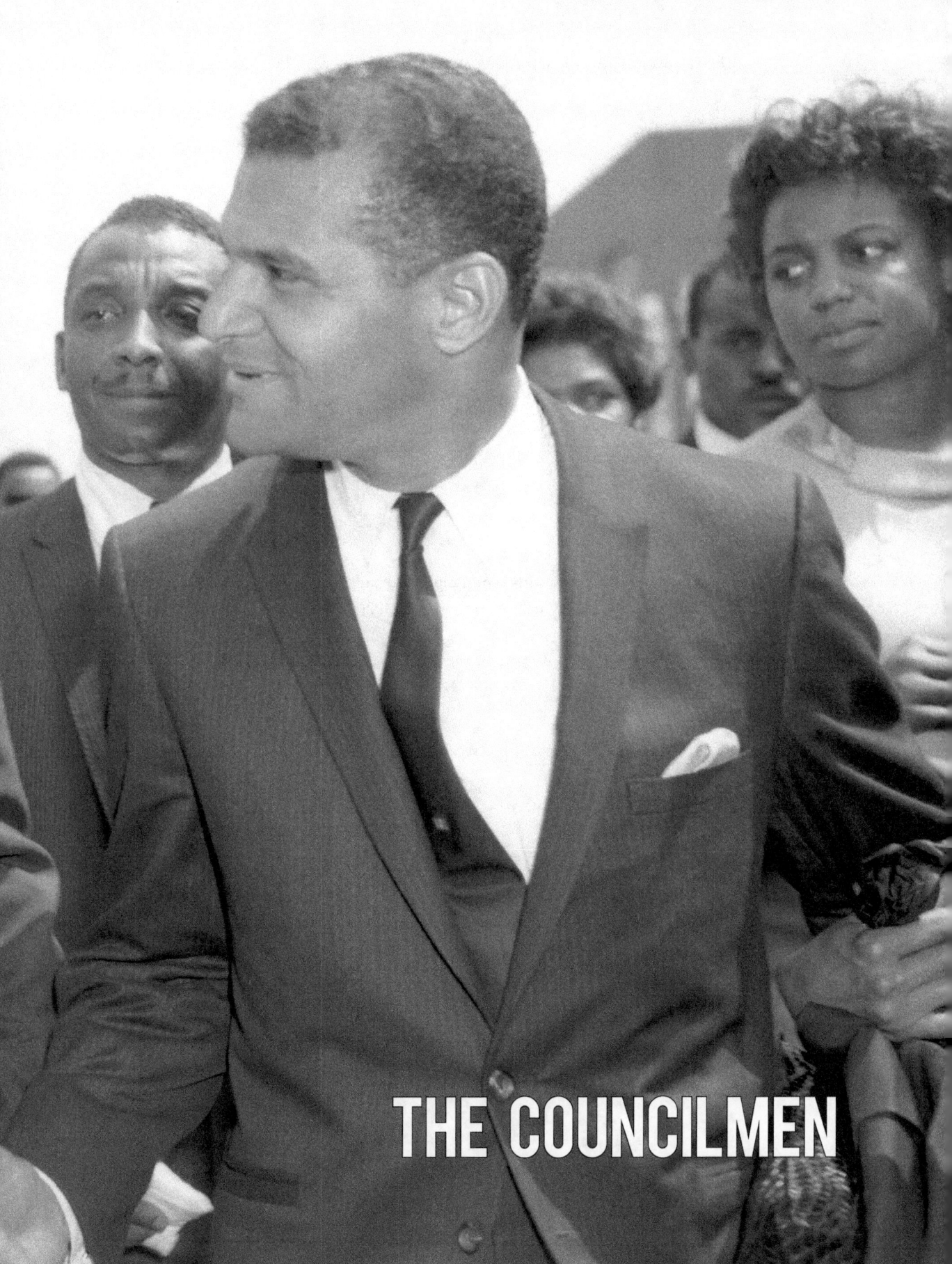

THE COUNCILMEN

*Overleaf*: Robert Kennedy (*standing*) with Leon Ralph (*left*) and Billy G. Mills (*sitting*) on the way to campaign at the Watts Writers Workshop. March 26, 1968

*Opposite*: Billy G. Mills (*right*) with Attorney General Robert Kennedy (*left*). c1968

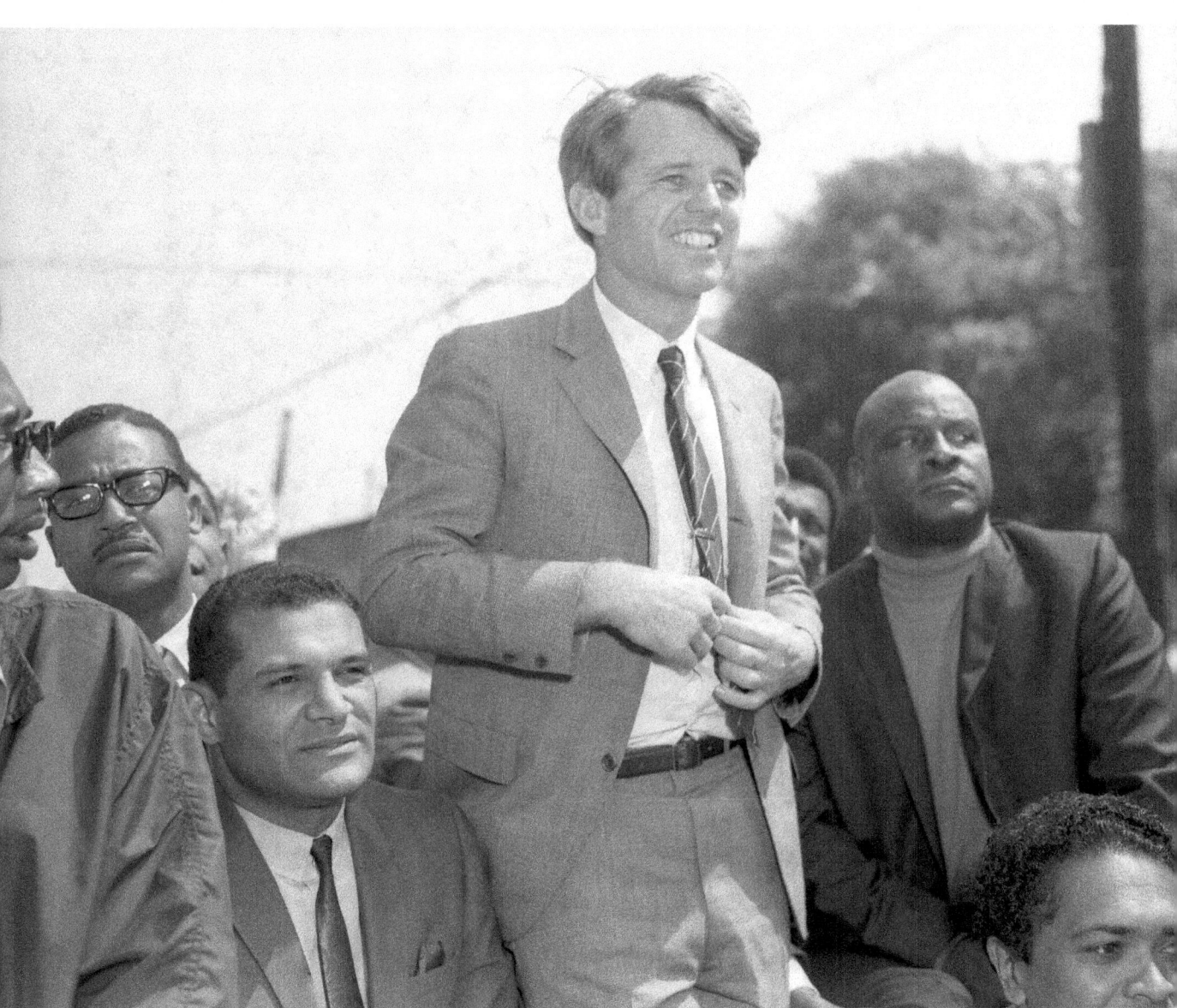

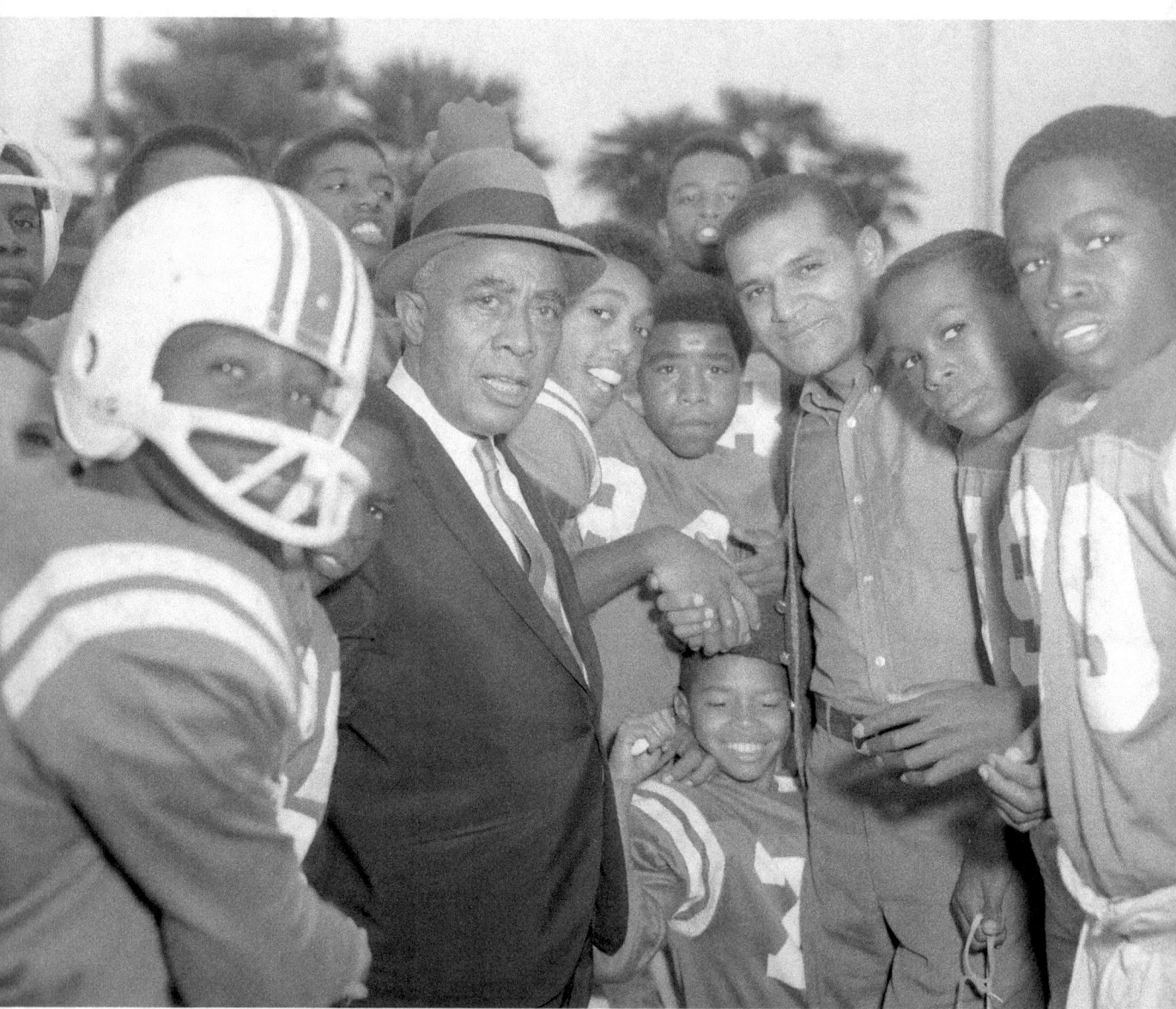

Gilbert Lindsay (*left*) with Billy G. Mills (*right*) and boys at Wrigley Field. Gilbert Lindsay was born on a cotton plantation in Mississippi, where he later picked cotton for 50 cents a day. In 1928, he moved to Los Angeles and became a janitor for the DWP. By 1963, at the age of 62, Lindsay became the first African American to join the city council. Appointed to fill a vacancy, he was reelected consistently until his death in 1990. c1964

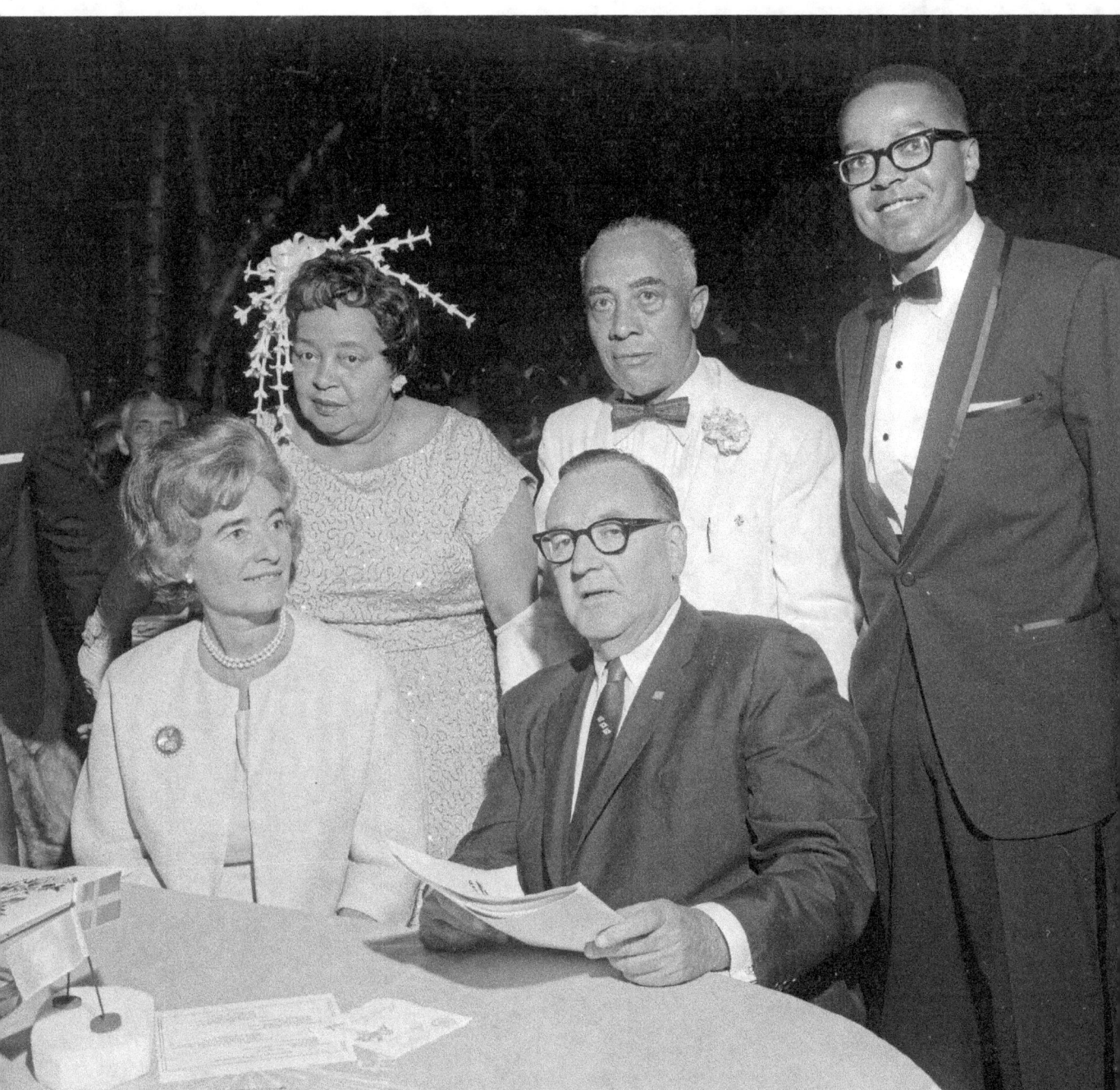

The Cinderella Internationale Beauty Pageant at the Cocoanut Grove. Councilman Billy G. Mills (*far left*), Theresa Lindsay, (*left*), Councilman Gilbert Lindsay (*right*), Sherrill Luke (*far right*), Bernice Brown, (*bottom left*), and Governor Pat Brown (*bottom right*). October 1, 1964

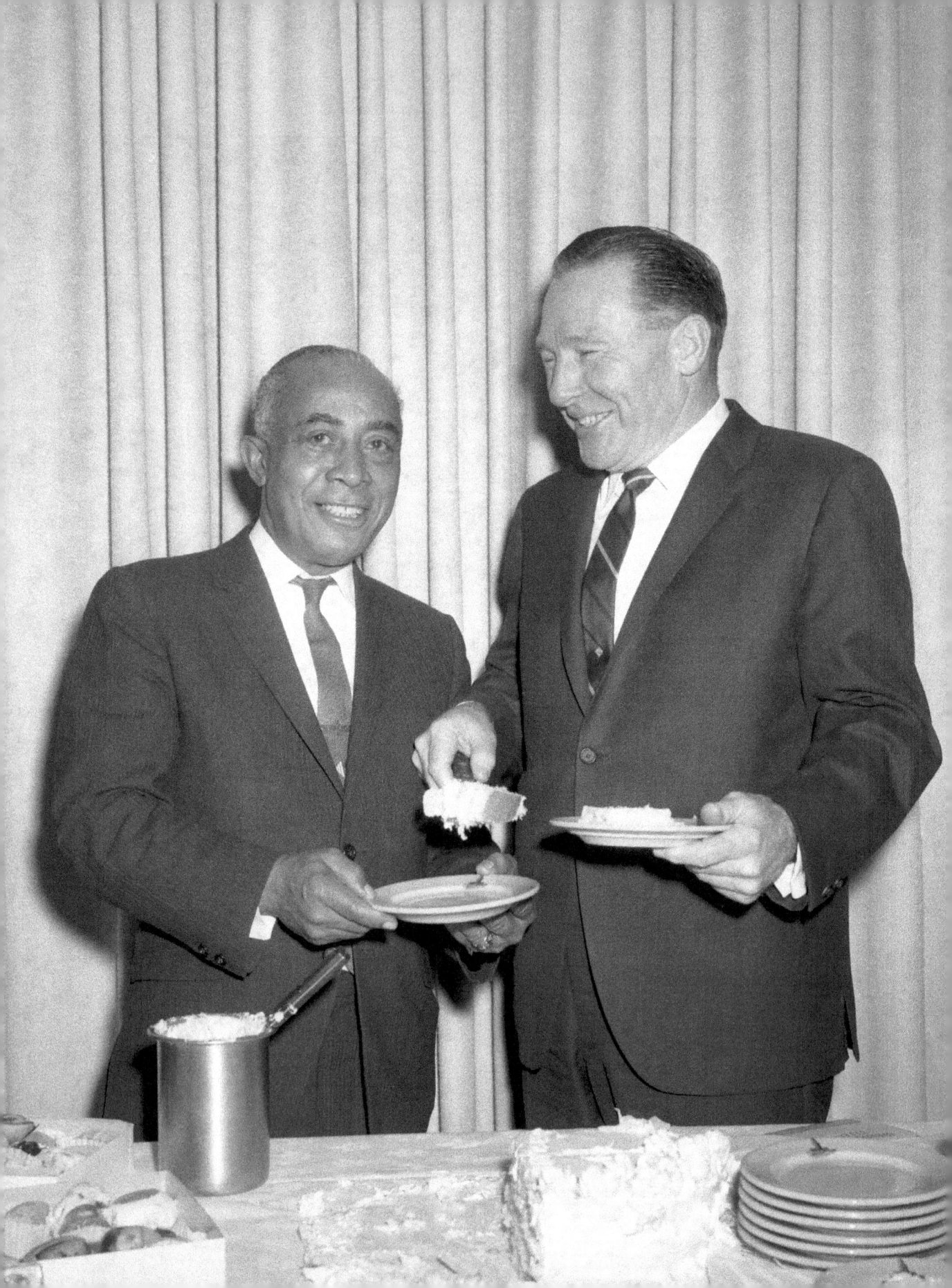

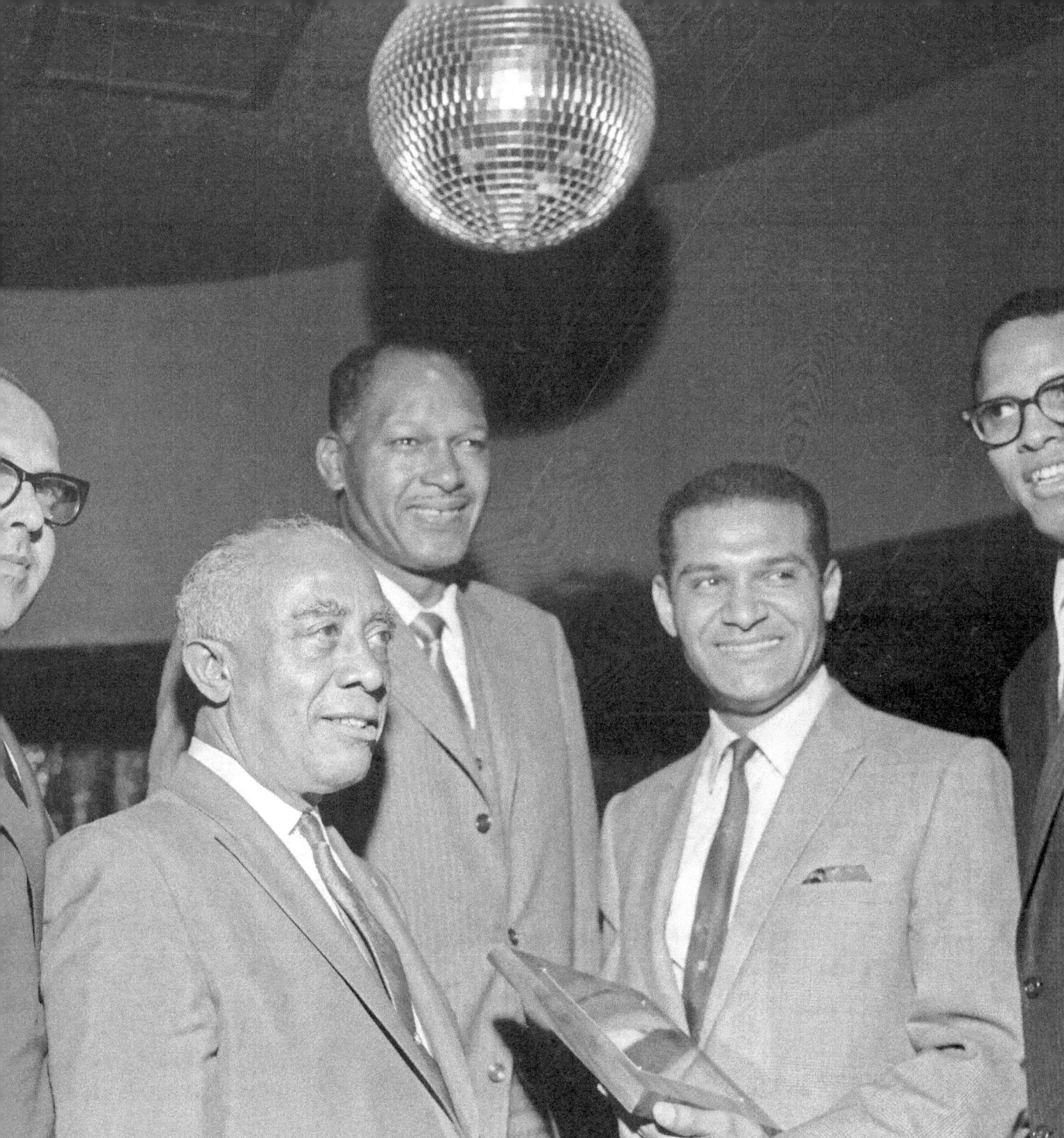

Gilbert Lindsay (*left*) with Tom Bradley (*center*) at Bill of Fare honoring Billy G. Mills (*right*). c1968

*Opposite*: Councilman Gilbert Lindsay (*left*) enjoys cake with Mayor Sam Yorty (*right*). c1964

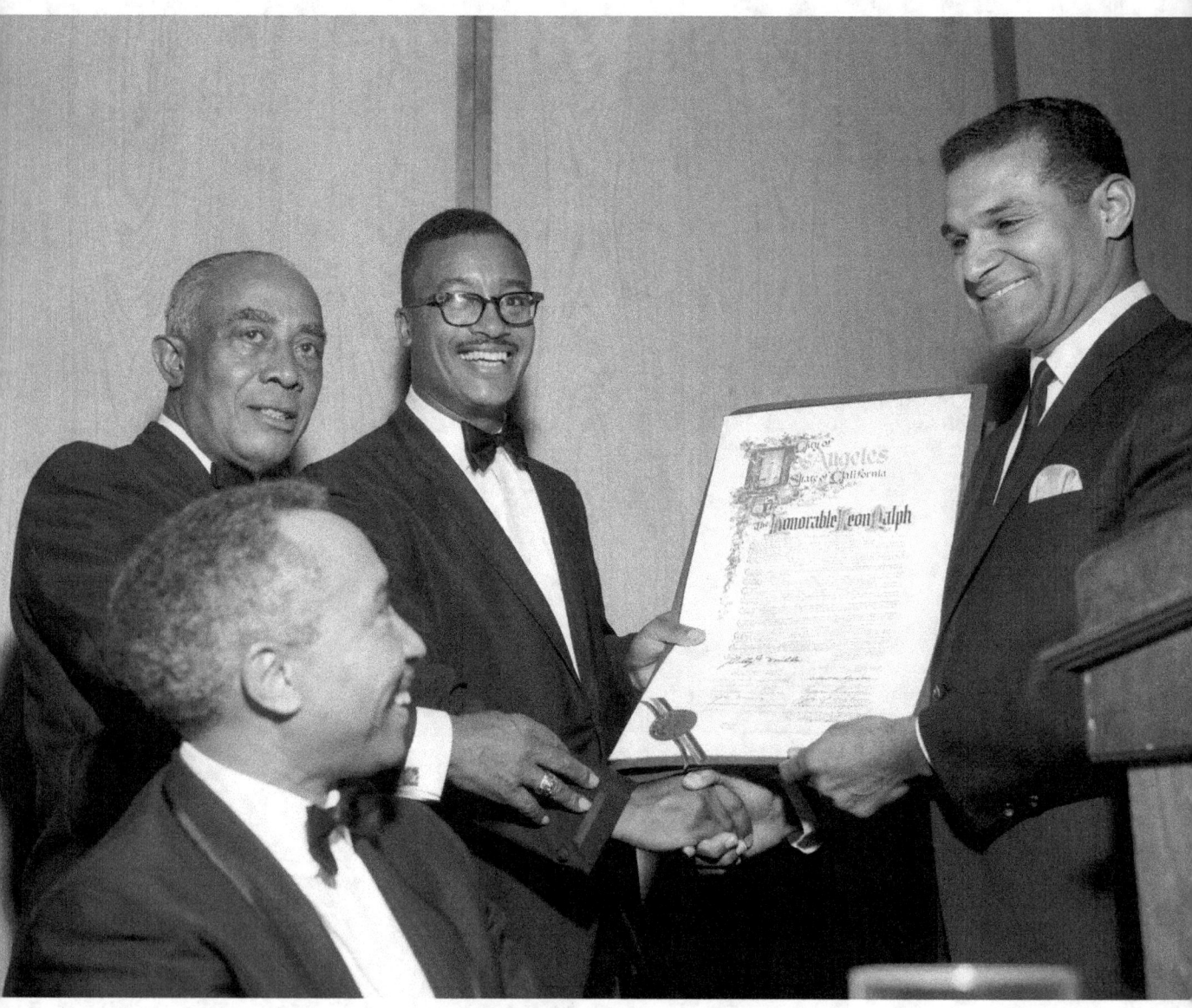

Gilbert Lindsay (*left*) at dinner in honor of Assemblyman Leon Ralph (*center*). Billy G. Mills (*right*) presents Ralph with a resolution. November 19, 1967

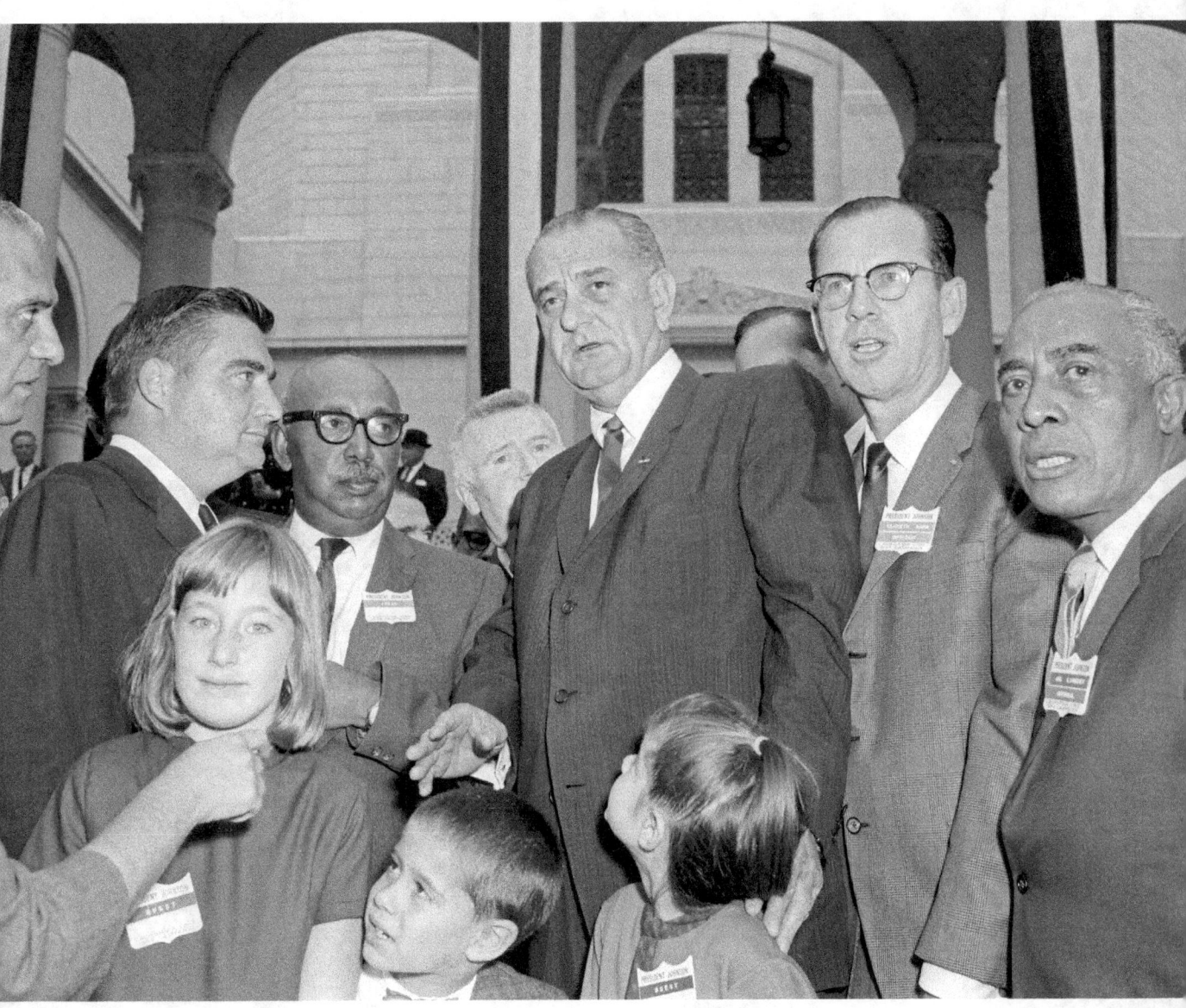

Gilbert Lindsay (*far right*) with Kenneth Hahn (*right*), President Lyndon B. Johnson
(*center*), Leon Washington (*left*), Pierre Salinger (*far left*) and Edward Roybal (*farther left*),
during the president's visit to City Hall. c1964

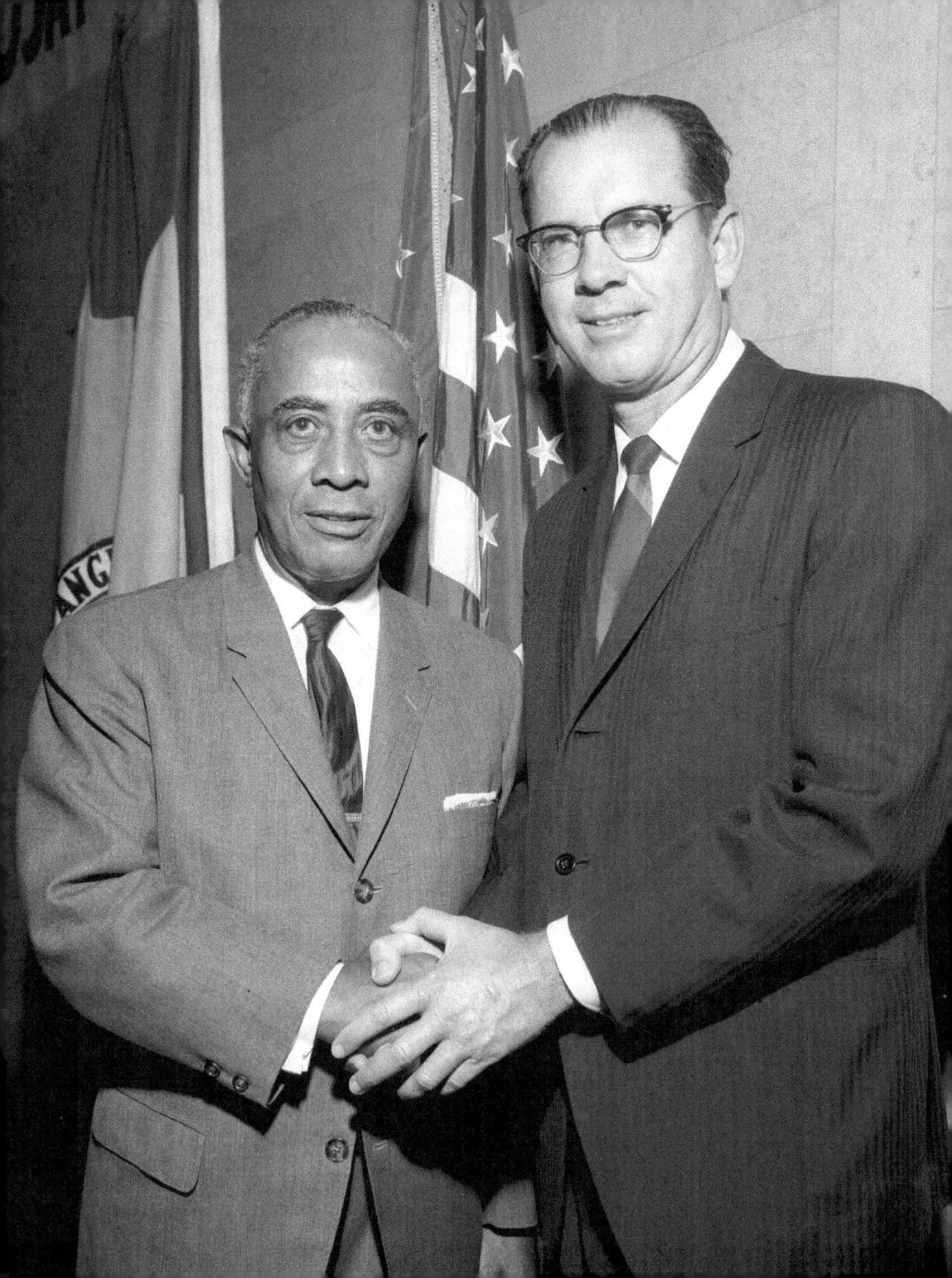

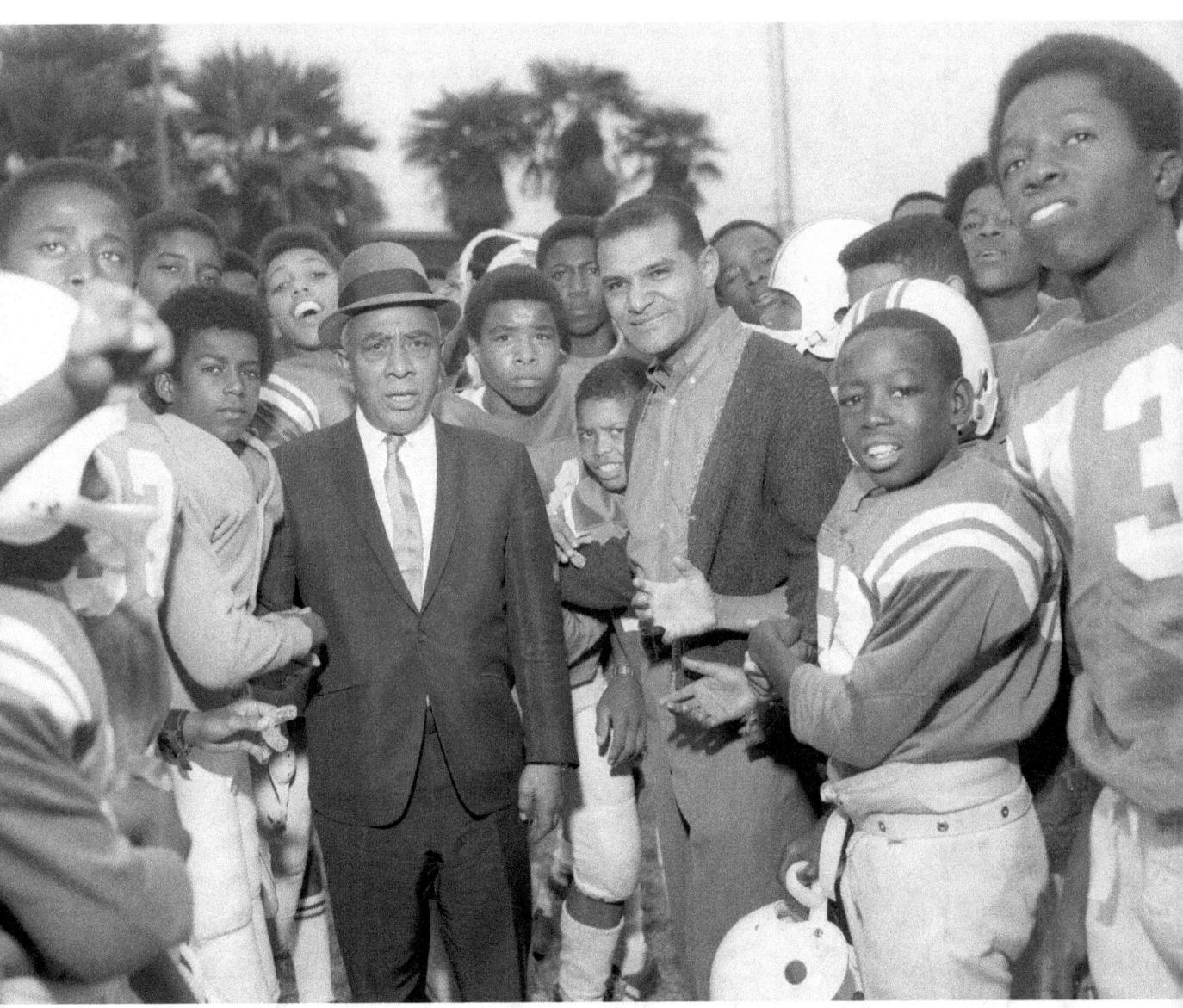

Gilbert Lindsay (*left*) and Billy G. Mills (*right*) visit youngsters at Wrigley Field. c1964
*Opposite*: Gilbert Lindsay (*left*) shakes hands with Kenneth Hahn (*right*) at his campaign
victory celebration. c1964

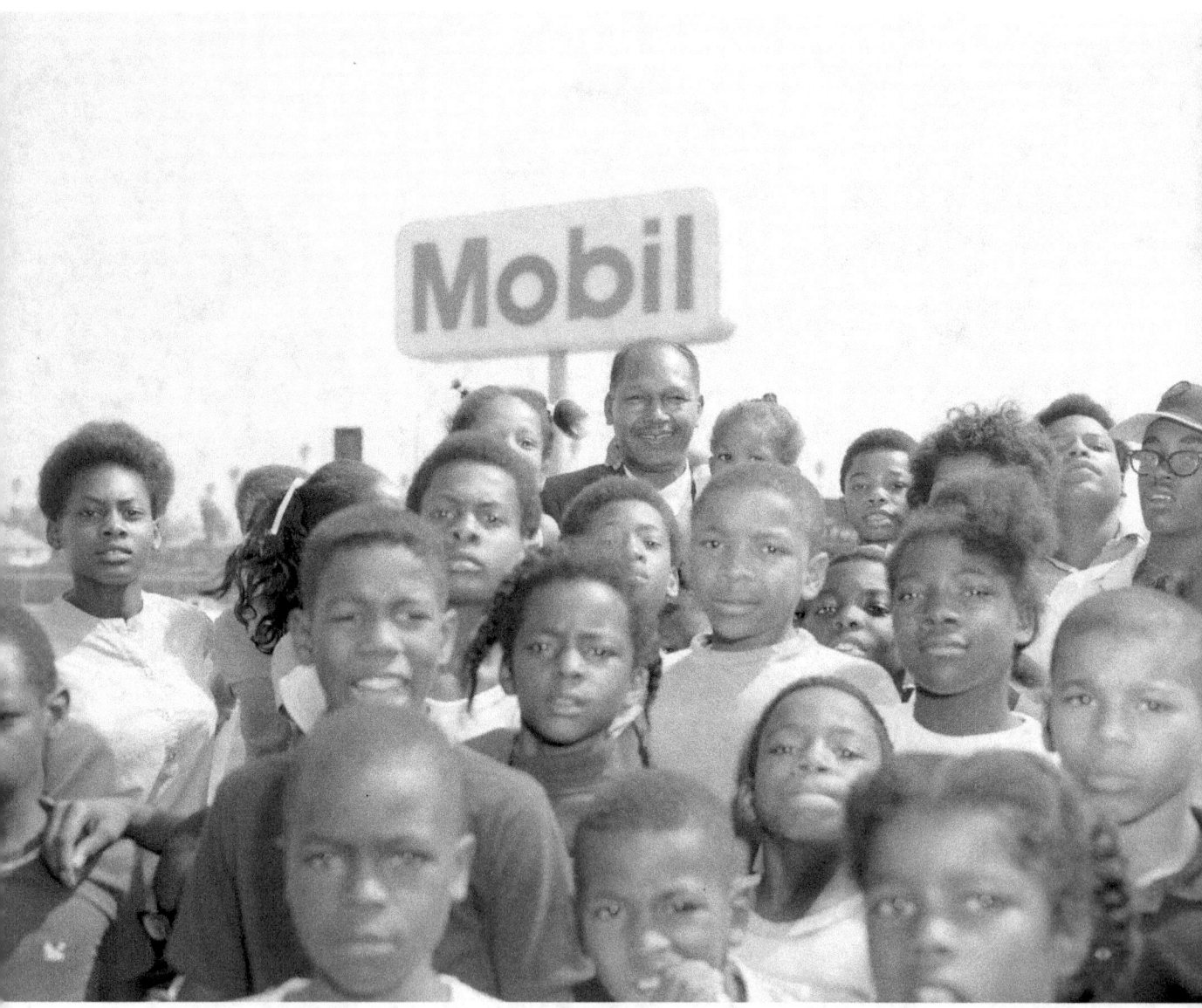

Tom Bradley campaigns with children at Mobil gas station. In 1940, Bradley was one of 400 African Americans in a racially-segregated LAPD. Bradley was the second African American to join the Los Angeles city council, representing the 10th District in 1963. He was also the first and only African American to become mayor of Los Angeles, and the second African American mayor of a major city in 1973. His twenty years in office marked the longest mayoral term in the city's history. c1969

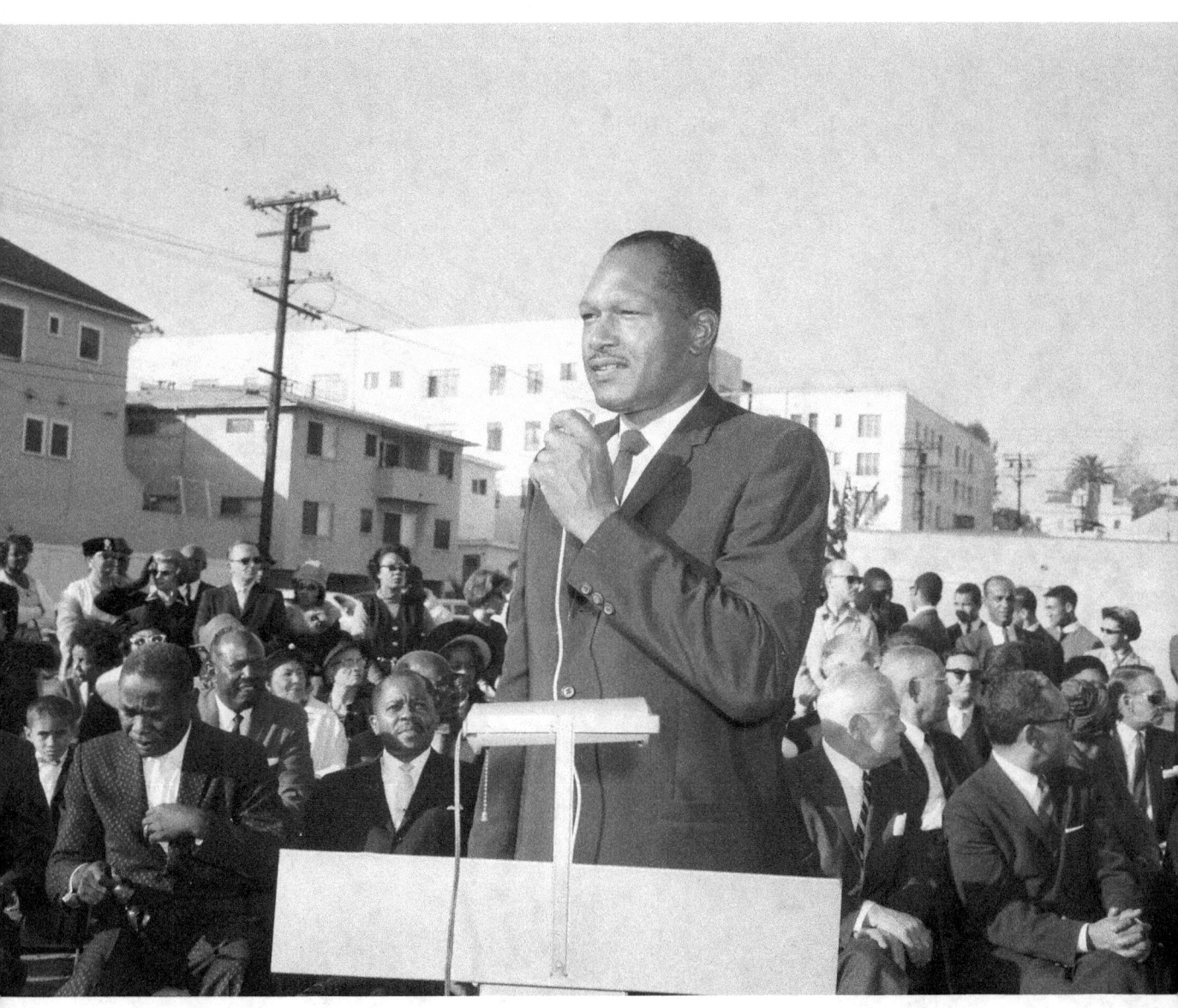

Tom Bradley speaks at the groundbreaking ceremony for the Bank of Finance. c1964

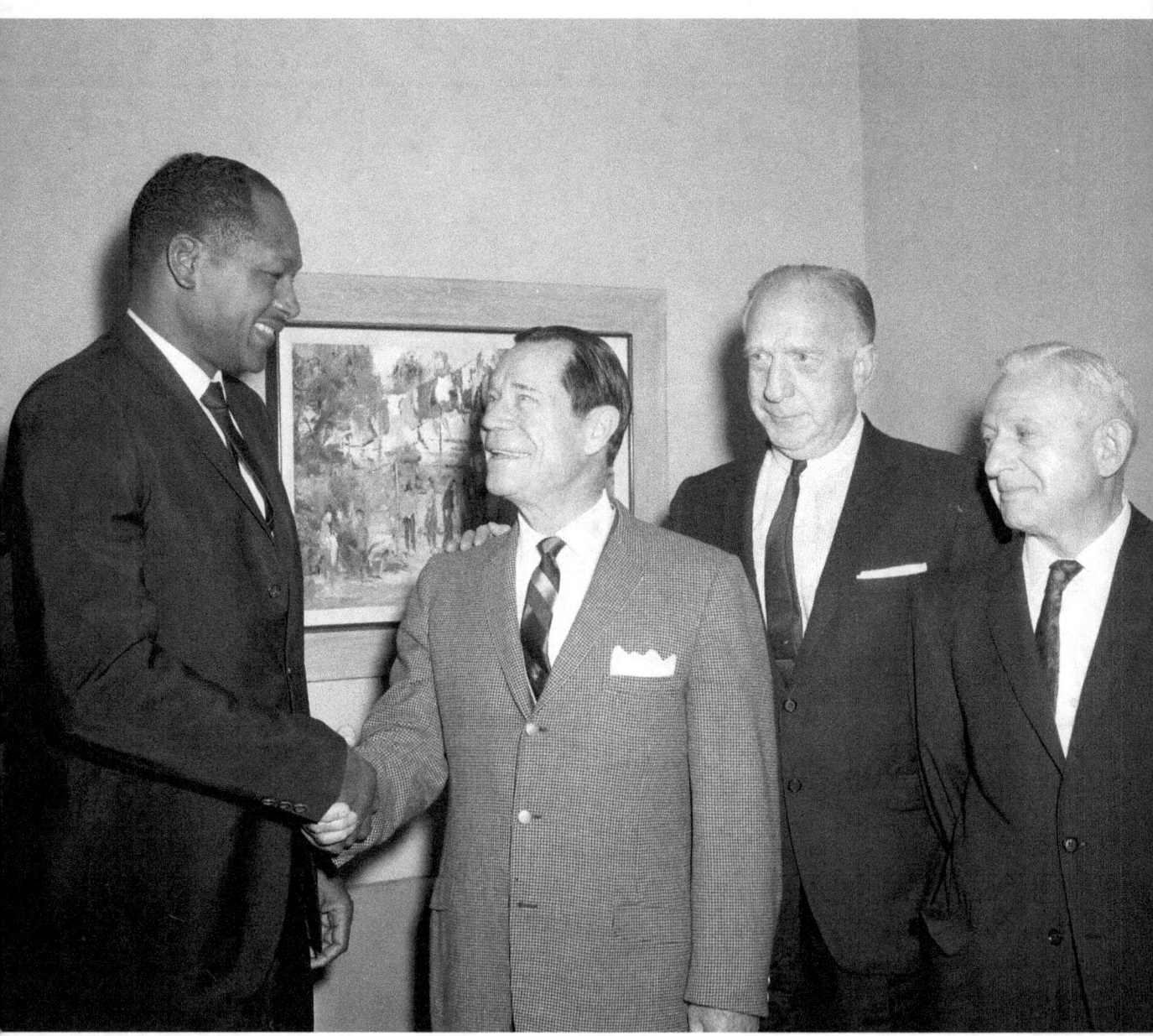

Tom Bradley meets actor Joe E. Brown at his office. c1964

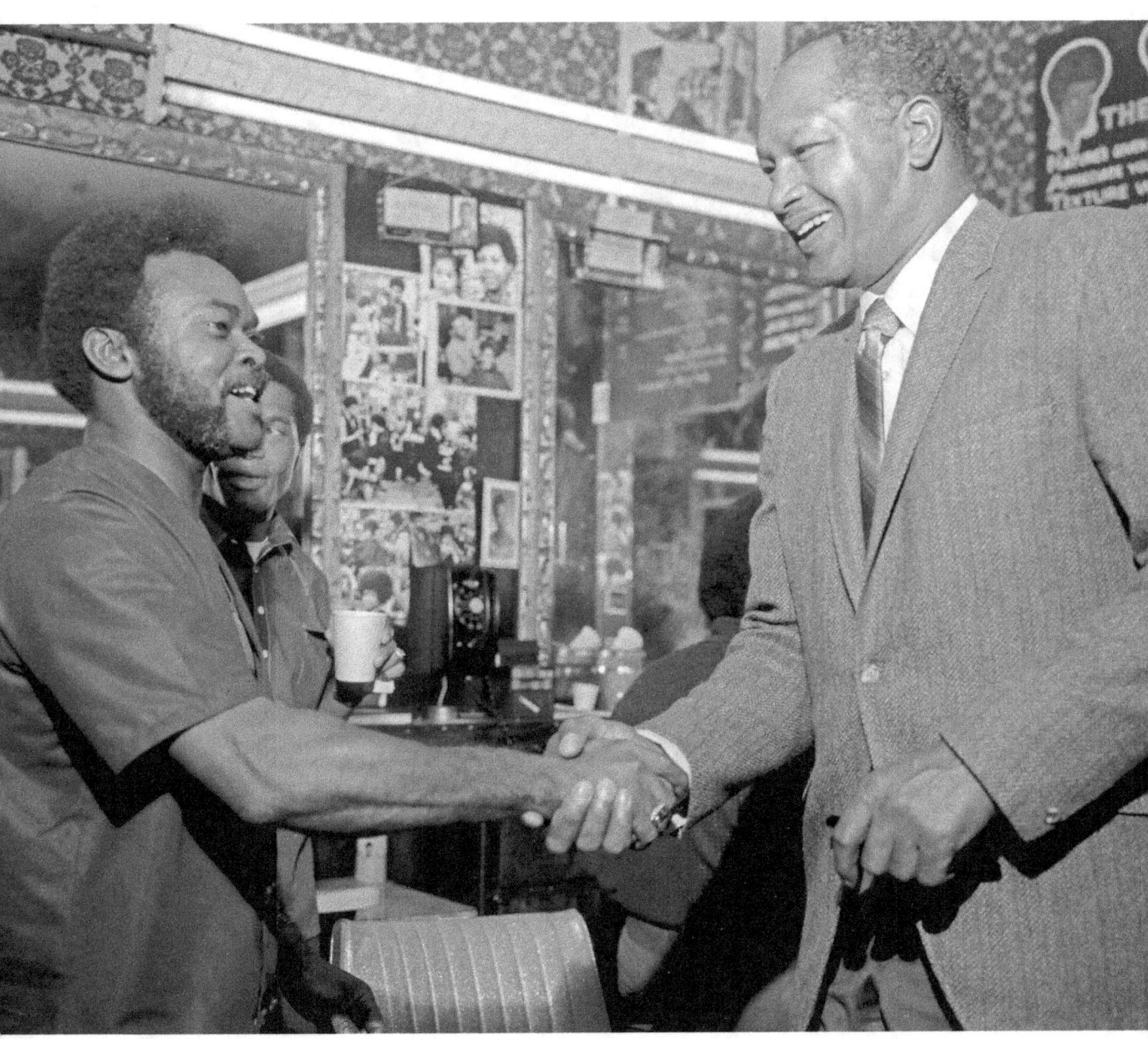

Tom Bradley (*right*) campaigns at the Magnificent Brothers Hair Salon 2. c1970

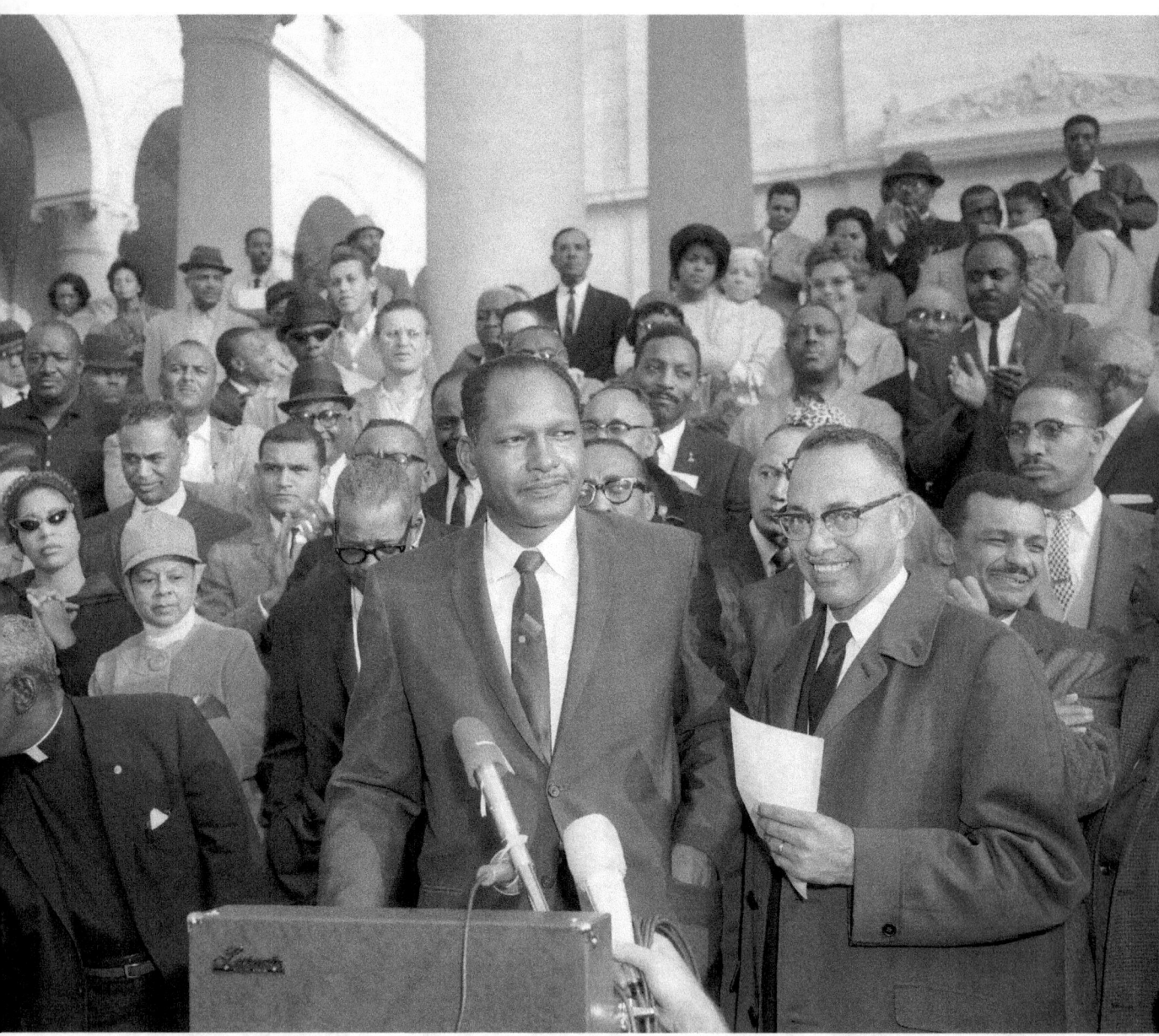

Tom Bradley speaks to crowd at the steps of City Hall. He is joined by Rev. Thomas Kilgore (*right*). c1964

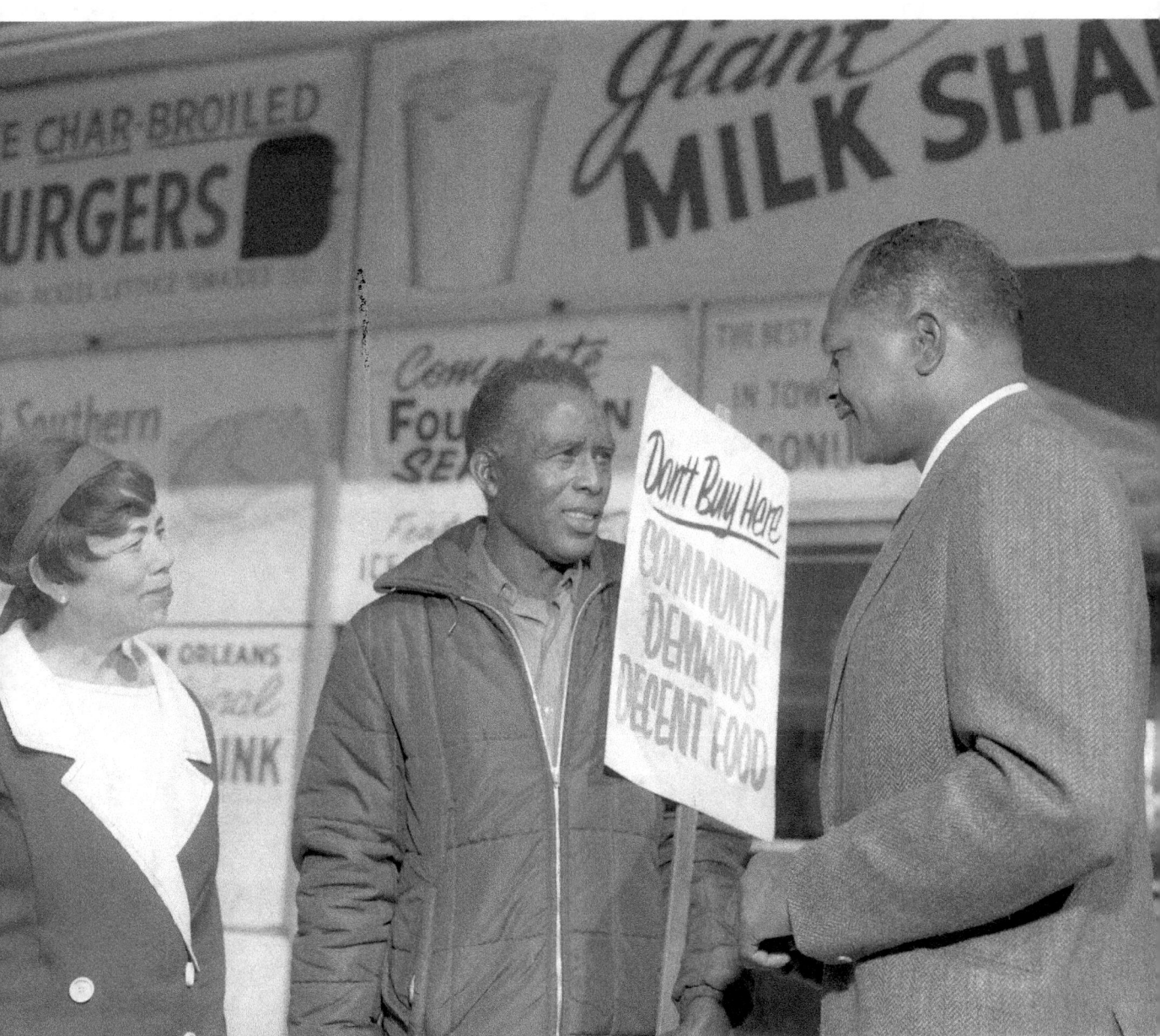

Tom Bradley (*right*) speaks to protestors during the Donre Market boycott. c1970

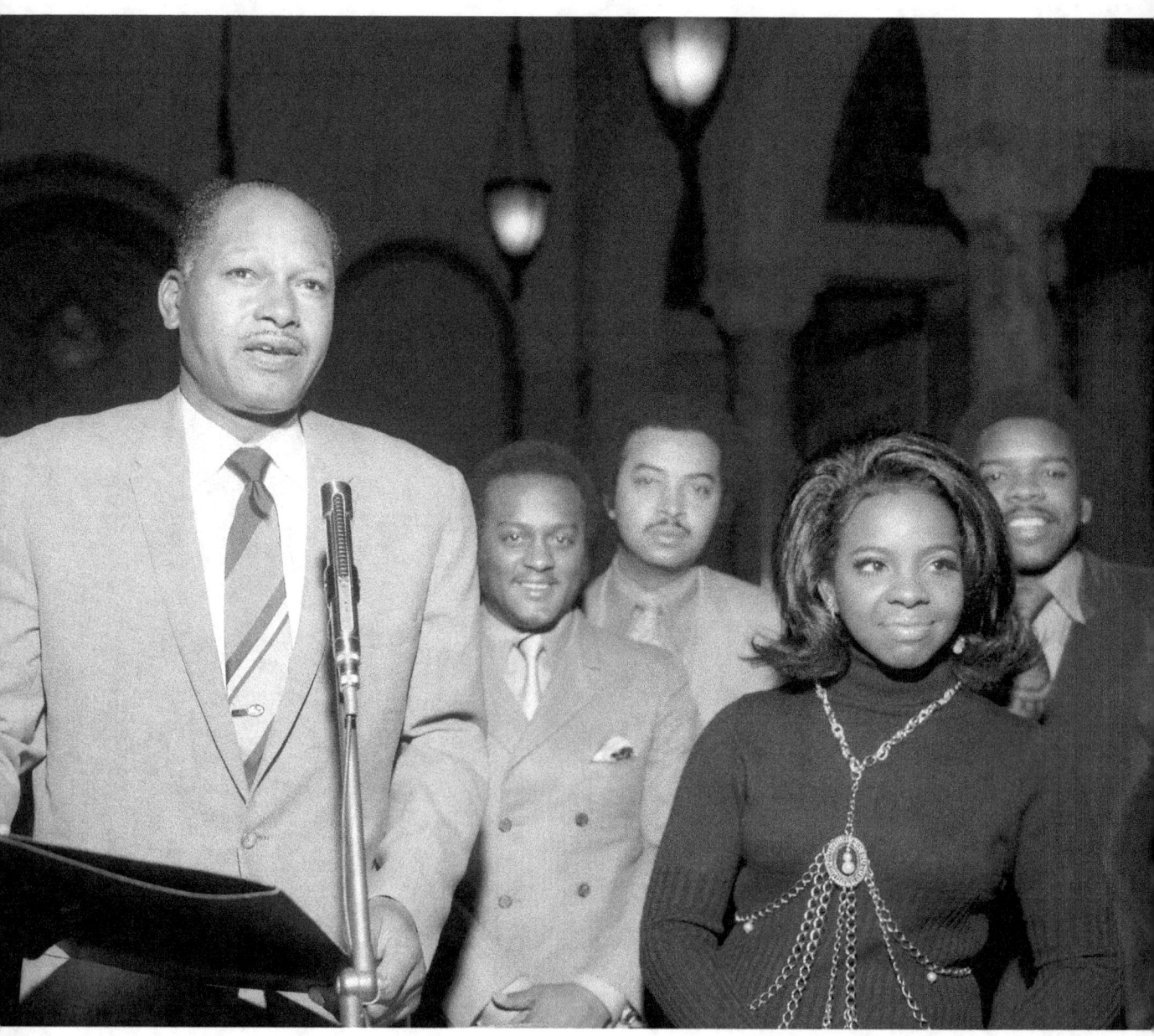

Tom Bradley (*left*) presents a resolution to Gladys Knight and the Pips. February 13, 1970

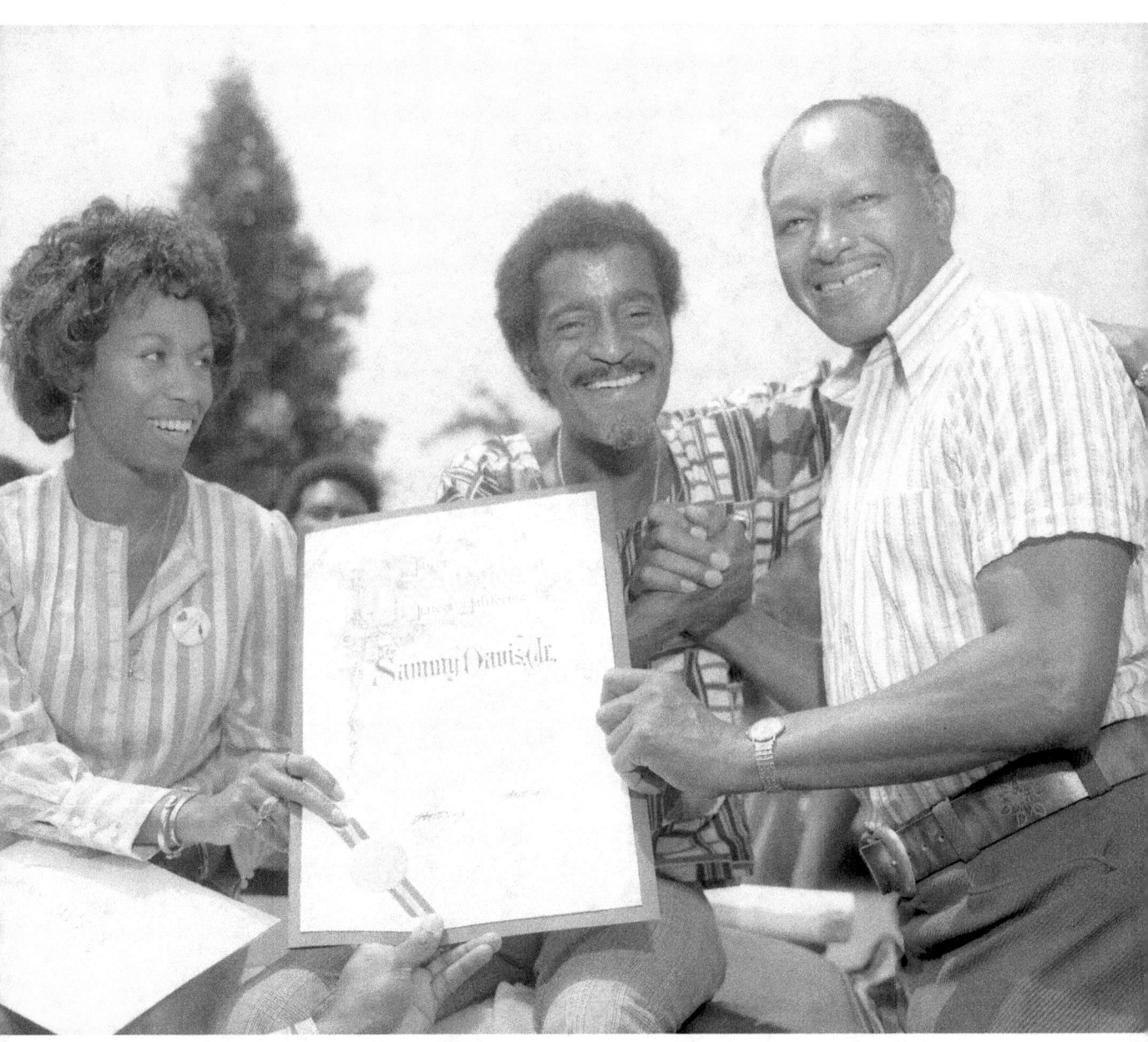

Tom Bradley (*right*) presents a resolution to actor and singer Sammy Davis Jr. (*center*), with his wife Altovise Davis (*left*), at the Watts Summer Festival Parade. August 22, 1971

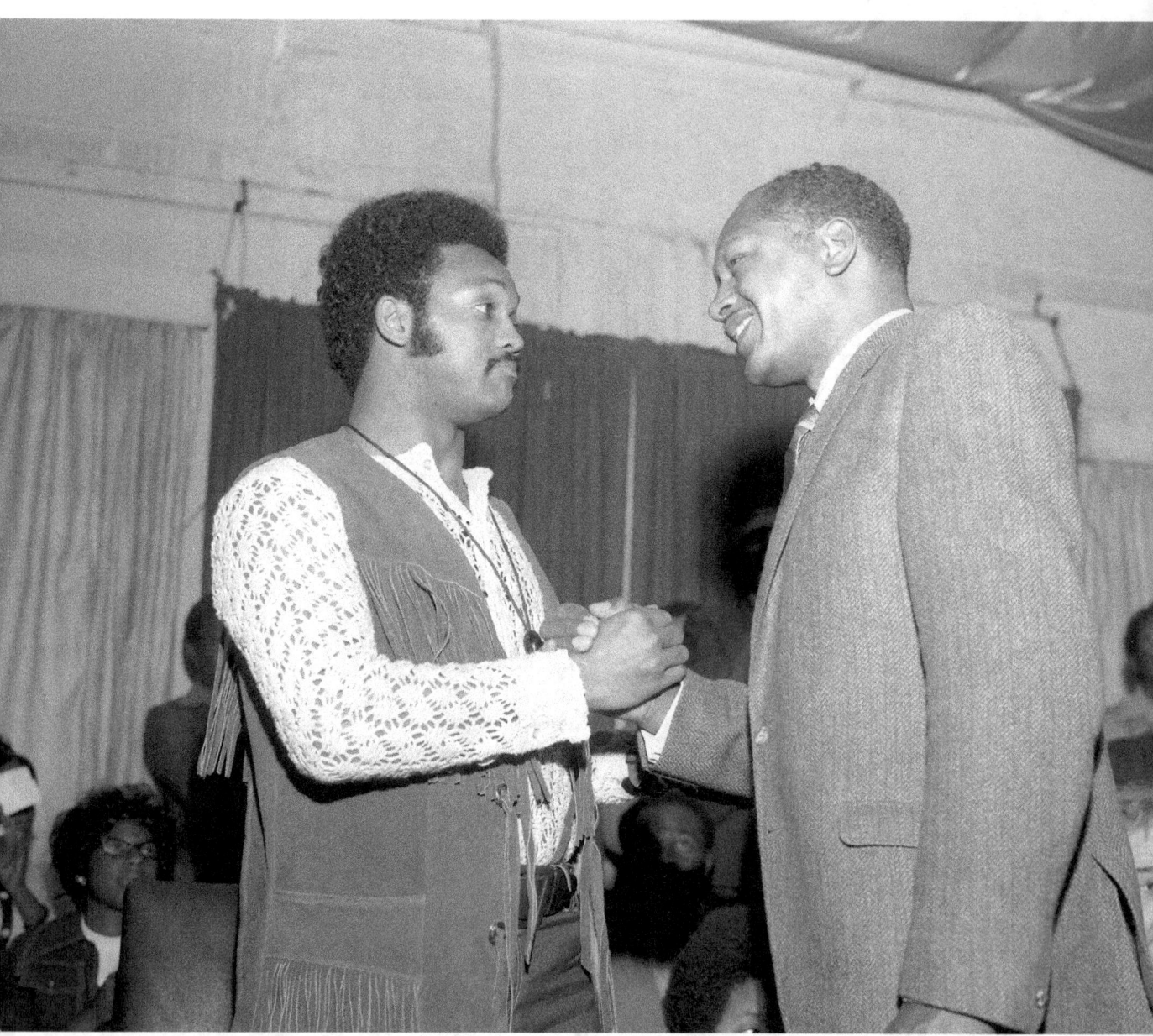

Reverend Jesse Jackson (*right*) with Tom Bradley (*left*) at the First AME Church.
May 7, 1970

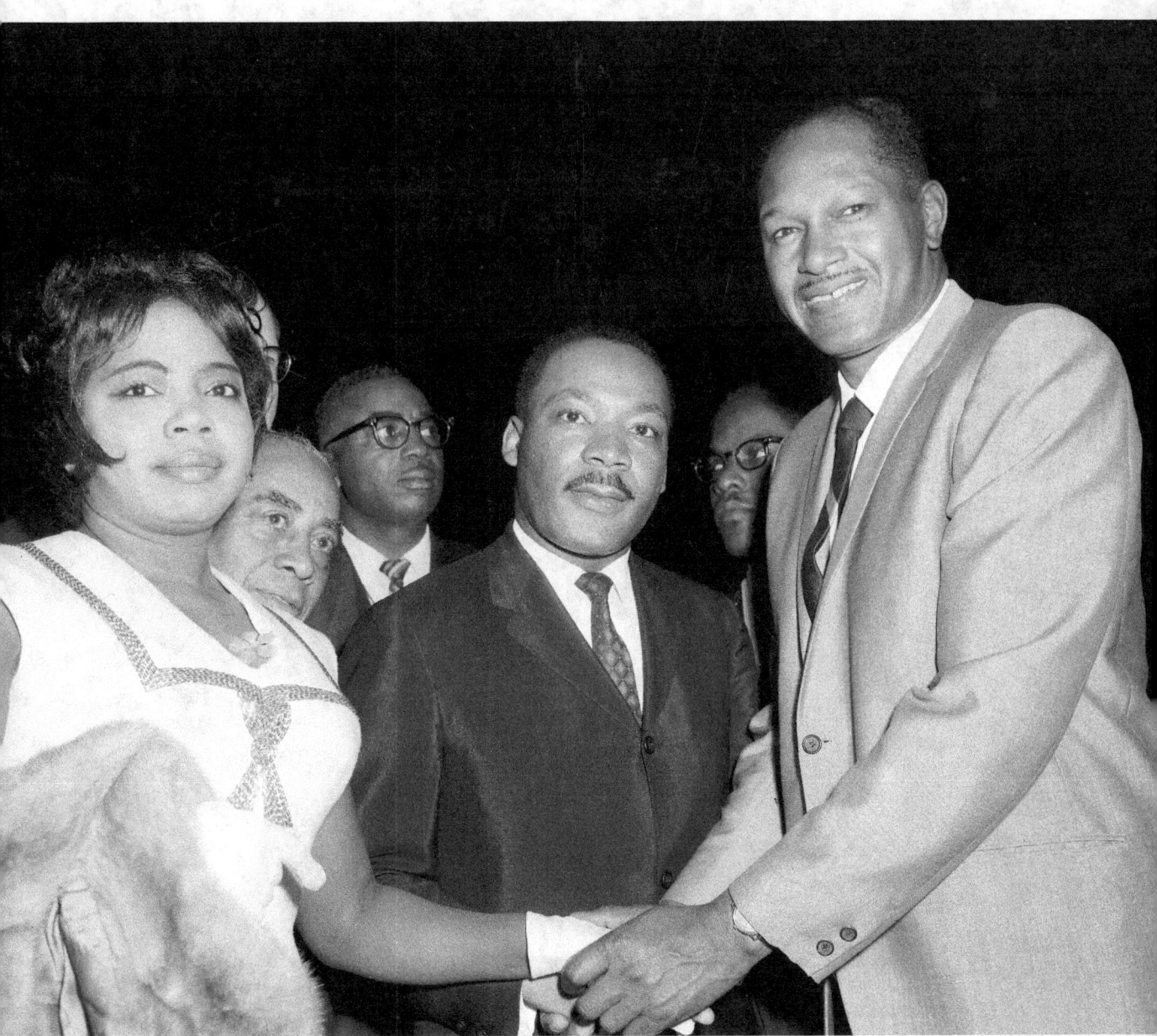

Tom Bradley (*left*) presents a resolution to Martin Luther King Jr. (*center*).
February 24, 1965

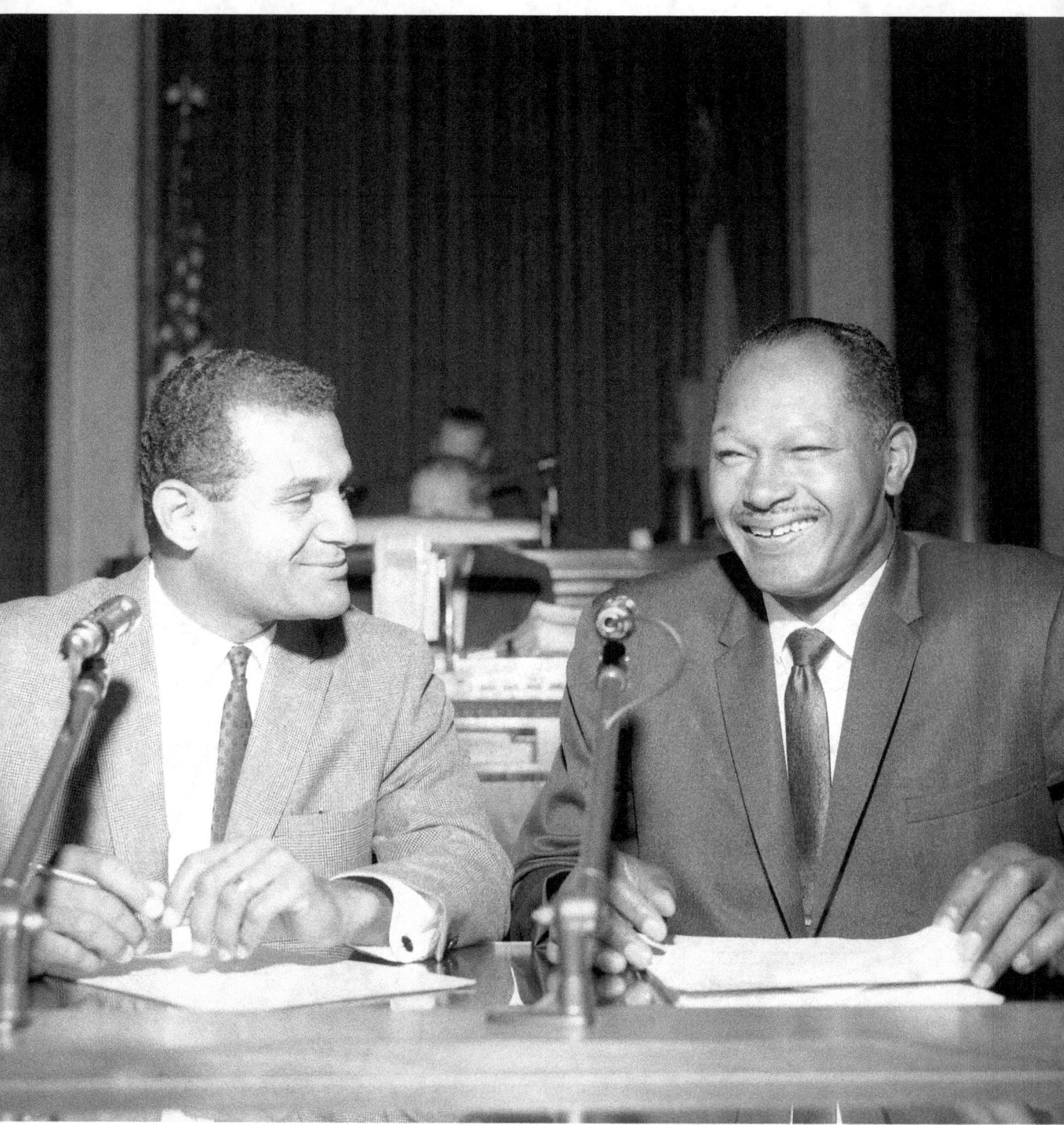

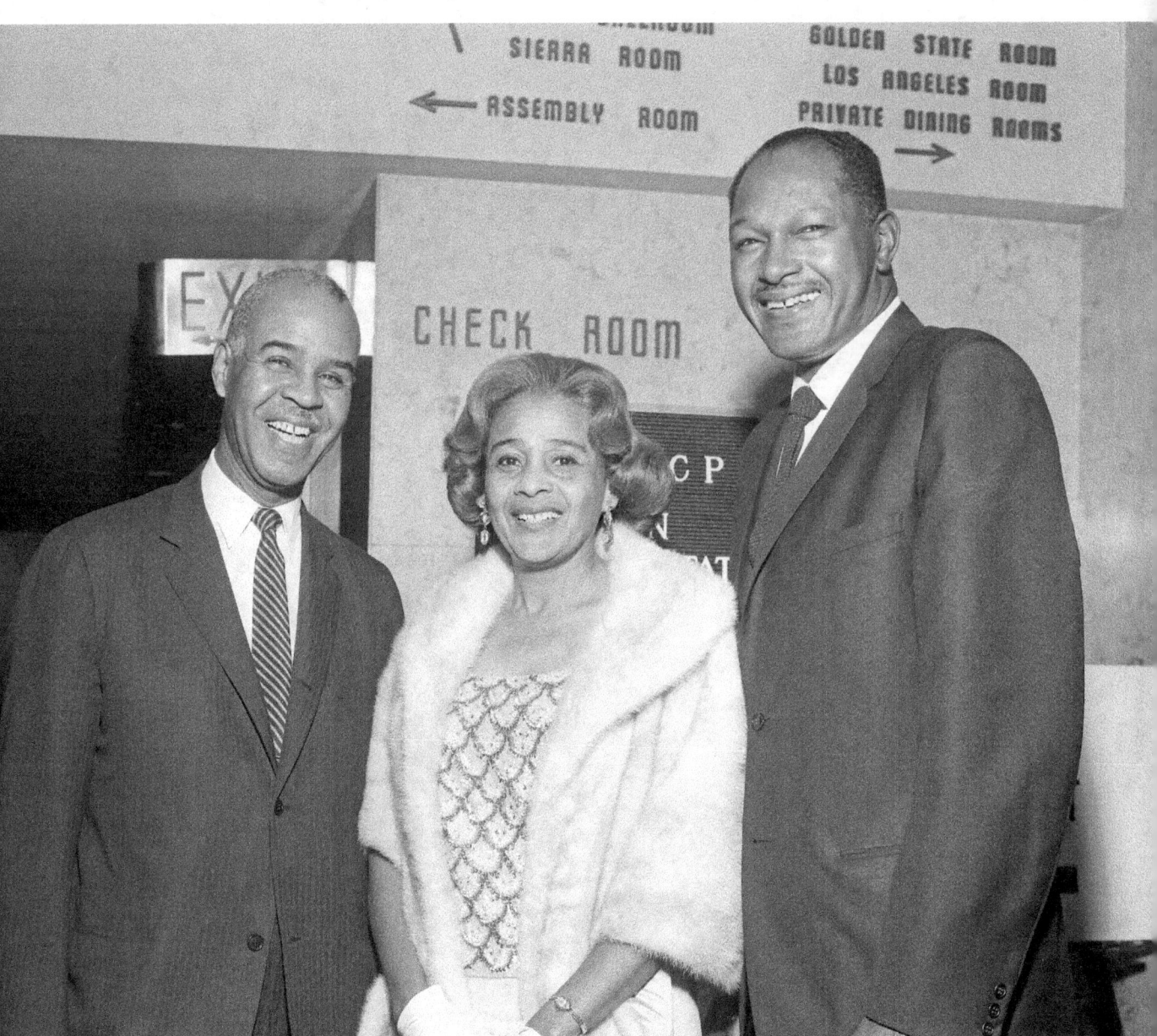

Tom Bradley (*right*) and wife Ethel Bradley (*center*) with NAACP leader Roy Wilkins (*left*)
at NAACP life membership banquet. November 11, 1965
*Opposite*: Tom Bradley (*right*) with Billy G. Mills (*left*) at city council chambers. 1963

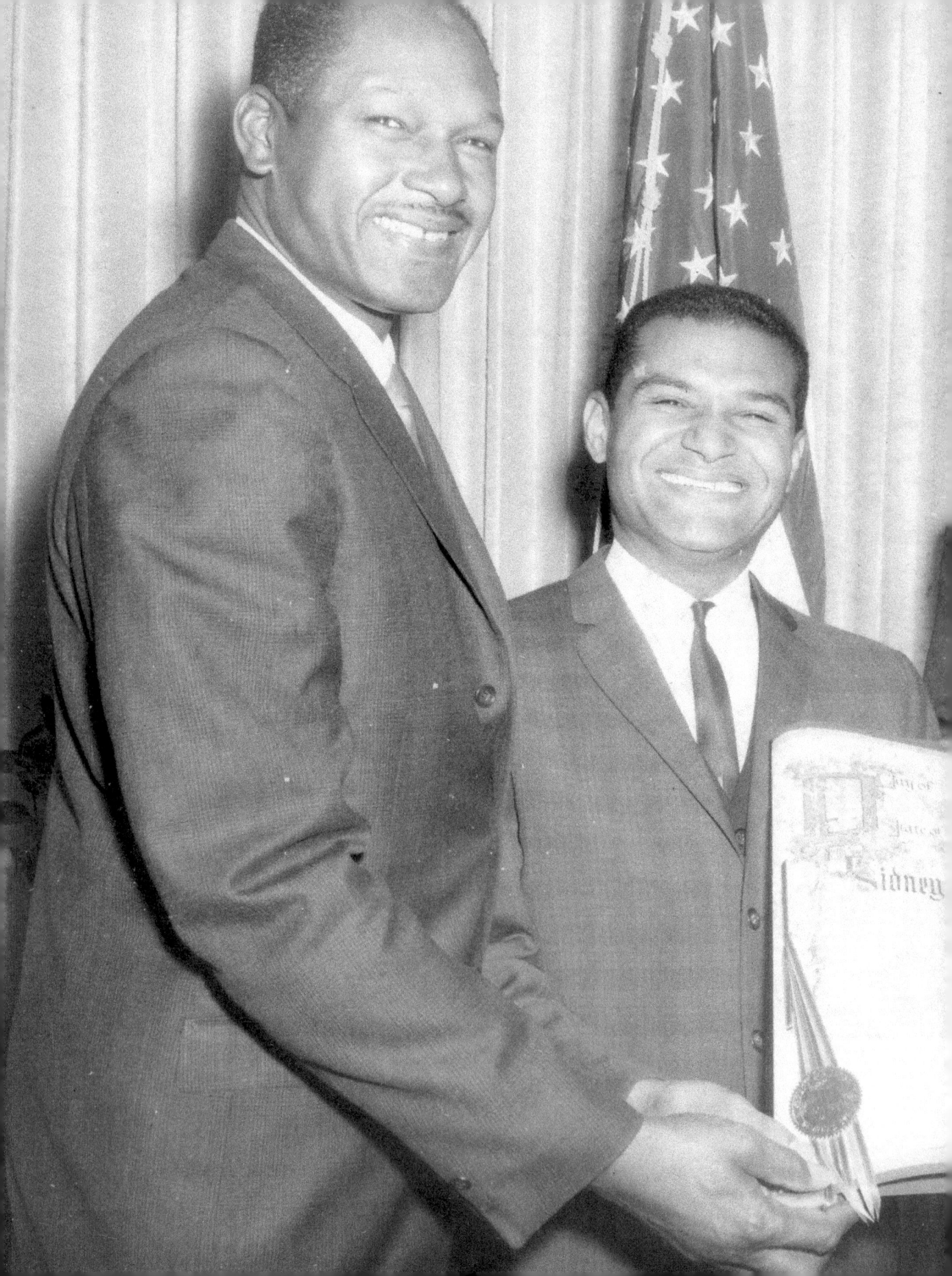

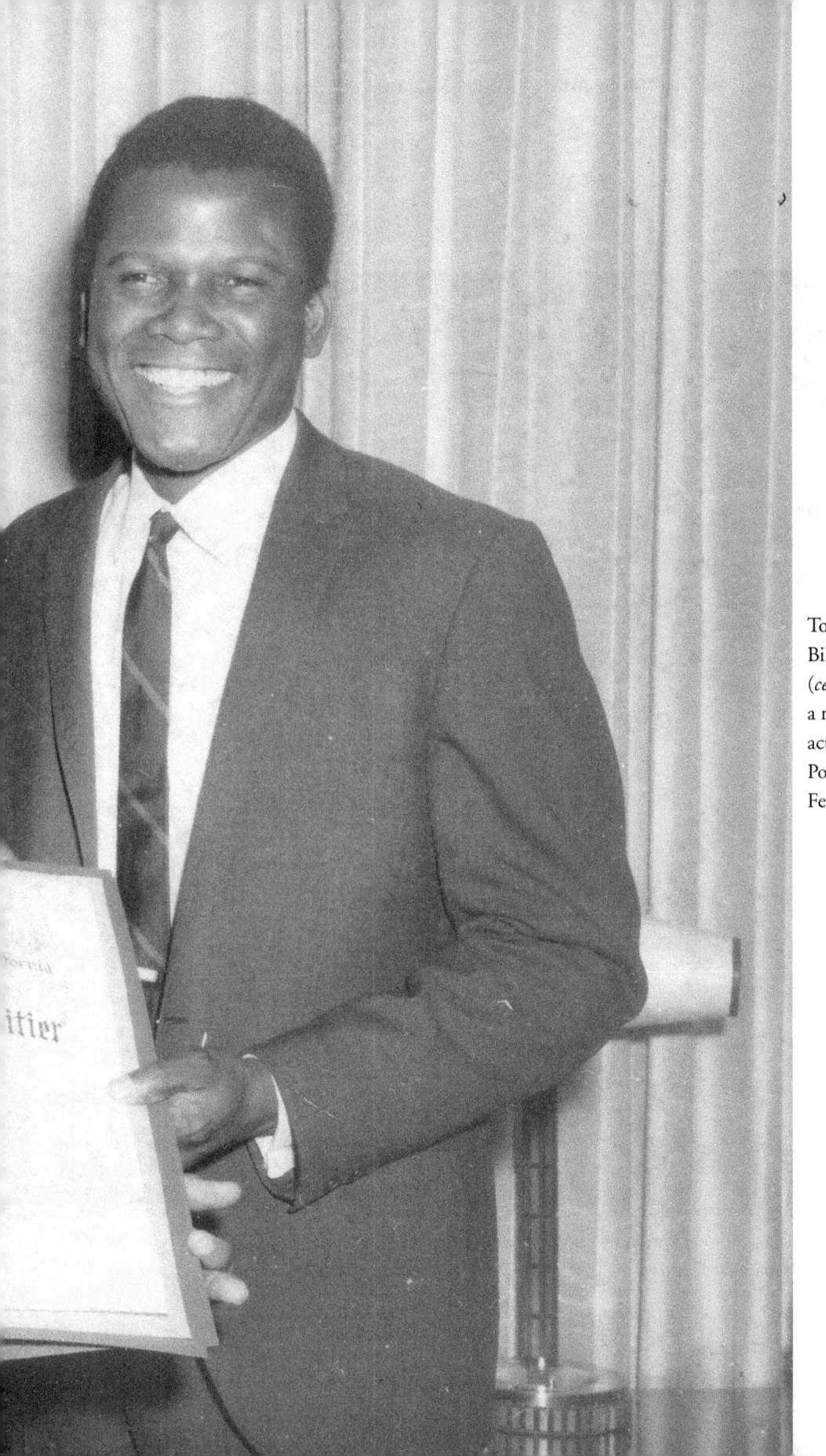

Tom Bradley with
Billy G. Mills
(*center*) presenting
a resolution to
actor Sidney
Poitier (*right*).
February 10, 1964

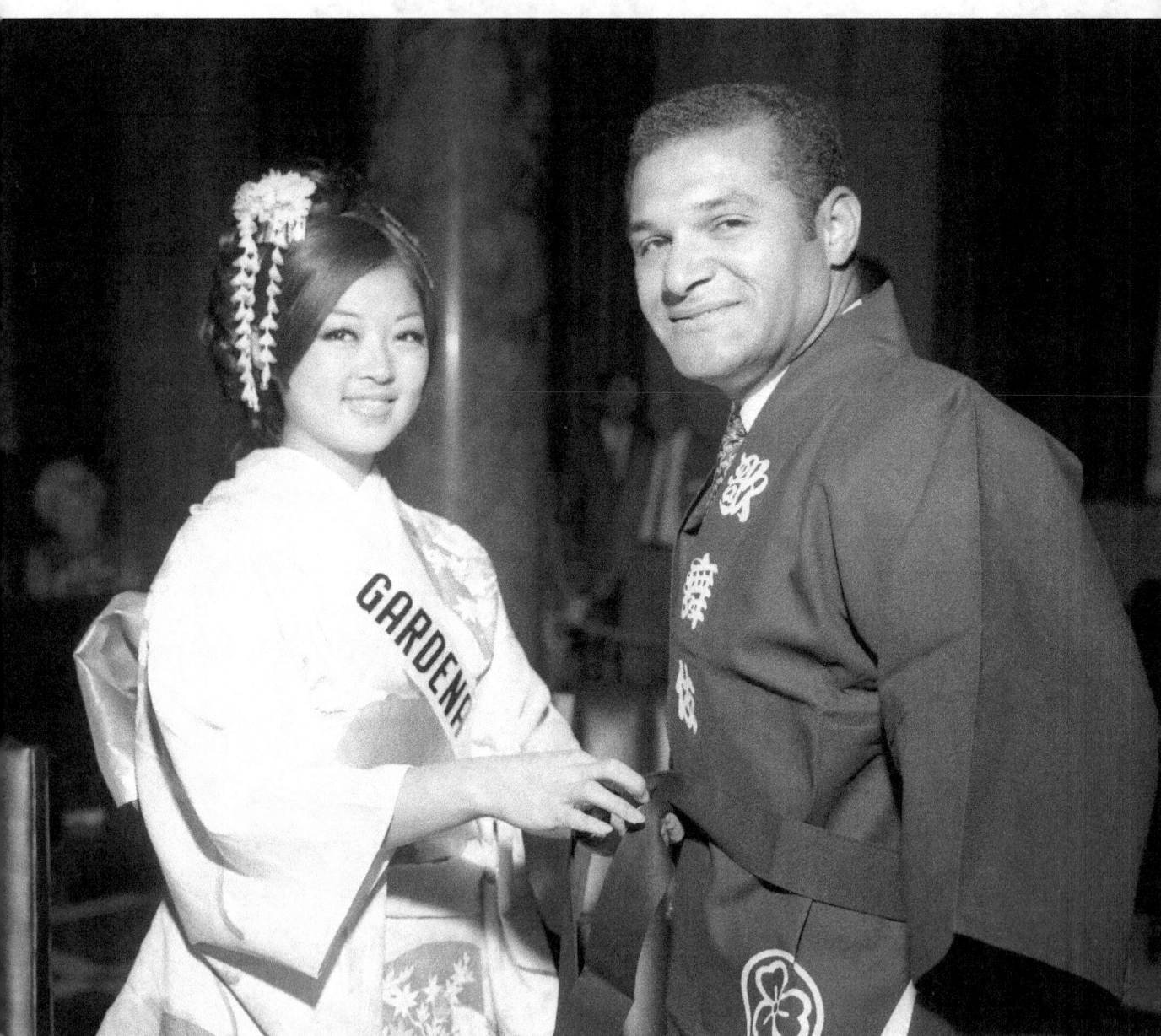

Billy G. Mills dons traditional kimono with the help of Joyce Yukiko Uyeda, the contestant representing Gardena Valley, during the 29th Nisei Week Festival. August 19, 1969

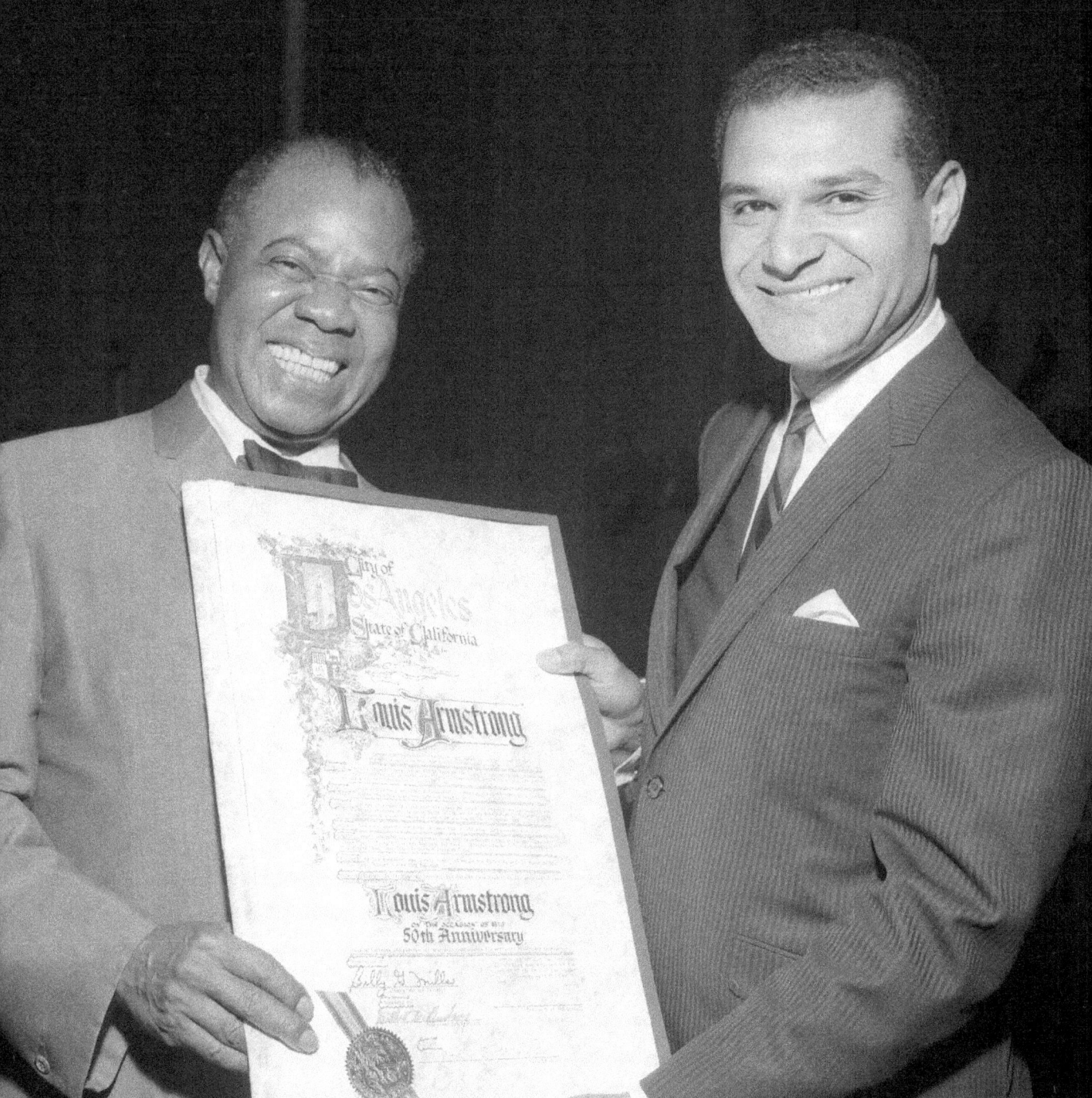

Billy G. Mills presents a resolution to musician Louie Armstrong. Mills was the first African American to graduate from the UCLA Law School in 1954. Elected in 1963, Mills was the third African American to serve on the Los Angeles City Council, a seat he held until 1974 when he became a Los Angeles Superior Court judge. He was the first African American chairman of the Democratic County Central Committee, winning over fellow Councilman Tom Bradley by just three votes. October 26, 1966

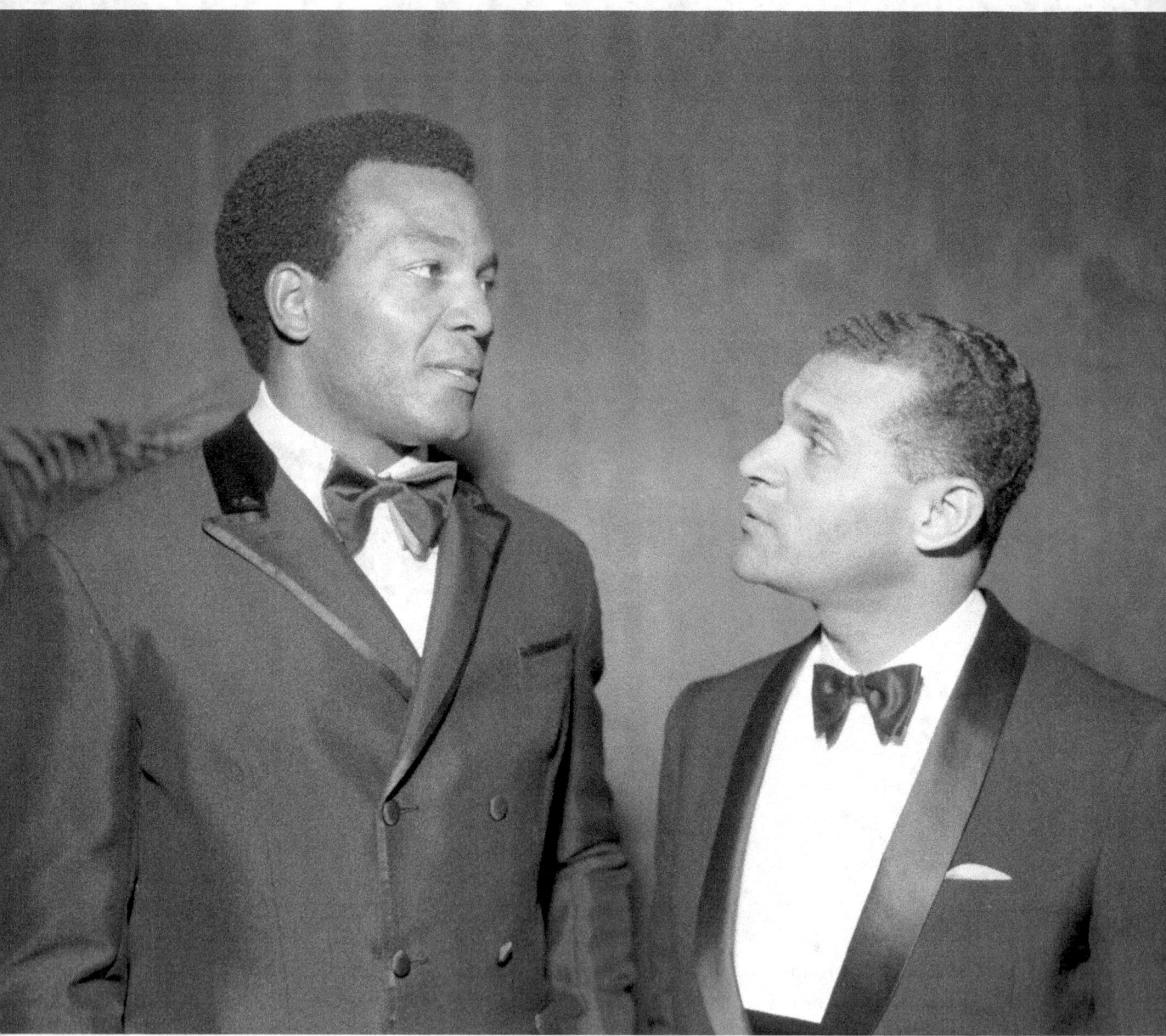

Billy G. Mills (*right*) with football player and actor Jim Brown (*left*) during Jefferson–Jackson Day Dinner. May 14, 1968

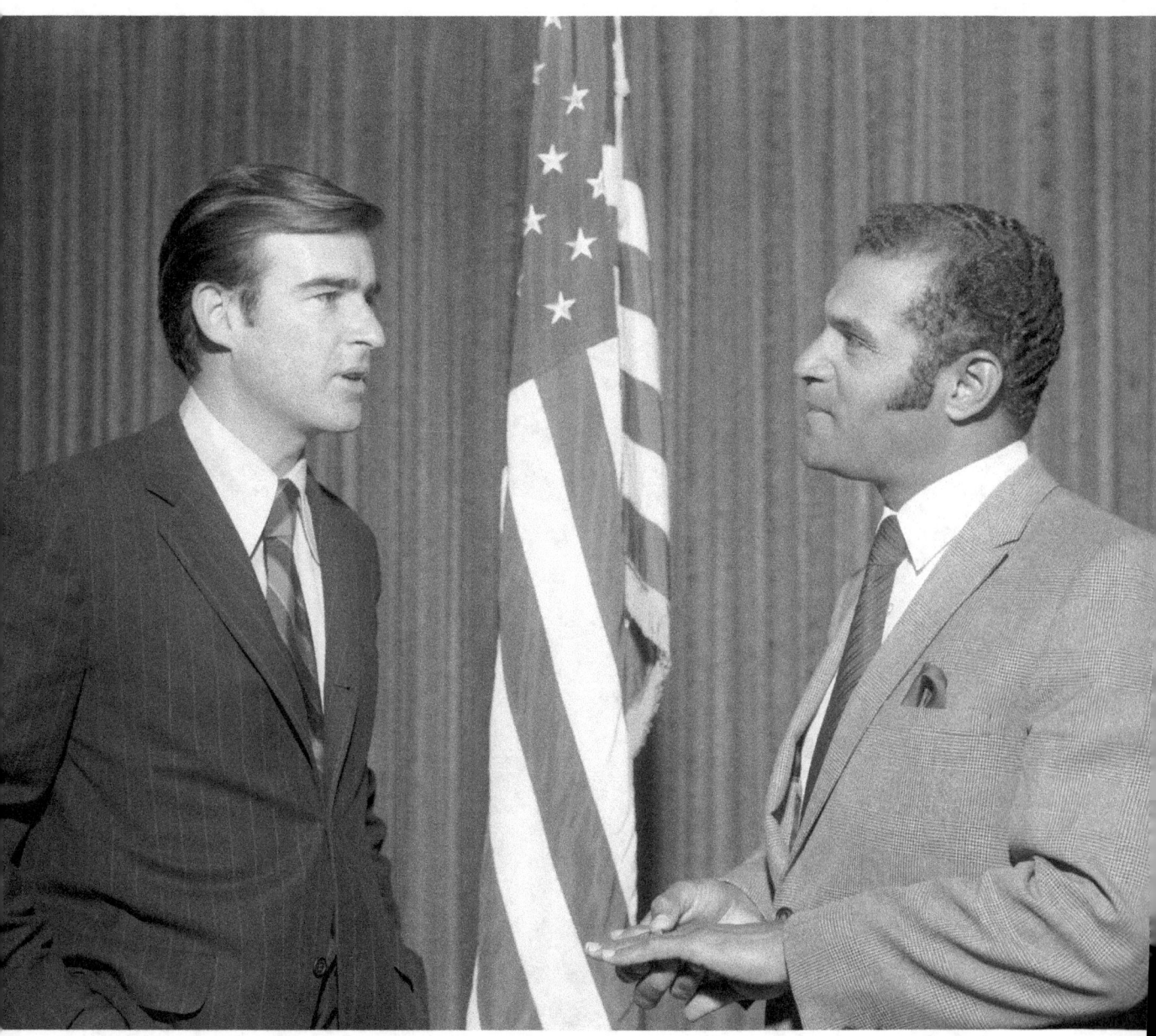

Governor Jerry Brown (*left*) speaks to Councilman Billy G. Mills (*right*). c1970

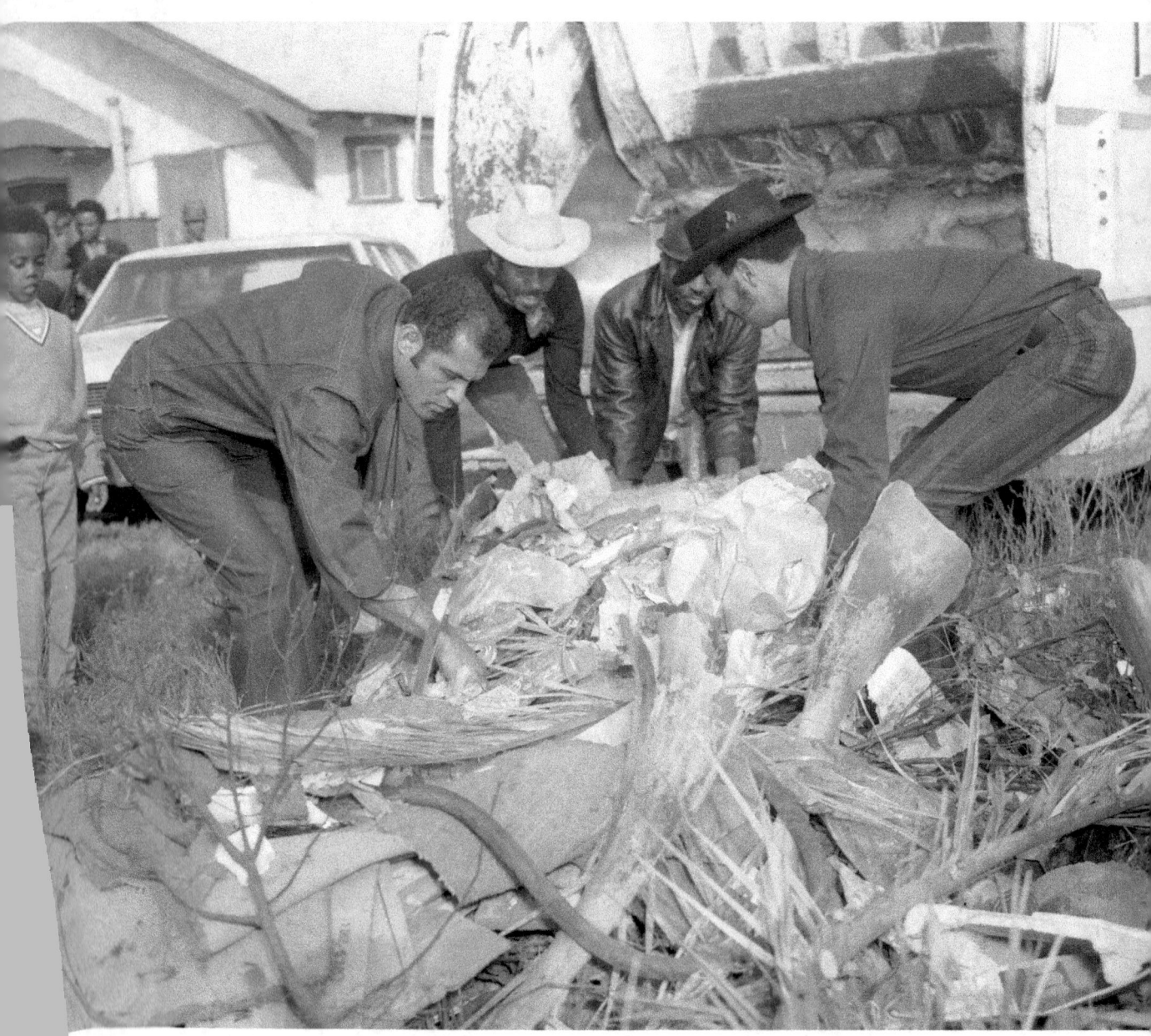

Billy G. Mills (*jean jacket on the left*) at Clean L.A. Committee clean-up. c1971

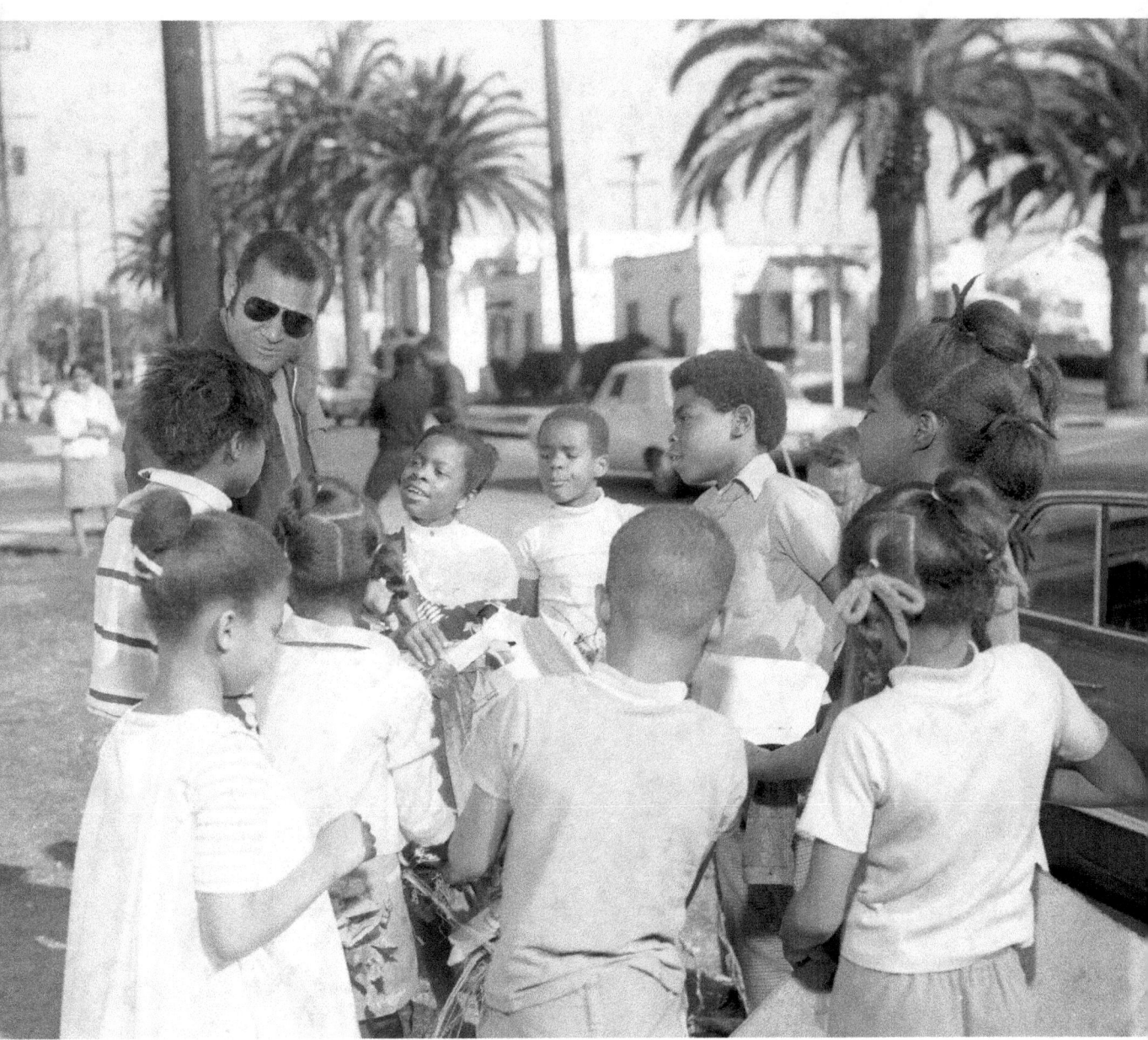

Billy G. Mills (*sunglasses*) talks to neighborhood kids during Clean L.A. Campaign. c1970

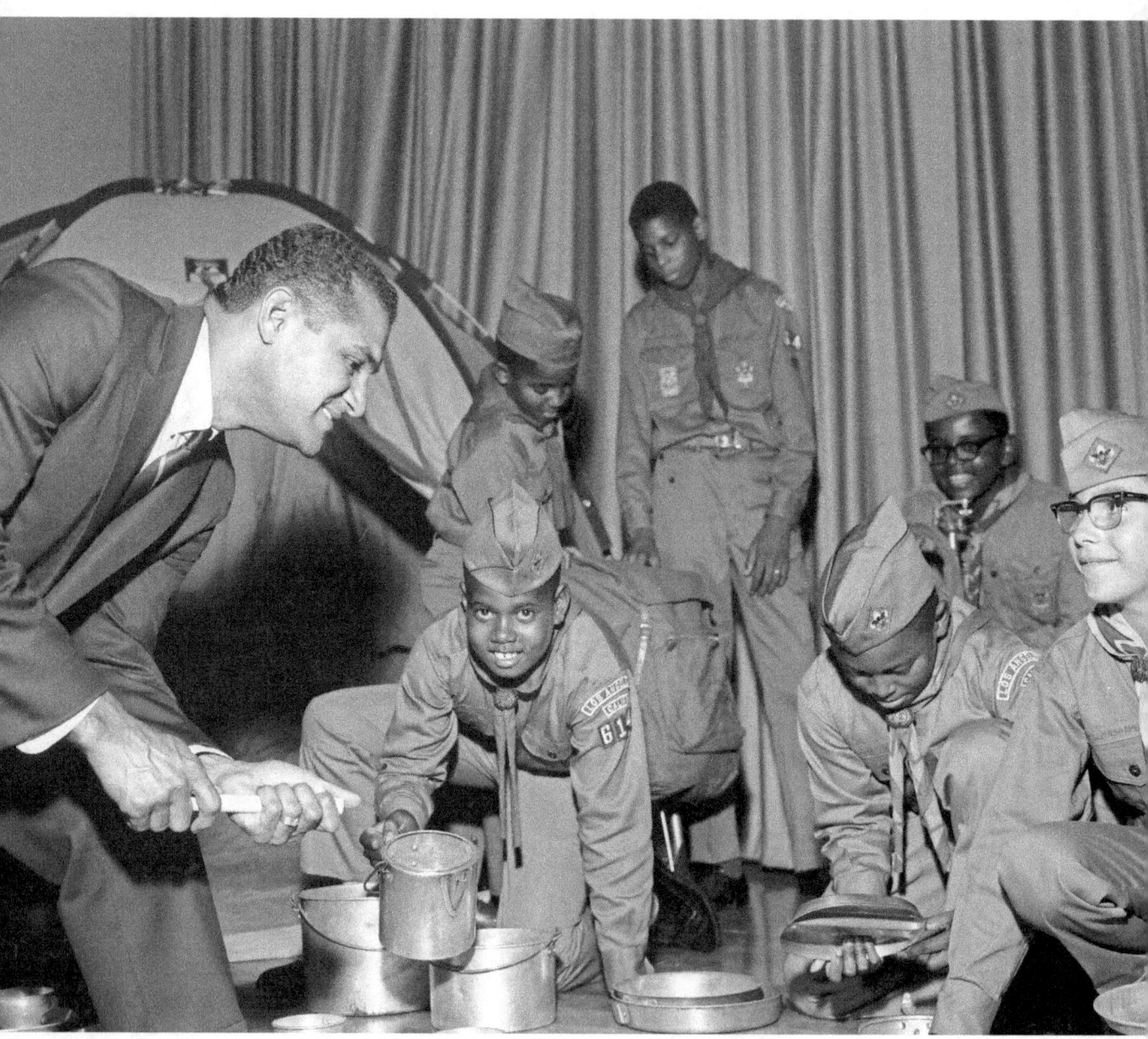

Billy G. Mills (*far left*) with Boy Scout troop. c1965

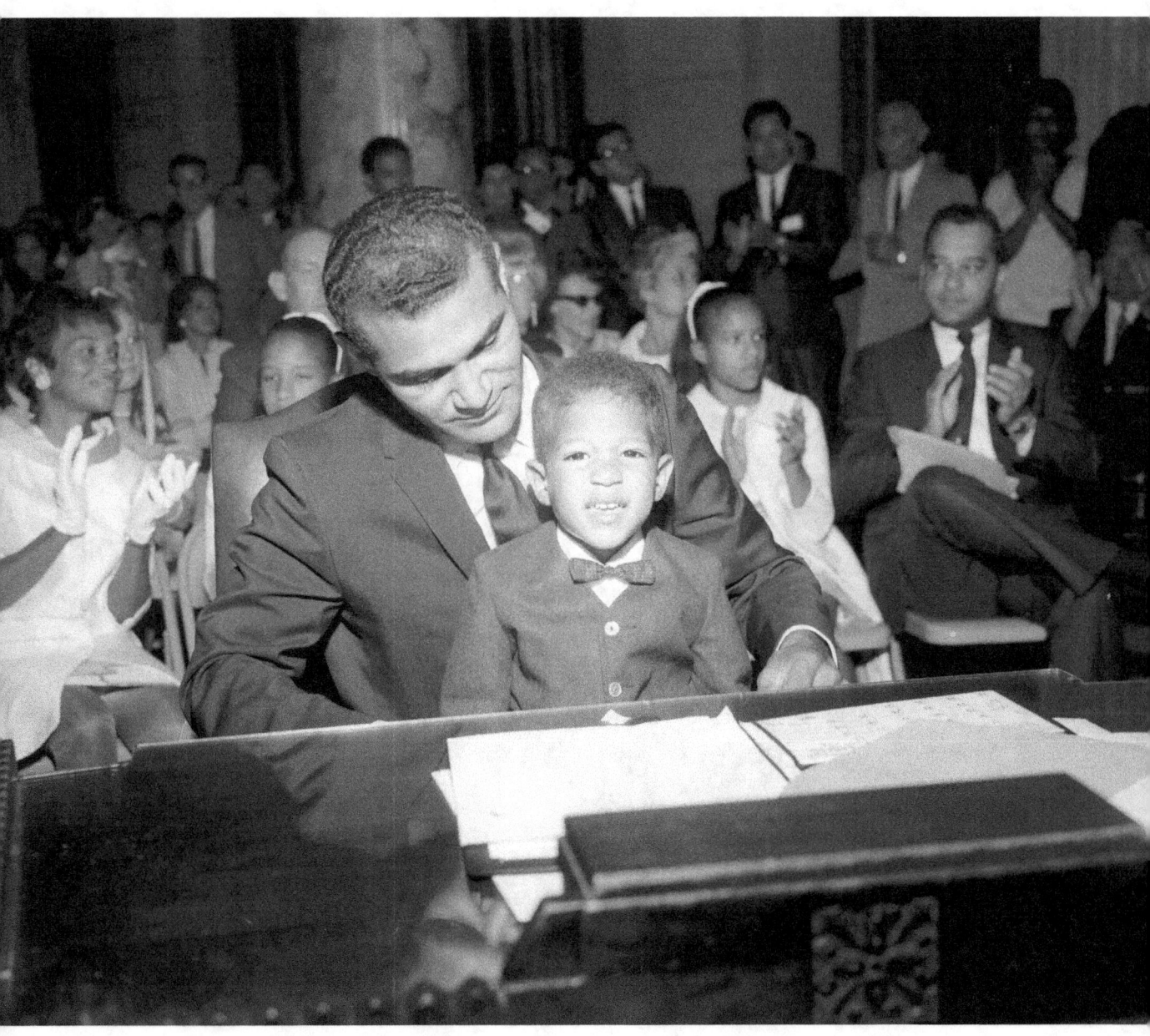

Billy G. Mills at council chambers with son, John Mills. c1967

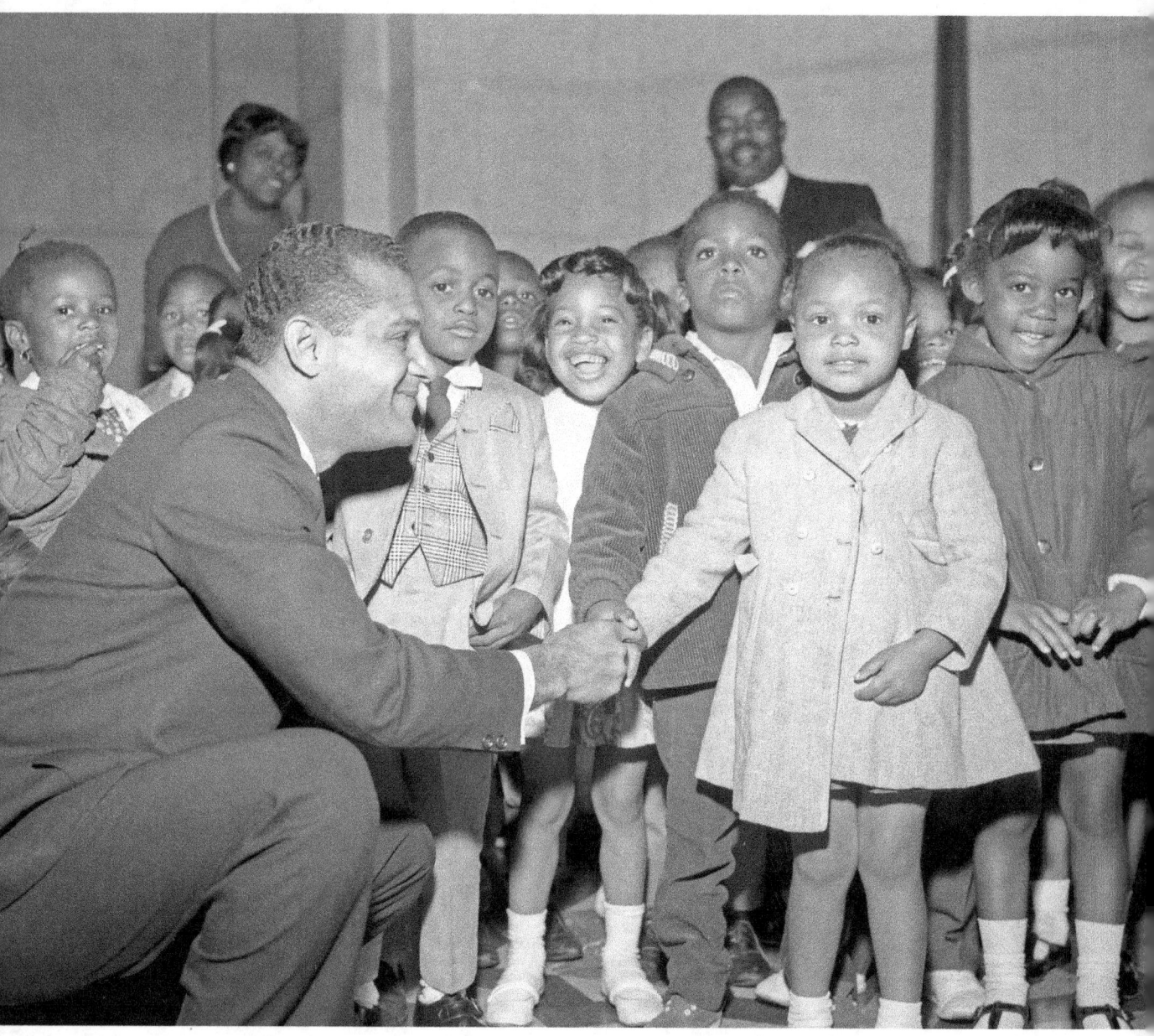

Children visit Billy G. Mills (*left*) at City Hall. c1966
*Opposite*: Councilman Billy G. Mills speaks at Ladies of Paradise meeting. c1967

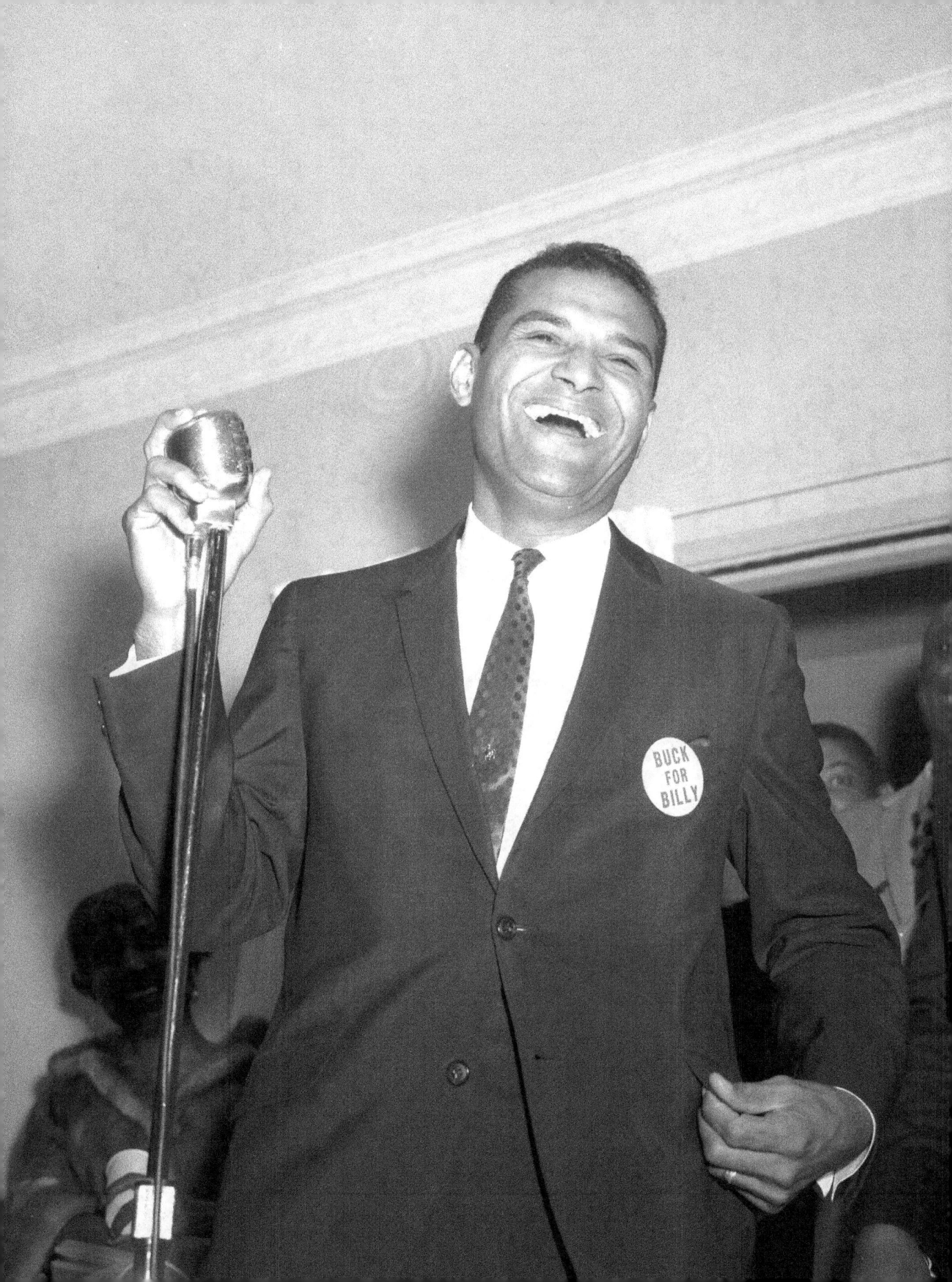

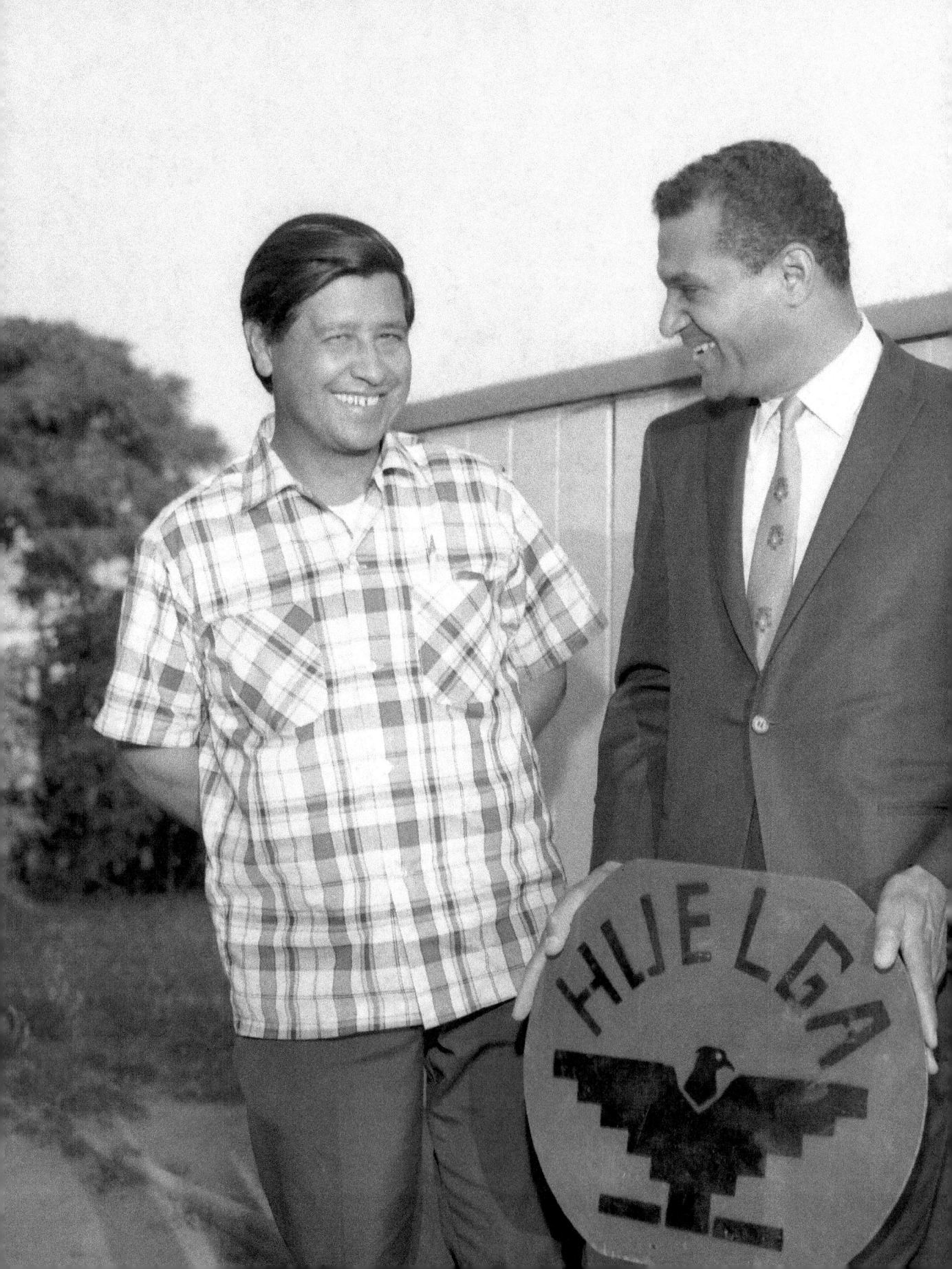

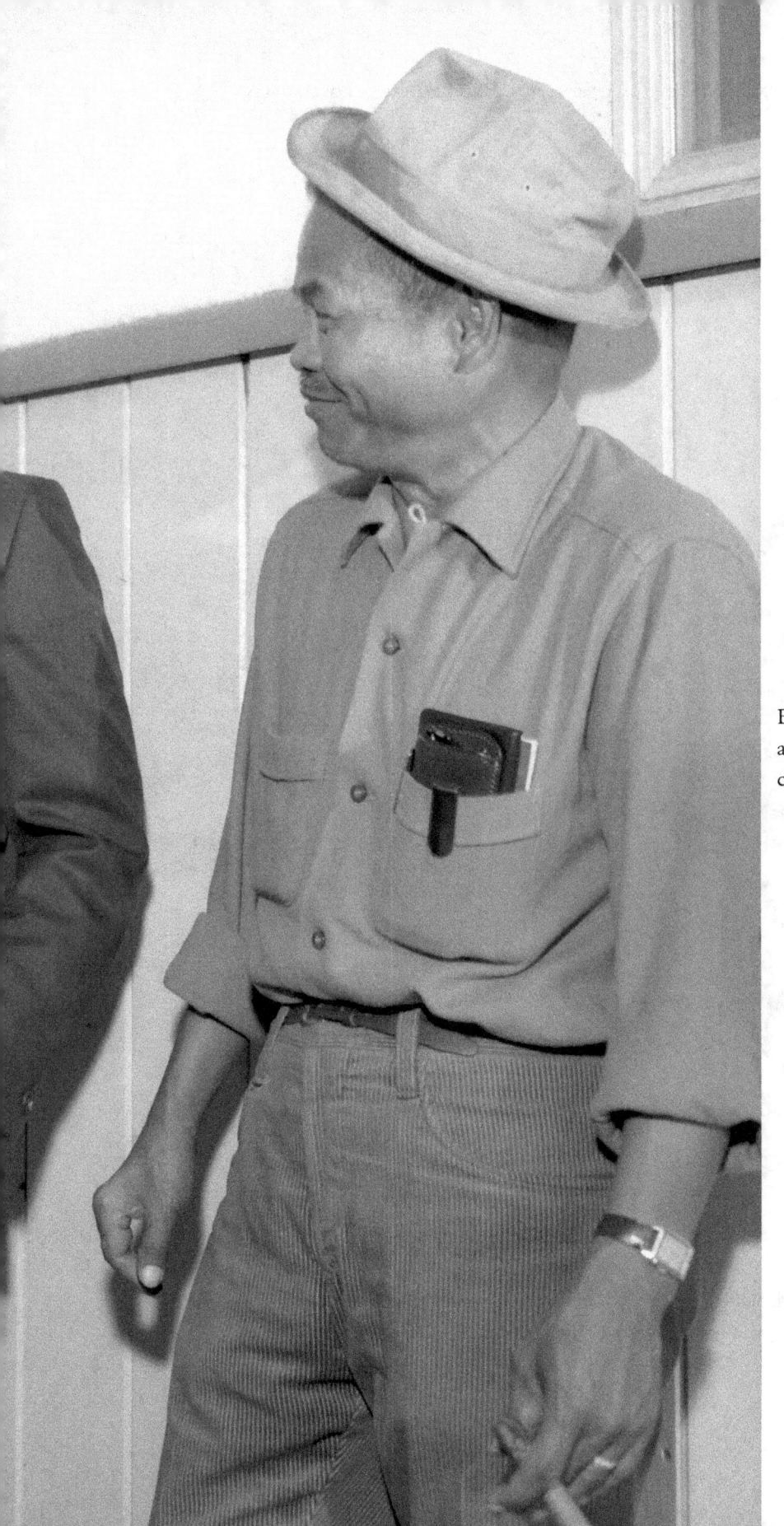

Billy G. Mills (*center*) with activist Cesar Chavez (*left*). c1966

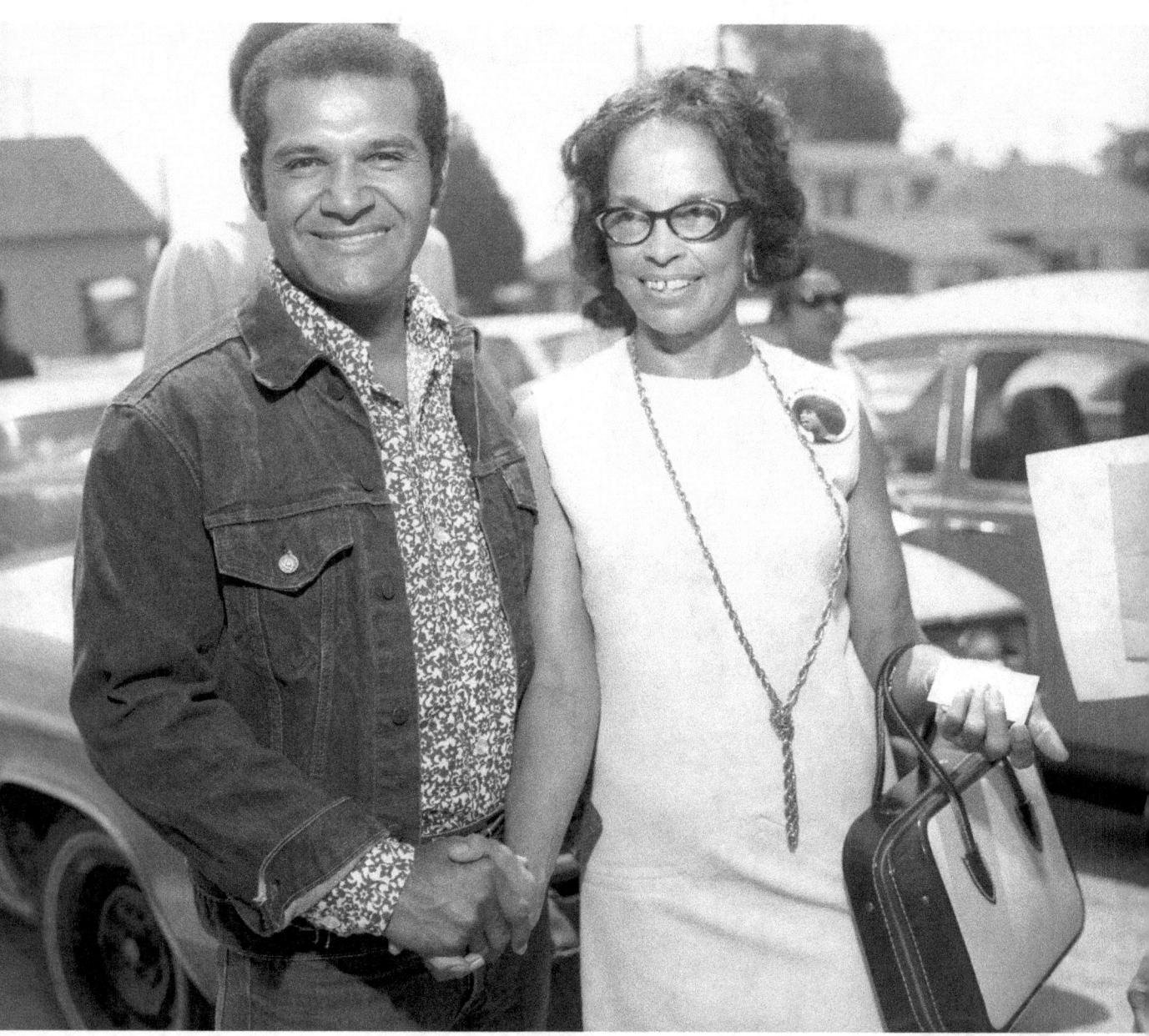

Billy G. Mills (*left*) with Sallye Davis (*right*), mother of Angela Davis, at Elks Hall during an Operation Breadbasket meeting. July 15, 1971

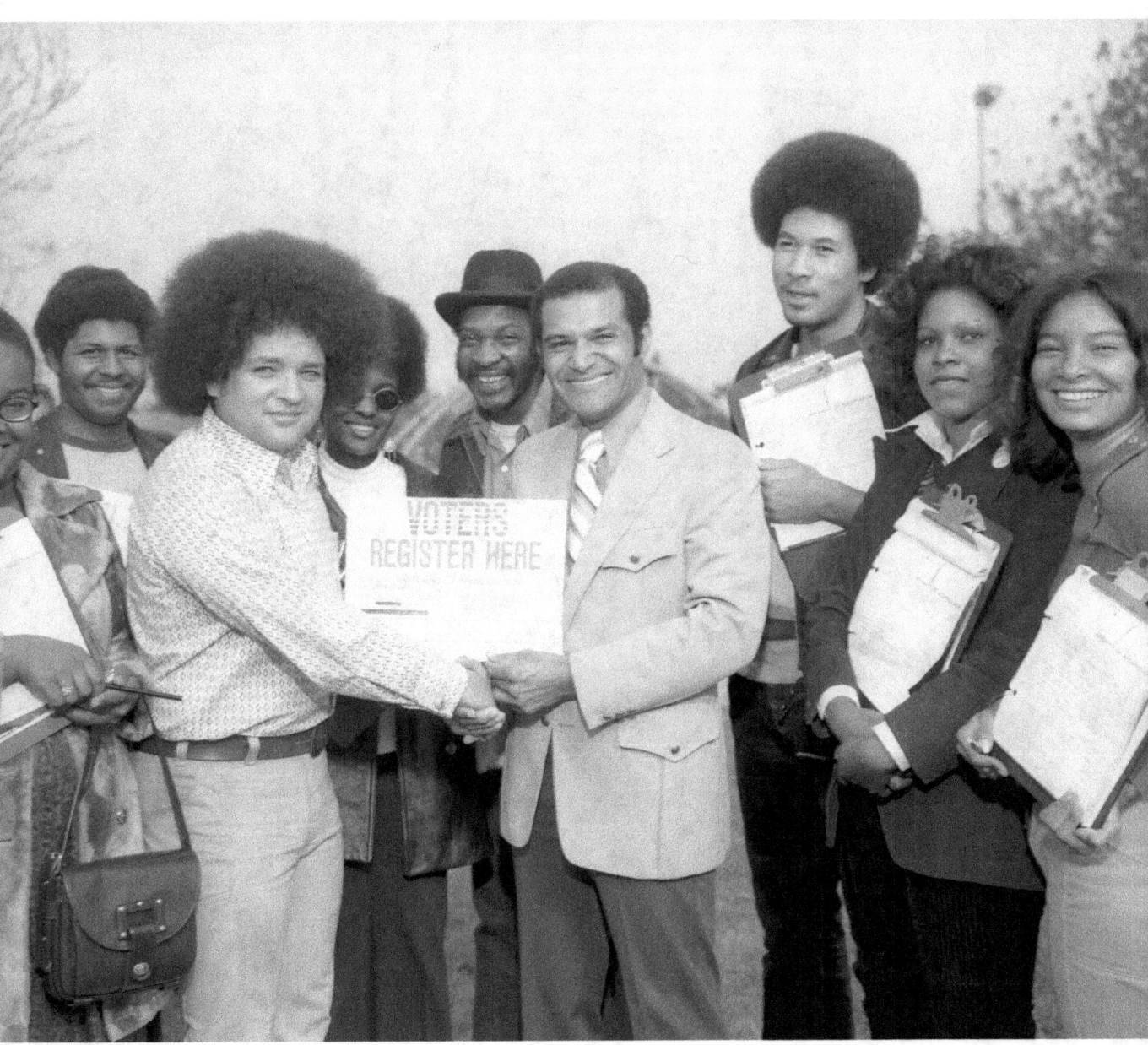

Billy G. Mills (*center*) with student volunteers for student voter registration drive. c1970

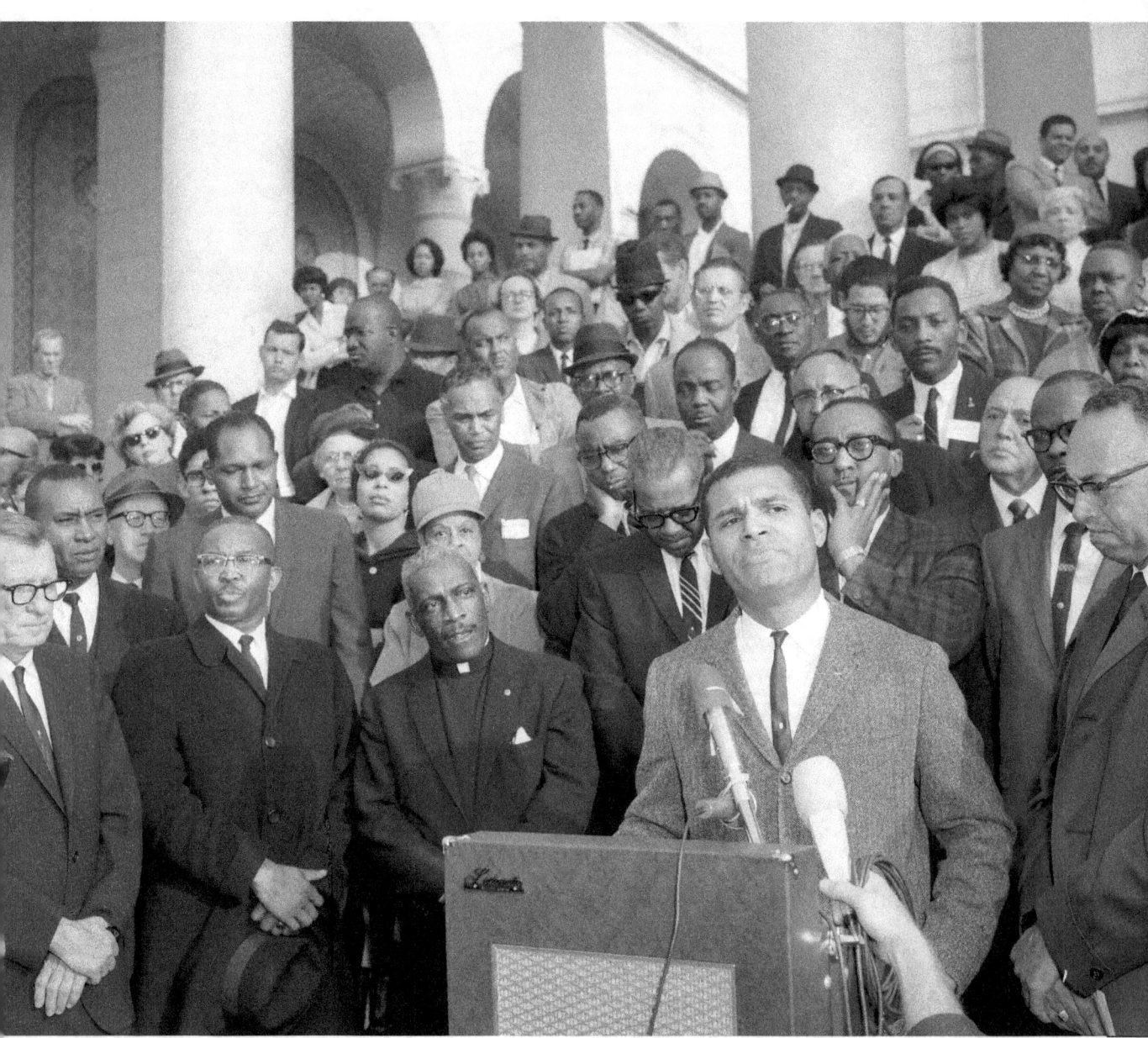

Councilman Billy G. Mills speaks at protest in front of City Hall. c1965

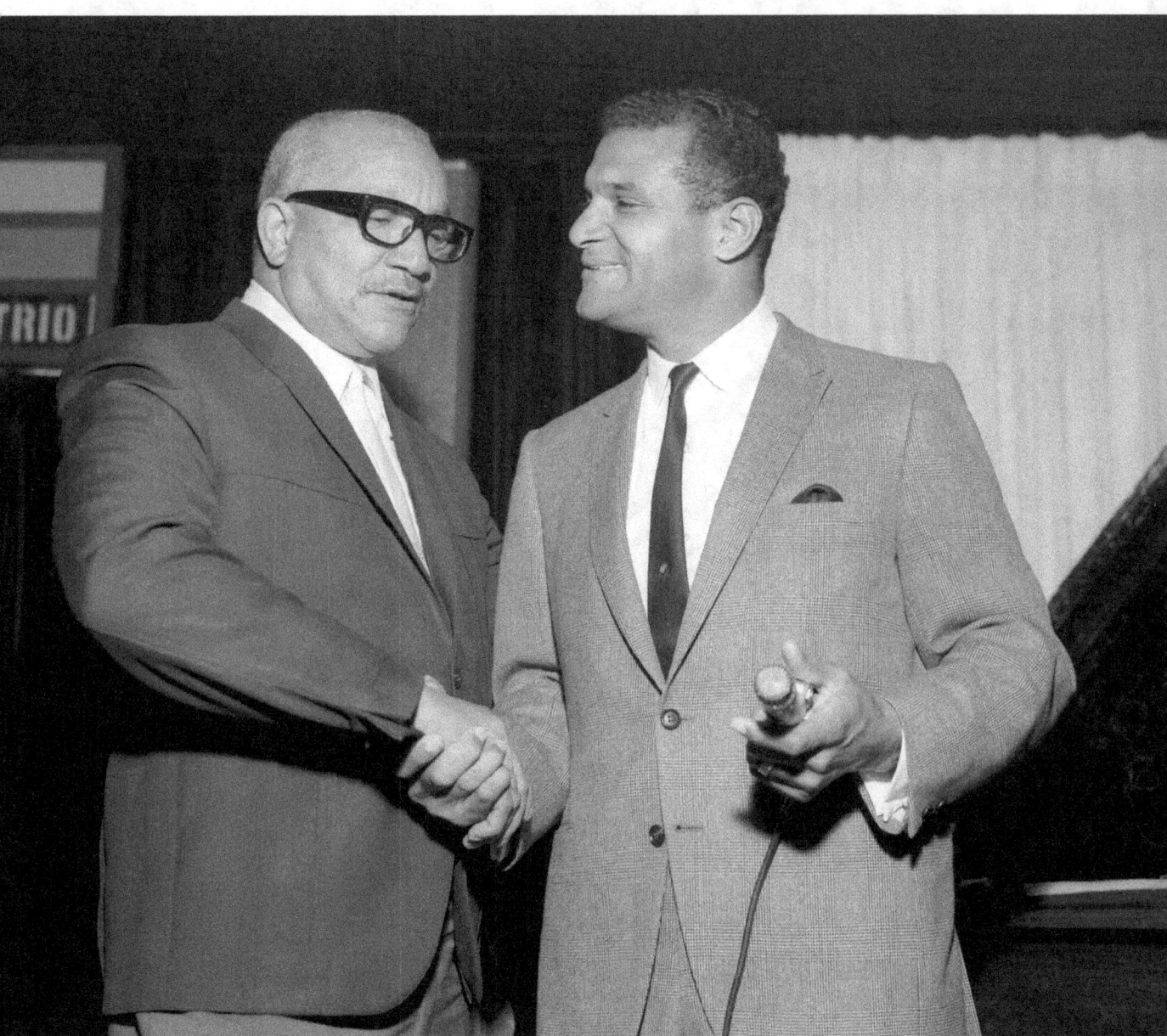

Billy G. Mills (*right*) with comedian Redd Foxx (*left*) at the cocktail party in Mills' honor at the Playboy Club. April 25, 1968

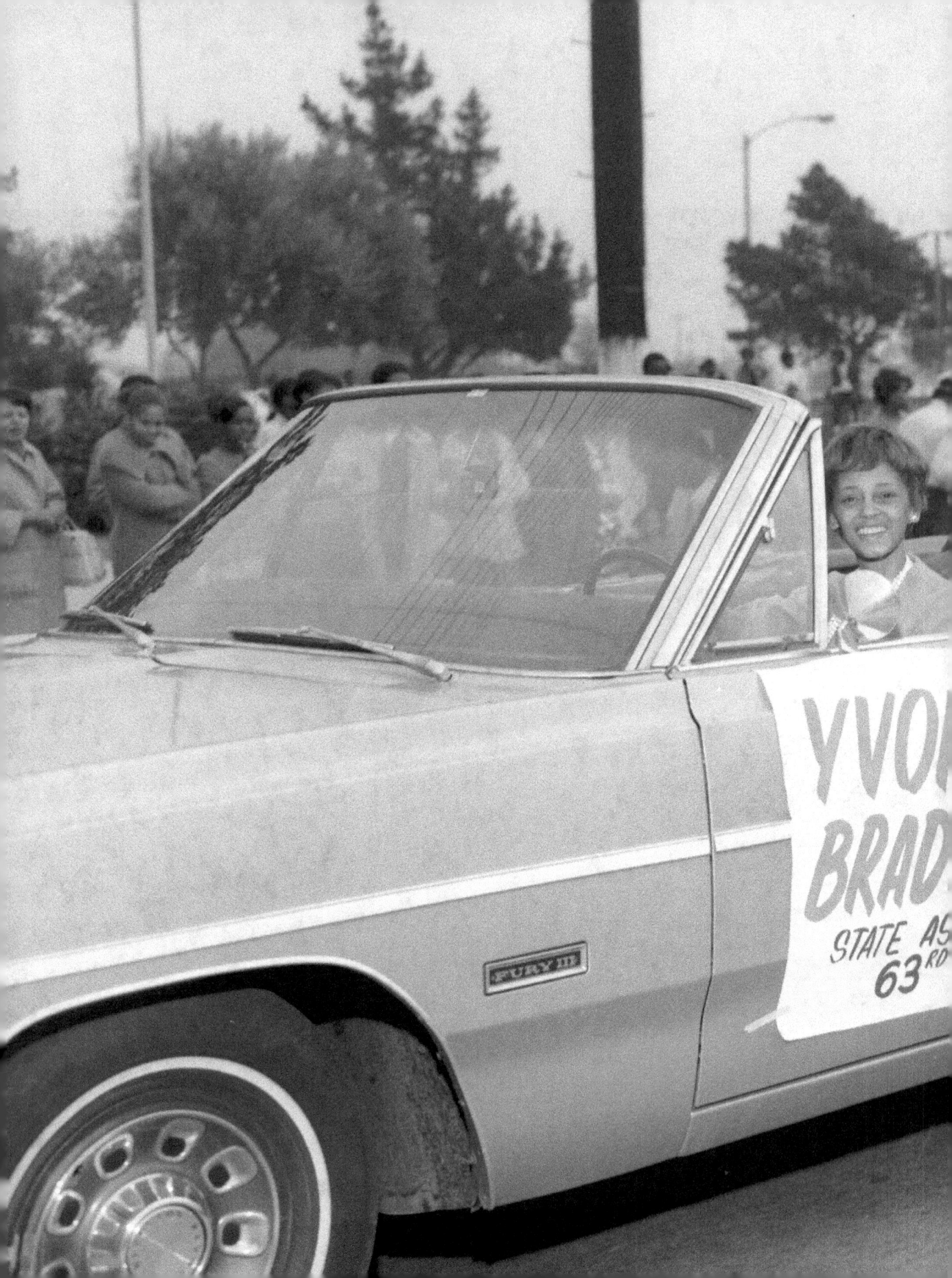

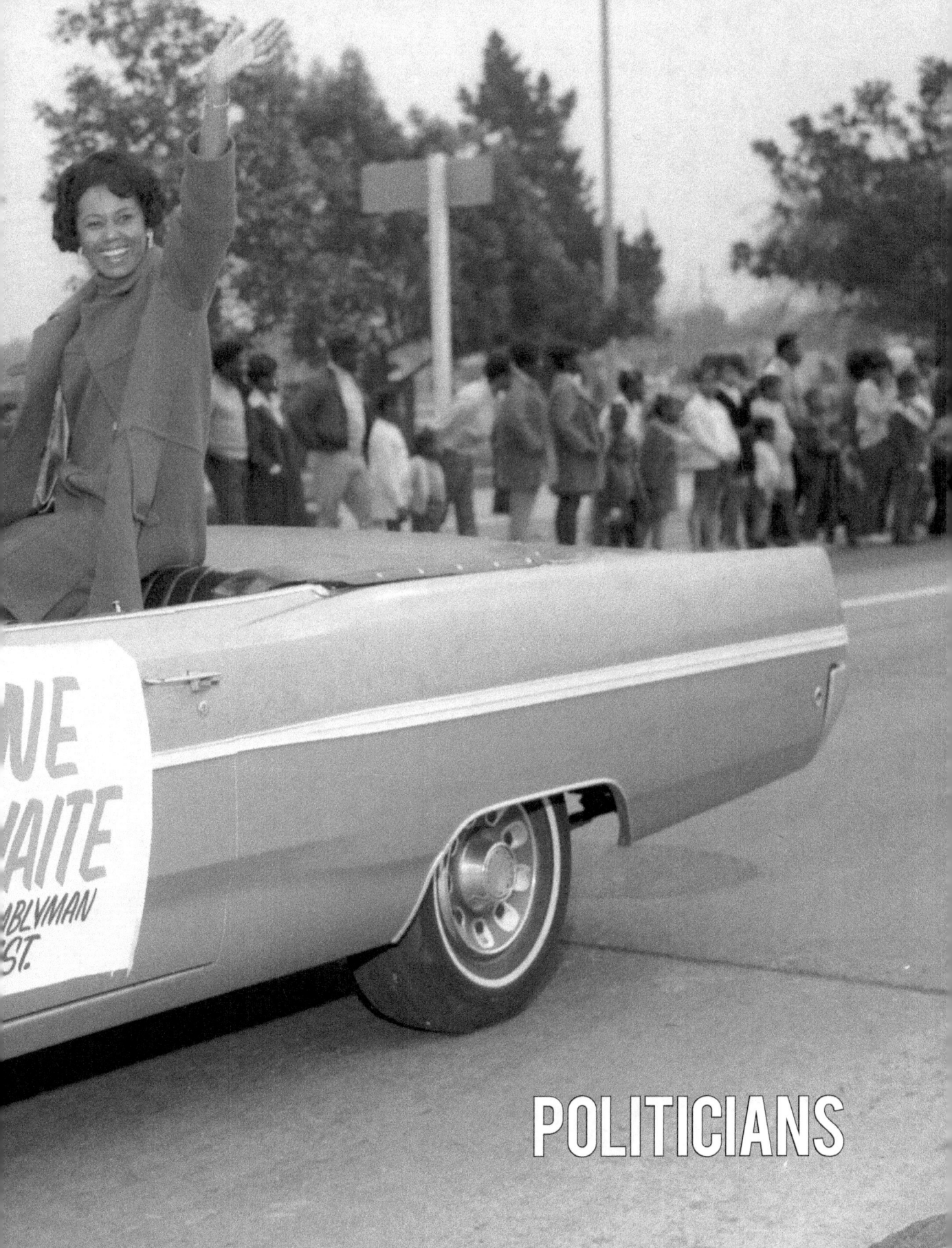

POLITICIANS

*Overleaf*: Yvonne Brathwaite Burke waves to the crowd during Watts Parade. c1964

*Opposite*: Yvonne Brathwaite Burke throws out a pitch during opening of Little League season at Denker Park. May 18, 1967

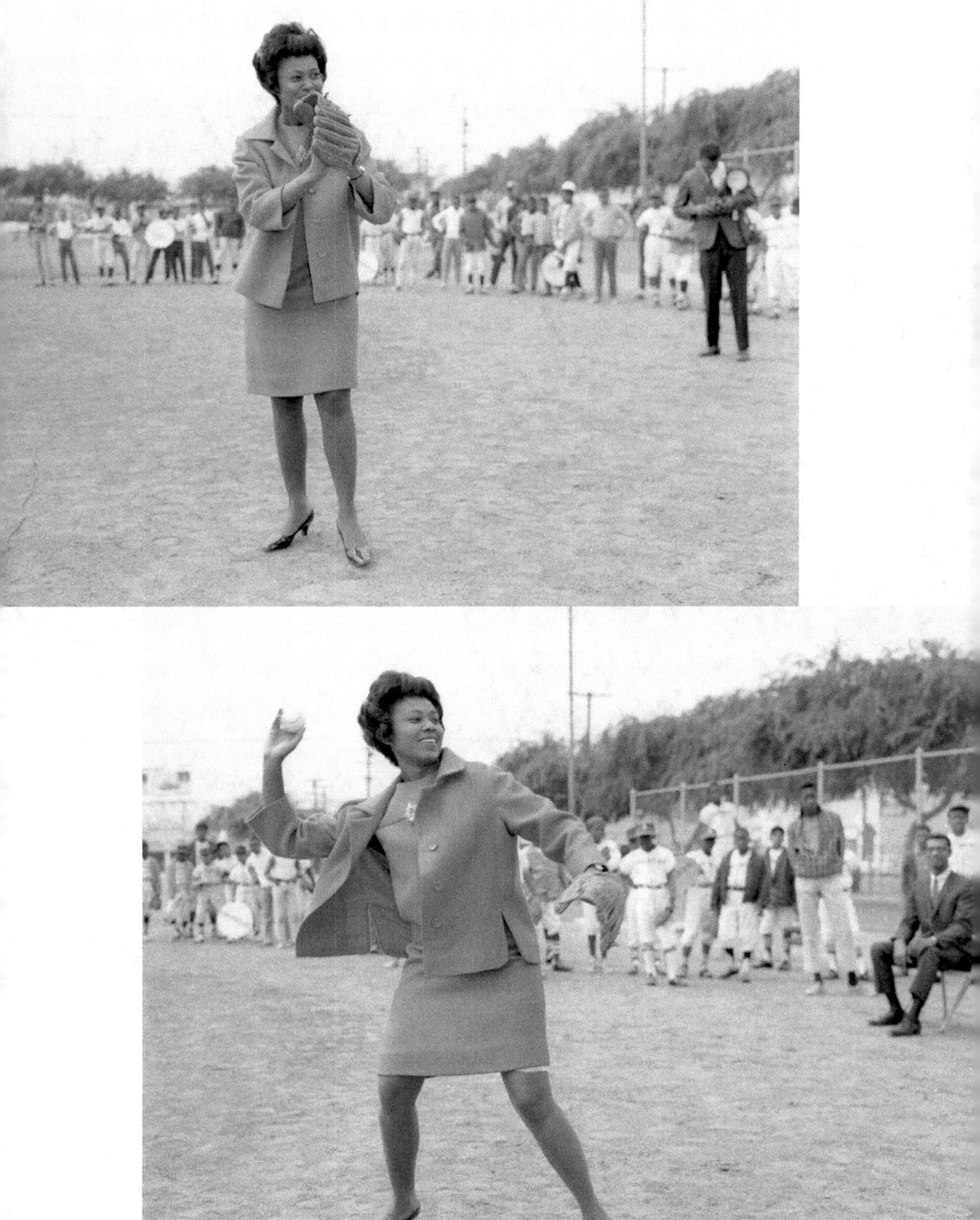

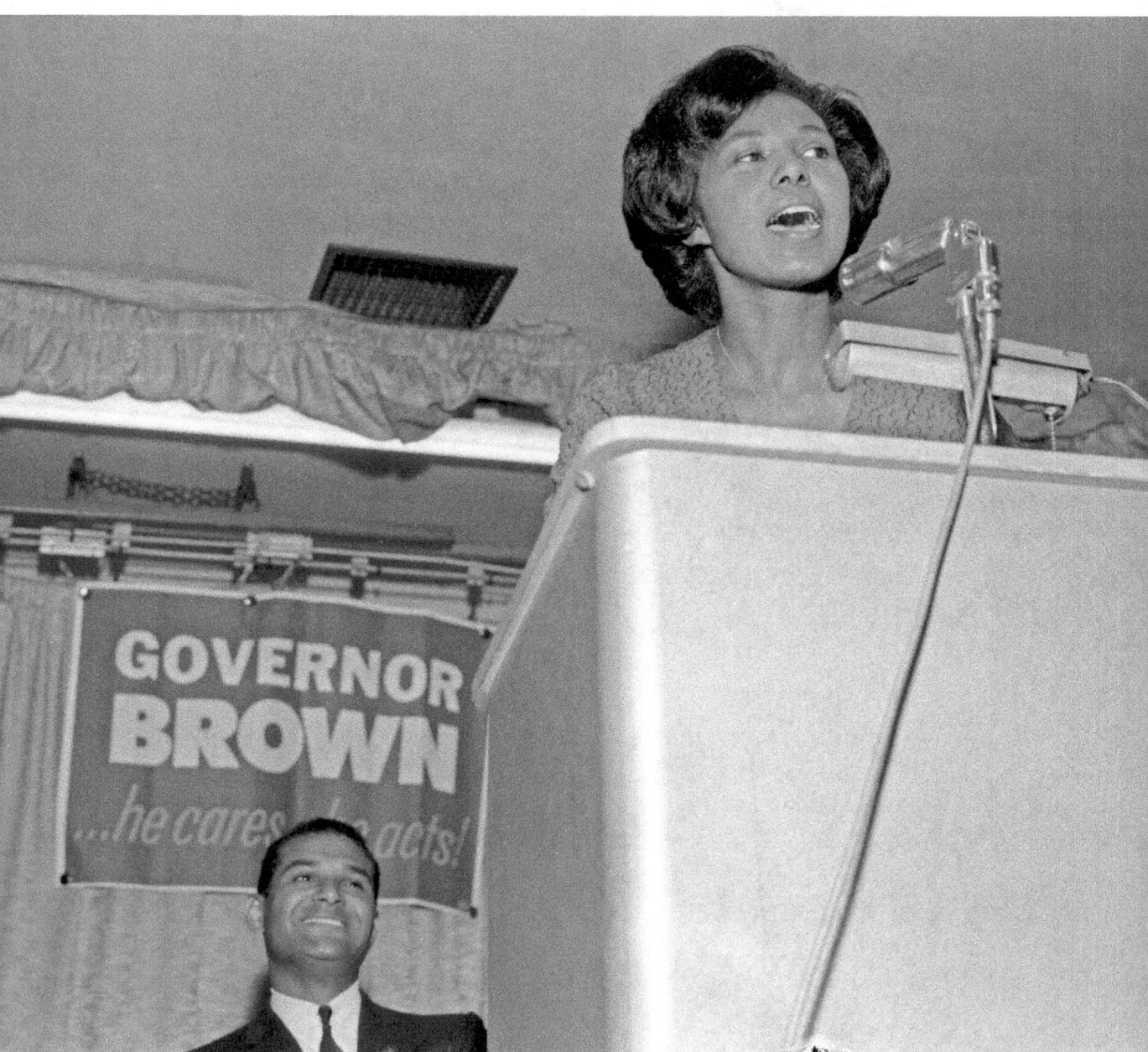

Yvonne Brathwaite Burke speaks at a rally for Pat Brown. In 1966, Burke became the first African American woman elected to the California Assembly, and in 1972, was the first woman elected to the House. She was also the first woman to chair the Congressional Black Caucus. In 1972, she became the first congresswoman to give birth and be granted maternity leave while serving Congress. c1966

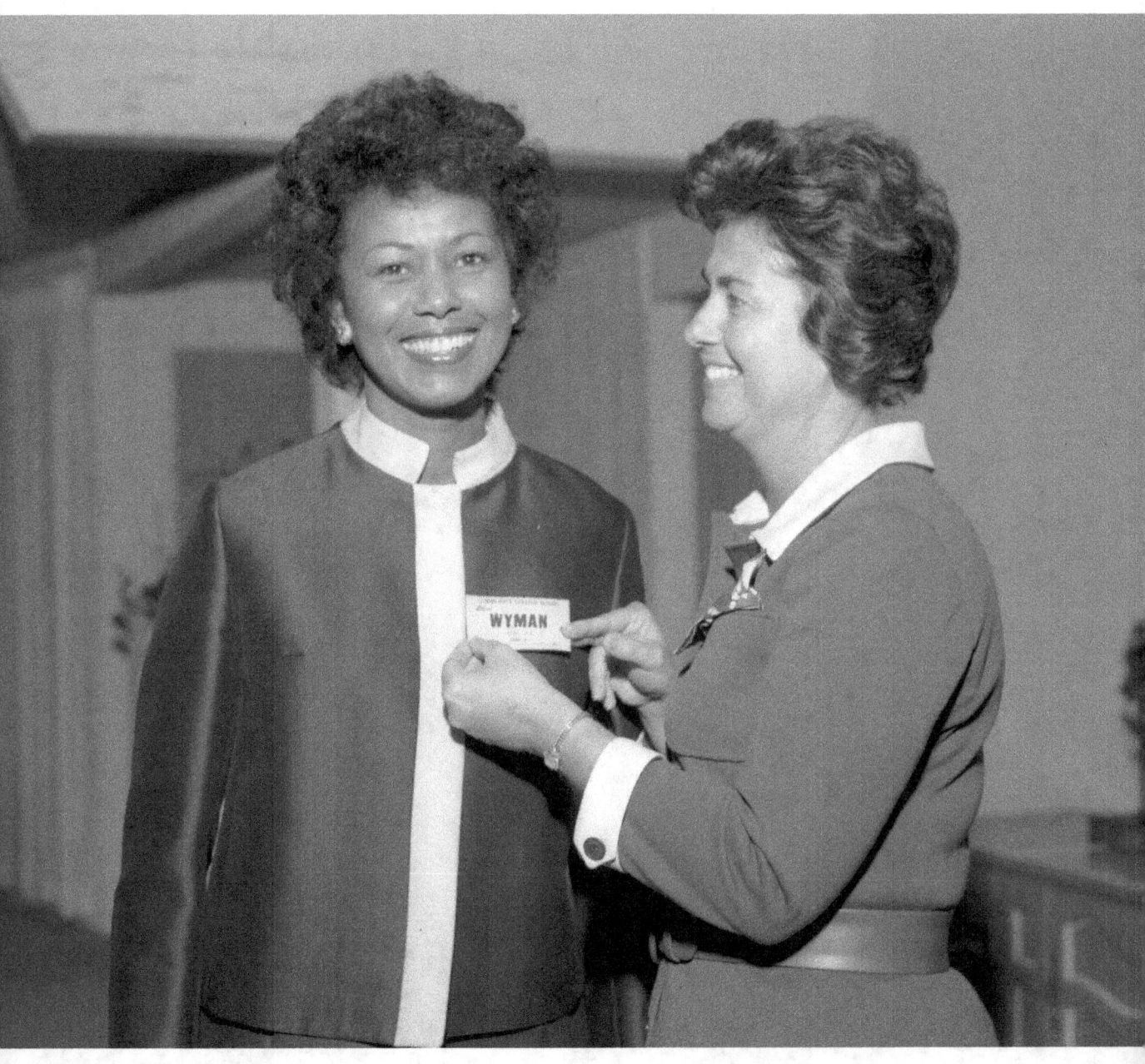

Rosalind Wyman pins a button to Yvonne Brathwaite Burke during Wyman's campaign for community college board. c1971

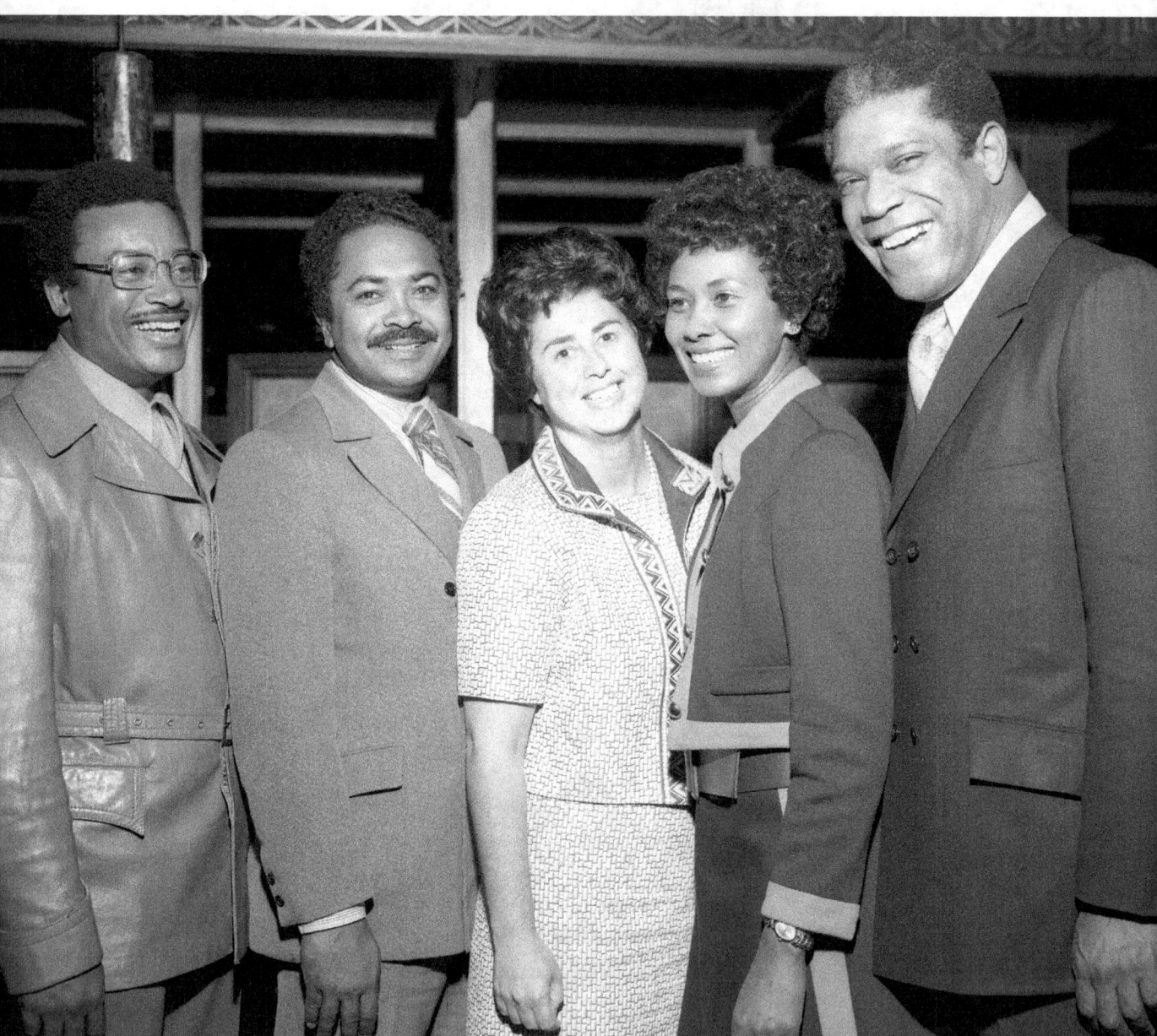

Yvonne Brathwaite Burke (*right*) with Assemblyman Leon Ralph (*far left*), Senator Mervyn Dymally (*left*), Rosalind Wyman (*center*) and Assemblyman Bill Greene (*far right*) at Operation Breadbasket meeting. 1971

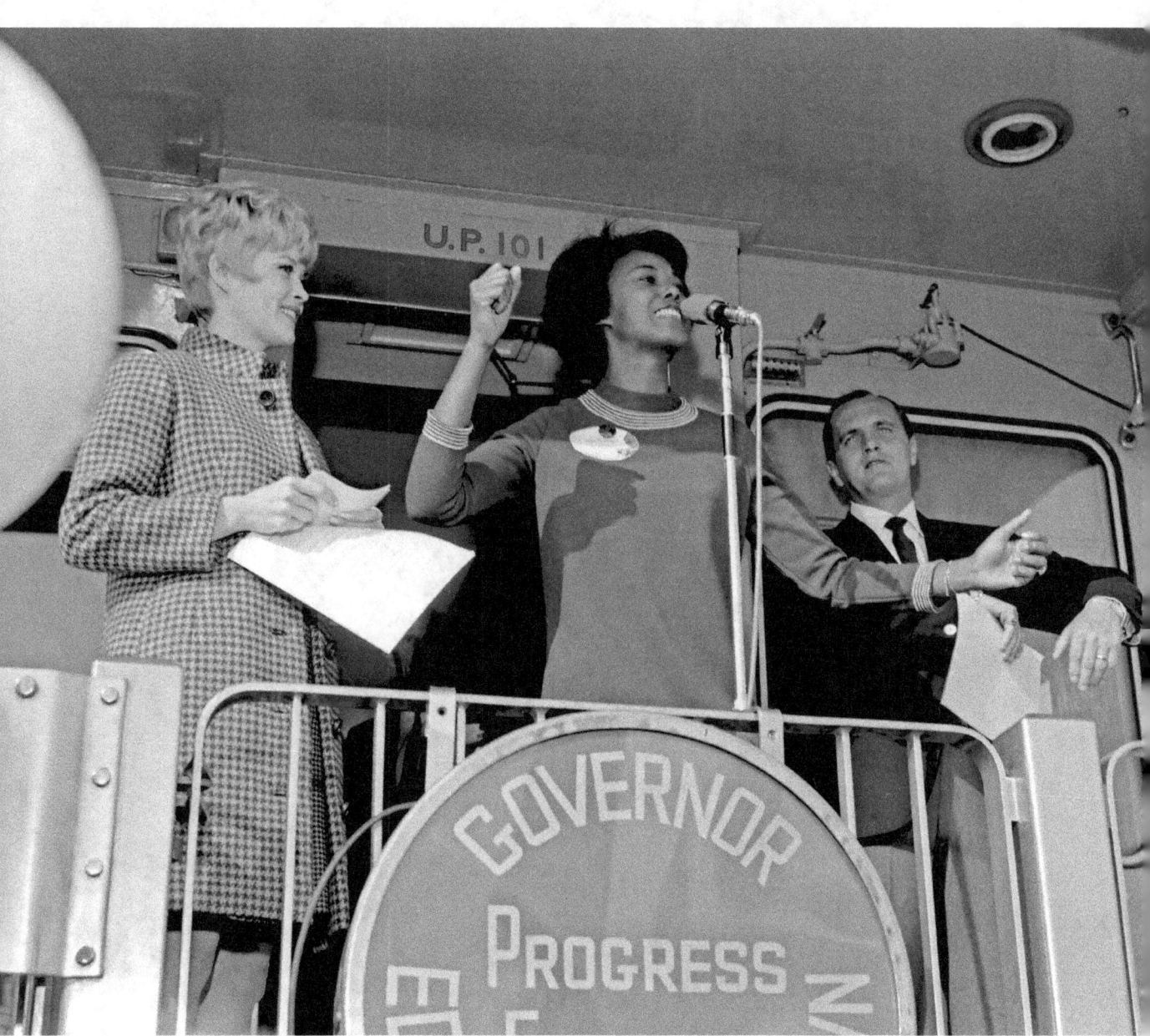

Yvonne Brathwaite Burke (*center*) speaks for Pat Brown during rally. She is joined by actress
Dorothy Provine (*left*) and actor Bob Newhart (*right*). October 30, 1966

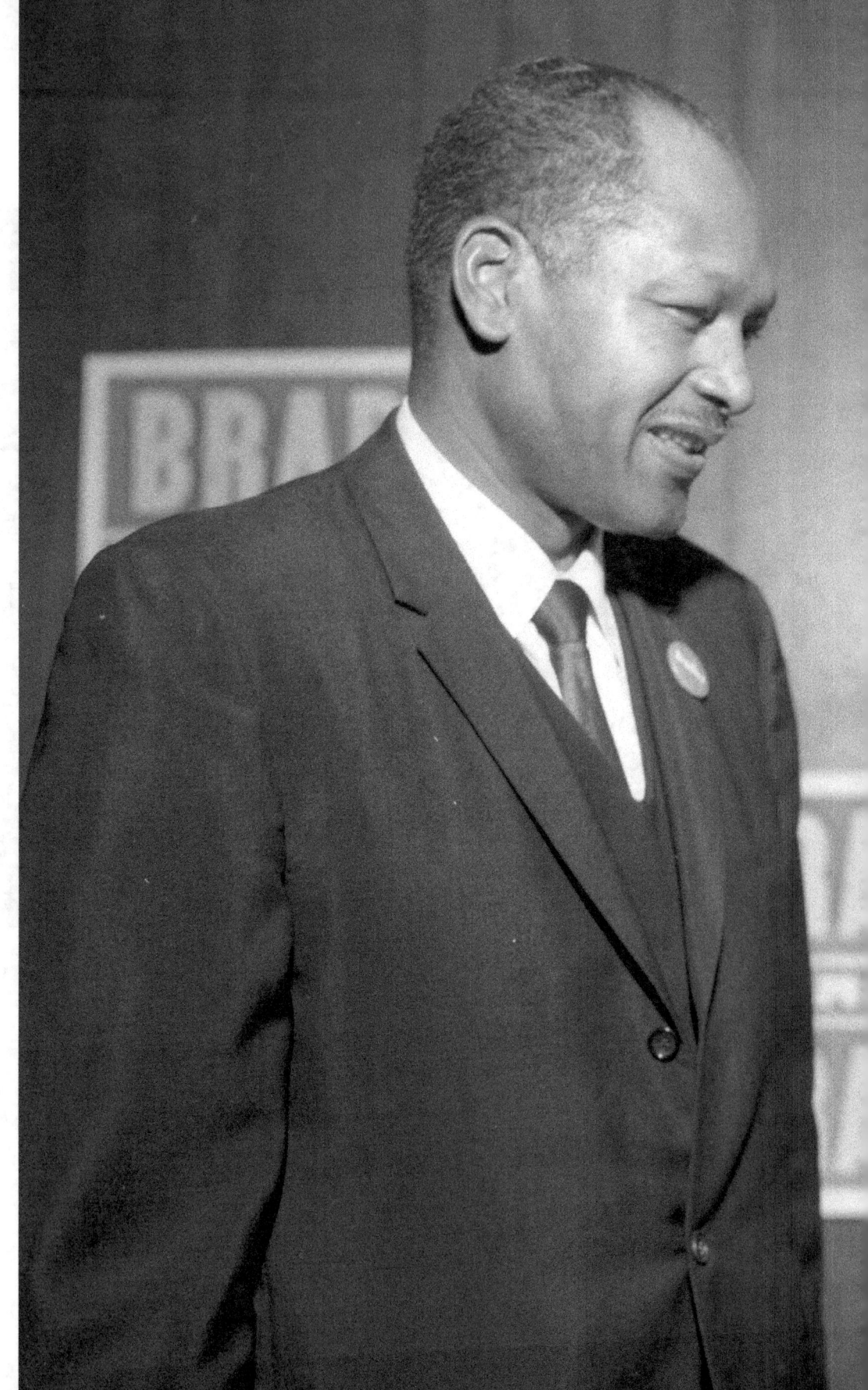

Tom Bradley
(*left*) with
Yvonne
Brathwaite
Burke (*right*)
at his mayoral
campaign
headquarters.
c1965

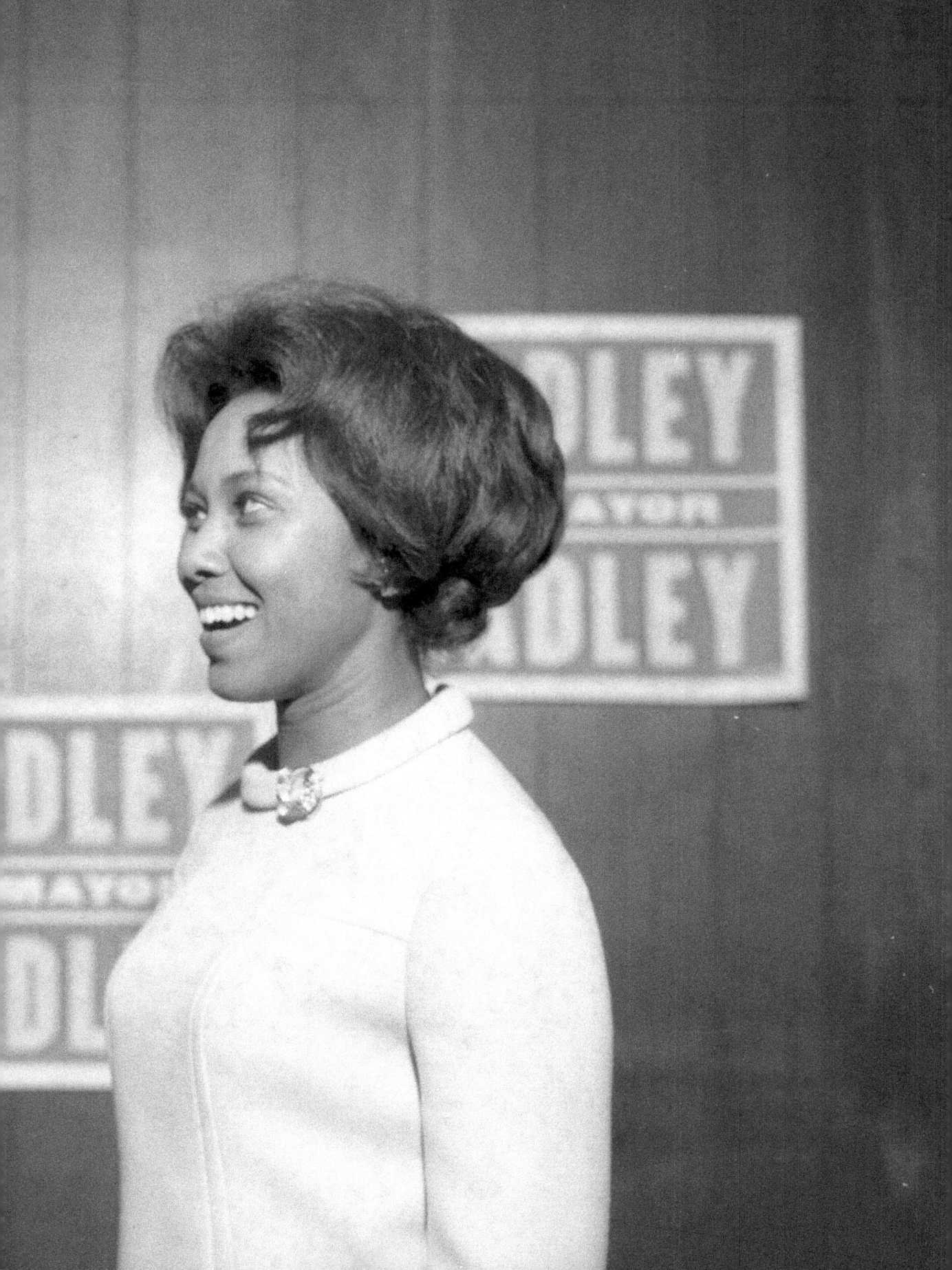

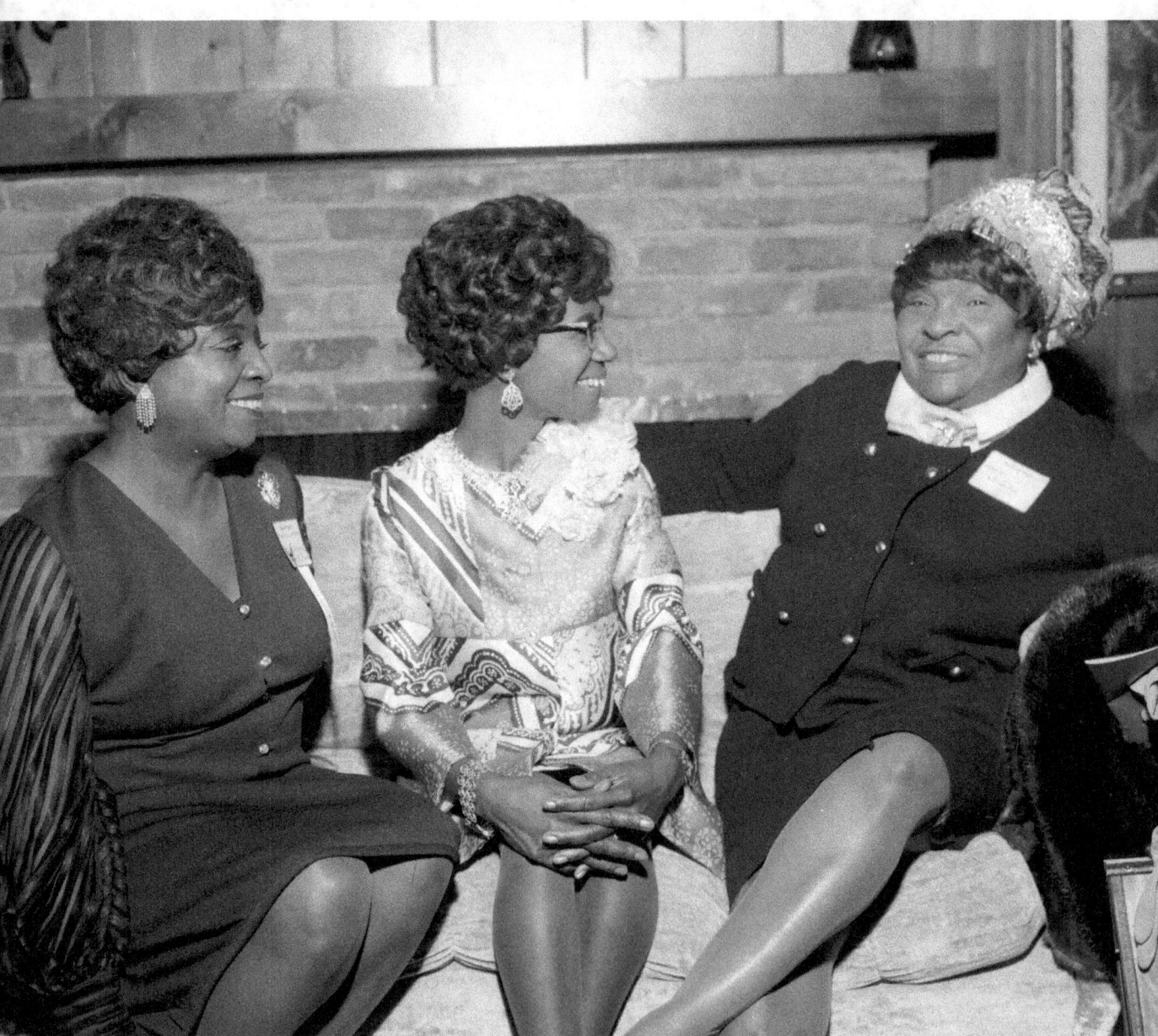

Shirley Chisholm (*center*) with ladies from the Committee of 19. January 1, 1970

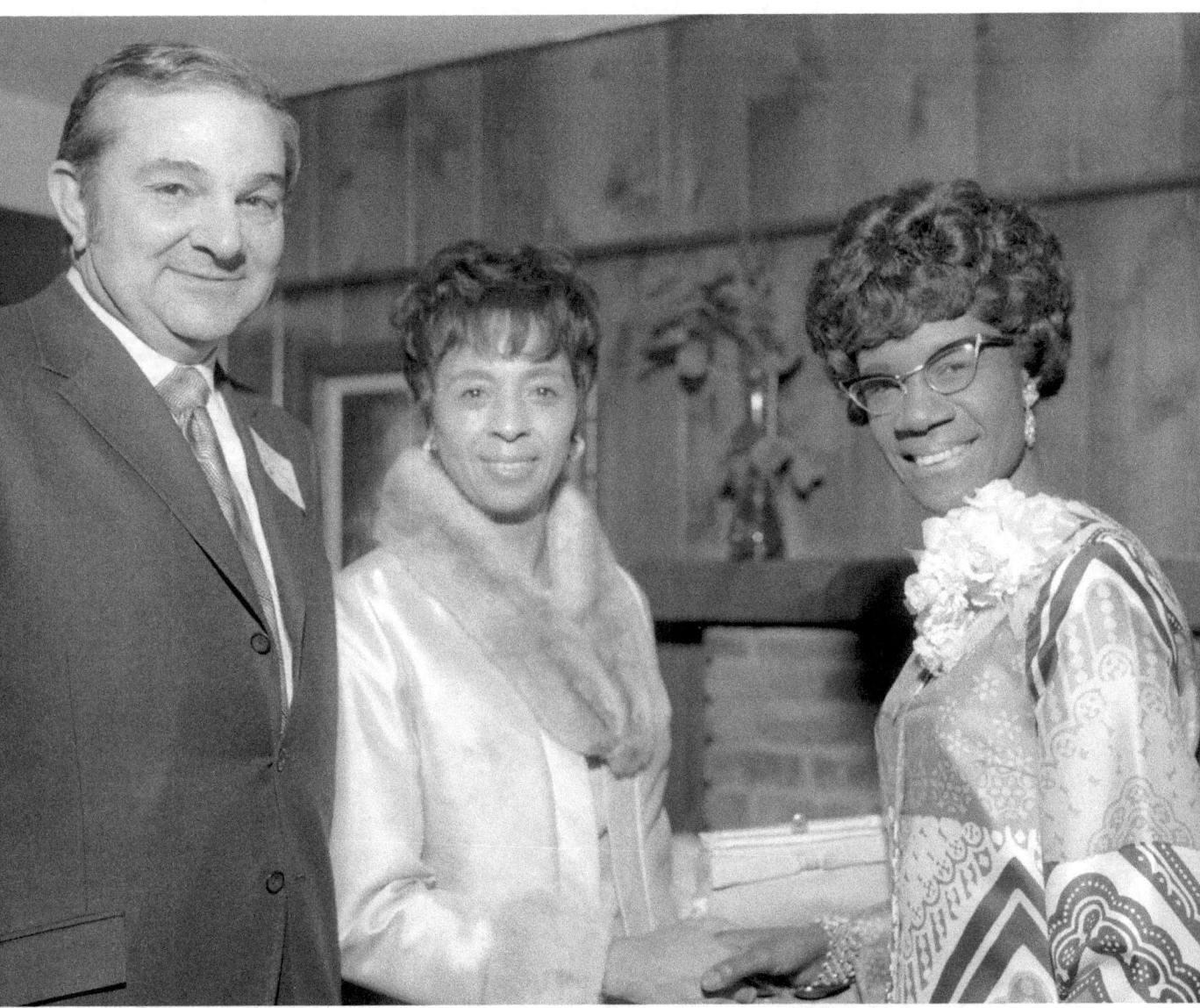

New York Congresswoman Shirley Chisholm is shown with Maria Cole (*center*) and George Brown (*left*), visiting Los Angeles at the invitation of the Committee of 19 Women for Better Government. Before Barack Obama and Hillary Rodham Clinton ran for president in 2008, Shirley Chisholm paved the way for both. Chisholm was the first African American woman elected to congress in 1969, and in 1972 she became not only the first African American to run as a major party candidate, but also the first woman to run for the Democratic presidential nomination, and the second woman ever to run as a major party candidate (second only to Margaret Chase Smith, who ran as a Republican). January 1, 1970

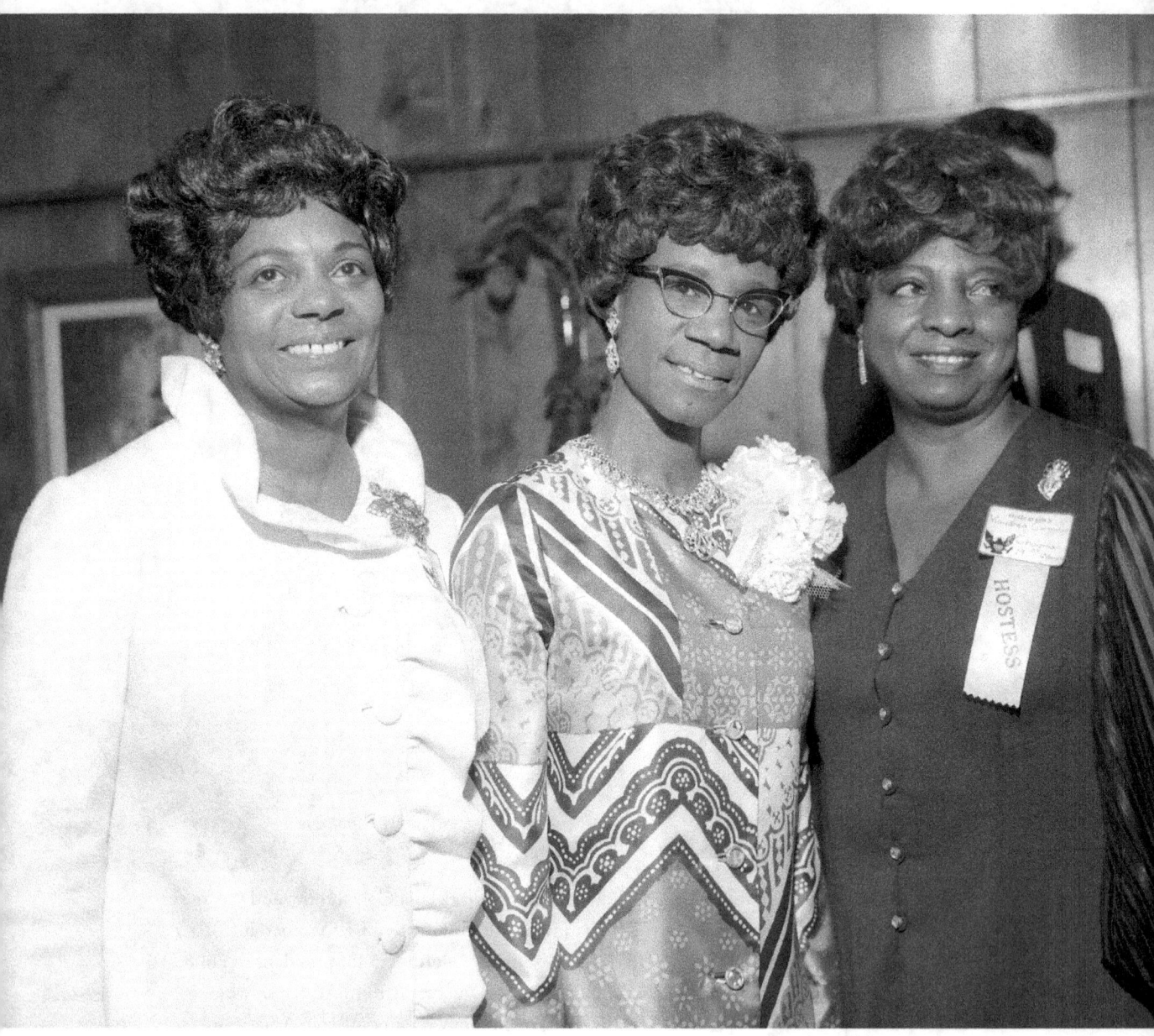

Shirley Chisholm (*center*) with ladies from the Committee of 19. January 1, 1970

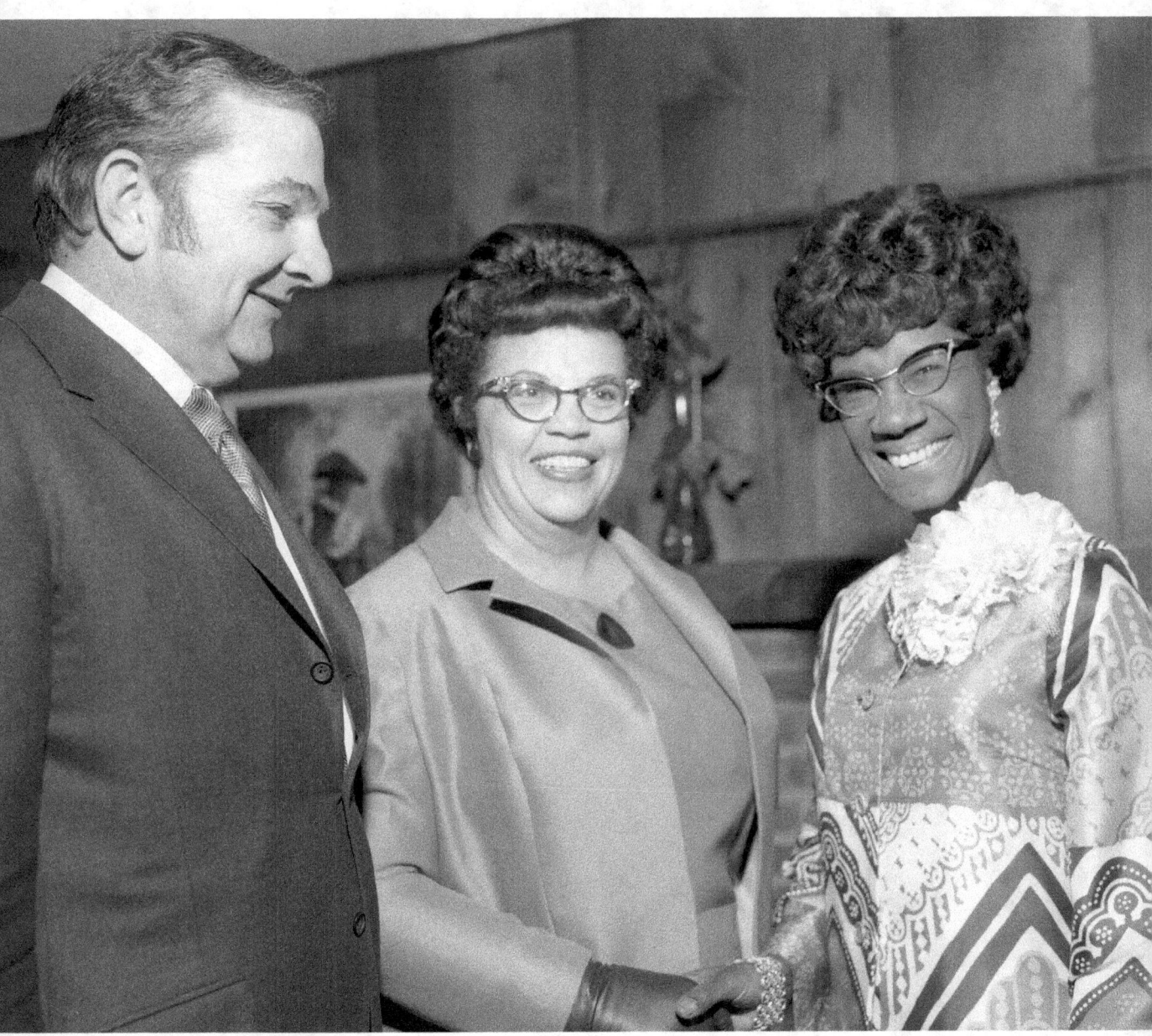

Shirley Chisholm (*right*) with Gloria Curtis (*center*) and George Brown (*left*).
January 1, 1970

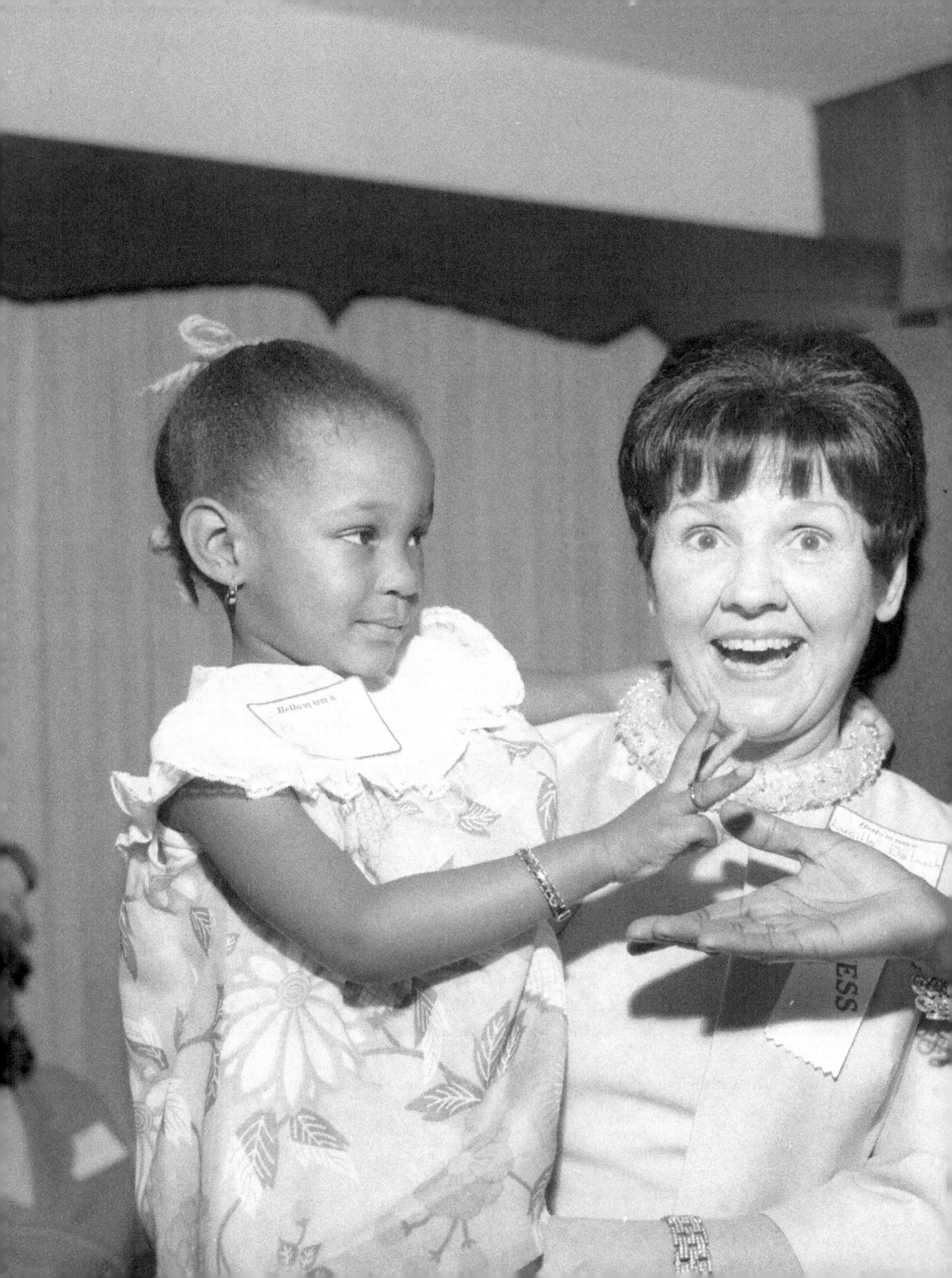

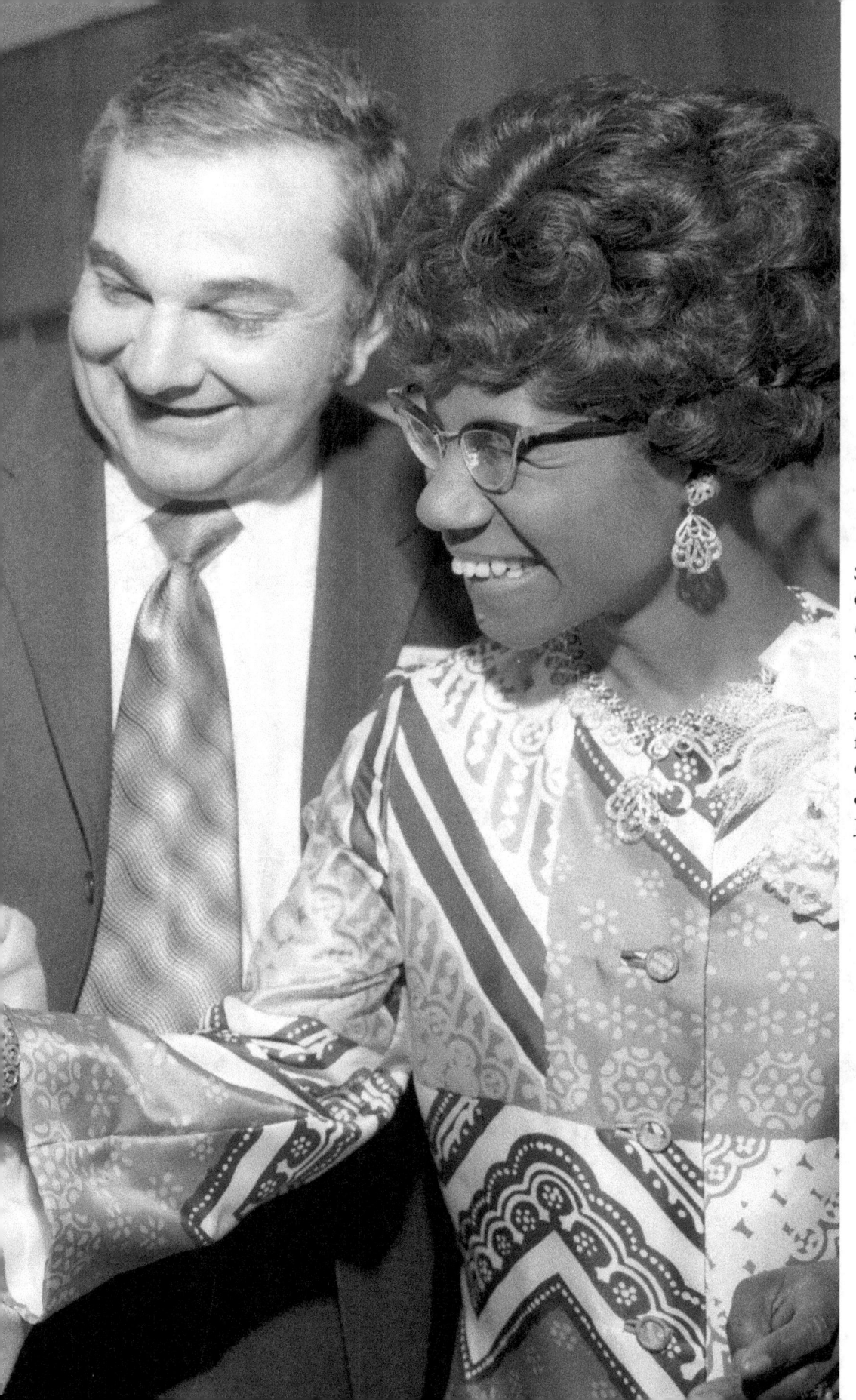

Shirley
Chisholm
(*far right*)
with George
Brown (*right*)
at reception
for the
Committee
of 19.
January 1,
1970

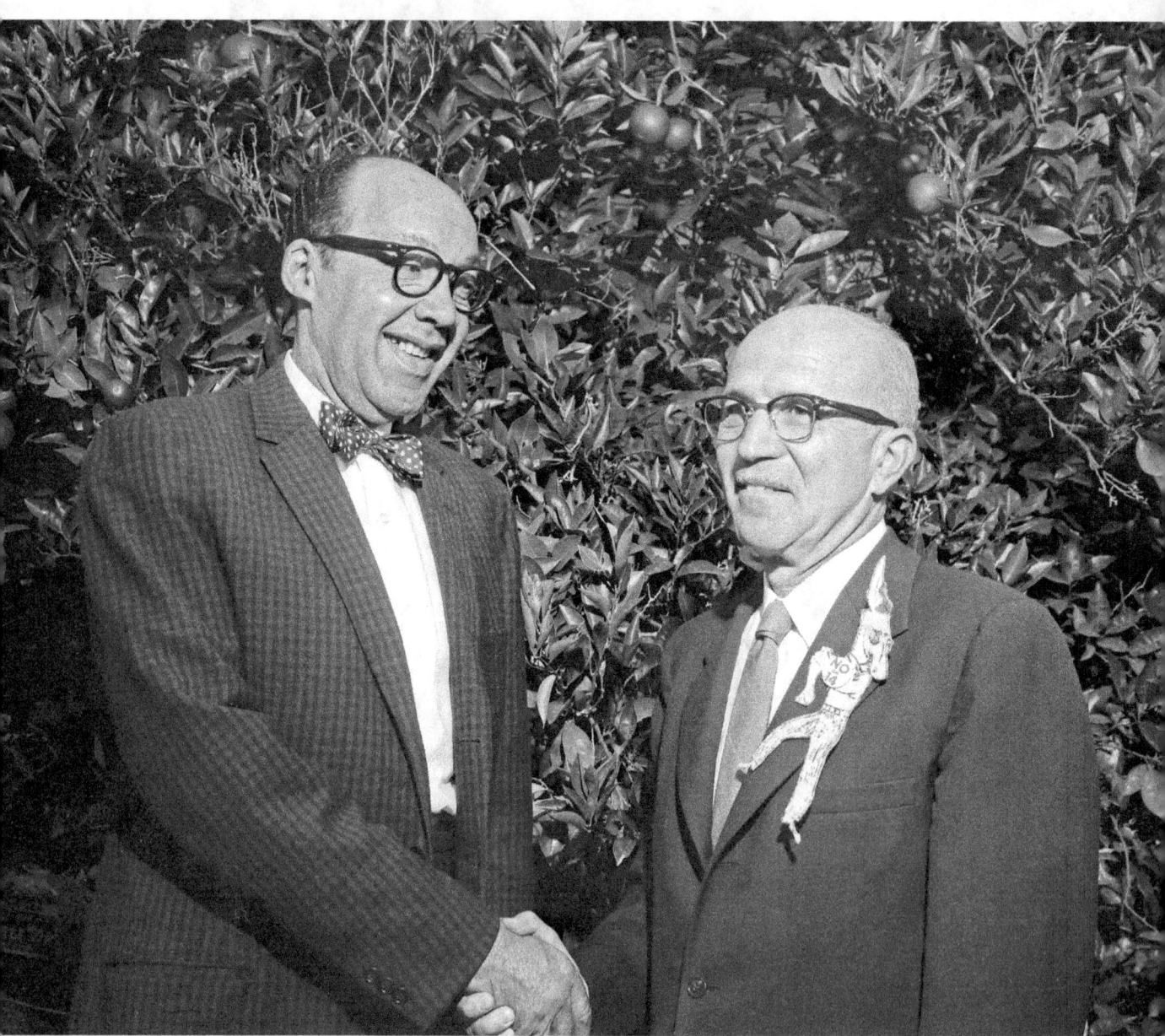

Augustus Hawkins (*right*) at garden party for Byron Rumford. September 17, 1964

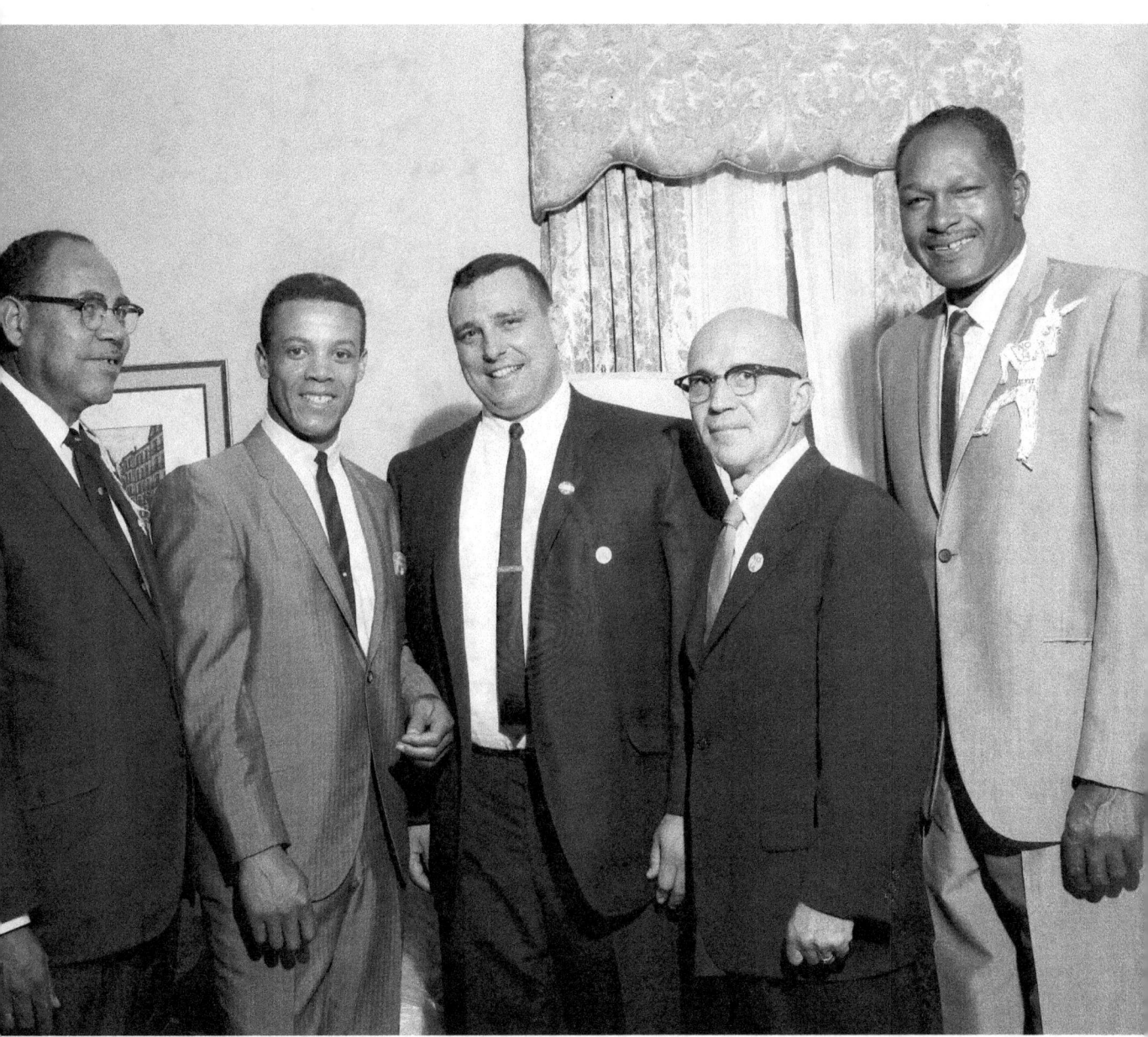

Augustus Hawkins (*right*) with Assemblyman Byron Rumford (*far left*), baseball player
Maury Wills (*left*) and Tom Bradley (*far right*) at garden party for Byron Rumford.
September 17, 1964

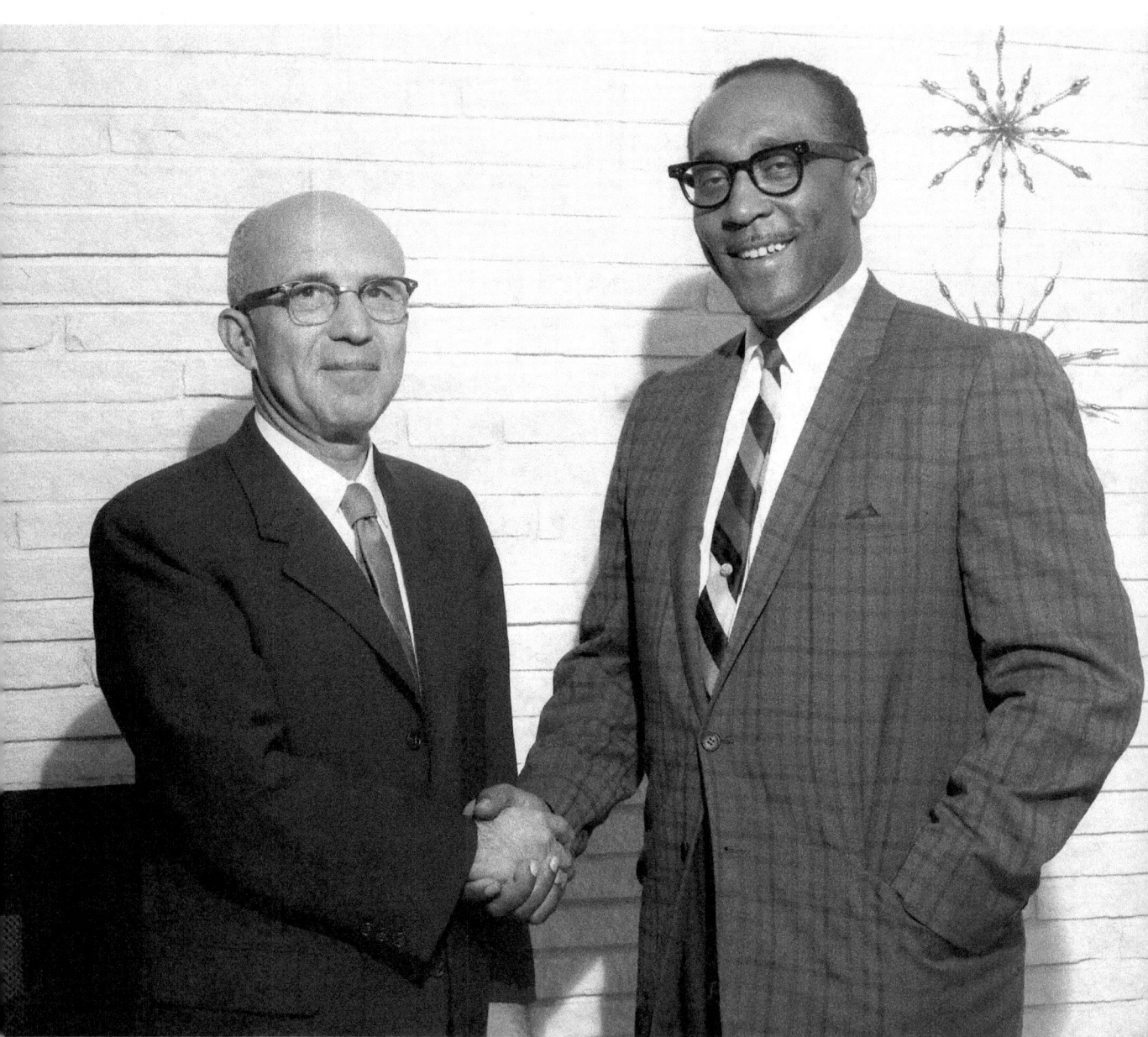

Augustus Hawkins (*left*) shakes hands with Rev. H.H. Brookins (*right*). c1963

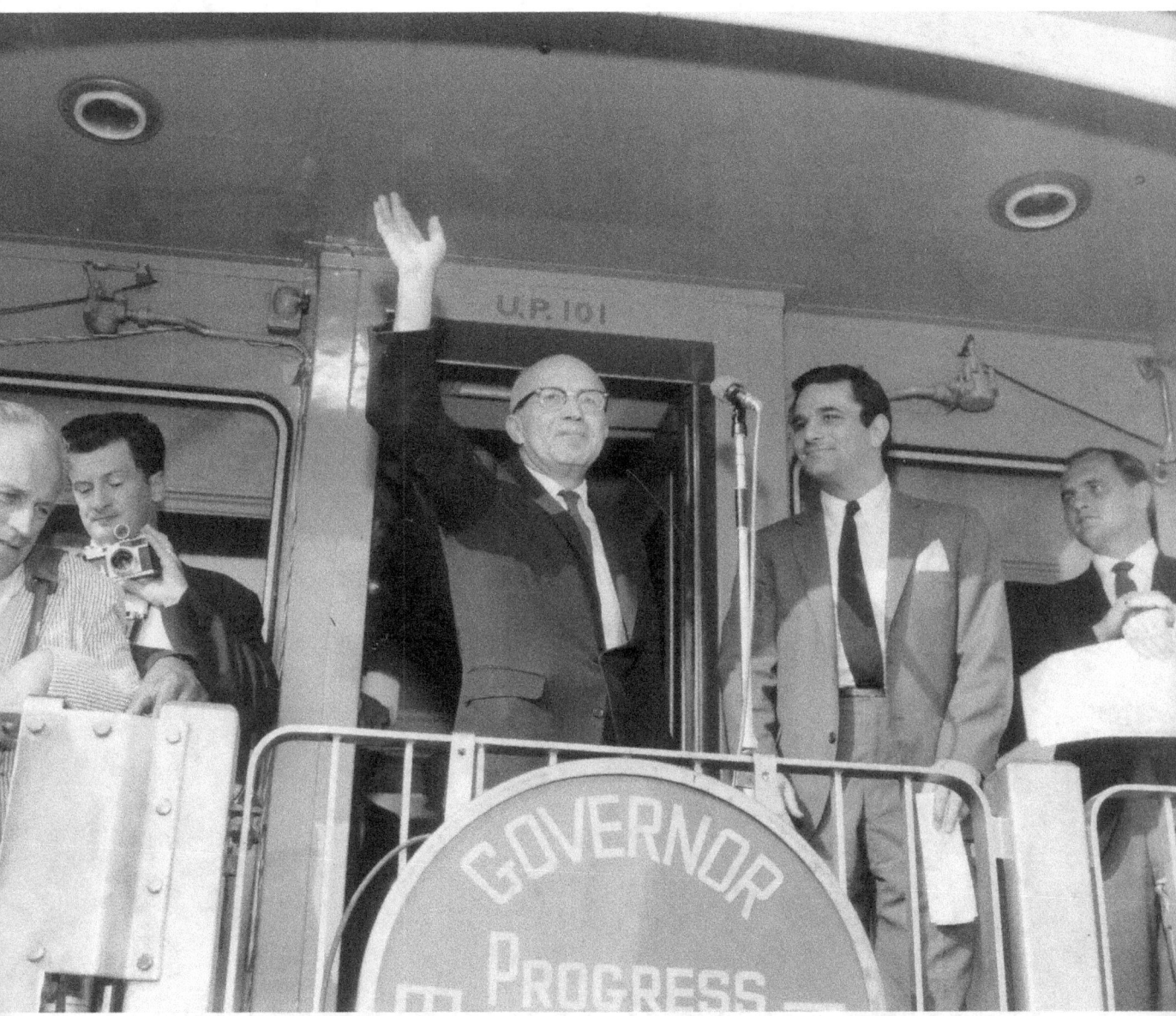

Augustus Hawkins (*center*) with Peter Falk (*right*) and Bob Newhart (*far right*), was the second African American elected to the California assembly, the first African American to serve California in Congress and the first black politician west of the Mississippi River elected to the House of Representatives. Hawkins was fair skinned, often being mistaken for white and given preferential treatment on buses while growing up, much to his anger. He chose to walk instead. He was a champion of equal employment opportunities, fair housing and civil rights. October 30, 1966

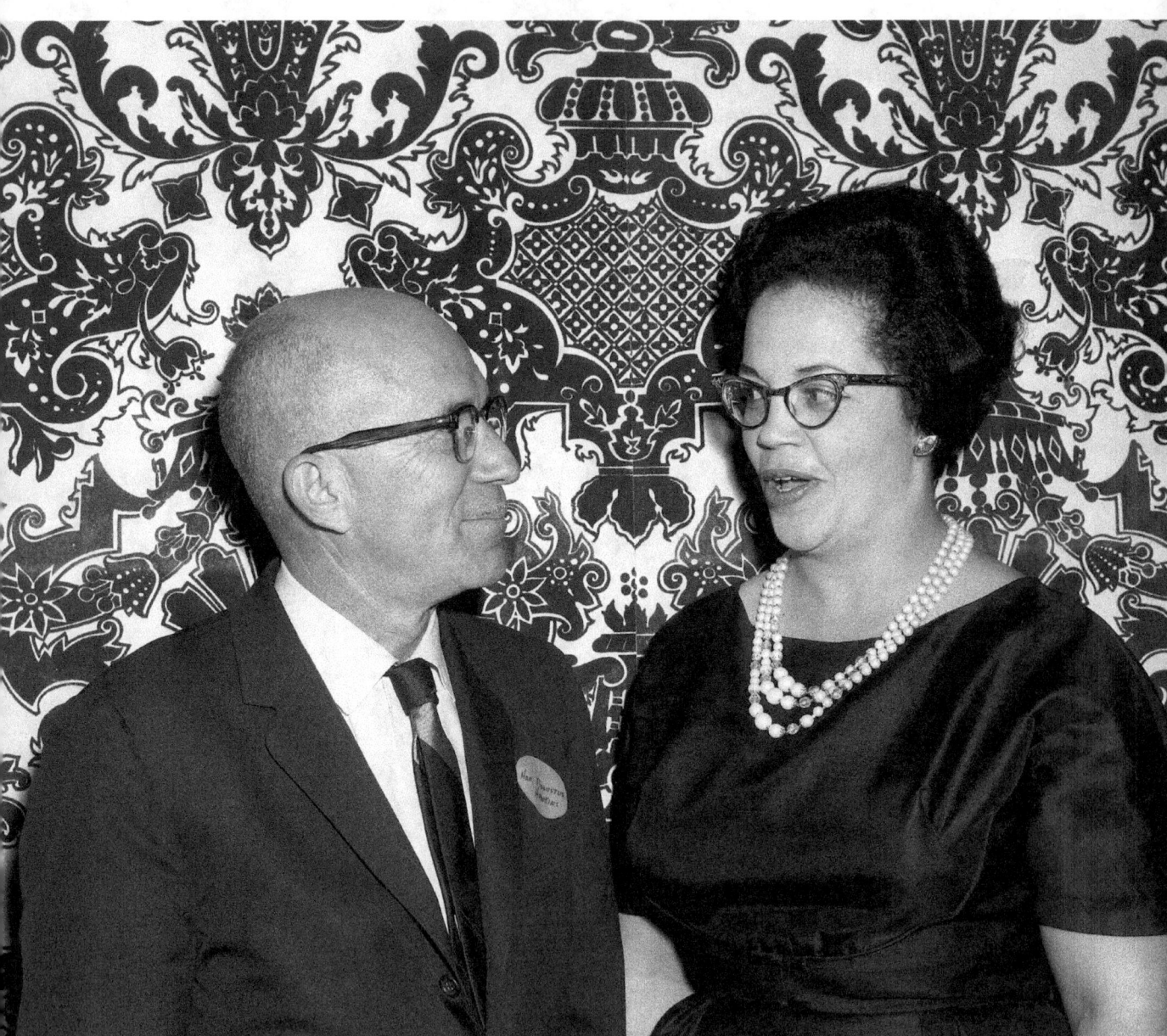

Augustus Hawkins (*left*) with Gloria Curtis (*right*) at the Ambassador Hotel. c1964
*Opposite*: Mervyn Dymally (*right*) with City Councilmen Billy G. Mills (*far left*), Tom Bradley (*left*) and Gilbert Lindsay (*far right*). c1964

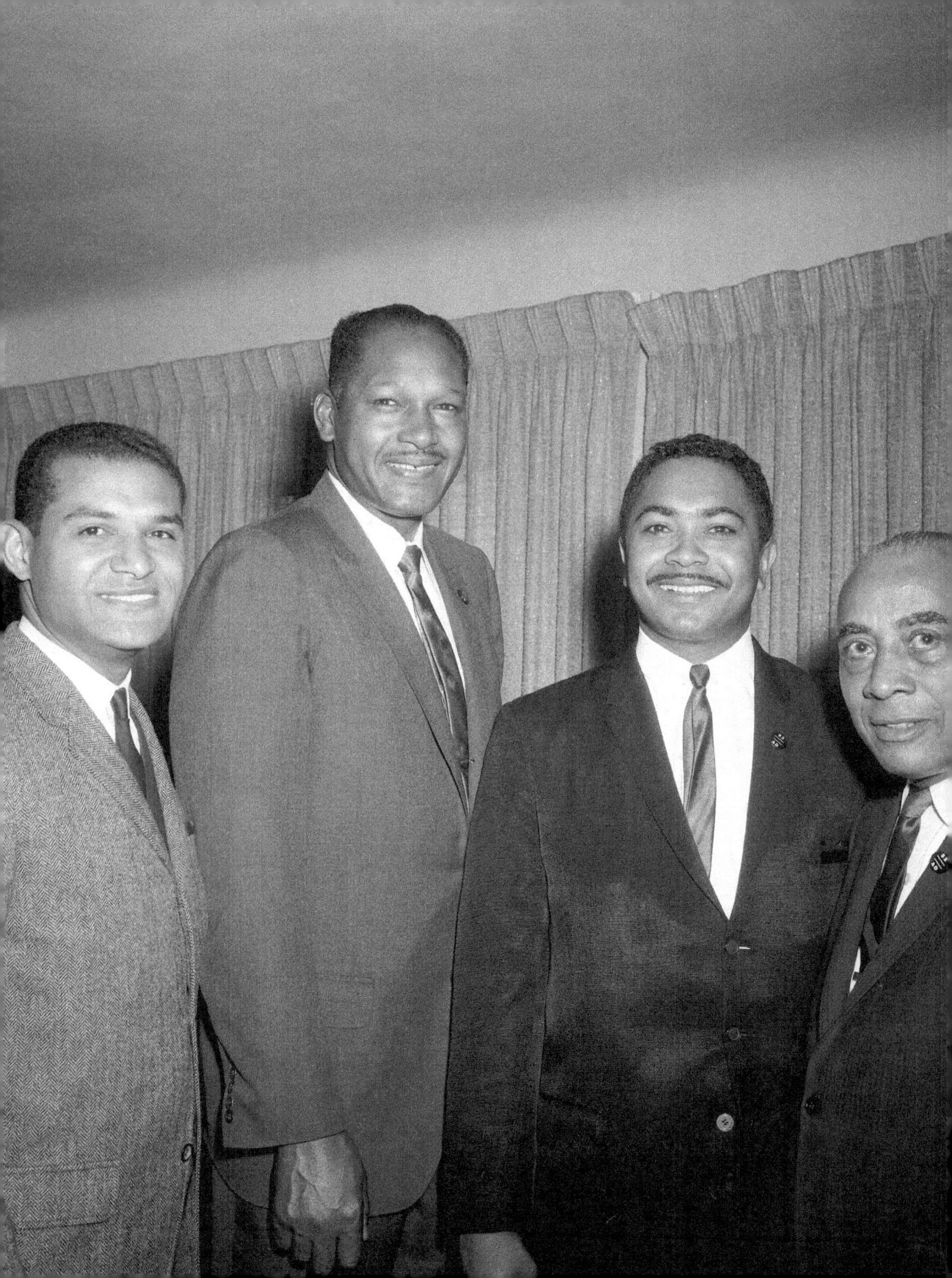

*Opposite*: Mervyn Dymally (*right*) meets Muhammad Ali (*left*) at a Compton NAACP meeting. Born in Trinidad, Dymally moved to the U.S. at the age of nineteen and became a citizen in 1957. In 1962, he became the first foreign-born black lawmaker elected to the assembly. In 1966, he was the first African American elected to the state senate, and California's first African American lieutenant governor in 1974. Dymally had amazing staying power. In 2002, he found himself dissatisfied with the candidates for his original assembly seat and chose to run again, winning back the seat he'd left at the age of 76. October 20, 1966

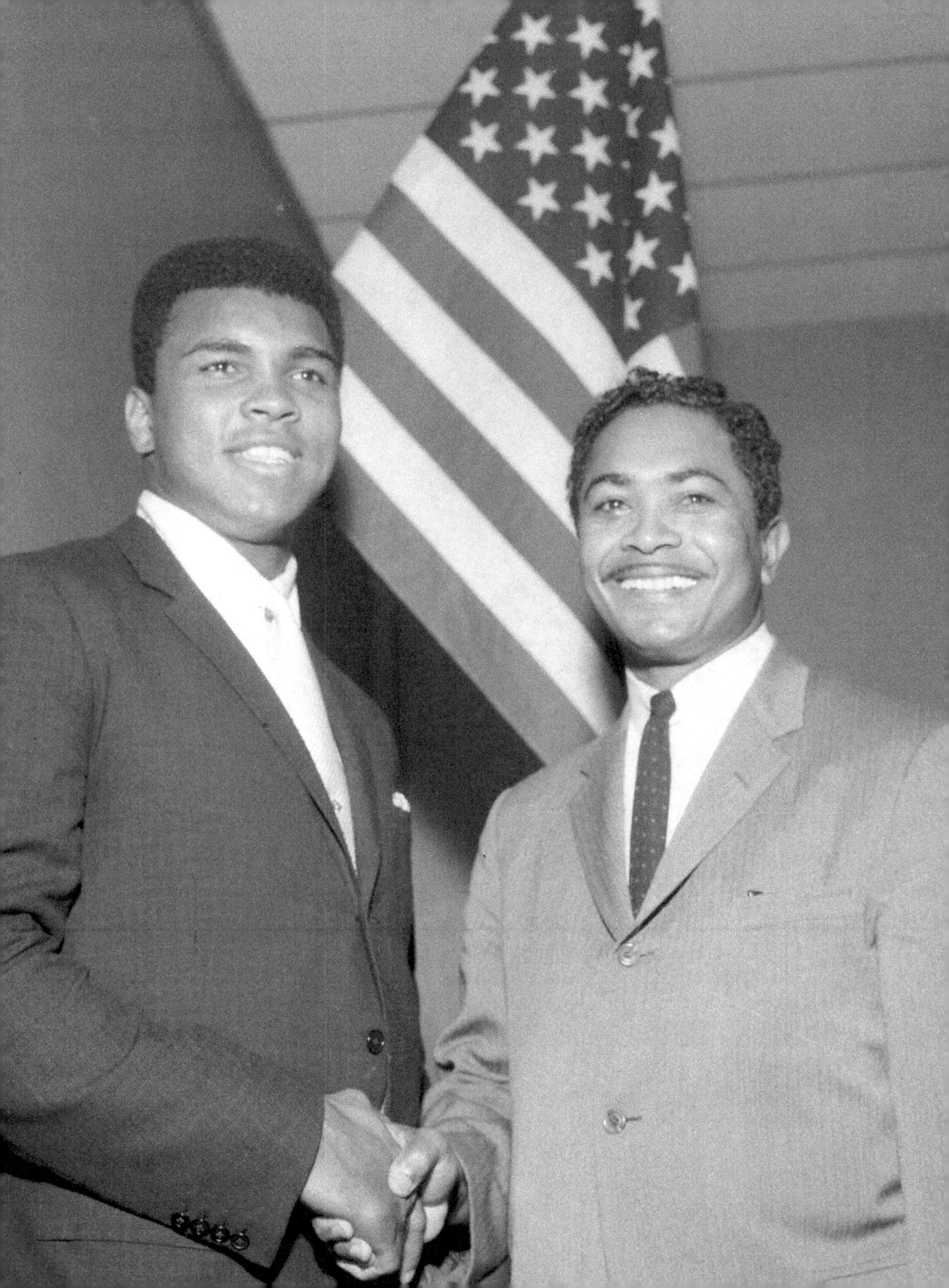

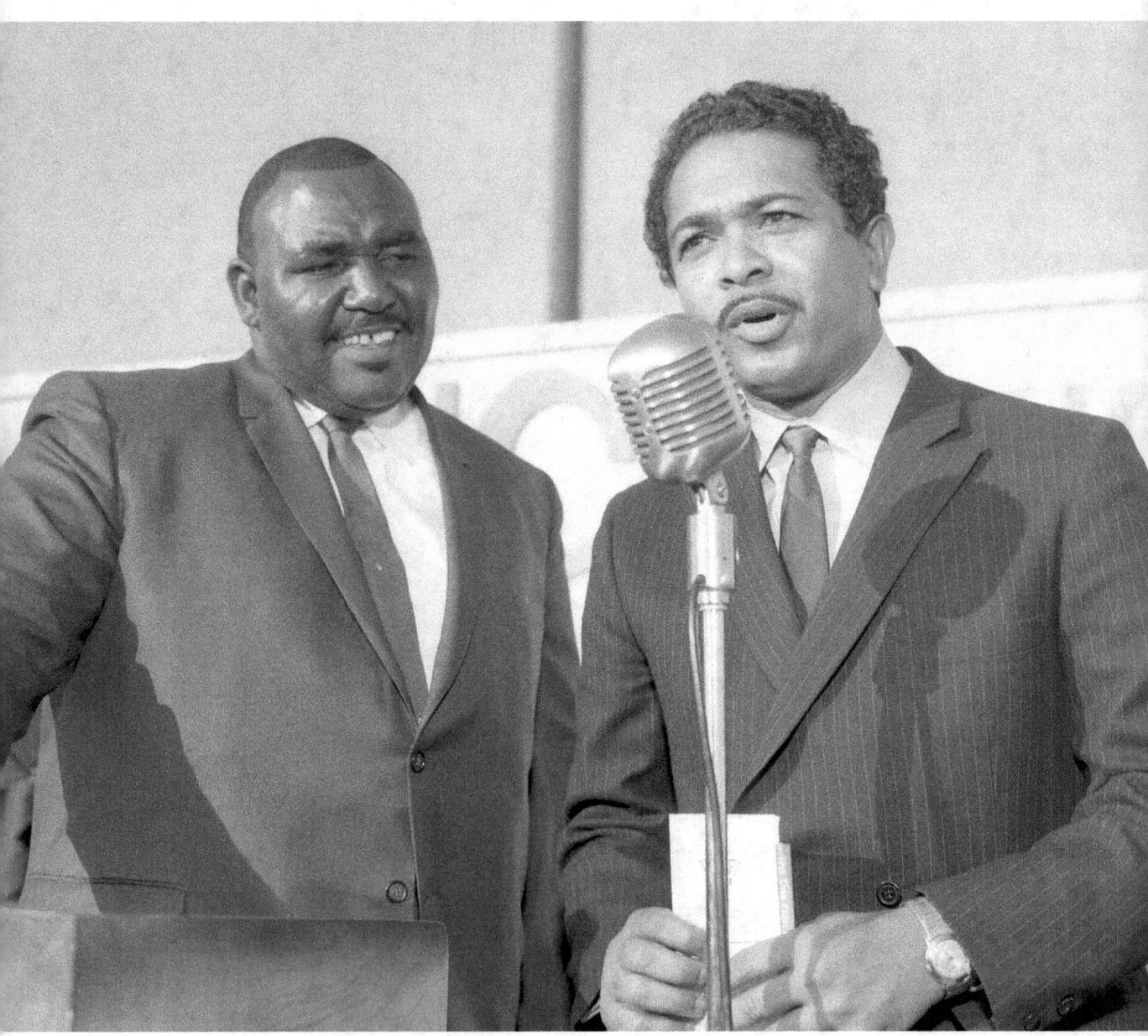

Mervyn Dymally (*right*) speaks during award ceremony outside of CCC Mission Possible headquarters. February 29, 1968

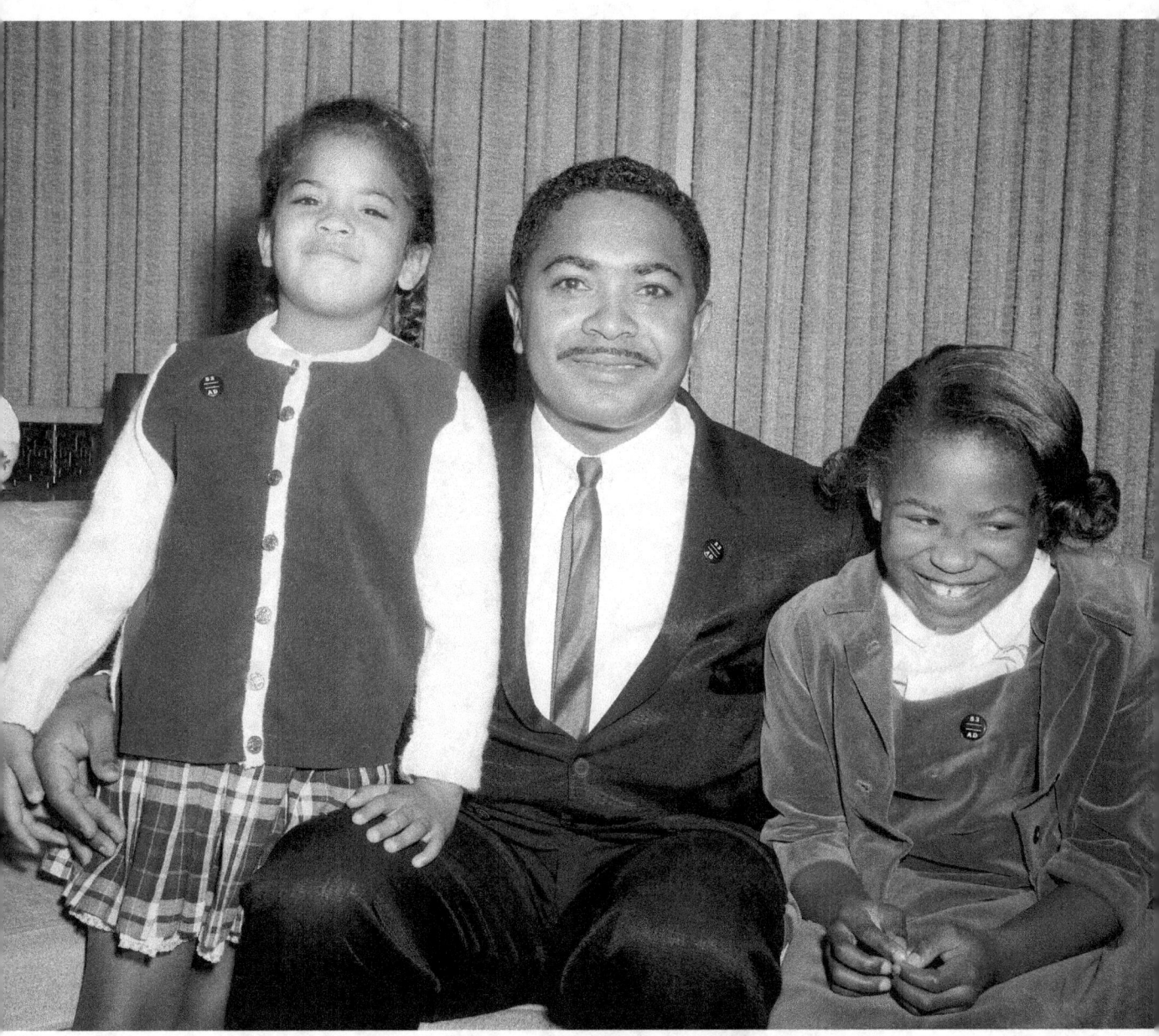

Mervyn Dymally with children at city council office. c1964

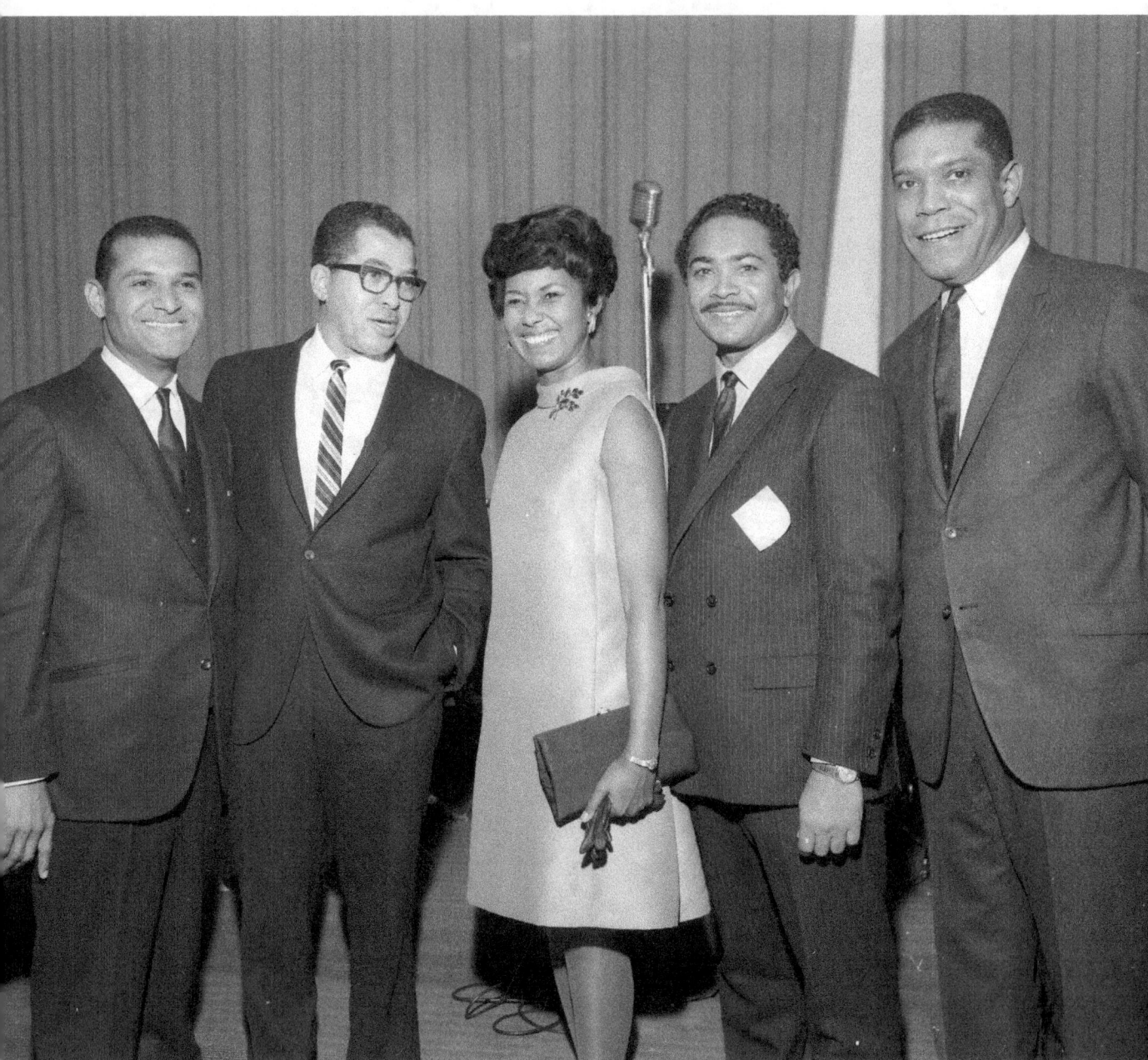

Mervyn Dymally (*right*) with Billy G. Mills (*far left*), Yvonne Brathwaite Burke (*center*) and Bill Greene (*far right*).

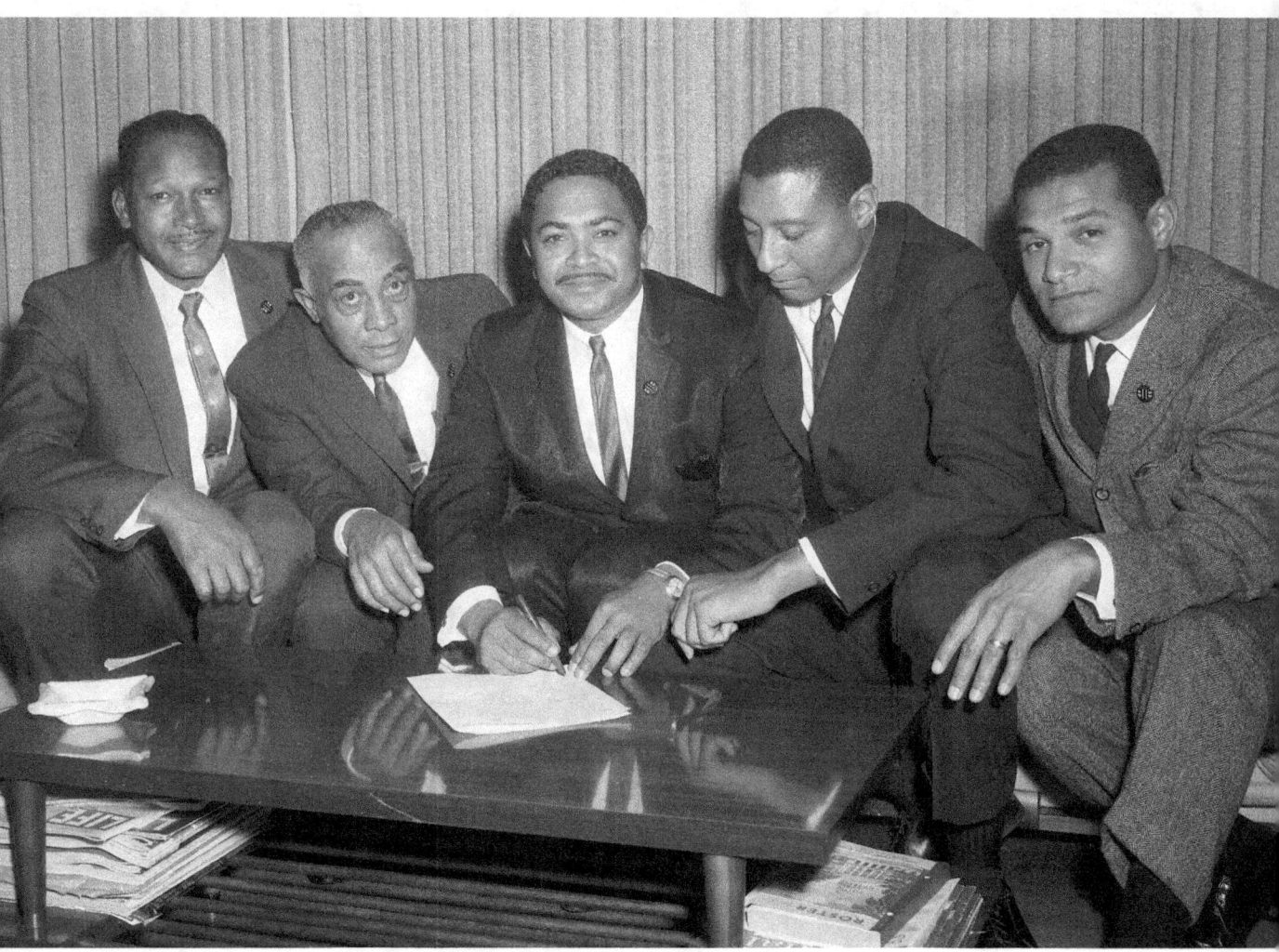

Mervyn Dymally (*center*) with Tom Bradley (*far left*), Gilbert Lindsay (*left*), William Williams (*right*) and Billy G. Mills (*far right*). c1964

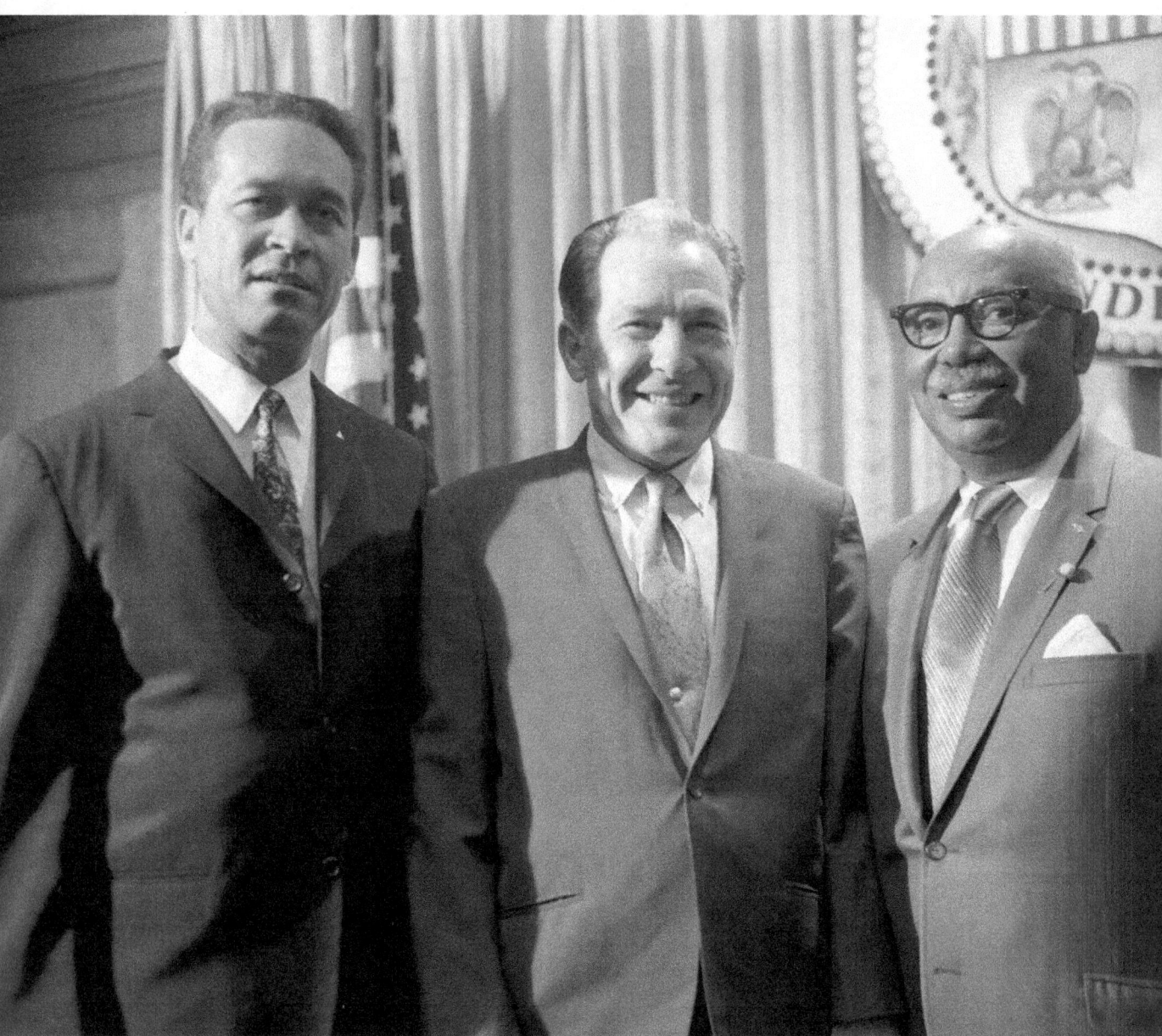

Douglas Dollarhide (*left*) receives plaque from Mayor Sam Yorty (*center*) with Leon Washington (*right*). Dollarhide was the first black city councilman elected in Compton in 1963. By 1969, he was the mayor of Compton, a city that had been predominantly white, but by 1969 had become 65% black. Compton became the largest city west of the Mississippi to elect a black mayor when they elected Dollarhide, who began his career as a mail carrier. August 14, 1970

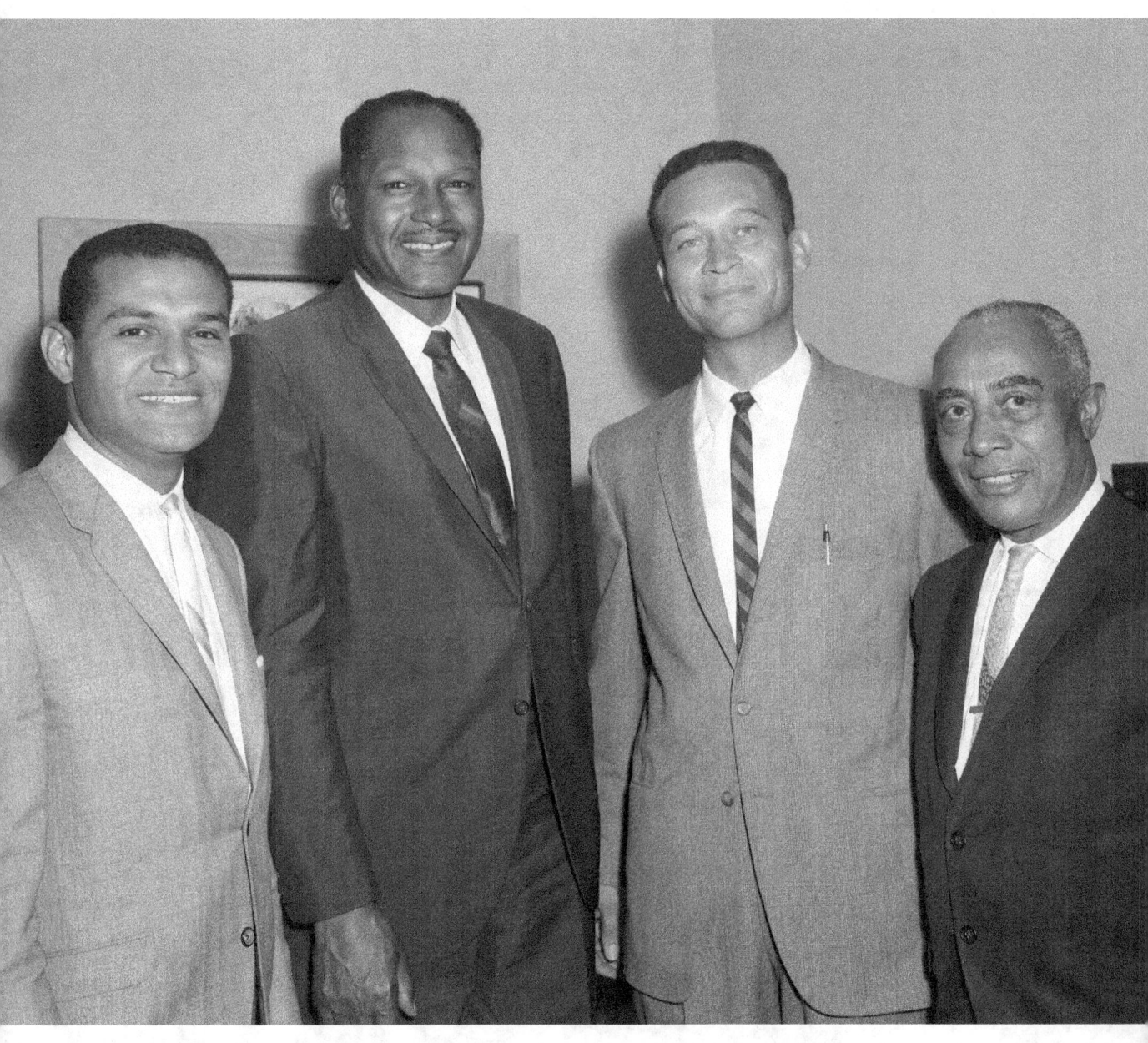

Douglas Dollarhide (*right*) with City Councilmen Billy G. Mills (*far left*), Tom Bradley (*left*) and Gilbert Lindsay (*far right*). c1960s

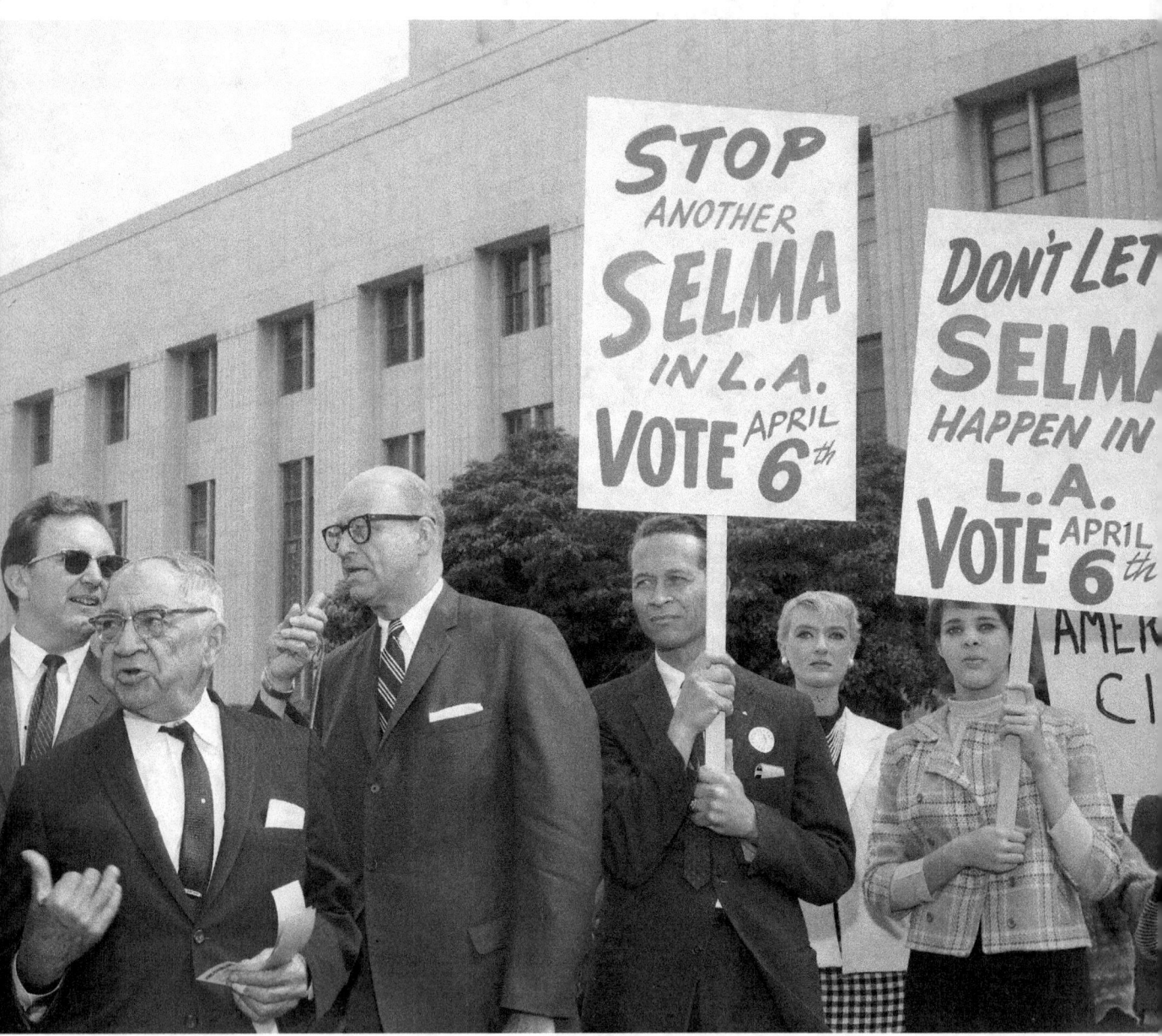

Douglas Dollarhide (*center*) with Claude Hudson (*far left*) and Congressman James Roosevelt (*left*) at Prop. 14 protest. c1964

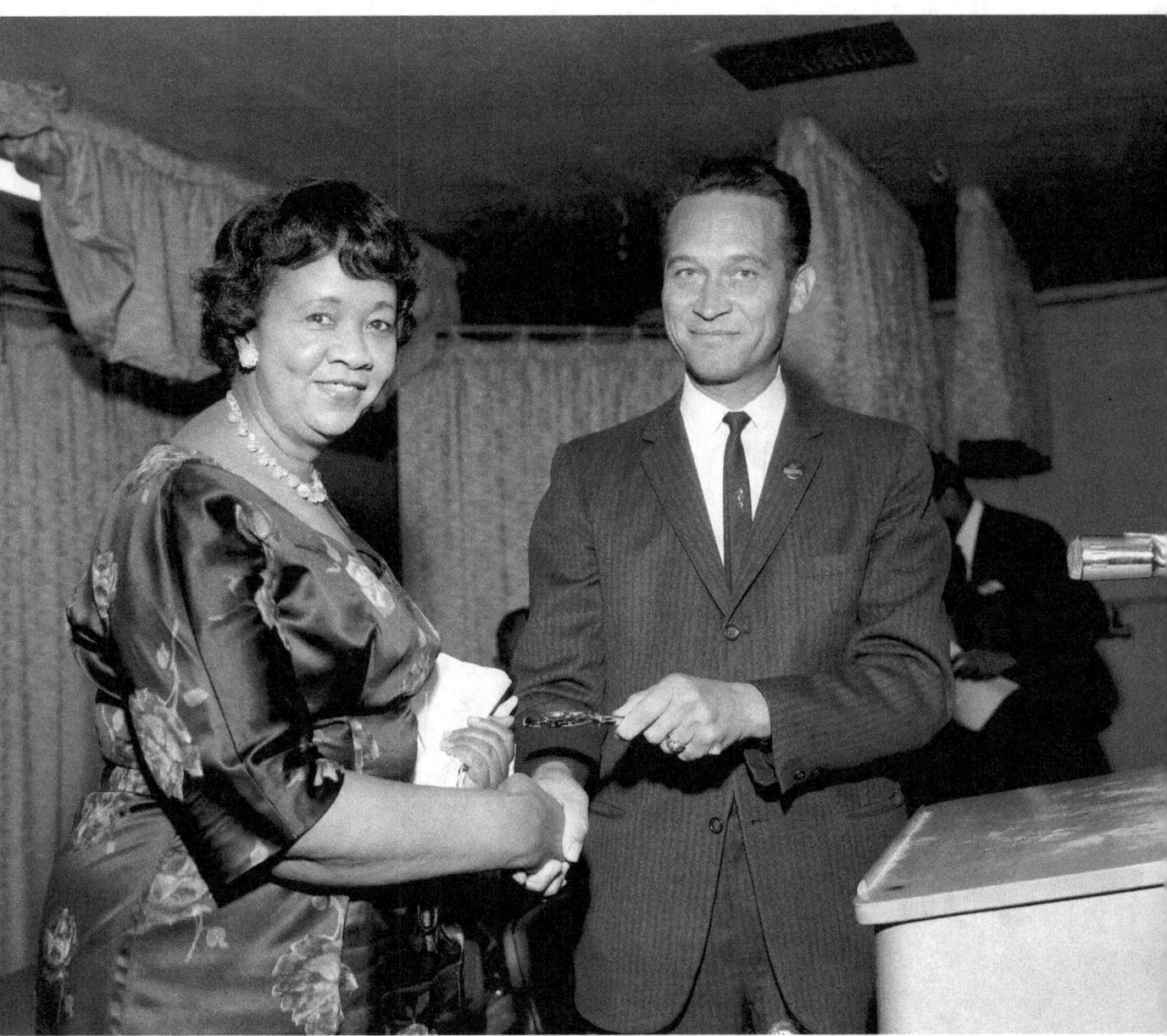

Douglas Dollarhide (*right*) shakes hands with Dr. Dorothy Height (*left*), the "Queen Mother of Civil Rights" at a rally for Pat Brown. c1966

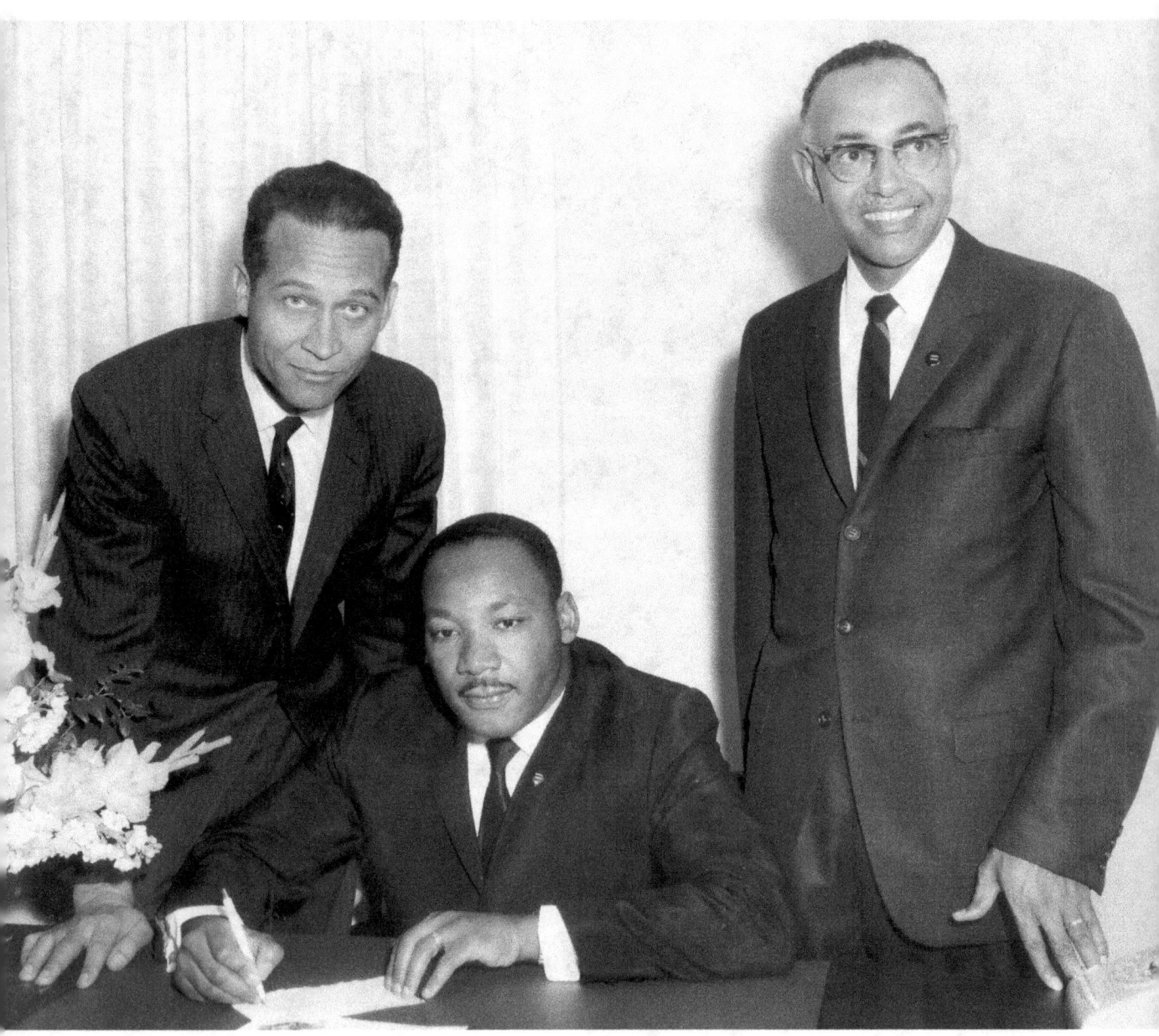

Douglas Dollarhide (*standing left*) with Martin Luther King (*center*) and Rev. Thomas Kilgore (*standing right*). c1964

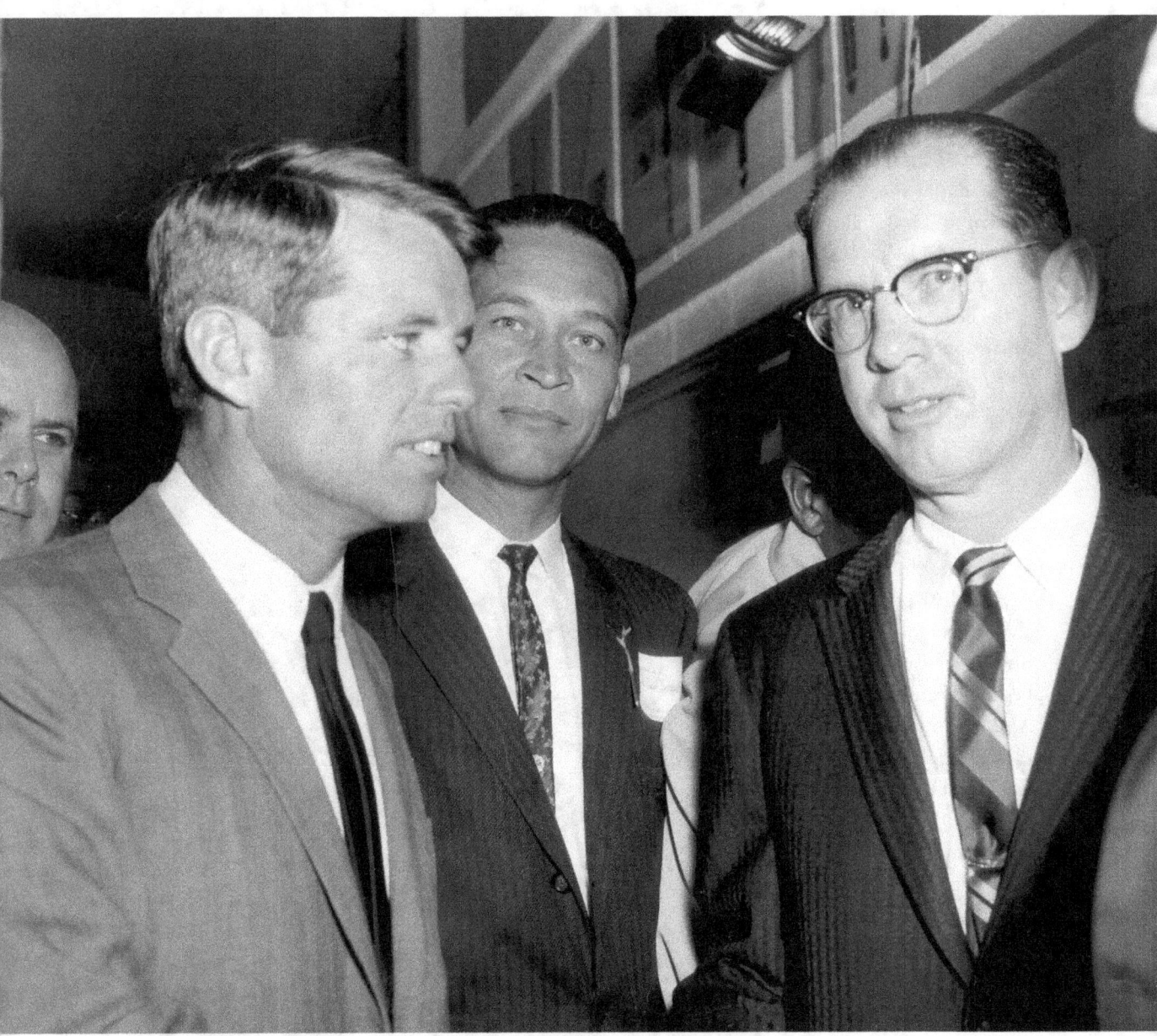

Douglas Dollarhide (*center*) with Robert Kennedy (*left*) and Kenneth Hahn (*right*) while campaigning at Markham Junior High. June 9, 1964

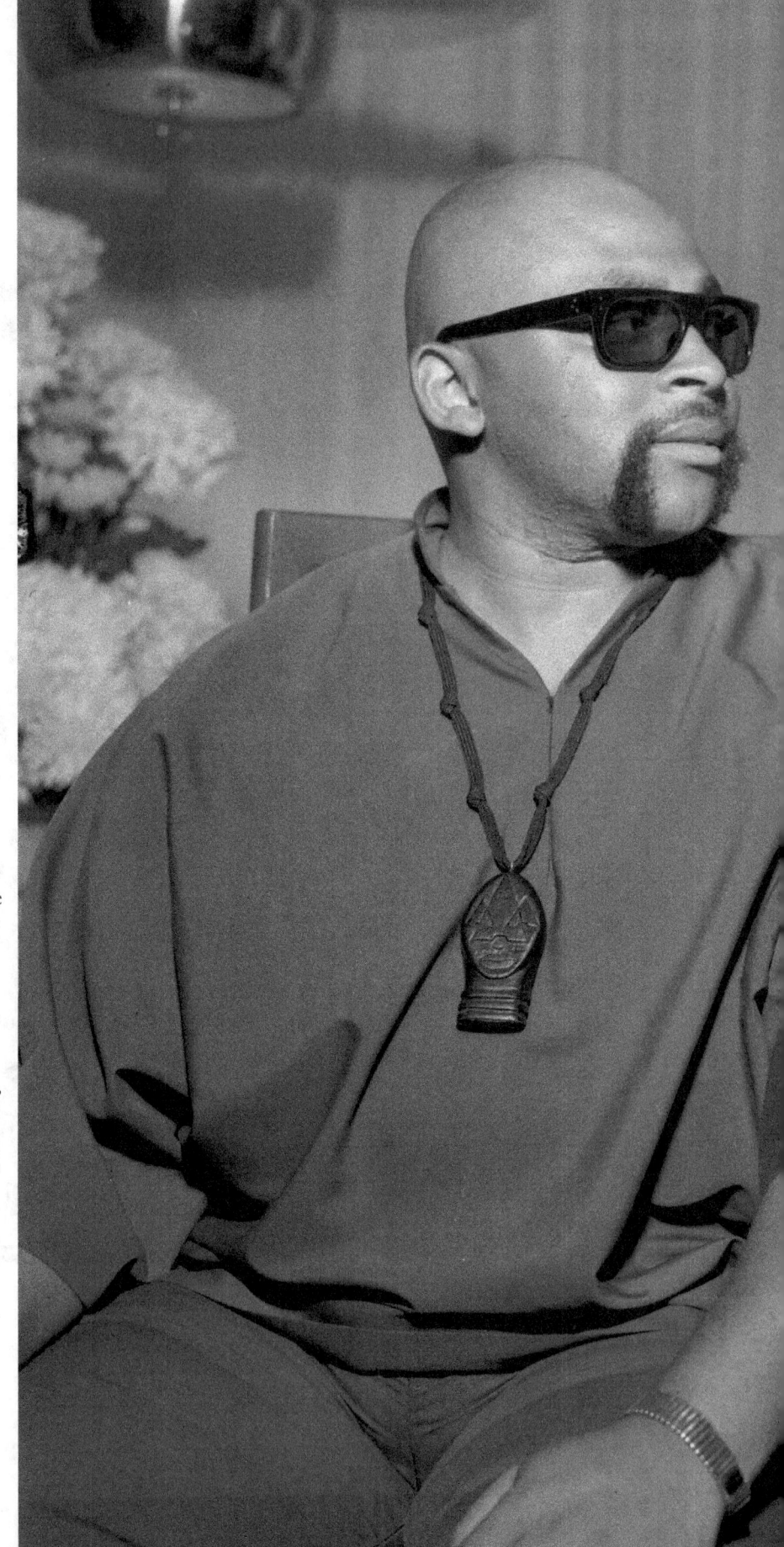

Bill Greene (*right*) with Ron
Karenga (*left*). Bill Greene
was a freedom rider in the
South, during the violent
years of the Civil Rights
Movement. Having served a
prison sentence for his part
in the demonstrations in
Mississippi, he escaped from
a Louisiana jail after another
arrest and became a fugitive,
shortly before becoming
engaged to his wife. "I spent
most of our honeymoon
sewing up his ragged clothes.
He was one of the larger
guys, and the police force
always went for him first,"
his wife remembered. Greene
began his career as the first
African American clerk in
the California Assembly.
By 1967, he had succeeded
Mervyn Dymally, taking
over Dymally's assembly seat,
and again in 1975, claiming
Dymally's recently vacated
senate seat. c1970

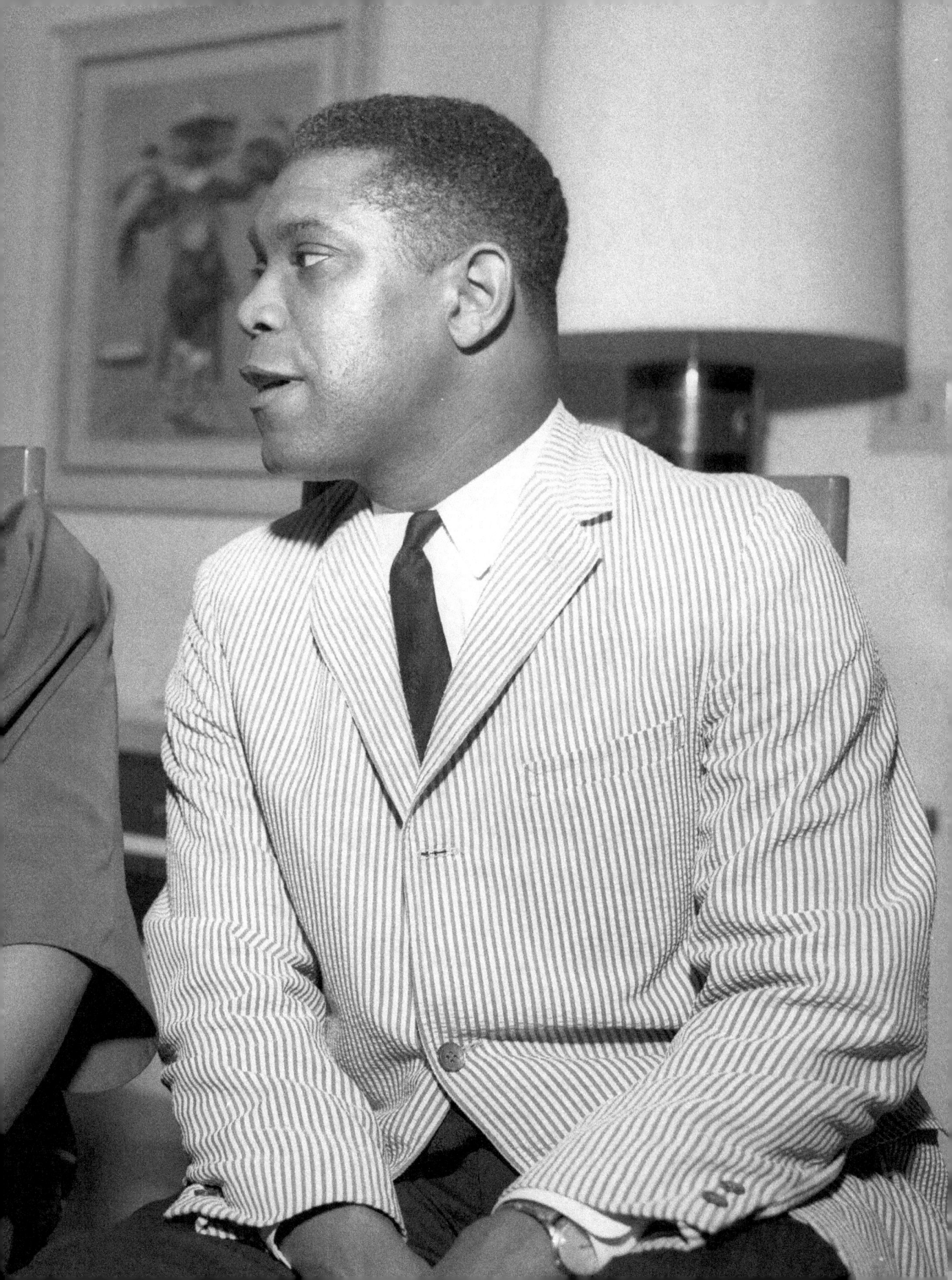

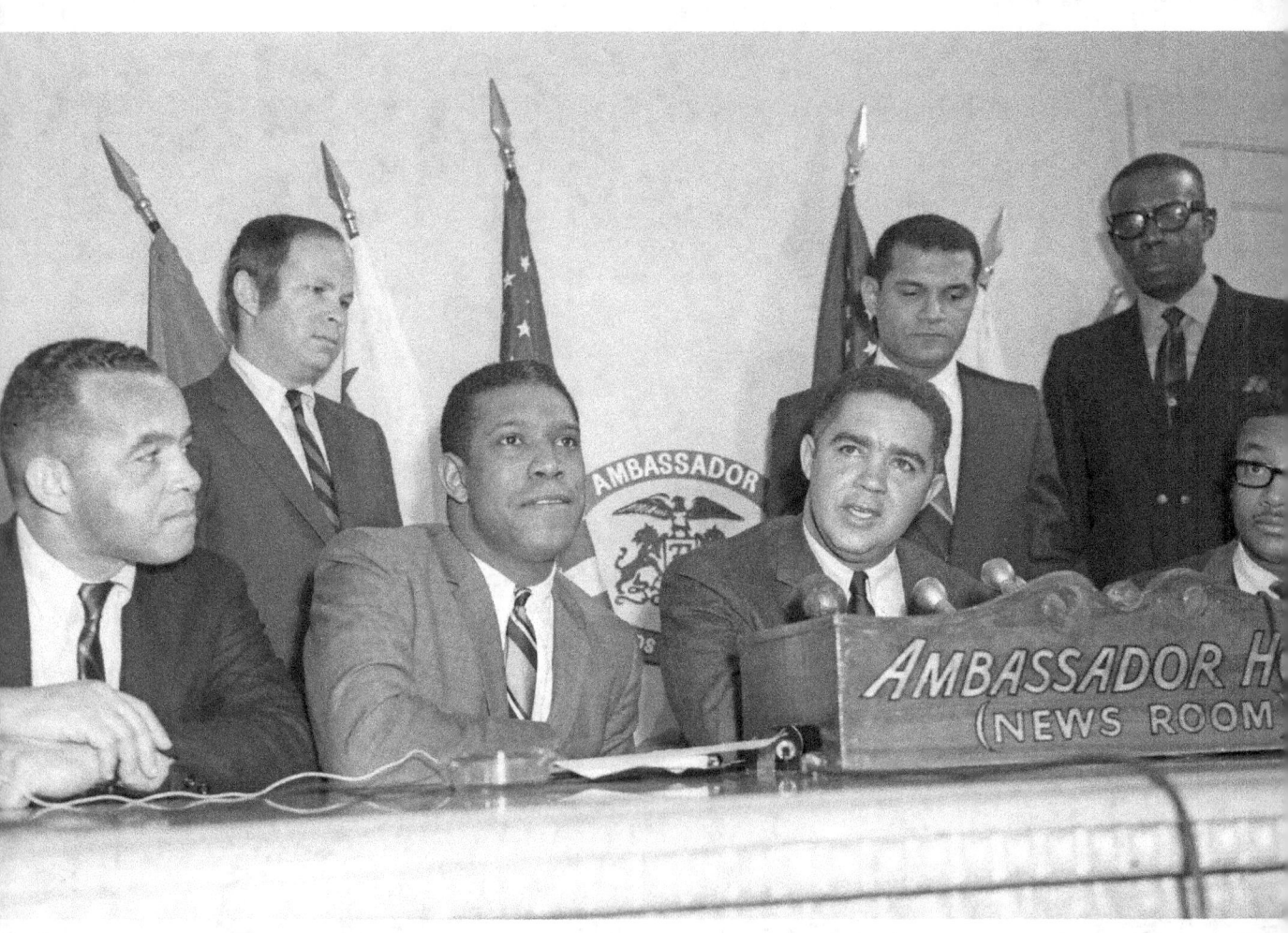

Bill Greene (*seated left of center*) with Leon Ralph (*far right*) and Billy G. Mills (*standing, right*) at press conference in the Ambassador Hotel. c1960s

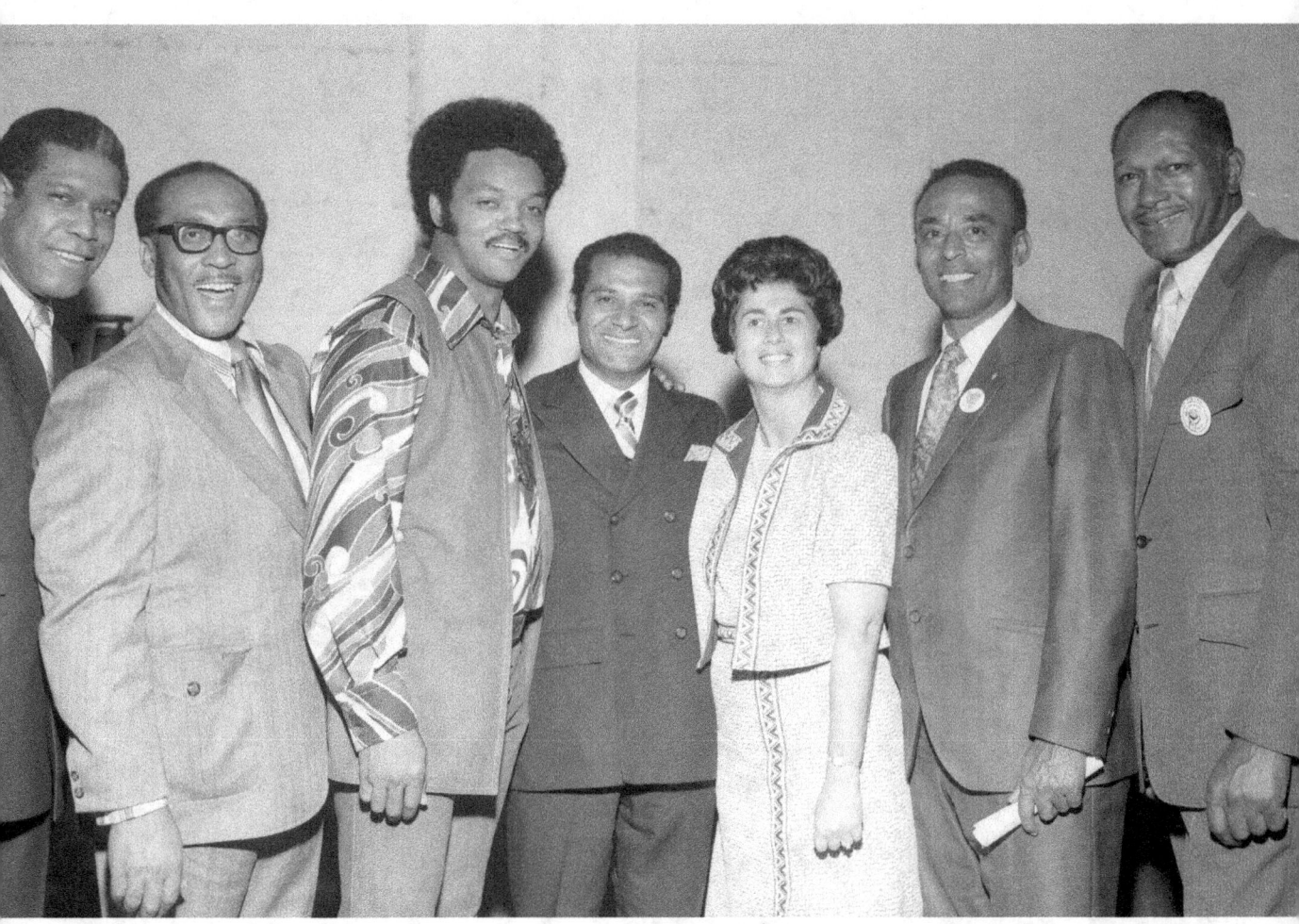

*Left to right*: Bill Greene with Rev. H.H. Brookins, Rev. Jesse Jackson, Billy G. Mills, Rosalind Wyman, Arnett Hartsfield and Tom Bradley at Operation Breadbasket meeting. c1970s

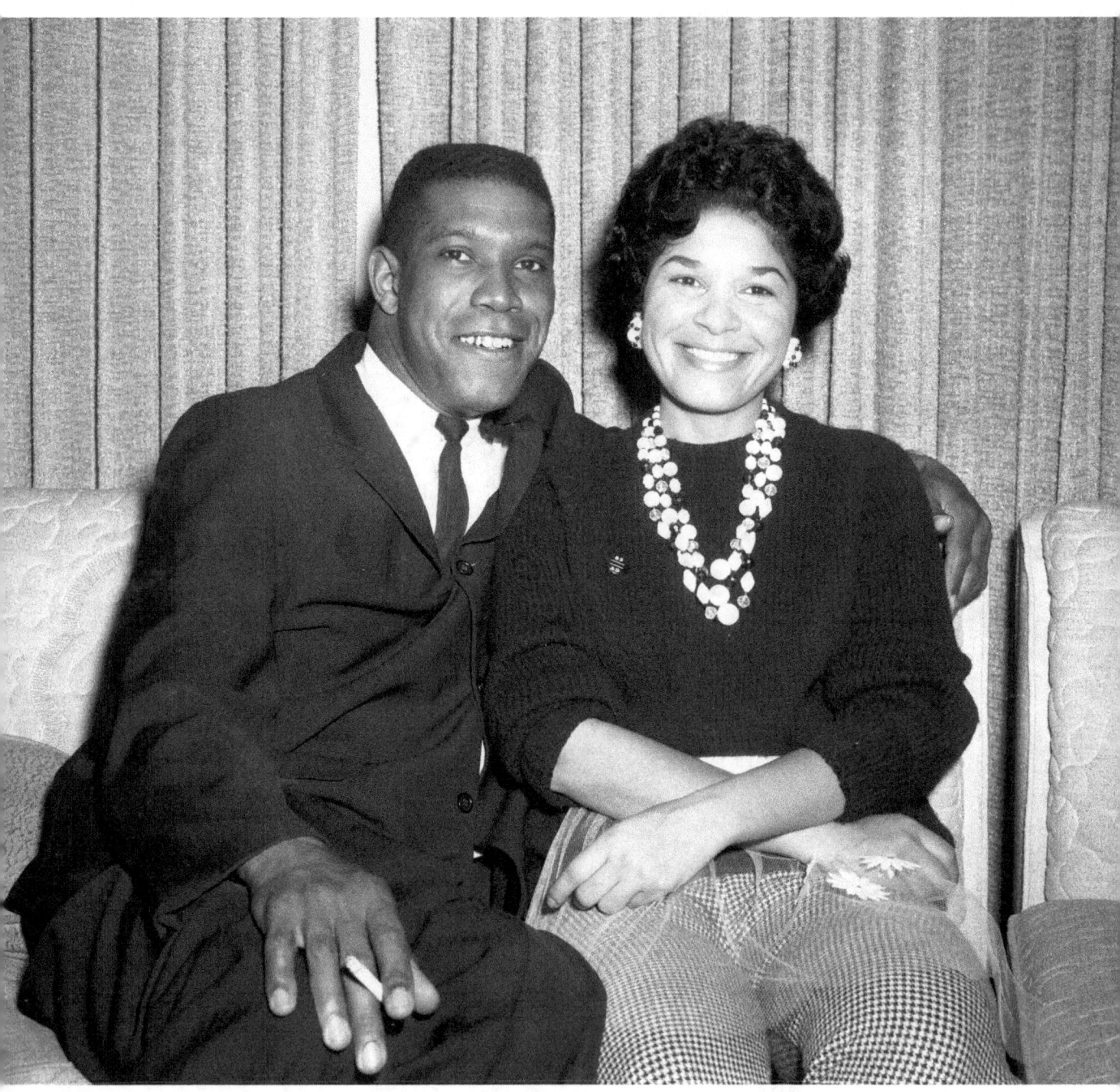

Bill Greene with wife Yvonne Greene at city council office. c1964

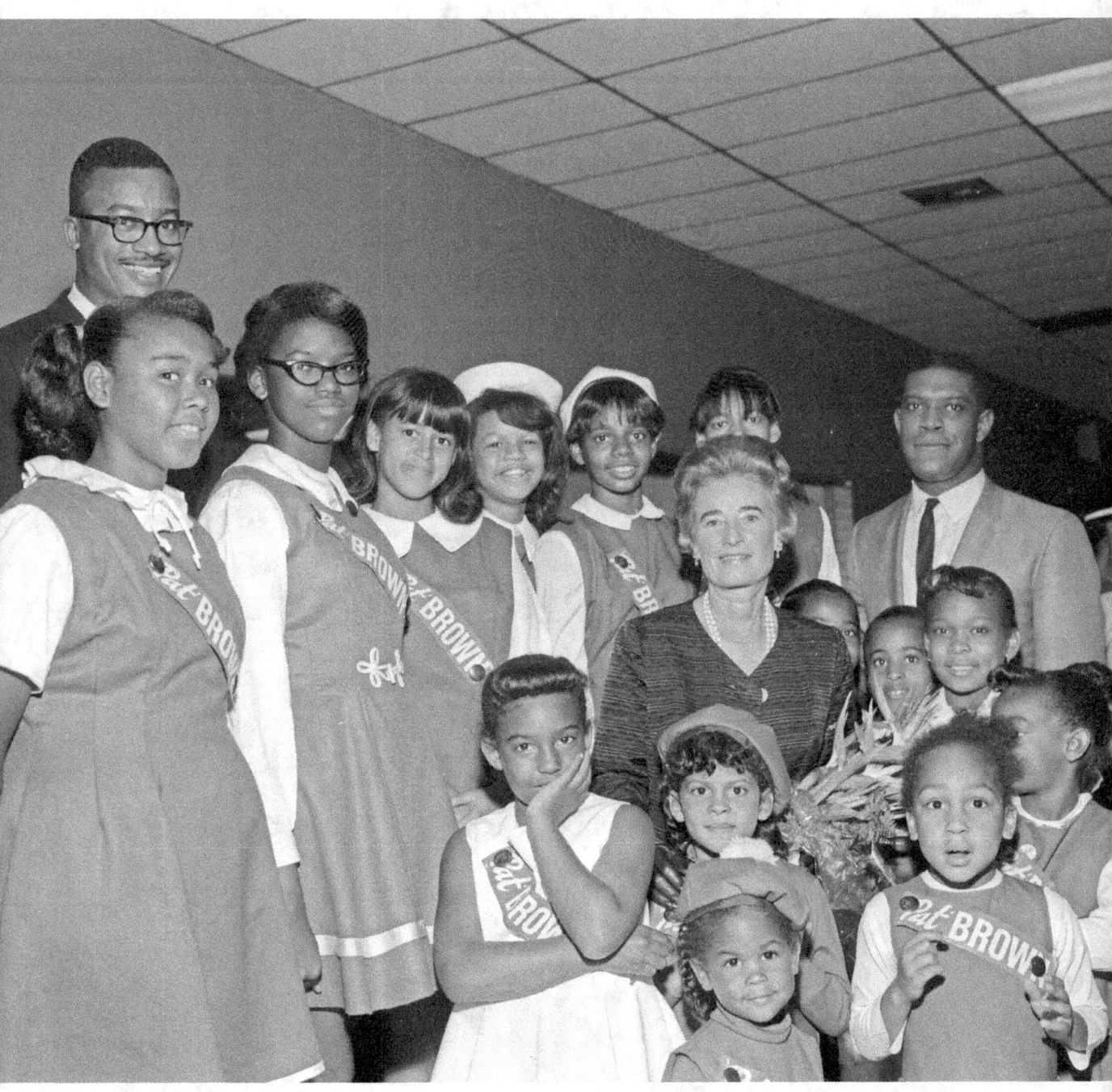

Bill Greene with Leon Ralph (*far left*), and Bernice Brown (*center*) at Pat Brown rally.

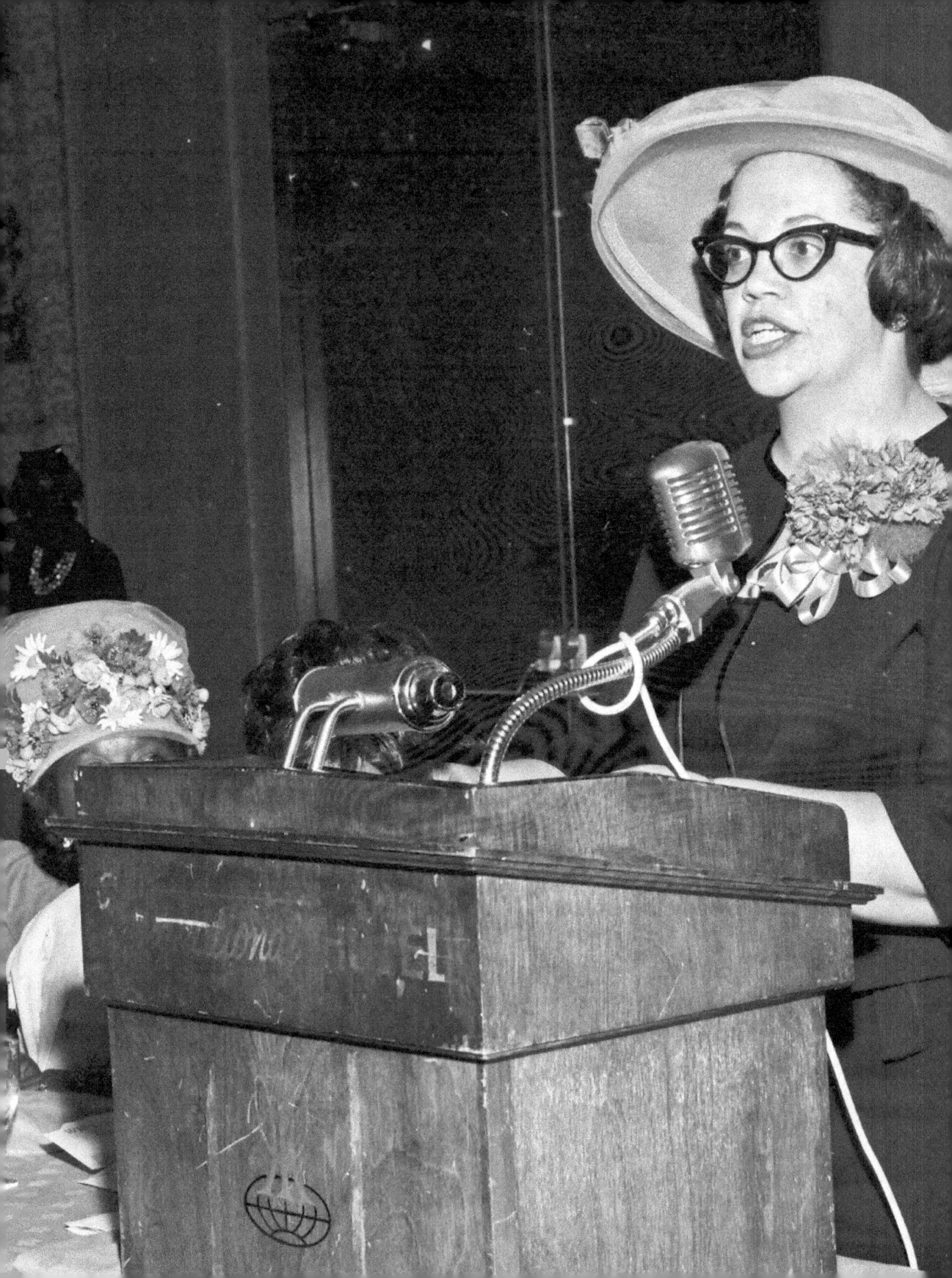

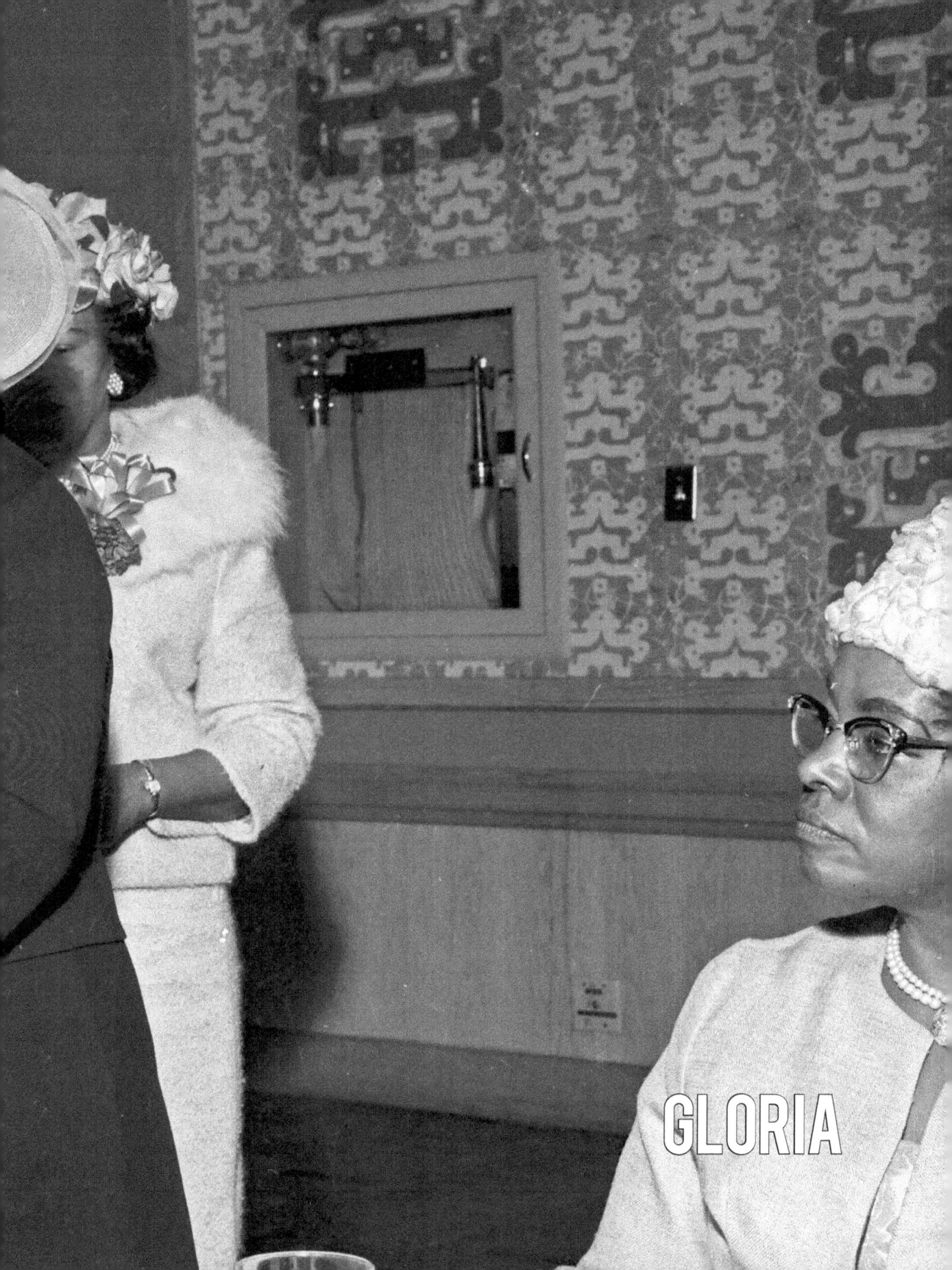

GLORIA

*Overleaf:* Gloria Curtis speaks at the Zeta Phi Beta Sorority Awards and Fashion Show. c1965

*Opposite*: Portrait of Gloria Curtis in library. Gloria Curtis was an elementary school teacher and the wife of Rolland Curtis. She began her career in education in 1953. She retired as director of volunteer programs for the LAUSD in 1988. In 1964, Gloria was tasked with researching and writing biographies of famous African Americans to incorporate into existing textbooks, which lacked heroes of color. She went on to co-author several textbooks highlighting minorities in history. It is because of Gloria's kind generosity that the Rolland J. Curtis Collection is a part of the Los Angeles Public Library's Photo Collection. c1960

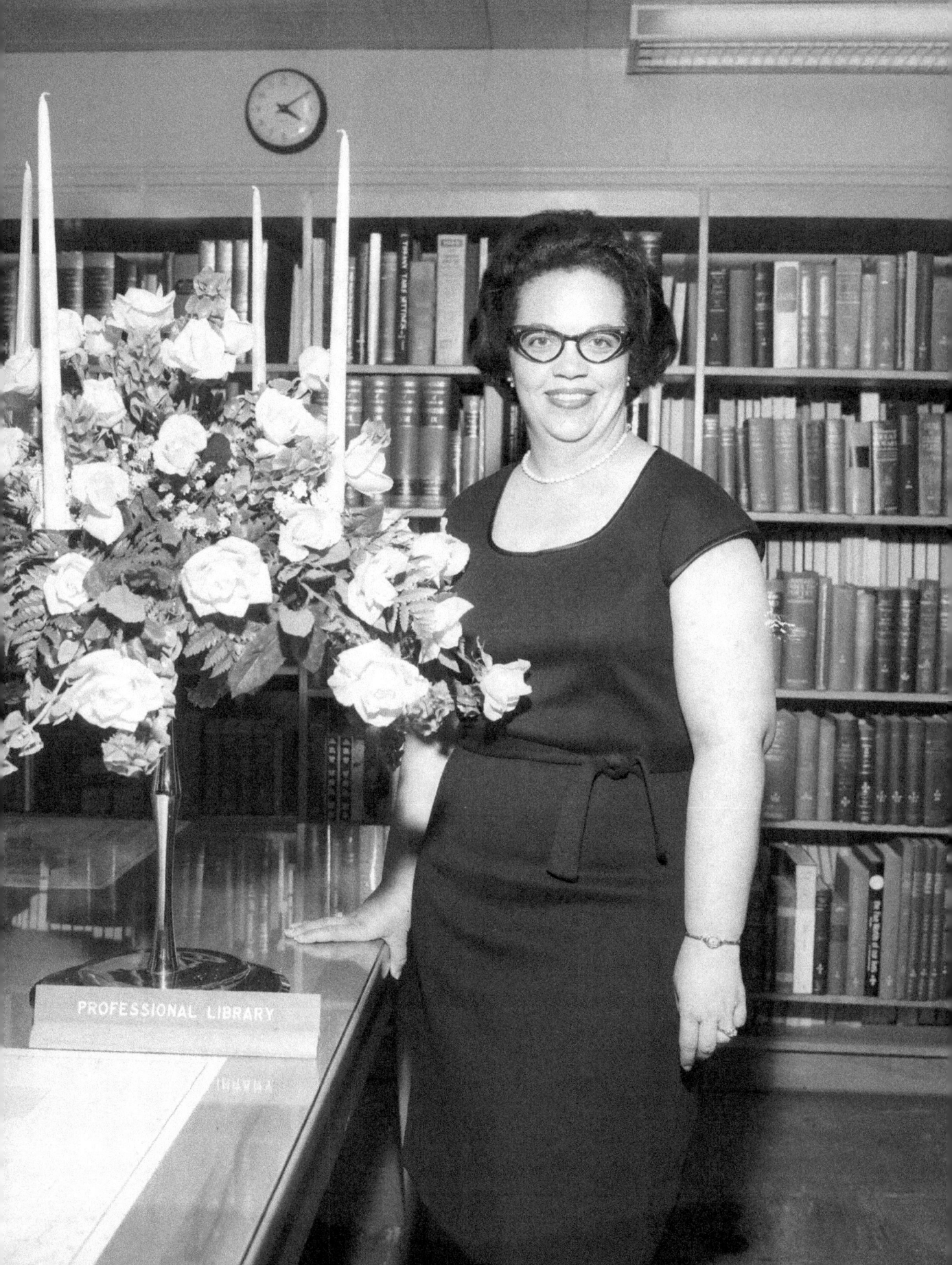

PROFESSIONAL LIBRARY

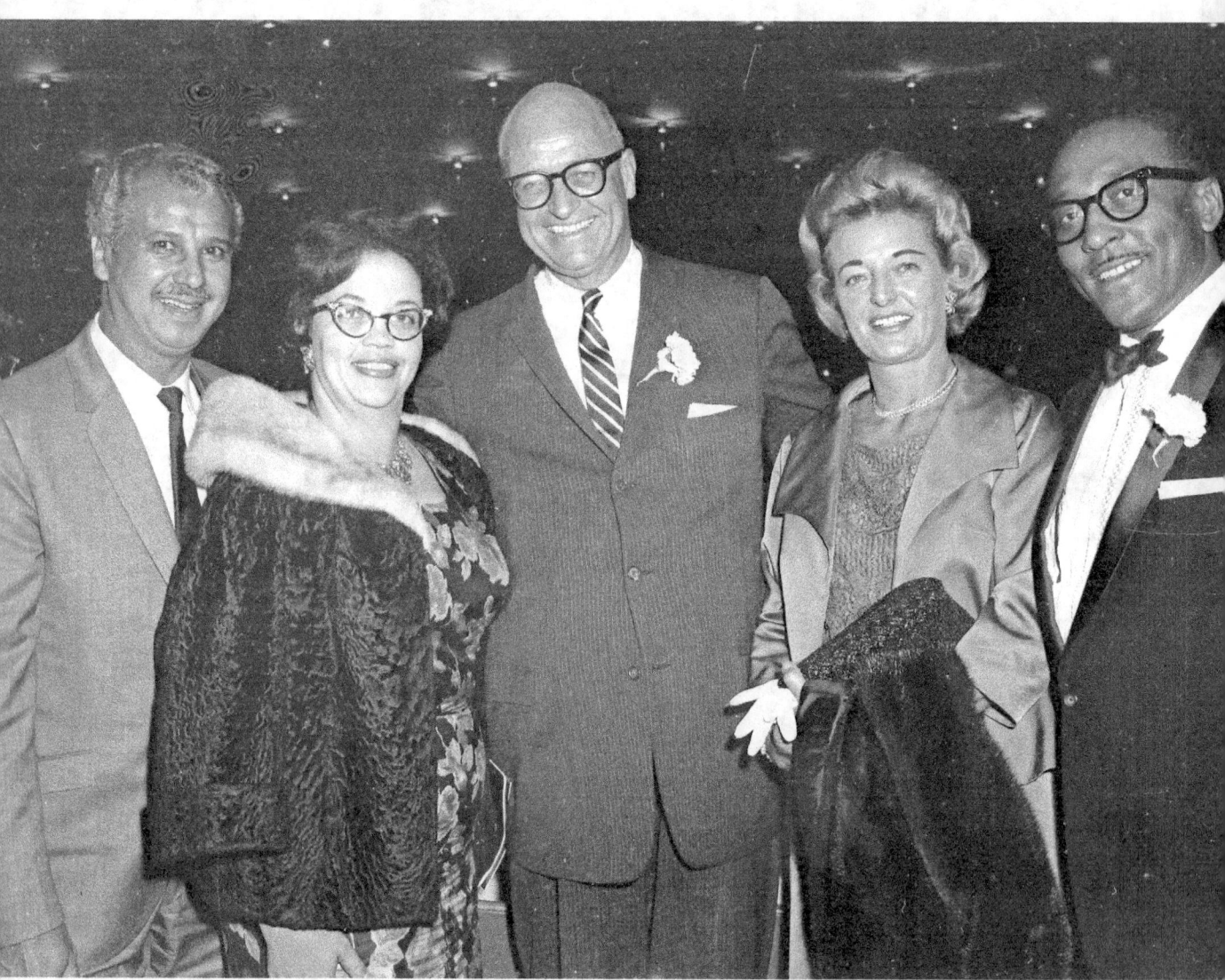

Gloria Curtis (*left*) with (*right to left*), Leon Aubry, James Roosevelt, his wife Irene Roosevelt and Rev. H.H. Brookins at the First AME's Church Elevation Banquet at the Biltmore Bowl. November 5, 1964

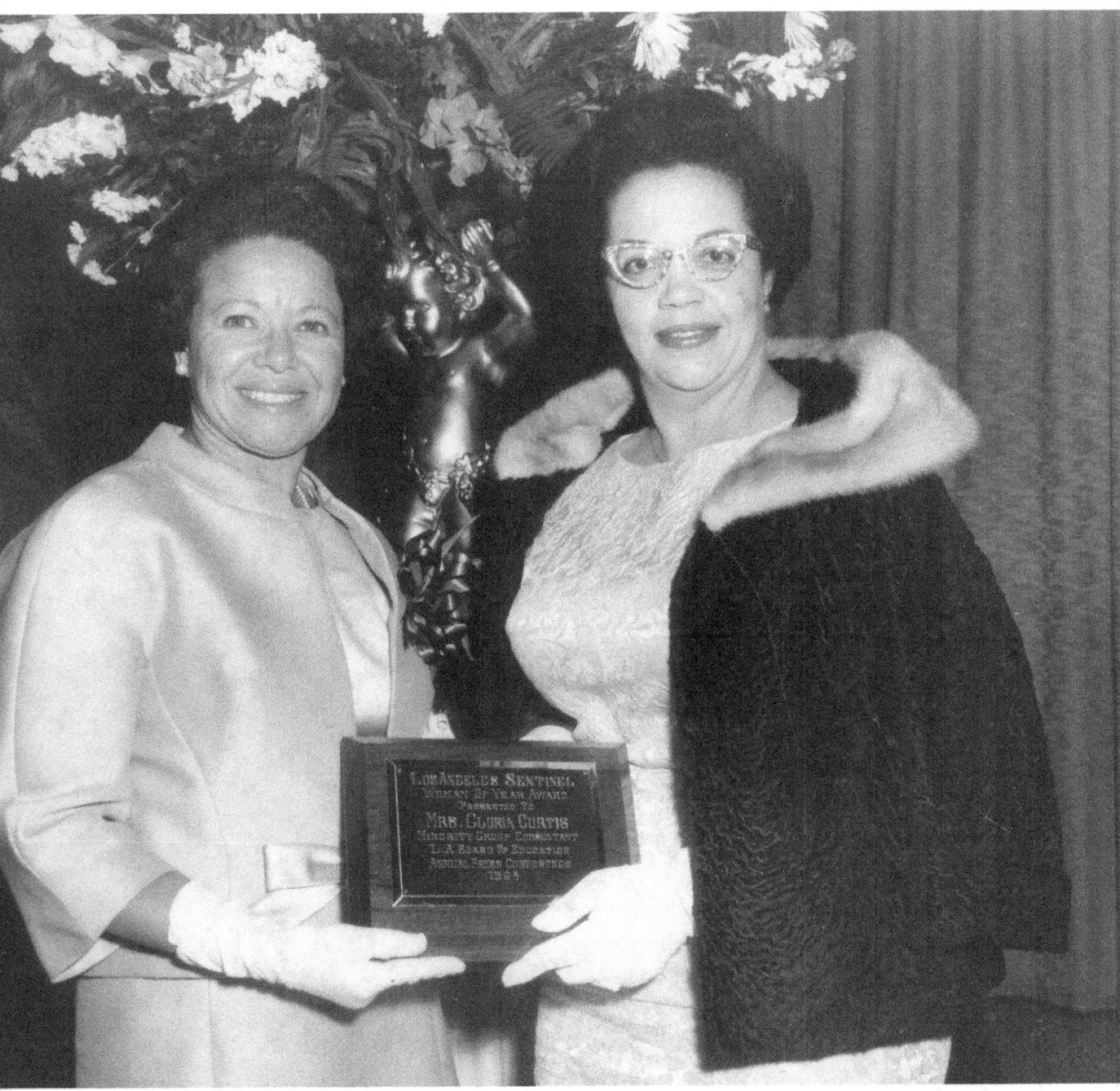

Ruth Washington (*left*) presents Gloria Curtis (*right*) "Woman of the Year" award from the *Los Angeles Sentinel*. November 5, 1964

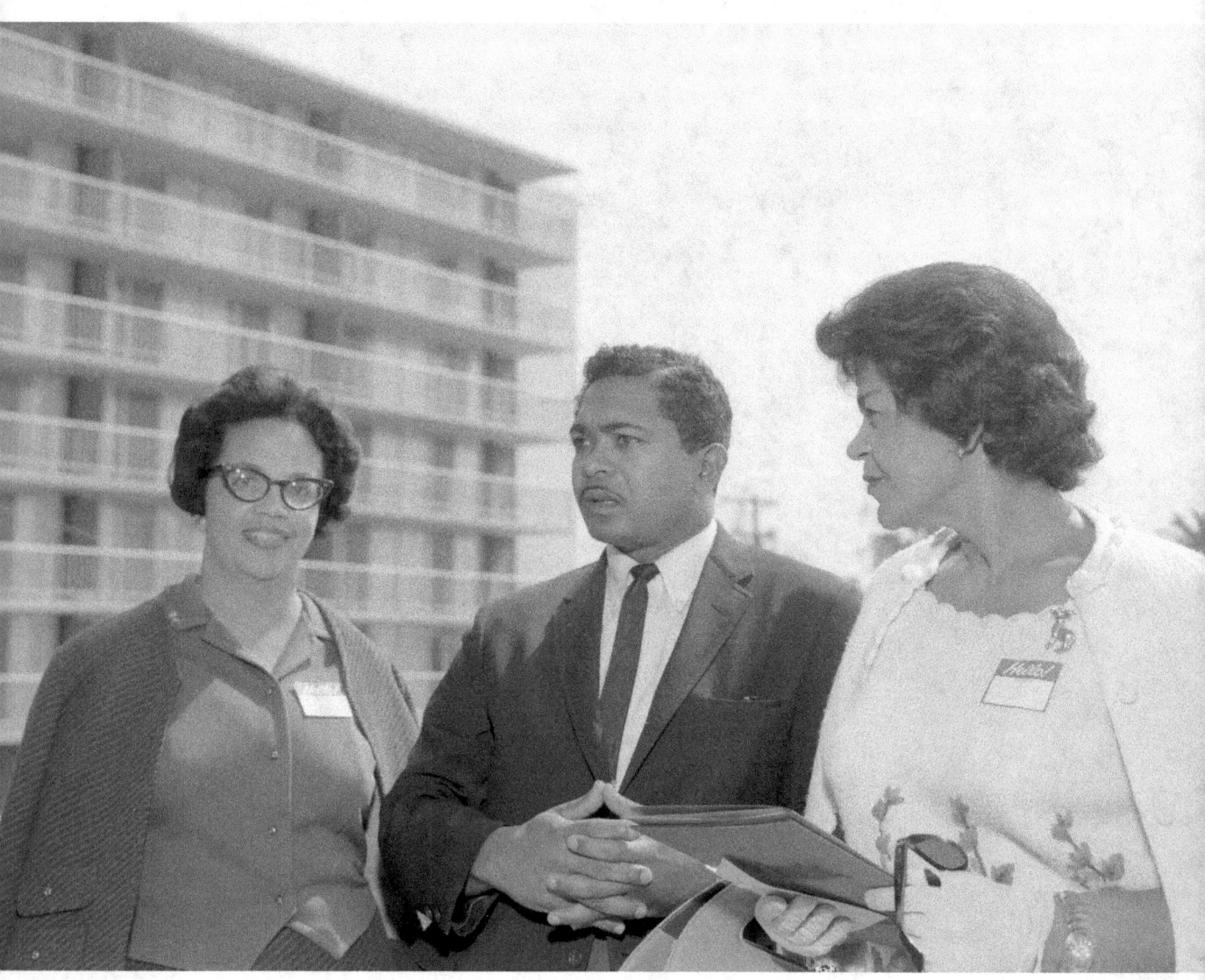

Gloria Curtis (*left*) with Mervyn Dymally (*center*), Marguerite Justice (*right*) during meeting. c1966

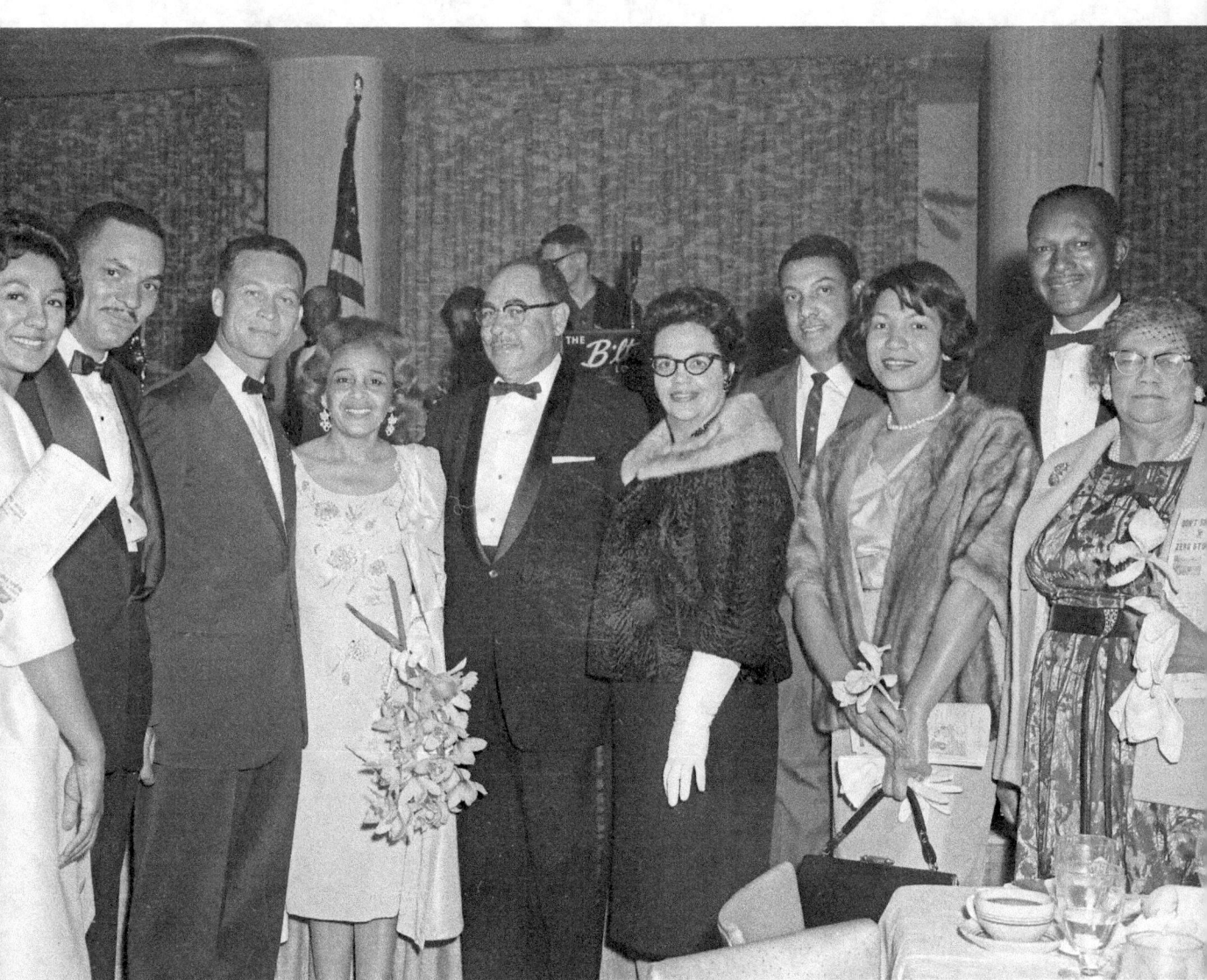

Gloria Curtis (*right from center*) with (*right to left*), Mathilda Curtis, Tom Bradley, Irene
Yopp Curtis, Charles Curtis Jr., Byron Rumford, Ethel Bradley and Douglas Dollarhide at
*Los Angeles Sentinel* salute for Leon Washington. April 23, 1964

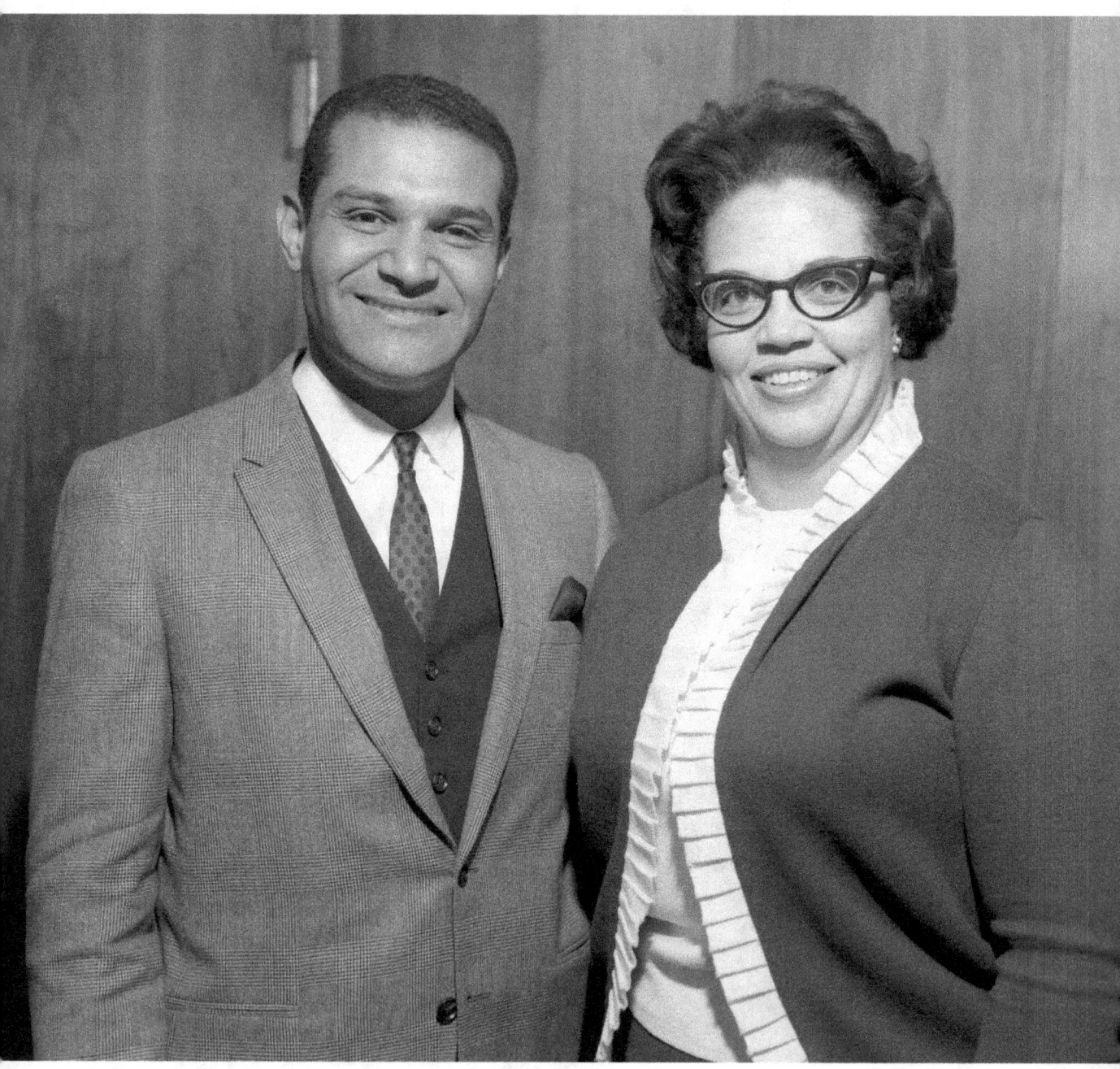

Gloria Curtis (*right*) with Billy G. Mills (*left*). c1966
*Opposite*: Portrait of Gloria Curtis at home. c1960s

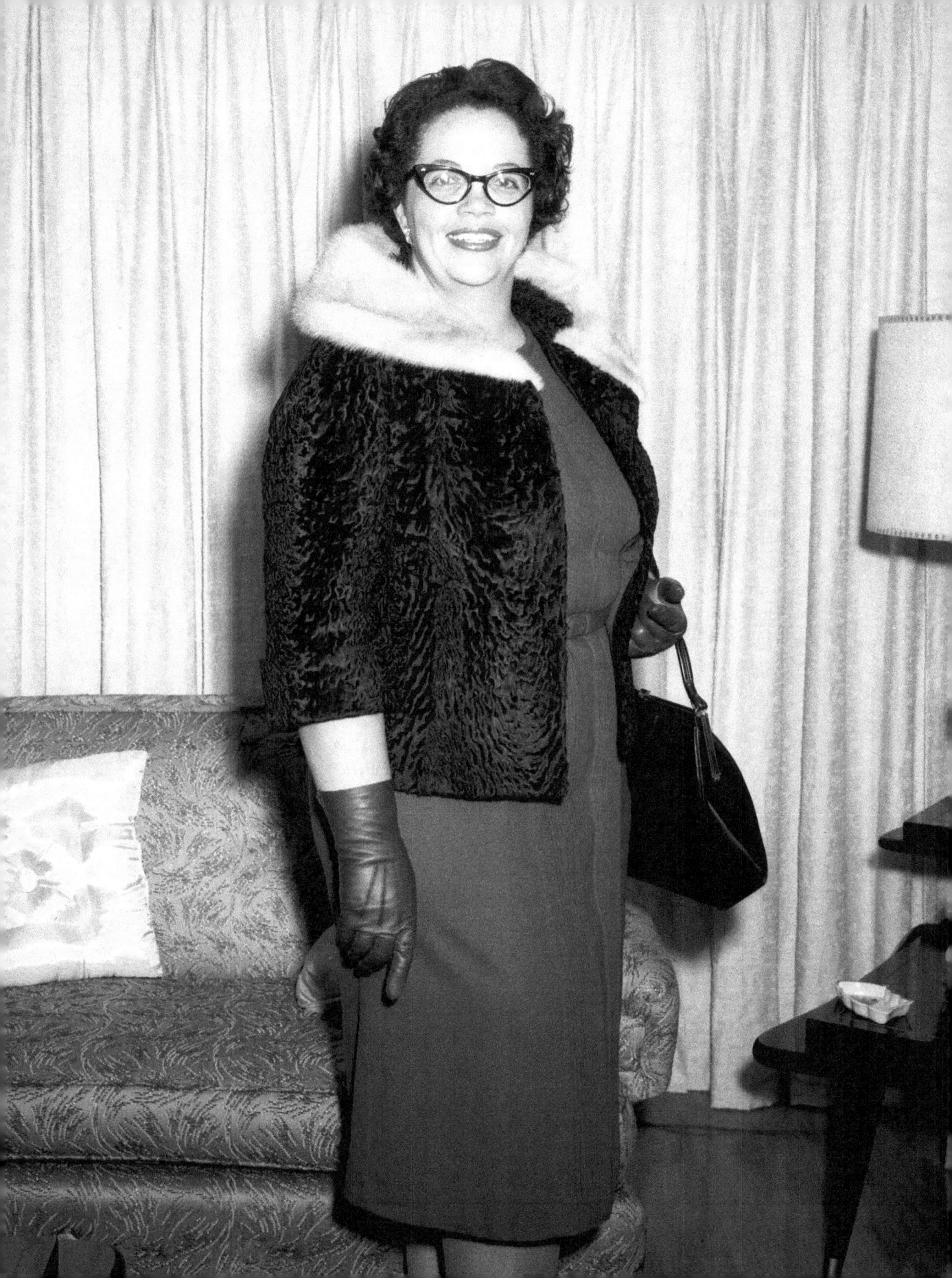

# ABOUT THE AUTHORS

**Kristine Protacio** emigrated with her family from the Philippines in 1989. She lived in Los Angeles until 2011, where she finished her Bachelor's degree in History from Cal Poly Pomona. Looking for adventure, she moved the Pacific Northwest and, with a little luck, found a husband, two cats, a Master's program, and a new place to call home. In 2015, she completed two Master's degrees, an MLIS and an MAS, from the University of British Columbia in Vancouver. Where does adventure call her next? She'll have to wait and see. She plans to return to the Pacific Northwest and enjoy some much needed time off and wait for the next opportunity for archiving history.

**Christina Rice** is a librarian, archivist, author, wife, and mother. She obtained an MLIS from San Jose State University and now oversees the Photo Collection at the Los Angeles Public Library. She is the author of *Ann Dvorak: Hollywood's Forgotten Rebel* (University Press of Kentucky) and multiple issues of the *My Little Pony* comic book series (IDW Publishing). She lives in Los Angeles with her husband, writer Joshua Hale Fialkov, their daughter, two dogs, and a disgruntled cat. One day, she hopes to live in a house big enough to fit her Guns N' Roses pinball machine which has been in her mom's garage for way too long.

# ABOUT THE PHOTO COLLECTION

The Los Angeles Public Library (LAPL) began collecting photographs sometime before World War II and had a collection of about 13,000 images by the late 1950s. In 1981, when Los Angeles celebrated its 200th birthday, Security Pacific National Bank gave its noted collection of historical photographs to the people of Los Angeles to be archived at the Central Library. Since then, LAPL has been fortunate to receive other major collections, making the library a resource worldwide for visual images.

Notable collections include the "photo morgues" of the *Los Angeles Herald Examiner* and *Valley Times* newspapers, the Kelly–Holiday mid-century collection of aerial photographs, the Works Progress Administration/Federal Writers Project collection, the Luther Ingersoll Portrait Collection, along with the landmark *Shades of L.A.*, an archive of images representing the contemporary and historic diversity of families in Los Angeles. Images were chosen from family albums and copied in a project sponsored by Photo Friends.

The Los Angeles Public Library Photo Collection also includes the works of individual photographers, including Ansel Adams, Herman Schultheis, William Reagh, Ralph Morris, Lucille Stewart, Gary Leonard, Stone Ishimaru, Carol Westwood, and Rolland Curtis.

Over 100,000 images from these collections have been digitized and are available to view through the LAPL website at **http://photos.lapl.org.**

# ABOUT PHOTO FRIENDS

Formed in 1990, Photo Friends is a nonprofit organization that supports the Los Angeles Public Library's Photograph Collection and History & Genealogy Department. Our goal is to improve access to the collections and promote them through programs, projects, exhibits, and books such as this one.

We are an enthusiastic group of photographers, writers, historians, businesspeople, politicians, academics, and many others, all bonded by our passion for photography, history, and Los Angeles.

Since 1994, Photo Friends has presented a series called *The Photographer's Eye*, which spotlights local photographers and their work. These talks are presented bi-monthly. In 2011, Photo Friends inaugurated *L.A. in Focus*, a lecture series that features images drawn primarily from the Photo Collection, and other topics on Los Angeles themes. We have presented programs on L.A. crime, the San Fernando Valley, Kelly–Holiday aerial photographs, and L.A.'s themed environments, among others.

With initial funding from the Ralph M. Parsons Foundation, Photo Friends sponsored *L.A. Neighborhoods Project* by commissioning photographers to create a visual record of the neighborhoods of Los Angeles during the early part of the 21st century (all now part of the collection). To ensure the Library's Collection will continue to reflect such an important part of Los Angeles's history, a generous grant enabled Photo Friends to hire five contemporary photographers to document present-day industrial L.A. These images have become part of LAPL's permanent collection and are available through the library's photo database. Photo Friends also curates photography exhibits on display in the History Department and locations around the city.

Photo Friends is a membership organization. Please consider becoming a member and helping us in our work to preserve and promote L.A.'s rich photographic resource. All proceeds from the sale of this book go to support Photo Friends's programs.

**www.photofriends.org**

This catalog was published in conjunction with
*Firsts, Seconds and Thirds:*
*African American Leaders in Los Angeles During the 1960s and '70s*
*from the Rolland J. Curtis Collection*
a photo exhibit on display in the
Los Angeles Central Library History & Genealogy Department Jan. 21–July 2, 2016

# THANK YOU!

Kim Creighton, Diana Sauceda, Matthew Mattson, Joyce Arnold, Carolyn Cole, Gloria Curtis, David Davis, Cindy Olnick, Natalie Mallard, and the John Randolph Haynes & Dora Haynes Foundation.

*Firsts, Seconds and Thirds: African American Leaders in Los Angeles During the 1960s and '70s from the Rolland J. Curtis Collection*
Edited by Kristine Protacio
Copyright © 2016 Photo Friends of the Los Angeles Public Library
Images © Los Angeles Public Library Photo Collection

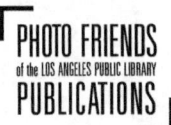

Published by:
Photo Friends of the Los Angeles Public Library
c/o Future Studio
P.O. Box 292000
Los Angeles, CA 90029

www.photofriends.org

Designed by Amy Inouye, Future Studio Los Angeles

Special quantity discounts available when purchased in bulk by corporations, organizations, or groups. Please contact Photo Friends at: **photofriendsla@gmail.com**

ISBN-13: 978-0692703472

Printed in the United States

photo
friends
LOS ANGELES PUBLIC LIBRARY

www.ingramcontent.com/pod-product-compliance
Lightning Source LLC
Chambersburg PA
CBHW080957170526
45158CB00010B/2832

*9780692703472*